Creating the Hudson River Park

Creating the Hudson River Park

● ●

Environmental and Community Activism, Politics, and Greed

TOM FOX

Rutgers University Press

New Brunswick, Camden, and Newark, New Jersey

London and Oxford

Rutgers University Press is a department of Rutgers, The State University of New Jersey, one of the leading public research universities in the nation. By publishing worldwide, it furthers the University's mission of dedication to excellence in teaching, scholarship, research, and clinical care.

Library of Congress Cataloging-in-Publication Data

Names: Fox, Tom, 1947– author.
Title: Creating the Hudson River Park : environmental and community activism, politics, and greed / Tom Fox.
Description: New Brunswick ; Camden ; Newark ; London : Rutgers University Press, [2024] | Includes bibliographical references and index.
Identifiers: LCCN 2023028910 | ISBN 9781978814011 (cloth) | ISBN 9781978814028 (epub) | ISBN 9781978814042 (pdf)
Subjects: LCSH: Hudson River Park (New York, N.Y.) | Urban renewal—New York (State)—New York—History. | Public spaces—New York (State)—New York—History. | Manhattan (New York, N.Y.)—Environmental conditions. | Manhattan (New York, N.Y.)—Social life and customs. | Manhattan (New York, N.Y.)—Politics and government.
Classification: LCC F128.65.H83 F69 2024 | DDC 974.7/1—dc23/eng/20231018
LC record available at https://lccn.loc.gov/2023028910

A British Cataloging-in-Publication record for this book is available from the British Library.

References to internet websites (URLs) were accurate at the time of writing. Neither the author nor Rutgers University Press is responsible for URLs that may have expired or changed since the manuscript was prepared.

♻ The paper used in this publication meets the requirements of the American National Standard for Information Sciences—Permanence of Paper for Printed Library Materials, ANSI Z39.48-1992.

rutgersuniversitypress.org

This book is dedicated to individuals and organizations who fought the exploitation of the Hudson River and envisioned and championed the creation of the Hudson River Park over the past forty years.

Five individuals deserve my deepest appreciation for their critical leadership at various stages of effort to build our park.

Financier Arthur Levitt Jr.
Labor leader Thomas P. Maguire
Investment banker Michael Del Giudice
Environmental attorney Albert K. Butzel
Philanthropist Douglas Durst

Contents

Preface

I have had a unique opportunity to participate in the creation and protection of the Hudson River Park since its inception in 1986, and this book, written in the first person, describes the journey. I have kept much of the nautical terminology and the political, governmental, financial, and land-use information, and I have included a brief glossary for the reader's use. The work includes numerous citations to sources of information to ensure accuracy and transparency. Many citations, particularly in the early chapters, are primary source materials that predate the internet and include minutes of meetings, letters, memos, reports, plans, media coverage, editorials, and other documents.

CUNY Brooklyn College Archives has graciously agreed to support the publication of this book by scanning primary source citations. Reference materials that can be placed online can be found at https://tinyurl.com /Creating-the-Hudson-River-Park in the Brooklyn College Archives. The documents expand and enrich the story, and as they say, "the devil is in the details." I am thankful that readers will have access to this important information. The complete Fox Collection describing urban greening and environmental initiatives between 1975 and 2023, primarily in New York City, will be publicly accessible for research and education at the CUNY Brooklyn College Archive in the coming years.

This story is told chronologically. It includes the twelve years of controversy and compromise that preceded the 1998 Hudson River Park Act, which officially designated the waterfront as a public park. My initial advocacy was financed by foundations, corporations, and individuals who support charitable initiatives in the city. After working for the government briefly, my last twenty-five years of contributing to the park has been as a volunteer. I have participated in the project as an environmental advocate; a gubernatorial appointee; a founding president of the public authority established to plan, permit, build, and operate the park; a nonprofit board member; a tenant; a citizen; a litigant; and most recently, a member of the park's official Advisory Council.

Initial design and construction proceeded smoothly in the spirit of the original plan to preserve the natural habitat, expand maritime activities, open public access to the Hudson, and create recreational opportunities for adjacent communities and millions of New Yorkers. However, over time, the city and state starved the park for public funding, focused on other new park initiatives, and encouraged commercial development in and adjacent to the park. As a result, progress in completing the park has ebbed and flowed like its namesake river.

The strategies and tactics used by various parties working to create, complete, oppose, and exploit the park should be of interest not only to park professionals, urban planners, policymakers, community organizers, waterfront advocates, environmental activists, landscape architects, urban ecologists, and designers but also to park visitors, members of adjacent communities, and anyone interested in how cities work—or do not.

I have been privileged to work shoulder to shoulder with talented and energetic men and women, of all ages and from many walks of life, who have shared their passion and vision and have overcome substantial challenges to create the park we have today. However, the park is yet unfinished and will certainly be reimagined in the future. Therein lies another opportunity—and potential peril. Failing to create a financing mechanism to capture a portion of the increased value the park created in the adjacent neighborhoods before it was built has led to commercialization of the park as the city and state redirected this increase tax revenue to their pet projects and other municipal priorities.

As I complete this manuscript in the fall of 2023, I am reminded of how much we have won over the past forty years and what was at stake. Despite a recent trend toward commercialization, the creation of the Hudson River Park is a tremendous victory for public participation and the preservation, restoration, and enjoyment of nature.

Parks contribute to physical and mental health, the city's tax base, climate resiliency, energy conservation, and tourism. They reduce air and noise pollution, absorb stormwater, and enhance the image of the city as a place to live, work, and visit. In the long run, public parks pay for themselves. More importantly, they are critical to the city's physical, social, and economic well-being.

New financing mechanisms must finally be developed to support the Hudson River Park and other public parks without commercializing them; otherwise, we will kill the goose that laid the golden egg. We must fund the construction and long-term maintenance and operation of public parks via the significant economic, environmental, and public benefits they create.

The stewards of Central Park have kept true to the 1858 vision of Fredrick Law Olmsted and Calbert Vaux for more than century and a half. My hope is that future generations not only maintain and protect the Hudson River Park but also increase its public benefit as they shape the park's future and correct some of the flaws that have resulted from forcing the park to meet too many different agendas! Its only agenda should be the protection and restoration of the Hudson River and its nearshore habitat, and the public use and enjoyment of this magnificent urban waterfront.

Excelsior!
Tom

Creating the Hudson River Park

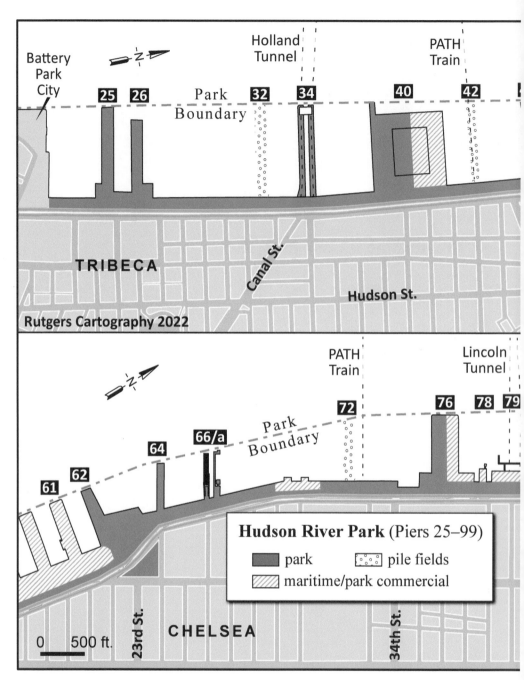

Hudson River Park. (Created by Mike Siegel)

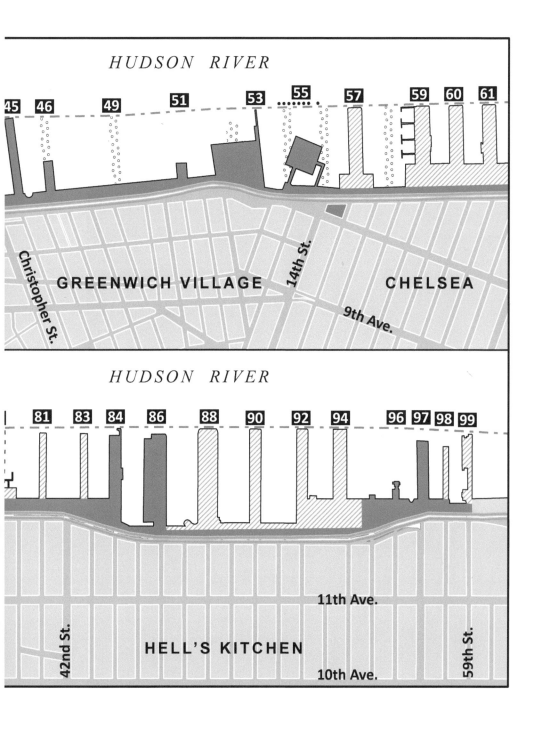

HUDSON RIVER

45 46 49 51 53 55 57 59 60 61

Christopher St.

GREENWICH VILLAGE

14th St.

CHELSEA

9th Ave.

HUDSON RIVER

81 83 84 86 88 90 92 94 96 97 98 99

11th Ave.

42nd St.

HELL'S KITCHEN

59th St.

10th Ave.

Introduction

● ● ● ● ● ● ● ● ● ● ● ● ● ●

> I know that every good and excellent
> thing in the world stands moment by
> moment on the razor's edge of danger
> and must be fought for.
>
> **THORNTON WILDER**

The 4-mile-long, 550-acre Hudson River Park is nearing completion and is the largest park built in Manhattan since Central Park was established more than a century and a half earlier. It has transformed a derelict and dangerous waterfront, protected the Hudson River estuary, created new recreational opportunities for millions of New Yorkers, enhanced tourism and the image of the city, preserved maritime commerce, stimulated redevelopment in adjacent neighborhoods, and set a precedent for waterfront redevelopment. The park attracts seventeen million visitors a year.

This story is a first-person account of how the park came to be. Community groups, civic and environmental organizations, labor unions, the business community, government agencies, and elected officials worked together and won a historic victory for environmental preservation, the use and enjoyment of the Hudson River, and urban redevelopment. However, the park is also the embodiment of a troubling trend toward the commercialization of America's public parks.

Major public works that reshape world-class cities are traditionally crafted by planners, architects, engineers, and elected officials. The effort to reimagine the West Side of Manhattan began in 1974 with a proposal for a massive undertaking known as Westway. Westway was planned as a 4.2-mile limited-access interstate highway burrowing through 234 acres of new landfill and platforms at a cost of over $2 billion. The plan was supported by city, state, and federal officials, the real estate industry, the building and construction trades, the business community, and the media.

Those of us who opposed Westway celebrated in 1985 when the project was defeated after a bitter decade-long legal battle that ended with one of the earliest victories of the urban environmental movement.

Between 1986 and 1998, a new vision for the future of the West Side waterfront was forged through a unique participatory planning process involving all the competing stakeholders. Working together over ten years, city, state, and federal agencies, environmental, civic, and community organizations, elected officials, construction unions, and the business community captured a once-in-a-lifetime opportunity to revitalize Manhattan's West Side waterfront. The highway became a tree-lined urban boulevard, landfills and platforms were prohibited, and a world-class maritime park was planned on the waterfront.

My Brooklyn roots, warrior spirit, and love of nature and urban life came together in a lifelong passion for public open space. In addition to playing a bit part at the end of the Westway saga, I was an early leader in the community gardening movement and the fight for Brooklyn Bridge Park. I initiated the plan for a forty-mile Greenway through Brooklyn and Queens and led a citywide coalition of 120 park, community, environmental, sports, and civic organizations committed to research, planning, and advocacy to expand and enhance the city's open spaces.

In 1986, Governor Mario Cuomo appointed me to the West Side Task Force, a twenty-two-member group charged with recommending alternatives for Westway. We recommended a surface roadway and waterfront esplanade, but determining the fate of the miles of underwater property proved so contentious an issue, it was left to a future planning entity. In 1988, I was appointed to the West Side Waterfront Panel, which ruled out landfill and platforms, and in 1990, we recommended that the roadway become a tree-lined urban boulevard and the entire waterfront a world-class maritime park.

To finance the construction and maintenance of the project, we recommended using a variety of funding sources, including city, state, and federal funding, and designating three locations within the park—locations that offered structures with more than four million square feet of space atop existing piers—for park-related commercial development, and retaining that revenue. We also suggested the use of a creative financing mechanism to capture a portion of the value created by the appreciation of adjacent real estate that we agreed would result from the park's construction.

In 1992, the city and state each committed $100 million toward the construction of the park and established the Hudson River Park Conservancy to oversee its design, construction, and operation. I was appointed the conservancy's first president, and by 1995, we had completed the Concept and Financial Plan for the park. I resigned shortly afterward as Mayor Giuliani began to remove certain properties from the park and Governor Pataki sought greater control of the project.

In 1997, I joined the Hudson River Park Alliance, a coalition that grew to over thirty environmental, civic, and community organizations that helped negotiate and advocate for the passage of the 1998 Hudson River Park Act. That legislation designated the 550 acres of upland property, underwater property, and the piers as a public park. It established the Hudson River Park Trust to design, build, and operate the park and set aside all the underwater property as an estuarine sanctuary to support research, restoration, and preservation of this unique habitat. After the passage of the act, I joined a group of community, business, environmental, and maritime advocates to form an organization called "Friends of Hudson River Park" to support the park.

As expected, the Hudson River Park and the new urban boulevard that ran alongside it were significant catalysts in the revitalization of Manhattan's far West Side south of 59th Street. They made it easier for people and vehicles to move along that part of the island, opened the waterfront so it could be used and enjoyed by the public, protected the estuary, improved the image of the city, and made the adjacent neighborhood a more desirable place to live, work, and visit. They increased tourism, the value of adjacent real estate, and the city's tax base. All in all, the project seemed poised to be a win-win undertaking.

In fact, the planning and construction of both projects proceeded smoothly at first. The roadway was completed in 2001, and the first section of the park, in Greenwich Village, opened in 2003 to rave reviews. In 2002, however, Michael Bloomberg was elected mayor, and his agenda was pro-development. Under Bloomberg, the entire West Side of Manhattan adjacent to the waterfront was rezoned to allow for increased development, but no mechanism was instituted to earmark any new revenue generated for supporting the Hudson River Park.

The lack of adequate public funding seriously impeded the effort to build and maintain the park. By 2008, Friends of Hudson River Park had secured approximately $100 million for the park through public advocacy, private fundraising, and legal action against city agencies that failed to relocate inappropriate and now-illegal facilities from the waterfront. We conducted a multiyear study that showed that the initial $75 million public investment in the strip of parkland in Greenwich Village, the first segment of the park, had increased the value of real estate within three blocks of the park by $200 million.

This success validated the study and financing recommendation of the West Side Waterfront Panel and confirmed the benefit of building the park. But by this point, the Hudson River Park Trust was under new development-oriented leadership, and the classic conflicts between public and private uses resurfaced. In 2011, they forced Friends to reorganize as a fundraising organization. The community leaders, environmentalists, and civic leaders who worked with the government to plan the park and begin construction were replaced by real estate developers, attorneys, investment bankers, and consultants. The city and state effectively put a For Sale sign on the park, and the trust became a real estate broker.

The new leadership of the trust and a reconstituted Hudson River Park Friends then lobbied for multiple changes in the legislation governing the park. One of these changes was selling development rights from the piers to properties along the park, which were recently rezoned to permit residential and commercial office space and now could be developed even more densely. Others were extending the term for commercial leases to ninety-nine years, allowing office development in the park and retaining and possibly expanding a heliport.

Trust leadership allowed Citigroup to build and install a private water taxi dock for their employees without public review and worked secretly with a donor to design a 260-million-dollar theater complex on a new "island" built in the sanctuary. That proposal led to a bitter legal battle that did not end until 2017, when the island was allowed to be built under the condition that the government provide the money to complete the park and restore the estuarine sanctuary.

Within two years, more than $146 million in new public funding for the park was approved. In 2019, I was elected to the Hudson River Advisory

Council, a fifty-member body composed of community, environmental, and civic organizations and all the West Side elected officials, a precedent that was established by the West Side Task Force. After several years of quiescence, the council has begun to play a more active role in planning and policy for the park.

Protecting public parks and keeping them free of commercialization has always been an enormous challenge. Over the past century and a half, for example, there have been many plans for commercial development in Central Park, but none have been implemented. Why should our new generation of urban parks be any different?

As we are increasingly coming to realize, parks perform a wide array of functions necessary to support and enhance life in the city. They contribute to physical and mental health, reduce air and noise pollution, conserve energy, absorb storm water, support wildlife, enhance the image of a city, and make it a more desirable place to live, work, and visit. For these reasons, public officials should not be allowed to sell pieces of our parks to the highest bidder to wring more revenue from these valuable public assets. Parks already increase real estate, payroll, and sales tax revenues, and their contributions to the city and urban living far exceed revenues received from exploiting this asset and undermining public use.

Twenty-five years after state legislation created the Hudson River Park, the city, state, trust, and the reconstituted Friends have new leadership. Residential and corporate investment in adjacent neighborhoods has matured, and soon no more commercial development will be allowed in the park. People who live on the West Side need the park to maintain both their quality of life and the value of their property—so do corporations ranging from Google and Citigroup, to Disney, RXR Realty, and Related Companies, to name just a few that have invested heavily on the far West Side.

It is clearly in everyone's interest to secure stable, long-term public funding if the park is to succeed. To this end, the new neighbors should work with elected officials to craft a financing mechanism that finally meets the park's needs for long-term maintenance, operation, and capital replacement. Without such a mechanism, the park and adjacent communities will suffer; we saw this happen in the 1980s when we failed to maintain public spaces like Bryant Park, Union Square, Washington Square, Prospect Park, and even Central Park.

The struggle to ensure that the Hudson River Park becomes the world-class waterfront park originally envisioned by its creators is far from over. Commercial interests have recently played a greater role in the park and the

Hudson River Park Trust's efforts to limit the involvement of the community and other stakeholders in planning and decision-making have led to public mistrust and frustration.

City and state officials and the new trust leadership must embrace the public involvement that created the park to ensure its completion and long-term care. Without an informed and engaged citizenry working in partnership with government agencies, elected officials, philanthropists, and enlightened business interests the Hudson River Park, along with many others across the country, can never realize their full potential.

The U.S. Army Corps of Engineers 2022 resiliency plan includes building a twelve-foot-high concrete flood wall along three miles of the park. The wall would diminish public use and enjoyment of the park, impede public access to the river, undermine the quality of life in adjacent neighborhoods, and erode the value of adjacent real estate and the city's tax base. I am hopeful that the governor and the mayor answer the growing public appeal to establish a task force to oversee a more coordinated approach to ensure that investments in new waterfront infrastructure complete the transformation of Manhattan's lower West Side waterfront spurred by the creation of the park.

This story was written to accurately document the history of the Hudson River Park, to recognize both those who made it happen and those who made it difficult, and to offer lessons that may help citizens, planning and park professionals, public servants, and elected officials expand and protect the public parks and natural systems that are so critical to the well-being and even the survival of urban society.

1

Starting the Journey

● ● ● ● ● ● ● ● ● ● ● ● ● ●

The first time I saw the waterfront along Manhattan's West Side was from the back seat of a '49 Ford as my parents drove up the old Miller Highway—better known as the West Side Highway—from the Brooklyn Battery Tunnel. My Aunt Irene was sailing to Europe, and we were headed to Midtown Manhattan to see her off.[1]

It was sometime around 1955. The cobblestone roadway was elevated, and we drove past piers with tugs, barges, cargo vessels, and ocean liners sporting multicolored flags from around the world. In those days, you could go aboard an ocean liner for a bon voyage party right up to the time the ship sailed. As an eight-year-old, running up and down the ship's corridors with my younger brother Gordon was one of the most exciting experiences of my brief lifetime.

It seemed like there were parties in every cabin; animated conversations, laughter, and music filled the air. Then the chimes sounded, and the loudspeakers intoned, "All ashore that's going ashore!" and it was time to leave. Crestfallen that the party was ending, we went down the gangway and joined waving throngs on the pier as confetti filled the air and the ship's horns blasted farewell. It was magical.

Ocean Liner Row and the West Side waterfront circa 1955. (Alamy)

Ferries, Tugs, Cargo Ships, and Ocean Liners

Throughout the seventeenth and eighteenth centuries, maritime activity in the city was primarily along the East River on the Brooklyn waterfront and in Lower Manhattan, where sailing ships were more likely to find favorable winds. In the early days, sailing ships had no specific departure time; they sailed with the tide when the vessel was full. Ships might remain docked for days awaiting cargo or sail to other ports to fill their holds before heading to Europe. It was not until 1818 that the Black Ball Line initiated the first scheduled transatlantic schooner service in the nation—one regularly scheduled crossing a month, from New York to Liverpool.[2]

Technological innovations of the early nineteenth century jolted Manhattan's West Side into commercial importance—specifically, steam power, the building of the Erie Canal, and the invention of the screw propeller. Steam power enabled ships to dock more easily in the strong westerly winds that buffeted the West Side. The *North River Steamboat*, colloquially known as the *Claremont*, introduced steam navigation to the world when she departed Greenwich Village for Albany in 1807.[3]

The waterfront got a major boost in the fall of 1825 with the opening of the Erie Canal.[4] Agricultural products, grain, lumber, and raw materials from upstate New York, the Great Lakes, and the Midwest arrived on the West Side piers, destined for the factories and warehouses that were rising rapidly along the waterfront. The raw materials, and finished goods, were then shipped to Europe or to ports up and down the East Coast. In 1836, a Swedish engineer named John Ericsson invented the screw propeller, which gave vessels a shallower draft and greater control over tides and currents.[5]

Because there were no bridges or tunnels connecting the island of Manhattan and the mainland United States, railroad barges crisscrossed the Hudson River from New Jersey, disgorging their contents for West Side factories and meat and produce markets that served a growing city. Eleventh Avenue was known as Death Avenue because freight trains traveling to and from the piers killed hundreds of people who were crossing the avenue.[6] Hundreds more were maimed as the tens of thousands of ferry commuters swarmed ashore from Hoboken, Weehawken, and Jersey City every morning and evening. Maritime commerce was the lifeblood of both the neighborhoods on Manhattan's West Side and the rest of the city.

In the first half of the twentieth century, new technology again disrupted the West Side maritime industry and the manufacturing, warehouse, and distribution facilities that lined its waterfront. In 1909, the first Port Authority Trans-Hudson trains, soon known as the PATH, began operating between Hoboken and Lower Manhattan.[7] In 1927, a revolutionary air-ventilated vehicle tunnel beneath the Hudson River opened. The tunnel, designed by a civil engineer named Clifford Milburn Holland, linked New Jersey and Lower Manhattan.[8]

Using the same technology, the Lincoln Tunnel was built in 1937, joining New Jersey with the "middle" of Manhattan.[9] John Roebling's suspension-bridge technology, first used to build the Brooklyn Bridge, which opened in 1883, had matured and was used to build the George Washington Bridge, which opened in 1931 and connected Upper Manhattan to northern New Jersey and its network of roadways.[10] Together, these technological advances had a profound impact on the trans-Hudson commuter ferry industry.

By the 1960s, the manufacturing jobs that filled many West Side buildings began moving to southern states to take advantage of cheaper labor. At the same time, the practice of prepackaging goods in containerized shipping made it easier to protect maritime cargo, reduced theft, and minimized the labor required for cargo handling. This development displaced tens of thousands of stevedores who worked the docks and ended the days when a guy in your neighborhood would pop open the trunk of his car to sell items that "fell off the back of the truck"—cheap.

Because there was not enough room to maneuver and store containers on Manhattan's West Side, the Port Authority of New York and New Jersey—the interstate agency in charge of port infrastructure—began constructing container ports on vast stretches of wetlands in the cities of Newark and Elizabeth, New Jersey, in 1962.[11] The port construction was a death blow to maritime commerce along the West Side waterfront.

Making matters worse, commercial jetliners replaced ocean liners as the preferred way to travel to Europe. It was faster and cheaper to fly to Europe than to make your way to New York City and sail the Atlantic. Cruise ship companies began partnering with airlines to offer fly-and-cruise packages and relocated their ships to Miami and other points south.[12] Passengers could quickly and inexpensively fly to Florida to start their Caribbean vacation. Although this system saved the cruise industry fuel and travel time, tens of thousands of direct and indirect jobs disappeared from Manhattan's West Side virtually overnight.[13]

The maritime industry, once the linchpin of the West Side economy, was on its deathbed, and the once-vibrant riverfront became abandoned, derelict, and dangerous—and home to a host of activities that residents did not want in their neighborhoods: concrete plants, bus garages, sanitation facilities, vehicle tow pounds, auto body shops, and even a prison.

The City's Master Builders

The twentieth century was an era of big ideas and bigger egos. Robert Moses excelled in both as the planner and master builder responsible for major public works that shaped New York City and the surrounding region between the 1920s and the 1960s. At one time or another, and often concurrently, Moses led multiple planning and development agencies, which was questionable but gave him tremendous power.[14]

He built highways, bridges, tunnels, parks, public housing, zoos, and Flushing Meadows Corona Park, the site of the 1964–1965 World's Fair. In the process, Moses filled miles of wetlands with the construction of Jacob Riis Park, Jones Beach, Robert Moses State Park—originally established as Fire Island State Park and later renamed to honor its "progenitor"—and the Belt Parkway.

He also bulldozed through traditional neighborhoods in the name of urban renewal to redesign the city and region to accommodate the automobile. In 1929, the Regional Plan Association, a nonprofit planning group, proposed a network of expressways to relieve traffic congestion and reshape regional transportation.[15] One of the most notorious was the Cross Bronx Expressway, which plowed through the mid-Bronx. The Major Deegan and Brooklyn Queens Expressways devastated city neighborhoods as well and cut local communities off from the waterfront.[16]

As the Moses era waned, new quasi-governmental authorities were established to expedite redevelopment. New York City created the Public Development Corporation in 1966, and New York State established the Urban Development Corporation in 1968.[17] That authority's 1971 Wateredge Study was the progenitor to the proposed highway that would become known as Westway.[18]

Westway, one of the more controversial infrastructure projects in the city's history, was seen as a more reasonable alternative to the Robert Moses approach.[19] It would avoid destroying existing neighborhoods by creating new "land" on landfill, concrete piles, and platforms in the Hudson River to support a limited access interstate highway, along with housing, commercial development, and a water's edge park on Manhattan's West Side. Both the city and state agreed to support this West Side redevelopment effort.[20]

By this point, the Rockefeller family had already made significant "private" contributions to help shape the city. In the 1930s, Nelson helped his father build Rockefeller Center, which became a symbol of the city's resilience during the Great Depression. He and his brother David secured the East River site for the United Nations to ensure that the institution called New York City "home."[21] David was particularly focused on preserving the economic viability of the Financial District in Lower Manhattan and was executive vice president for planning and development at Chase National Bank in 1955, when it merged with the Bank of Manhattan Company.

The newly expanded Chase Manhattan Bank needed a large headquarters. In 1958, older brother Nelson was elected governor, and by 1964, Chase Manhattan Plaza—a sixty-story office tower on Pine Street and the first rectilinear, tinted-glass building in lower Manhattan—opened. The plaza provided 2.5 acres of open space in the crowded financial center, and the project helped stimulate a resurgence of the Financial District.[22]

At that time, I was working in the mailroom of a brokerage house, adjacent to the recently completed superstructure. During lunch hour, my coworkers and I would eat our brown-bag lunches out on Chase Plaza.

Isamu Noguchi's sunken rock garden and fountain was my first exposure to public art; I was impressed. On other days, we would head down to Radio Row to gawk at the gadgets for sale in the shops lining the block and listen to auctioneers offer lots of cargo from the ships docked on the nearby waterfront.

Love of the Outdoors

I had come along early in the baby boom and grew up in the 1950s and early '60s in Flatbush, a middle-class neighborhood in the heart of Brooklyn. We lived in a four-story walk-up on Ocean Avenue, a major street that was lined with apartment buildings for miles and had tree-lined side streets containing large private homes—many of them Victorians. Because there were not many parks or playgrounds, we spent untold hours playing in the streets, alleyways, schoolyards, backyards, basements, and coal bins, or on fire escapes and rooftops. The neighborhood was our playground.

Scores of boys and girls my age learned friendship, teamwork, competition, and collaboration. We played games like Ring-a-Levio, Johnny on the Pony, Mum Freeze, stickball, and box baseball. We would choose up sides. You might be picked last, but everyone got to play. Rules were enforced collectively. As with all children, we could sometimes be petty, jealous, and spiteful. But we learned there was no benefit in making enemies or holding grudges, and differences were often worked out with the "Odds or Evens" formula. This was where I learned the importance of loyalty, being a team player, and keeping your word and understood the value of cooperation, leadership, and taking responsibility.

I never met my grandparents. My maternal grandfather was killed when he was thrown from a sidecar in a motorcycle accident on his way to work at a Queens dairy. My grandmother, who had emigrated from Ireland and died the month before I was born, raised nine children. On my mom's side, I was part of large a working-class family. My dad was Irish too and had a brother and two sisters, but I never met his parents, who died when he was young. We lived in a two-bedroom apartment, and my father was a union electrician, working with Con Edison down in the manholes every day. He left for work about 5:30 every morning because we did not have a car, and he rode buses or the subway to get to various jobs around Brooklyn and Queens.

Like most men of his generation, my father did not think that my mother should take a job outside of the house. My mother did a great job raising us, helping us with our homework, and taking us to church every Sunday and to activities like Boy Scout meetings. We helped her string beads and bundle Raleigh cigarettes and S&H Green Stamp coupons she collected to win prizes. My younger brother and I went to Catholic grammar school, but the family could not afford a Catholic high school education for both of us, so my brother went to Midwood High School.

When I was thirteen, I started high school and worked after school every weekday to contribute to the family; my younger brother did the same. I rode the streets of Brooklyn, in all kinds of weather, on a heavy single-speed delivery bike and found that working outside was tough—and was terrible for academic achievement. I had been an A student in grammar school, but I attended two high schools and summer school at three other high schools. I graduated with a 66 average—just enough to get my Regent's diploma.

I thought I had become stupid, but later in life I realized that working every day did not allow me to study or participate in extracurricular activities. At my fortieth reunion of St. Augustine's High School, in Park Slope, a classmate approached me at the bar and said, "We would've voted you the 'Most Changed' guy in the class of '64, but nobody knows who the hell you are!"

'Nam

Playing on the street and working outdoors made being "outside" routine to me, but my two tours in Vietnam added new dimensions to the experience. Besides drudgery, chaos, and adrenaline, 'Nam introduced me to nature, something I really had not experienced growing up in Brooklyn. The jungles, rivers, and rice paddies were alive with monkeys, snakes, lizards, parrots, and water buffaloes that were fascinating. The insects, however, were everywhere. They were annoying, and sometimes dangerous, but I eventually got used to them. I had no idea how the natural world worked, but I decided I wanted to find out someday.

I was a U.S. Navy Gunner's Mate guarding supply lines that supported the U.S. Marine Corps in the northernmost combat zone in South Vietnam—I Corps. In 1966, when I arrived, our small Naval Support Detachment in Chu Lai was primitive. We lived in tents and sandbag bunkers behind a few coiled rolls of concertina (or barbed) wire on a bay that was fed by three rivers and protected from the ocean. Just like New York Harbor, the entire area was a tidal estuary, although at the time I had no idea what that was.

Fishing villages were strung along the shore, and the villagers headed out to sea each sunrise in small fishing junks, or even smaller basket boats, to pit their skills against a sometimes-merciless ocean. Being a fisher was difficult and dangerous work, but I was taken with village life. An Hai was a small village just outside our perimeter that had bamboo huts with thatched reed roofs dotted along the river's edge. There was no plumbing, electricity, or windows—just shutters that were lowered when it rained.

Pigs searched for scraps along the shore while ducks swam close by. In the evening, the boats were turned over between the trees, and the nets were hung to dry and mend. Behind the homes there were vegetable gardens where chickens scratched at the earthen mounds and ate insects. A narrow dirt road separated the village from the rice patties. It was a simple life—difficult but rich in many ways—with your family, your livelihood, and your food all in one place. The villagers were self-sufficient.

Life in Vietnam offered an important education about enduring difficult circumstances and sharpened my survival skills. The experience also began a lifelong fascination with the natural world.

I had volunteered for both of my tours in Vietnam, from 1966 to 1968, and most of us were shocked and confused to return home to public scorn and isolation. We had been overseas for a year—in my case, two—and were proud of our service but forced to conceal it as we struggled to fit back into a changed society. We went to 'Nam individually and came home the same way. With no support system for returning vets, nothing prepared us to go from "in-country"—as we called 'Nam—armed to the teeth, to standing on a street corner in Brooklyn in civilian clothes a week later, watching the world go by as if nothing had changed. But we had changed.

We were all promised we would get our jobs back after our service, but there was a recession in 1969, and the Wall Street brokerage house where I worked had gone bankrupt.[23] I was told that, given my skills as a gunner's mate, I could be an armorer or work in law enforcement. I'd had enough of guns and violence, but I needed to earn a living.

My first job was repossessing cars. I got dinner and $10 for every car I helped repossess while prowling Crown Heights, Bedford Stuyvesant, Red Hook, and Cobble Hill neighborhoods in Brooklyn looking for cars whose owners were three months behind in their payments. I was used to working nights, but I was not armed, and taking people's cars was risky business. In addition, it was not cool being a white boy jacking cars in Crown Heights in 1969. I heard some incredible threats screamed out of windows as we broke into cars and raced away. However, I did like the "juice," that occasional adrenaline rush from 'Nam that was hard to find at home.

I wanted to get a college education, so in 1970, using the GI Bill, I got into Pace University in Lower Manhattan. I went to school at night and started what turned out to be a long college career.

Getting an Education

Initially, I gravitated toward classes in business and law with the vague aim of returning to Wall Street. But I found shifting legal rulings confusing and realized that what I wanted most in life was some certainty. I found it in science. There was order in natural systems. When you drop something, gravity pulls it down, while every day, the sun comes up on the same side of the earth. No one would change the laws of physics the way some people changed the rules about respecting patriotic young men who answered their nation's call to service.

My grades at Pace were good enough to allow me to transfer to Brooklyn College as a daytime student in 1972 when I was twenty-five years old. At Brooklyn, I took every science course I could—from meteorology and oceanography to physiology and astronomy. I loved exploring how the real world works, and I loved natural systems and being outdoors. And because I was not very good with physics formulas and found chemistry too much like cooking, I majored in biology. My fascination with nature in the jungle made field botany and ecology quite appealing, and I began to understand that, in one way or another, everything in nature was indeed interdependent.

I wanted to focus on urban ecology, a field that did not exist at the time. So I quit my job and became a full-time graduate student at City College of New York and studied ecology—minus the "urban." I had come to understand that in cities, people and nature are interdependent. Natural systems are strongly influenced by people—the dominant biological variable in the urban environment. But city residents were often oblivious to their natural surroundings, and their primary influences were their families, social status, and job opportunities.

I believed that, in addition to the physical sciences, sociology, political science, and economics were essential to understanding the urban environment. That did not go over well with my biology professor, who thought that studying social and political sciences was a waste of time. The sociologists saw the physical sciences as a waste of time and advised me to switch my major. So I found myself in a difficult situation—with no support for what I was passionate about and unemployed for the first time since I was thirteen.

Gateway NRA

Kids who grew up in Brooklyn often took the Green Line bus down Flatbush Avenue and over the Marine Parkway Bridge to swim at Bay 14 in Jacob Riis Park. Just on the other side of an overgrown chain link fence was Fort Tilden, an abandoned U.S. Army fort with gun emplacements that had protected the entrance to New York Harbor during World War II. In 1938, the Army had built two huge sixteen-inch gun bunkers about five stories tall with artillery shells that were carried to the guns on railroad cars. The concrete bunkers were camouflaged by a small forest of white poplars (*Populus alba*) interspersed with Japanese black pines (*Pinus thunbergia*) and Russian olives (*Eleagnus augustifolia*). I decided to write my master's thesis on one of the oceanfront plants in the Fort, seaside goldenrod (*Solidago sempervirens*).

It was April 1975, and as I was traipsing through brambles, I found six small American holly (*Ilex opaca*) trees scattered in this ninety-eight-acre woodland—all of them less than five feet tall. Mature barrier beaches in the New York/New Jersey metropolitan feature beech/holly forests. There is one on Sandy Hook in New Jersey and another on Fire Island. I was certain that the holly seeds were being deposited by migrating birds defecating as they passed through the area and that I was observing ecological succession in action.

Because I had no basic information about Fort Tilden, I drove over to Gateway National Recreation Area headquarters in Floyd Bennett Field to see what I could find. Gateway was the nation's first urban national recreation area. Established in 1972, it included Jamaica Bay and surrounding properties—among them, Floyd Bennett Naval Air Station, two landfills in Brooklyn, Jacob Riis Park, Fort Tilden, and Breezy Point in the Rockaways. The remainder of Gateway included Staten Island's south shore beaches, Miller Field and Great Kills, as well as Sandy Hook, New Jersey. The park was 26,000 acres.[24]

I found the chief of interpretation, Sam Holmes, on the second floor. I had never actually met a National Park Service ranger before, but Sam was certainly not what I expected. He wore black glasses and a sweater, had a shock of white hair, and sat in an office crammed with piles of paper. When I asked him for topographical studies, water table analyses, and/or vegetation surveys of Fort Tilden, he looked at me over the top of his glasses. "We don't have any of that," he replied. "Do you want a job?"

Having recently decided to become a full-time graduate student, I thanked him but demurred. As I headed home on my motorcycle, I realized that I was not happy with my graduate studies. Even more, I felt uncomfortable not working—and this was a new urban park! I swung my bike around, returned to Sam's office and accepted the job on the spot. I had absolutely no idea what the job was, and neither did he, but it changed my life. Sam became my mentor and remained a friend for more than forty-five years until he passed away, as quietly and gently as he lived, at ninety-six, in 2021.

We made things up as we went along. I had a badge, a ranger's hat, a nifty World War I Park Service uniform, and a chance to design and implement environmental education programs. One of our most successful programs was Operation Explore. Sam had colleagues at the New York City Board of Education, Cornell Cooperative Extension, and the New York State Office of Parks, Recreation, and Historic Preservation and believed strongly in the power of partnerships.

Pooling limited resources, we brought inner-city youth to the seashore to learn about nature at the Gateway Environmental Study Center and to regional farms and fisheries to understand where their food came from.[25] Operation Explore provided environmental education opportunities for tens of thousands of inner-city youths for more than twenty years.

We introduced a new form of access to the park when we brought four thousand people out on Circle Line boats for the first time during the 1976 Bicentennial Celebration.[26] In preparation for my trip narration, I joined Peter Stanford, founder of the South Street Seaport Museum, aboard a U.S. Coast Guard cutter. I was overwhelmed by the maritime history and geology of the New York Harbor, and that interest has stayed with me ever since.

Most Gateway rangers had arrived via the Tetons, Grand Canyon, and other "crown jewels" of the National Parks system, and they were shocked to find themselves on a polluted waterway, under an approach to Kennedy Airport, working in abandoned military facilities and teaching inner-city kids about nature. They were sure they had pissed someone off to get the assignment. But I was a city kid who had never been to a national park, and I thought this was heaven.

After a while, I tired of showing the kids something else that they could not have and then sending them back to the 'hood. I asked Sam if we could bring our programs out to the surrounding neighborhoods but was told that the National Park Service did not allow that. Instead, he suggested that I check out a volunteer group called the *Green Guerillas*, whose members were planting street trees and breaking into vacant lots to create community gardens and parks.

Guerillas? Like freedom fighters? The lack of a second *r* in guerilla was supposed to indicate their peaceful intent. Why not?

Back to the Streets

I met Liz Christy, the founder of Green Guerillas, in 1976. I joined the group and worked on projects like the Bowery Houston Community Farm and Garden (now the Liz Christy Community Garden, named in her honor), which is located on the Lower East Side—then a rough and tumble neighborhood with a high crime rate, rampant drug use, and plenty of vacant lots and abandoned buildings.[27]

We helped residents build community gardens from Hell's Kitchen to Bedford-Stuyvesant, mucked out stables at the New York Police Department Mounted Unit on Varick Street for the manure, and gathered discarded Christmas trees to create mulch. When we stripped Christmas trees for chipping, we sometimes found ornaments that we stuffed with wildflower seeds and created "seed grenades" to toss into the vacant lots. Seed "bombs" have endured and become more environmentally friendly over time.[28]

My fellow Green Guerillas were teachers, secretaries, merchants, horticulturalists, graphic designers, senior citizens, government officials, and municipal employees. Our mission was to expand public open space by helping folks in low-income neighborhoods convert vacant lots into community gardens and parks. Many inner-city neighborhoods were lawless then, and the city had more than two thousand acres of vacant lots. When a local community group asked for our help, we would help them cut through fences with bolt cutters and start their garden.

As technical assistants, we provided expertise and some plant material, but only a minimal amount of labor; residents did most of the work. We did not have permits or insurance, but I was finally working in the urban environment. I figured that the cops had better things to do than come after us, and if we did get caught, I thought to myself, "What were they going to do, send me to 'Nam?" Having no fear is liberating. And I decided to dedicate my life to working with people who wanted to create and protect nature in the city.

After leaving the National Park Service, I became a co-director of urban agriculture at the Institute for Local Self-Reliance, a small alternative non-profit think tank in Washington, DC, supporting local solutions for sustainability.[29] We advised nonprofit organizations and built community gardens and parks in Washington, DC, and in the South Bronx—as that neighborhood was burning. In 1979, after two years of splitting my time between Washington, DC, and New York, I moved to Greenwich Village to find my place in what was then a struggling city.

The West Village

Greenwich Village of the early 1980s seemed the perfect place to forge a fresh future. The block of Bank Street, where I lived, just west of St. Vincent's Hospital and the Village Green Recycling Center, was tree-lined and flanked with small apartment buildings and classic brownstones.

Many of the mid-block brownstones were set back from the sidewalk and had small yards in front, which gave the whole street a spacious feeling. And like the rest of the Village back then, our block offered an eclectic mix of residents: older beatniks who had bought their homes in the 1950s, young families who had inherited property from their parents and were raising their children or still partying, and a range of ordinary, interesting, sometimes-celebrated neighbors.

My next-door neighbor Ruth, a woman in her sixties, had bought her four-story building for $38,000. It was just a few doors down from the building that disgraced film producer Harvey Weinstein sold for $25.6 million in 2018.[30] The television journalist Charles Kuralt lived across the street in the garden apartment, and the drummer for the British rock band Dire Straits was on the second floor. There were retirees, musicians, immigrants, actresses and actors who waited tables between gigs, lawyers, real estate agents, families with children, and folks like me—a thirty-year-old Vietnam veteran struggling to make the city a greener, more livable place.

The Village had a lot to offer and was a great place to hang out. Hanging out was a skill I had learned as a teenager growing up in Flatbush. When you were not at school or working, you were hanging out—in this case, strolling along streets like West 4th and Bleecker, checking out the passersby, and popping in and out of local shops like Zito's Bakery, Ottomanelli & Sons Meat Market, Faicco's Italian Specialties, Murray's Cheese, and Matt Umanov Guitars.

There was a constant ebb and flow on the streets where tourists and students passed Mafiosi and musicians. The only thing the Village did not have was public open space.

Native American history of Greenwich Village is thought to have begun 6,500 years ago, and by the seventeenth century, when the area was known as Noortwyck, the Dutch had cleared pastures and planted crops.[31] The area's population grew rapidly after the American Revolution when, in the 1780s, an eight-acre parcel was purchased as a potter's field and public gallows.[32] A series of yellow fever and cholera epidemics between 1799 and 1821 ravaged Lower Manhattan, forcing those who could escape to move north to what is now known as Greenwich Village.

The abundance of nature must have been taken for granted as the neighborhood developed because little attention was given to providing public open space. Two centuries later, the area represented by Community Board 2, which encompasses the West Village, ranked second from last in the city for parks and open space per capita.

The biggest park in the Village was Washington Square, the former potter's field a half mile from my apartment. It was usually a busy place. Tourists and what we called the bridge and tunnel crowd—kids from the city's outer boroughs and the suburbs—bought skinny, two-paper joints, sometimes actually containing pot, from dealers stalking the funky rubber padded mounds on the west side of the park.

The chess tables in the park attracted serious players and hustlers, and the park's amenities included benches, a playground, and space for roller skating— and, most notably, for singing and dancing around the fountain at the center of the park. Washington Square Arch, designed by Stanford White, was built in 1890, gave the park its name, and was a historic landmark.[33] The so-called Hangman's Elm, the oldest tree in Manhattan, was another local attraction.[34] Above all, however, Washington Square Park was the "quad" for New York University during the academic year, so there was not a lot of open space that community residents could use.

The other park space in my neighborhood was Abingdon Square, which was not a square but two small triangles farther west on Bank Street at Bleecker Street. Because the triangles were split in two by the heavily trafficked Hudson Street, Abingdon Square was not the greenest of green spaces. One triangle was a well-loved but decrepit playground, while the other had a weathered bronze statue of a World War I doughboy on a granite pedestal. The benches surrounding that memorial were mostly occupied by senior citizens during the day and by the homeless at night.

Sunning on Pier 51 at Jane Street in Greenwich Village, 1986. (Tom Fox)

The major open space in our West Village neighborhood was three blocks farther west down Bank Street at the abandoned piers on the Hudson River. The working waterfront and local bars teeming with longshoremen and truckers had been a popular place for gay men to find companionship since the 1930s. As the advent of containerization prompted the maritime industry to abandon the waterfront, the piers in Greenwich Village became a place where the gay community could find camaraderie and companionship at a time when social and sexual revolutions were sweeping the country. The abandoned piers were for sunning and socializing, and the now-empty pier sheds seemed well suited for trysts, as were the backs of the trucks left empty and unlocked at night to prevent theft.[35]

The native Lenape, the Delaware people indigenous to the area, called the Hudson River *Mahicantuck*, loosely translated to "the river that flows both ways."[36] The mighty Hudson is indeed tidal and empties to the Atlantic, forming one of the nation's most biologically productive tidal estuaries, subject to both marine and riverine influences. Salt water from the Atlantic can travel as far north as Poughkeepsie when the tide runs high. Yet it was not until the nineteenth century, and even more so in the early twentieth century, that the West Side waterfront became an incredibly important economic engine for New York City.

2

Westway
(1974–1985)

●　●　●　●　●　●　●　●　●　●　●　●　●

The mega-development project known as Westway was an ambitious $2.3 billion plan to fill in the Hudson River shoreline from Chambers Street to 36th Street, bury a limited-access interstate highway underneath, and cover it with three million square feet of residential and commercial office development and a ninety-eight-acre water's edge park. Its genesis has roots in the early 1960s when the initial planning for modern-day Lower Manhattan began.

Governor Nelson Rockefeller supported large-scale redevelopment projects in the city—among them, residential development on Roosevelt Island, a narrow island in the East River and later a mixed-use community at Battery Park City. As chairman of the Downtown-Lower Manhattan Association, his brother David pushed for the construction of the World Trade Center—yet another way to secure Lower Manhattan's economic revival.[1]

To anchor its foundation, builders excavated seventy feet down to bedrock because the site was once offshore and over the centuries had been covered with landfill. The bedrock is called Manhattan schist, a unique metamorphic rock formation. In Lower Manhattan, the bedrock averages between ten and forty feet deep. It is eighteen feet deep at Times Square and 260 feet deep in Greenwich Village.[2] That is why most skyscrapers are clustered in either Midtown or Lower Manhattan.

To save time and money, the builders of the World Trade Center dumped one million cubic yards of excavated material into the Hudson River across West Street, which became the initial landfill for the ninety-two-acre planned community at Battery Park City.[3] Battery Park City contains 9.3 million square feet of commercial space, 7.2 million square feet of residential space, and thirty-six acres of parks. Another major redevelopment project that David Rockefeller supported was a plan to reimagine the entire West Side waterfront with a project that would become known as Westway.

The Westway Battle

The Miller Highway, named for Julius Miller, who was the Manhattan Borough President when construction began in 1929, remained unfinished until the southern section between Chambers Street and the Brooklyn Battery Tunnel was completed in the 1940s.[4] By 1957, this narrow cobblestone roadway carried almost one hundred thousand vehicles a day and allowed movement north and south along the waterfront without limiting access to the West Side's commercial maritime piers.

But the highway was poorly maintained, and in 1973, it collapsed under the weight of a dump truck, which, along with a passenger car, fell to the street below near Little West 12th Street in Greenwich Village.[5] In 1974, city, state, and federal officials announced a new West Side revitalization project—a highway that would carry 135,000 vehicles a day and connect the newly redeveloping Lower Manhattan with the rest of the city and surrounding region.

The proposed highway was a limited-access interstate highway from West 42nd Street south to the Brooklyn Battery Tunnel. It would be tunneled under 234 acres of new landfill and platforms in the Hudson, extending from the bulkhead to the tips of the piers where the navigable waterway begins. The proposed landfill from the northern boundary of Battery Park City to West 36th Street, under which the highway would be built, stretched for 2.9 miles.

Project proponents planned to top this new Manhattan real estate with 110 acres of commercial and residential real estate and a ninety-eight-acre park along the water's edge. The plan was supported by city, state, and federal officials along with the real estate industry, the business community, the construction industry, building trades, and the city's major newspapers.

Business and real estate leaders were worried about the city's dire financial straits and its seeming inability to provide basic services. In 1971, real estate developer Lew Rudin and hotelier Robert Tisch had joined forces to form the Association for a Better New York to help address the city's growing problems.[6] By the 1980s, the association was advocating for a broad array of issues—including transportation. The Rudin family owned a significant portfolio of commercial real estate in Lower Manhattan, and the association had become a powerful business group by the time it threw its support behind Westway.

In 1979, David Rockefeller established the Partnership for New York City to help business leaders work more closely with the government to address pressing public issues.[7] The partnership also became a major Westway booster.

While the city and state governments were creating new administrative and financial tools to expedite large-scale urban redevelopment, grassroots community activism in the city was growing, especially in Greenwich Village, where writer and urban activist Jane Jacobs led neighborhood opposition to Robert Moses's plan for a Lower Manhattan Expressway that would have sliced through the neighborhood.[8] Jacob's groundbreaking 1961 book *The Death and Life of Great American Cities* decried the destruction of neighborhoods by urban renewal projects. Opposition to the project swelled, and the city abandoned it in 1969.

Starting with Earth Day, the 1970s brought increasing emphasis to protecting the environment. Environmentalists emphasized reducing air and noise pollution, protecting water quality, enhancing and expanding public open space, and preserving what remained of the city's natural habitat.

The battle over Westway seemed like the perfect storm, and the stakes were high for the groups pitted against one another. For Westway supporters, building the highway offered the opportunity to secure federal funding to help stimulate both the growth of Manhattan and the city. The project's opponents—largely community residents, environmentalists, and mass transit advocates—regarded Westway as a real estate development scheme disguised as a highway that would destroy a priceless aquatic habitat, increase traffic and air pollution, and further harm the quality of life in adjacent neighborhoods.

What became an eleven-year fight to stop the project began in 1974. Each opponent had reasons to oppose the project. The Clean Air Campaign warned of increased air pollution, and the Straphangers Campaign argued against increased automobile congestion at a time when the city's financially strapped subways were falling apart. The Sierra Club and Friends of the Earth opposed the project on environmental grounds. Residents of adjacent communities balked at the idea of being cut off from the Hudson by new residential and commercial development after commercial maritime activity had historically restricted waterfront access.[9]

Recreational fishing enthusiasts and marine scientists opposing the project ranged from the Hudson River Fishermen's Association, a group that later morphed into Riverkeeper, to Hudson River Sloop Clearwater, founded by folk singer Pete Seeger. They were concerned about the landfill's impact on the Hudson's unique estuary and fisheries habitat.

One unexpected opponent was real estate developer Seymour Durst. He formed the Committee for a Westway Alternative to advocate for building the highway on the land and rezoning inboard properties rather than developing in the Hudson. Durst became a plaintiff in the Sierra Club's lawsuit against the project and even funded a front-page *New York Times* advertisement opposing Westway in 1984.[10]

Landfill eventually proved to be the project's Achilles heel. This was because government officials and consultants failed to adequately address the project's environmental impact on fisheries and then colluded with one another to conceal their mistake.

Joining the Fight

Several years before I got involved with Westway, I worked at the Institute for Local Self Reliance, a nonprofit advocacy group in Washington, DC. On March 28, 1979, I accompanied two organizers from a demonstration community gardening project we had organized in the South Bronx to a meeting at the White House. Just before the meeting was scheduled to start, it was canceled, and we were told, "There's a small problem with a power plant in Pennsylvania." A nuclear reactor at Three Mile Island, not far from Harrisburg, had a radiation leak.[11]

The institute became a central player in organizing one of the nation's first large-scale nuclear power protests, an event scheduled for May 6. I remember watching people streaming from the assembly areas toward the stage in front of the fountain at the United States Capitol Building, where I was coordinating stage security. Tens of thousands of people arrived at The Capitol while marchers continued to depart the assembly areas half a mile away.[12]

Like many Vietnam veterans, I had never attended a public demonstration because the protests typically vilified the warriors as well as the war. Seeing almost one hundred thousand people from across the country, and from all walks of life, peacefully protesting in the nation's capital, I truly understood the value of democracy and freedom of speech. I was overwhelmed by the experience and the realization that citizens had the potential to change the world if they raised their voices in unison, believed in their cause, and were willing to sacrifice.

Working on the event also put me in touch with nonprofit organizers from around the country, notably Donald K. Ross of the New York Public Interest Research Group, known as NYPIRG.[13] Their staff organized college students across New York State to educate the public about important issues and legislation. I worked with NYPIRG on a series of No Nukes concerts that were held in the undeveloped northern section of Battery Park City and culminated in a finale in Madison Square Garden.[14]

But except for the time I retrieved a car in the middle of the night from the police department's tow pound on Pier 76, where it was hauled after a victorious Knicks playoff game in 1970, I had not seen the West Side waterfront until I moved to Bank Street in 1979. That visit, in the light of day, was a shock! Two former World War II Liberty ships were docked at the foot of Christopher Street and served as a maritime high school.[15] Other than that, the ships that once lined the waterfront had disappeared. Many of the pier sheds had been marred by fires and were abandoned, while the usable piers housed bus garages, sanitation facilities, tow pounds, concrete plants, and parking lots. Many of the remaining abandoned piers were home to drug dealing, prostitution, and makeshift homeless encampments.

The Neighborhood Open Space Coalition

Those were trying times in New York. The city was on the brink of bankruptcy, and nonprofit organizations were competing against one another. All of them were targeting the same philanthropists, foundations, and corporations for funding, trying to get local media coverage and trying to influence government agencies, budgets, and policies. But they were not working together, or sharing their plans, for fear that another organization might steal their ideas.

Believing there was a better way to influence public open space spending and policies, Lisa Cashdan (from the Trust for Public Land) and I started the Neighborhood Open Space Coalition in 1981. The coalition began at a desk in the trust's office across West 31st Street from Madison Square Garden and eventually made its home in a downtown loft three blocks from City

Hall. It was a perfect location for an advocacy group. The offices of city, state, and federal elected and appointed officials were all located within five blocks.

In June 1982, the coalition joined NYPIRG and other organizations in a nuclear weapons protest that drew a million people to the Great Lawn in Central Park.[16] Gene Russianoff, a tenacious lawyer who had established the Straphangers Campaign, later introduced me to Marcy Benstock, director of the Clean Air Campaign and a brilliant activist who was leading the opposition to Westway.

Marcy was a bright, passionate Radcliffe graduate who was deeply committed to the cause. Over the years, she worked tirelessly with a host of community, environmental, transportation, and civic organizations who opposed Westway, and she was supported by talented attorneys like Al Butzel and Mitch Bernard, who finally prevailed in court.

Most elected officials, Westway supporters, and the media denounced Marcy as an obstructionist, but she was incredibly knowledgeable about the issues, the players involved, the project finances, and the shortcomings of Westway. Gene's office was on Murray Street, three blocks from ours, and Marcy's office was on the other side of City Hall. Sometimes the three of us would have our brown-bag lunches together behind the Tweed Courthouse in City Hall Park to discuss strategy.

Gene and Marcy wanted the coalition and its members, which then included sixty-two organizations dedicated to parks, recreation, natural preservation, and public open space, to get involved in fighting Westway, but we had no expertise in federal regulations, highways, and mass transit. One thing I had learned as an advocate was not to speak out about issues you do not know much about because you will never be taken seriously. Even worse, doing that can affect your credibility on the issues where you are an expert.

As a result, the coalition only played a bit part in the epic Westway battle; we did not get involved until the endgame in 1983. We opposed the landfill and focused our research on the ninety-eight-acre Westway State Park planned for the river's edge atop the landfill. Government officials were holding a much-needed park hostage, insisting that the park could not be built without Westway. We knew that it worked the other way around as well: Westway could not be built without the park.

It was tough for a citywide open space advocacy group to argue against a new park in Manhattan. However, because city and state park agencies lacked adequate planning and management staff and were in dire financial straits, we focused our opposition on that weakness and the need to ensure that enough money would be available to maintain and operate the proposed park.

If the responsible agencies diverted resources to this new project, their ability to adequately maintain and operate their existing park systems, which were already suffering, would be diminished.

With our role defined, we joined the Westway opposition, first critiquing the state's three alternative plans for the park.[17] We did not comment on the impact on marine life or air quality but emphasized that our existing public parks were struggling and that scarce public resources should not be diverted away from them.

If new residential and commercial development was needed, we argued, there were opportunities to build in low-income neighborhoods throughout the city that had been devastated by abandonment, arson, and demolition. Those areas were largely vacant and were already equipped with the necessary infrastructure such as water mains, sewers, traffic lights, streets, and sidewalks, along with schools, firehouses, police precincts, and hospitals. Focusing on real estate development in the Hudson would only delay the redevelopment of struggling neighborhoods in Harlem, the South Bronx, Central Brooklyn, and the Lower East Side.

We explained how the proposed Westway Park could not work as planned and insisted that without identifying adequate funding to ensure long-term maintenance and operation, building the park would be irresponsible.

Testifying against Westway State Park

Their original plan was to make the new park part of the state park system, so the coalition staff reviewed recent agency budgets and management reports that reinforced our claim that the new park would drain critical funding from other state parks and endorsed our analysis.[18]

The New York State Comprehensive Recreation Plan of 1983 mandated three policies: little or no expansion of park acreage, rehabilitation of existing parks, and maintenance of current levels of recreation services.[19] But a budget analysis by the state Office of Parks Recreation and Historic Preservation showed that between 1975 and 1983 the agency had found it difficult to adhere to those policies. Permanent staffing had been reduced by 21 percent, and maintenance and operating budgets reduced by more than 14 percent. State and federal capital contributions had fallen by 50 percent, and the entire capital budget for the 770,000-acre state park system was only $12 million.[20]

Even more troubling was the fact that the state was still accepting property donations and adding new parkland to the system. Budget officials

painted a bleak picture of the current situation, noting that hours of operation were being cut back while both necessary maintenance and infrastructure repair were, at best, consistently deferred.

The U.S. Army Corps of Engineers held public hearings on the project's
draft supplemental environmental impact statement in June of 1984.
Estimates for the design and construction of Westway State Park ranged
between $54 million and $100 million. The coalition's analysis estimated that
the cost of maintenance and operation would be $7.7 million to $14.2 million each year, which represented almost 19 percent of the entire state park
system's operating budget.

We addressed four key issues. First, there was no mechanism to ensure
long-term funding for maintenance, operation, and replacement of items
like benches and lighting. Second, neither the city nor state parks agencies
were capable of building and managing a new park. Third, shrinking
budgets were hobbling the city and state park agencies that were already
struggling to maintain and operate existing park. And finally, tens of thousands of new residents and office workers in the proposed developments
atop the landfill would crowd the new park and make it less useful to existing
community residents.

Personally, I believed that the draft of the supplemental environmental
impact statement failed to seriously consider the most logical alternative to
Westway—namely, building the highway on the existing roadbed and creating a public park on the waterfront. The idea seemed radical, however, and I
was not comfortable proposing it publicly. Barry Benepe, co-founder of
Greenmarkets, was in the coalition's office as we were completing our testimony, and I mentioned the alternative but thought it seemed a bit far out and
asked him if we should include it in our testimony. He replied, "Why not!"

Our comments on the draft supplemental environmental impact statement
raised concerns about the cost of the park and its impact on a state park system in decline. We also questioned why an alternative plan for a roadway on
the upland property and waterfront park had not been analyzed.[21]

The Legal Victory

From start to finish, the battle over Westway was a wild and crazy ride—one
that seemed as if it would go on forever. Westway had been formally proposed in 1974, and opponents lost no time in suing to stop it.[22] Both Governor Hugh Carey and Mayor Ed Koch had opposed Westway when they

were candidates and then reversed themselves once they were elected—
Carey in 1974 and Koch in 1978.[23]

In 1977, the New York State Department of Transportation officially
applied for a permit to put landfill in the Hudson River—a permit issued by
the U.S. Army Corps of Engineers in 1981. Later that year, President Reagan
presented a ceremonial check for $85 million to the state to purchase the
city-owned land and underwater property south of 36th Street for Westway.
The city sued the state claiming the property that would now be redeveloped
was worth much more. That purchase would eventually prove important in
the fight for a Westway alternative.

Koch and Carey signed a memorandum of understanding agreeing on the
decision to build Westway three days before the deadline to apply for federal
funds to buy the right of way.[24] The federal government had previously agreed
to fund 90 percent of the cost of amenities, but there were concerns that the
new Reagan administration would remove those amenities from the project.
If so, the city and state agreed that they could trade in the highway funds to
support mass transit projects.

The state planned to begin the landfill operation when they received the
Army Corps permit—a permit that was almost always routinely granted.
However, in March 1982, the Clean Air Campaign, Clearwater, Hudson
River Fisherman's Association, and other organizations challenged the permit in U.S. District Court, claiming that the Army Corps of Engineers had
violated federal law by including invalid information about the impact of the
proposed landfill on fisheries.[25]

In addition, in 1982, Federal Judge Thomas P. Griesa of the Southern District of New York voiced concerns that the project's planners failed to adequately assess its impact on fish populations and barred the federal government
from reimbursing the state for the money it paid the city to buy the underwater property needed for Westway.[26] Judge Griesa dismissed all the environmental objections except the fish study and invalidated the permit; the
Corps of Engineers reconsidered the matter.

The Corps in turn asked the state Department of Transportation to
undertake the necessary fish studies. It was estimated that these studies
would take two years to complete because the sampling had to be done in
the winter when the striped bass, who are migratory, were in the harbor.[27]

Judge Greisa, however, allowed the state to receive limited federal funding for the project until the litigation was complete. While campaigning for
governor that year, Mario Cuomo asked Thomas Puccio, a former U.S. attorney, to review the Westway project and make recommendations. Puccio's

report, released in 1983, recommended scrapping the Westway plan, build-ing a more modest roadway, and using the money for the proposed project to pay for mass transit improvements instead.[28] Surprisingly, Cuomo rejected the recommendation.

During a 1985 trial, again before Judge Griesa, the Army Corps' district engineer for New York, Colonel Fletcher "Bud" Griffis Jr., testified that, in his opinion, the West Side would be redeveloped without Westway. Mitchell (Mitch) Bernard, the attorney for the opposition, suggested they should have withheld the permit and explored alternatives that did not require landfill.[29]

But a critical word was deleted between the draft and final supplemental environmental impact statement, released later that year. The draft version had determined that Westway would have no significant impact on the Hud-son's striped bass population. However, the final version omitted the word *significant*.[30]

Judge Griesa again ruled against the Army Corps and for the Sierra Club.[31] Sierra Club et al. v. U.S. Army Corps of Engineers et al. is a landmark legal decision that strengthens enforcement of the federal Clean Water Act and the National Environmental Policy Act protecting America's rivers, wetlands, and coastal waters across the nation.[32] At this point, everyone thought that Westway might finally be dead despite the fact that between 1974 and 1984, the state had received more than $227 million for the project and had already spent $87.5 million for items like legal fees, planning, and design.[33]

Attempting an End Run

But Westway supporters did not give up, and they set their sights on the Fed-eral Aid Highway Act, which is reauthorized every five years. New appro-priations are often used to fund specific pork barrel projects dear to one officeholder or another. There was a September 30, 1985, deadline to trade in the Westway funds. New York wanted the deadline extended and Westway included in the 1986 reauthorization. Leading the charge were the state's two U.S. senators: Daniel Patrick Moynihan (a Democrat) and Alphonse D'Amato (a Republican).

Several organizations opposing Westway had national constituents and reached out to colleagues to raise awareness about local opposition to the proj-ect's reauthorization, and the coalition joined the chorus. I was serving as the vice president of the American Community Gardening Association and had colleagues in cities throughout the country.[34] We began reaching out to folks at Philadelphia Green and Boston Urban Gardeners, as well as Shane Smith at the Cheyenne Community Solar Greenhouse.

Our pitch to Shane, for example, went something like this: "You've mentioned that Malcolm Wallop [the current three-term Republican Senator from Wyoming] isn't a big fan of New York City. There is a $2.3 billion highway project that's been delayed for the second time by a federal judge, but New York still wants to include it in the upcoming federal highway reauthorization. Your members and supporters might consider contacting Senator Wallop to suggest he vote against wasting taxpayer's money on a Manhattan highway that's been blocked in federal court twice."

Opposition to the continued funding for Westway grew[35] and Moynihan and D'Amato soon realized that they did not have the votes for an extension, or reauthorization, so the city and state withdrew the project from consideration and redirected the funding.[36] The city subway system got approximately $1.4 billion dollars, and $811 million was set aside for a replacement roadway on the West Side.[37] The action represented the final death blow for Westway, ending a bitter eleven-year environmental and legal battle that represented one of the earliest victories for the urban environmental movement.[38]

Major public works, intended to reshape world-class cities, were typically launched by elected officials, planners, architects, and engineers. Westway had been such a project, but it fell victim to regulatory review, community and environmental activism, and bureaucratic chicanery. Both the government and private sector, accustomed to winning with top-down planning and only cursory public review and participation, were certain that their plans for Westway would prevail—so much so that they did not bother to develop a Plan B.

The result was that a project that was supported for over a decade by every president, governor, and mayor, as they say in New York, "sleeps with the fishes"—especially the Atlantic striped bass. *Fighting Westway*, by William W. Buzbee, provides a great overview of the legal and regulatory fight against Westway.[39] This manuscript brings that story up-to-date and describes what has happened since.

The Aftermath

Westway was the beginning of my West Side story, and what followed took an entirely unexpected turn. Efforts to exploit the river did not end with Westway. Apparently, Meyer (Sandy) Frucher, then president of the Battery

Park City Authority and formerly the state's lead labor negotiator, was close to the governor and had sent memos to Cuomo requesting that the state consider a proposal to build parks, shopping centers, and housing on landfill between Chambers and 34th Streets. Frucher suggested funding for sixty-five acres of development between Battery Park City and the Holland Tunnel with revenues generated by Battery Park City Authority.[40]

The state's Department of Transportation began working with the city Department of Transportation and the city Planning Department on what was called the West Side Highway Replacement Study. The coalition had grown to include 112 member organizations, and we presented our testimony regarding the study at the initial public hearing.[41] We were among 218 participants—the full cast of Westway supporters and opponents girding for battle again—and, not surprisingly, the public comments were plentiful.[42]

In the spring following the Westway debacle, I found myself at a gathering held to discuss the aftermath of the project. Westway supporters along with civic, community, and environmental advocates gathered in the Villard Houses, a nineteenth-century Renaissance Revival mansion on Madison Avenue behind St. Patrick's Cathedral. Villard Houses was home to several nonprofit organizations including the Municipal Art Society, which was hosting the event.

One of the speakers was Sandy Frucher. Frucher explained that Cuomo was considering a new entity to review the four roadway options being proposed in a new study by the state Department of Transportation and make recommendations for both the roadway and future revitalization of the West Side.

"Will any citizens be appointed to the entity?" I asked.

Frucher replied that city, state, and federal officials responsible for planning, transportation, and economic development would be joined by individuals from the real estate industry, the building and construction trades, and other labor unions, but citizens would participate during the required public review process once a plan was developed.

"If you don't appoint citizens to this new group," I responded, "you'll run into the same problems you did with Westway when the plan comes out. Including citizens will help ensure that public concerns are taken into consideration, during the deliberations—not after the fact."

I believe that a successful community organizer is like a grain of sand ingested by an oyster—rough enough to be irritating but not destructive. To stop the irritation, the oyster coats the grain with layers of secretions that create a pearl. That was what I hoped to set in motion with my comment that evening.

3

The West Side Task Force (1986–1987)

● ● ● ● ● ● ● ● ● ● ● ● ● ●

The call from the office of Arthur Levitt Jr. office came as a surprise. Arthur was chairman of the American Stock Exchange and a pillar of the city's financial community and in June 1986, and I was asked to meet him for a 7:30 A.M. breakfast at Windows on the World, the famed restaurant atop the north tower of the World Trade Center.

The morning of the meeting, I traveled downtown on the subway instead of on my bike and took the elevator to the 107th floor where Arthur greeted me. He was a fit, soft-spoken man in his mid-fifties. We sat at a table with a spectacular view of the West Side waterfront, and after exchanging pleasantries, he said he had been asked to chair the West Side Task Force that was being established by the city and state to recommend a path forward for the West Side Highway, which was officially called Route 9A, and the redevelopment of the entire West Side waterfront.

The task force would complete its recommendations in six months. Task force membership would include city, state, and federal government agency and authority representatives, business and labor union representatives, and four public members. Arthur asked me to join. He told me that the "Second Floor"—political lingo for the governor's office, on the second floor of the capitol building in Albany—warned him that I was difficult to deal with. But the governor decided "he'd rather have you on the inside of the tent pissing out, than on the outside pissing in."

It was not the warmest invitation I had ever received, and I was skeptical about the deadline or reaching any sort of consensus. But this was an opportunity to be at the table during decision-making for the project, so I agreed.

In addition to creating awareness of the importance of the Hudson's marine habitat, Westway's defeat had apparently reinforced the importance of community participation. Arthur explained that he had grown up in politics—his father had been New York State Comptroller—but he had chosen a career in finance. I confessed that it would be very difficult to represent all the project opponents adequately, but I promised to do my best.

I liked Arthur and the fact that he was not involved in the Westway debate. He was a respected businessman with a gentle demeanor, he was direct, and he seemed genuine. Arthur was an avid outdoorsman and a supporter of Outward Bound, a program I held in high regard. It was a pleasant and productive breakfast. I later found out that Arthur liked those early morning breakfast meetings. All our task force meetings were then scheduled for 7:30 A.M.

Soon afterward, Arthur hosted a dinner in the boardroom of the American Stock Exchange so that twenty-two task force members could meet one another. I lived two miles away and it was a cool evening, so as an avid bicyclist, I biked down. As I was locking my bike to a parking meter in front of the exchange, I saw a Lincoln Town Car stop directly in front of the entrance, and a well-dressed man who walked with an air of confidence emerged.

As we both passed through the security check, he cast several questionable glances at the guy wearing a corduroy jacket and a white T-shirt with green print proclaiming, "Urban Gardeners Do It in Vacant Lots." I wore the jacket out of respect for Chairman Levitt, but I often wore jeans and sneakers when attending public events, giving testimony, and making presentations. Was I sending a message? Yes.

My "uniform" usually got people's attention because it was not a suit and tie like most professional men wore. I once dressed like a tree to testify at a city Park and Recreation Department budget hearing in the City Council Chambers.

City Council members are often represented by staff at hearings. When members did attend, they typically sat on the dais looking over papers, chatting with their colleagues, eating lunch, or reading the newspaper. You never knew if they were paying attention to what you were saying or had read the testimony you had submitted in multiple copies. Being decorated with leaves got everyone's attention. Of course, that was long before City Hall established any real security measures, and in those days, it was still possible to enter City Hall through the unlocked door at the back of the building.

We both ascended in a small elevator but did not speak to each other. As the door opened, Arthur greeted us, asking if we knew one other. When neither of us responded, he began introducing us. "Tom Fox," he said to me, "this is Tom Maguire, president of Local 15 of the International Union of Operating Engineers."

Arthur then turned to the other guy and said, "Tom Maguire, this is Tom Fox . . ." but before Arthur could mention my affiliation, Maguire interrupted, looking me in the eye. "I know who you are," he said. "You're one of those wacko environmentalists from Greenwich Village. I can't stand your guts."

"It's a pleasure to meet you too, Mr. Maguire," I replied.

I had learned not to gloat when I win. Sooner or later, I am going to lose, and I often learn more from my failures than my successes because the pain sears the lessons into my soul. Besides, it is good to have a reputation as a gracious winner, or loser. Maguire was one of the construction industry's leading Westway supporters. His job was making sure that thousands of operating engineers—the heavy equipment operators, mechanics, and surveyors at every public and private construction job in the city—kept working.

I then met the other task force members, most of whom I knew only by reputation: city and state transportation commissioners, current and former deputy mayors, civic and labor leaders, and my fellow citizen representatives. The task force was the first effort to include opposing parties in the planning of the West Side waterfront. Heated arguments were bound to arise.

The Task Force Mandate

Our initial scope of study was as follows:

To develop a consensus on long-range development goals that could serve as a framework for subsequent detailed consideration by the appropriate Federal, State, and City agencies. Among the questions to be examined by the Task Force are those involving: (1) alternative public transit and roadway improvements and financing mechanisms; (2) opportunities for open-space and public access to the waterfront; and (3) the scale, mix, and location of public and private development. Using the best information available to it, the Task Force will consider the new West Side alternative futures, evaluating in the process citywide and regional needs for office development, housing, parks and waterfront access, transportation, and similar considerations.[1]

Our focus was the strip of land described as "the West Side corridor," but what was that exactly? How far north did it go? The Westway plan had gone from the Battery to 42nd Street. Some of us thought our study should extend north to 72nd Street, where the Henry Hudson Parkway and Riverside Park began. However, at that time, the city was supporting a proposal by Donald Trump dubbed "Television City on the Penn Yards" along the waterfront between 59th and 72nd Streets.[2] In any case, the task force was told its northern boundary was 42nd Street and that was that.

When the task force was announced, Marcy Benstock of the Clean Air Campaign immediately attacked the governor for, as she put it, "resurrecting the worst part of Westway," even though the task force had not met yet.[3] At our initial 7:30 A.M. meeting in the Vista Hotel in the World Trade Center complex, members of the staff were introduced and ground rules were set.[4] Curtis Berger, Wein Professor of Real Estate Law at Columbia University, would direct the task force, and Ann Buttenweiser, an urban and waterfront planner, would be deputy director.

Arthur was committed to a strict deadline and wanted to "create the best and most orderly communication flow between the Task Force and interested community groups," so he first established a community outreach subcommittee to map out a strategy to ensure public involvement.[5] He also established a technical assistance subcommittee to analyze materials presented to the task force and select outside consultants. Members were told that three transportation studies were planned, or underway, that would provide additional information to help with our recommendations.

Updates were provided on the three studies:

- The New York State Department of Transportation had contracted with Vollmer Associates to analyze four roadway alternatives. That study would be completed in the fall.
- Parsons Brinkerhoff, an engineering firm, was undertaking a West Side opportunities study to assess mass transit options for the Metropolitan Transportation Authority (MTA). The firm's preliminary work indicated that alternatives proposed by Vollmer should include a thirty-foot right-of-way for possible bus, light rail, heavy rail, or monorail use.

- Finally, the Department of City Planning's West Side light rail feasibility study, which would begin in a month, would further develop the Parsons/MTA study. It would examine the feasibility of a light rail system extending from Inwood in northern Manhattan down the West Side and around the Battery to East River Landing, a proposed twenty-three-acre development on platforms between South Street Seaport and the Downtown heliport.[6]

Light rail was the pet project of task force member Herb Sturz, chairman of the City Planning Commission. However, another member, Damaso Seda, legislative director for Local 100 of the Transit Workers Union, opposed the light rail favoring an MTA alternative operated by his union.

The Neighborhood Open Space Coalition presented its testimony at public hearings regarding the roadway, so I had two opportunities to weigh in.[7] The cost of the four highway alternatives from the state transportation department ranged from $145 million to $585 million or more; the agency stated that up to $690 million of the $1.7 billion trade-in funds could be put toward the roadway, which would require a $121 million matching grant from the state.[8]

I have learned to view budget estimates with caution. Federal, state, and city estimates for the same project can often differ. The amount of money available, required, or generated by a project often varies depending on whom you ask and when you ask them. Changing estimates continued throughout my entire experience working on this project, and I soon realized that any government budget estimate should be considered "ballpark."

Only four citizen representatives were appointed to the twenty-two-member task force. David Sive, considered by many as a father of environmental law; Roberta Brandes Gratz, an urban historian and author from the Upper West Side; Robert Trentlyon, a Chelsea resident and the owner and publisher of two community newspapers; and me. David attended task force meetings but was not as involved as the rest of us, who spoke often and were skeptical that the lopsided composition of the task force would allow much room for compromise.

The four citizen members were at a disadvantage because we did not have support staff to digest the voluminous legal, financial, and technical information that we received regularly. Furthermore, we were supposed to represent a broad spectrum of constituents: environmentalists concerned with air and water quality, parks, and habitat protection; historic preservationists; small business owners; maritime interests; mass transit supporters; local neighborhood organizations; community boards; and local elected officials.

Arthur approved our request for a fifteen-member ad hoc advisory committee to help us digest the information we received and vet our response, which gave us hope that public participation was being taken seriously. I wrote memos about issues of importance to other task force members and copied members of our advisory committee, keeping them in the loop. My first memo, to Curt Berger, suggested issues that should "be on the table" early in the process, which included extending our project's boundary to 59th Street and questioning why we were not subject to open meeting requirements.[9]

Although the task force met once a month, members were expected to attend subcommittee and working group meetings—along with briefings, public meetings, field trips, planning workshops, and retreats—and to participate in innumerable phone conversations. The effect of the constant personal contact among members produced an interesting result: we began to feel like a team.

Most task force members were accessible, the staff was dedicated, the leadership was flexible, and I began to feel that we had a real opportunity to achieve something special. Given the top-down planning for Westway, however, the public was not convinced that the task force would be useful, and unless the public was convinced, we would not be. And so, our first challenge was to engage the public and increase their support.

Community Outreach

Our community outreach subcommittee was chaired by city Transportation Commissioner Ross Sandler, an attorney and avid bicyclist with a solid reputation in the environmental community. Our first move was to open our monthly meetings to the public and meet with members of interested civic and community groups, both to show respect and to better understand their concerns. With Arthur's approval, we invited the advisory committee members to the task force's meeting on September 3, with a follow-up meeting afterward at the nearby office of the Neighborhood Open Space Coalition—a practice that continued through the entire process.[10]

Not all our interactions with the public were smooth, however, and due to the bitter fight over Westway, uniformed police officers often attended our public meetings. At our first public meeting, in Chelsea, an agitated man sitting in the front row was speaking loudly to himself. Task force members were seated on a stage about three feet above the auditorium floor where our stenographer was recording the minutes. Suddenly, this fellow burst out of his seat and walked toward the stage, causing the stenographer to bolt from her chair. I jumped off the stage and pushed him back into his seat as a police officer rushed down the aisle and escorted him from the building. That is how contentious things could get in the early days.

We agreed to hire a community engagement consultant, someone to help coordinate and support our public participation efforts. We selected Alexia (Lex) Lalli, a well-respected professional who lived in the West Village. I requested that the task force create a library for research.[11] Curt suggested that Lex work both at the task force office several days a week and at her office on West 12th Street, and both should be open to the public.[12]

Lex was an important member of the team. She organized a boat tour, a daylong workshop to solicit ideas from the community, and a public hearing to review our draft report in December. She distributed fact sheets that described our efforts, and she organized field trips to revitalized waterfronts in Toronto, Chicago, Seattle, Boston, Baltimore, and Vancouver. Public participation became a primary focus of the task force.[13]

With the help of staff from the Manhattan Borough President's office, the Port Authority, and Battery Park City Authority, our technical assistance subcommittee interviewed several consultants. They recommended Gary Hack and Steve Carr of Carr, Lynch Associates in Cambridge, Massachusetts, as our planning consultant. We now had a top-notch team working on the project.

Expanding North

A key issue was how far "up" our West Side corridor went. Chairman Levitt had been told that the task force would be an independent entity and would be free to make any recommendations it agreed on. The last section of the Miller Highway, however, was still elevated between 43rd and 59th Streets and beyond our scope. Yet the state Department of Transportation planned to spend $80–$100 million to reconstruct that elevated section, and the city Department of Transportation advocated extending it a half mile farther south to 32nd Street to ease the downtown traffic flow through Midtown.

Curt realized that retaining the elevated roadway north of 42nd Street would force the task force to accept the idea of an elevated structure south of 42nd Street because it eventually had to come down to the surface. He insisted that this undermined the task force's independence, and Arthur agreed. The result was the state and city agreed to remove the last piece of the Miller Highway and extend our northern boundary to 59th Street, adding three-quarters of a mile to our roadway study area. However, our waterfront planning still stopped at 43rd Street.

New Working Groups

By early October 1986, the public was attending our monthly meetings. City Transportation Commissioner Sandler described our plans to hold a community workshop and introduced the team of specialists from Boston we had retained to facilitate the event.[14] We had established three formal working groups: transportation, waterfront-land use, and financial-legal-structural. The waterfront-land use working group included the major development proponents like Frucher, Sturz, and James Stuckey—the president of the city's Public Development Corporation—along with David Dinkins and me.[15]

The task force invited a hundred people representing different interests to the community workshop later that month and eighty-five accepted.[16] The meeting produced fifteen points that attendees thought important, the first of which was that there should be no landfill or development west of the bulkhead. Other requests included a low-speed, low-cost, at-grade roadway with signals, and there was also general agreement that the timeframe the task force was given to produce its report was too short.

At our November meeting, Gary Hack described possible outboard land-use scenarios, stressing that they were not blueprints but ideas whose components were interchangeable. Scenarios ranged from a recreational waterfront to housing, industry, and an urban-theme park.[17] Afterward, Gary, Curt, and Lex attended our ad hoc advisory committee meeting at the coalition where Gary again shared preliminary land-use scenarios. Hack's Scenario A contained fifty-six acres of outboard development, and Scenario C had 120 acres, which did not include the proposed Hudson River Center.[18] Advisory committee members requested that designs include development alternatives that did not require landfill or platforms in the river.[19]

Participants requested that all waterfront development be water-related, that inboard property rezoning be considered, and that more space be found for active recreation. They also requested that the task force recommend a long-term approach to West Side redevelopment.

Roadway Capacity

The task force had been charged with recommending a roadway design that would increase existing traffic capacity by 15 percent, and the state Department of Transportation released its West Side Replacement Study in August.[20] Two fortuitous events drastically changed both the planned capacity and the scale of the roadway.

The first was a report that the city was experiencing "considerable problems" meeting the State Implementation Plan, air pollution criteria established by the 1970 Clean Air Act.[21] Mayor Koch announced that traffic in the Midtown central business district had to be reduced by 25 percent to meet the State Implementation Program. Failure to meet these standards would drastically decrease federal funding for the city.

The second was the results of a one-day origin-to-destination study by our transportation engineering consultants who stopped motorists traveling along West Street and asked two simple questions: "Where are you going?" and "Where did you come from?" Up to this point, everyone assumed that the West Side Highway's critical role was to move vehicles through the city as well as to the central business districts. But the simple study showed that 85 to 90 percent of the cars and trucks traveling on West Street were going to or from Midtown or Lower Manhattan.[22]

By November, critical decisions were being made, and one of them involved how much traffic the new roadway would accommodate. Approximately 91,000 cars a day had used the old Miller Highway before its collapse, and more than 57,000 cars a day were using the West Side Highway when the task force was established.[23] Local residents believed that many of those trips had been diverted to neighborhood streets due to traffic congestion on Route 9A.

A week earlier, Sam Schwartz, the city's deputy transportation commissioner, had presented his department's plan for the replacement roadway with a ten-lane elevated highway at 59th Street narrowing slightly as it descended to the surface at 46th Street. A few days after the briefing, the task force was preparing for a pivotal weekend retreat at Mohonk Mountain House, a historic lakeside resort about ninety miles north of the city.

The two-day retreat would allow task force members to hash out an agreement on a new replacement roadway. One of our first briefings was again by city Deputy Transportation Commissioner Sam Schwartz, who presented the agency's plan for the replacement roadway. There was still a ten-lane highway, but it came down to the surface at West 57th Street.

Chairman Levitt noticed my surprise. "What's the matter, Foxy?" he asked. I replied, "Nothing. The plan looks great."

Mohonk Retreat

Our Mohonk retreat was a watershed. Task force members, staff, and consultants were together for two days in a rustic mountain resort on a brisk November weekend. Cell phones were not a thing yet, and our rooms had no telephones or televisions. The government officials were all accompanied by staff, and I had asked Arthur if citizen members could each invite a member of the ad hoc advisory committee.

Arthur agreed, and I was accompanied by Gene Russianoff of New York Public Interest Research Group—a lead Westway opponent, an attorney, brilliant tactician, and someone I trusted. I knew he would strengthen my resolve in an increasingly tense situation where the public members of the task force were outnumbered.

There were about thirty-five participants. We ate our meals together, received briefings, met in small groups, discussed alternatives, and mingled together at the bar in the evening. We got to know one another personally, not just by our positions on contentious issues. The retreat was one of Arthur's brilliant ideas that contributed significantly to building consensus.

The controversy over landfill in the Hudson had killed Westway and would kill any chance of a compromise. A smaller-capacity roadway could now be constructed without landfill in the river, but the pro-development members still supported landfill and platforms for residential and commercial development.[24]

In another stroke of genius, Chairman Levitt took that issue off the table, stating that a decision would be made by a subsequent entity after our work finished. Arthur assigned Gary Hack to develop options outboard of the roadway that Levitt suggested, ranging from park development—landscaped areas, playgrounds, pools, recreation facilities, amphitheaters, and esplanades—to such high-density development as commercial offices, luxury housing, and marinas. That decision proved critical, and thanks to it, I learned an important lesson: keep your eye on the prize and be willing to set aside some battles to fight another day. Neither side wins, but neither side loses.

Herb Sturz was focused on moving new residents and office workers in proposed developments to and from downtown without increasing traffic.

However, the Department of City Planning's light rail feasibility study would not be completed until six months after our report was due.

Some of us voiced concern that the light rail system would run north-south without any east-west connections and would not be integrated into the existing mass transit system. Sturz suggested that funding for the light rail come from new development, but that would divert money from mass transit and other amenities like parks and schools, which were frequently financed with revenue from new development.

Concerned about gentrification, some of us dubbed light rail the "Yuppie Express." A city proposal for 23 acres of platforms from the Battery to East River Park, called East River Landing, was on the table at the time.[25] We envisioned residents from Television City riding the light rail to work in Battery Park City, grabbing a drink and dinner at South Street Seaport, attending a game or concert at the new Madison Square Garden (proposed above the MTA's rail yards south of the Javits Convention Center), and traveling home to Television City without ever setting foot in Manhattan. (Of course, that was just what Sturz wanted.)

Our biggest fear was that a thirty-foot wide space for light rail between the roadway and the river would make the waterfront even less accessible and shrink the area we wanted for a public esplanade. Roberta led our opposition to the light rail. She and Herb Sturz had numerous private discussions and eventually compromised—a light rail right-of-way would not be included in our report either, but if additional transit on the West Side was needed, it would be built within the framework of the task force's recommended plan.

Our recommendations highlighted the potential for ferries and water taxis travelling north and south along the waterfront. There were several existing and proposed ferry lines between New York and New Jersey, and some of us were convinced that waterborne transportation allowed people to move about and experience the river without a designated right-of-way.

The light rail compromise reinforced the lesson learned from the decision to eliminate landfill. If no decision is made against someone's idea, it is easier to take that decision off the table. After all, it might eventually be implemented.

Grade separations are a safety measure. Where two or more roadways cross one another, separating traffic helps minimize the disruption of traffic flow. Task force members from the transportation and construction industry agreed on the need for grade separations at busy intersections—like 42nd Street and 34th Street, to ease traffic turning into the Central Business District—and at Canal Street, and entering the Brooklyn-Battery Tunnel.

Elevated roadways block views of the river and disperse air and noise pollution more widely, so the city Department of Transportation suggested that two lanes be depressed to move through traffic past 42nd Street and 34th Streets, claiming that traffic volumes called for a twelve-block tunnel estimated to cost $8–$10 million per block.

This stretch of the highway just happened to be home to several proposed developments, including Hudson River Center, a new Madison Square Garden, and an expansion of the Javits Convention Center. Some of us believed that the real purpose of this grade separation was to enhance movement between developments on either side of the roadway. The grade separations soon became a major factor in what was becoming a very expensive roadway.

Citizens on the task force believed that mass transit was more important for the city than an expensive highway. By keeping roadway costs low, more money could be allocated to a waterfront esplanade and/or the city's struggling subway system. Representatives of the building and construction trades, however, suggested that the entire available $811 million was exactly the amount that should be spent—not a penny less.

The $90 million to $120 million for the proposed grade separation in Midtown was nothing compared to the one proposed near the Brooklyn-Battery Tunnel, which would enhance the connection between Battery Park City and the World Trade Center, whose cost was estimated at $235 million. Citizen members argued that grade separations should be funded by the adjacent real estate developments they served. Although we lost that debate, we had an ace up our sleeve.

At the Mohonk retreat, members agreed to a narrow roadway and embraced the concept of a public esplanade between the roadway and the river—including a bicycle and pedestrian path. Creating a park was the primary goal of the Neighborhood Open Space Coalition. Vollmer Associates was working on roadway designs, and we held several meetings with them urging that the roadway be as narrow as possible to allow for a wider public esplanade to open the waterfront for community use.

However, Vollmer was told that the land between the road and the river should not be considered in their study and an esplanade would not be built with public money. If that area was developed as a public park, "others" would have to pay for it. That was how the city and state planned to hold public waterfront improvements hostage to new development. However, at Mohonk, task force members agreed to public funding for the esplanade. I was elated but apparently counting my chickens before they hatched.

Continuing Our Work

After our retreat, the task force issued a public report of several meetings we had held, including the deliberations at Mohonk, and described our preliminary recommendations.[26]

The highway would become an urban boulevard that would reduce costs, accommodate existing and projected traffic, and enhance pedestrian access to the waterfront. We would focus on land-use principles rather than specific land-use scenarios, including installing a continuous bicycle and pedestrian path along the waterfront, maximizing water-related activities such as kayaking, retaining piers where feasible, creating additional open space, and designating areas for maritime uses. We would continue to analyze future governance options and ways to pay for public amenities and recreational space.

Several agencies and institutions would have to be involved in implementing the task force recommendations, and we agreed that these efforts had to be coordinated. One proposal to implement our recommendations was creating a development authority with a small board that was controlled by the governor and the mayor. Another, which citizen members supported, was a planning group to continue our work until there were final plans that required a development entity be created. Public trust in the task force was not very solid, and proposing a development entity right away would undoubtedly generate significant opposition.

When we received the draft proposal for a follow-up entity, there were serious problems.[27] The proposed entity would be responsible for the planning and development of the highway, land, and in-water uses on the waterfront including the construction, condemnation, and disposing of property, and if necessary, it would override city zoning and regulatory requirements. It would also issue bonds "as required" to fund projects and could be established by the legislature or as an Urban Development Corporation subsidiary with all the requisite powers. My margin notes described the idea as outrageous.

Manhattan Borough President David Dinkins argued that the borough president should be a member of any new body. He also said that citizen membership, along with mandatory public participation and review requirements, were essential. The final compromise was recommending a planning entity that included the borough president and several citizens, appointed by the governor and the mayor, that would adhere to existing city and state land-use review procedures and include public participation.

Mapping the Waterfront as a Park

I followed up with a memo on my presentation at the Saturday night dinner in Mohonk, which laid out a rationale for building the esplanade with public money and designating the waterfront as a public park. Reading through the reams of briefing information that we had received for our retreat, I focused the statutory authority for the use of federal funds contained in 23 U.S.C. Section 319, Landscaping and Scenic Easement.[28] Advocates need to pay attention to the details. Even though it is a pain in the neck, they can contain treasures, as I learned in this case.

It seemed that preserving scenic areas adjacent to federally aided highways was an allowable federal transportation expense. I argued that designating the entire waterfront a scenic area might negate the need to repay the $90 million in federal funds used to build the right-of-way for Westway.[29] Governors and mayors, senators and congressmen, and unions and billionaires were interested in the future of the West Side waterfront. Working with sympathetic federal officials, they had received federal funding for Westway and could do it again on a much smaller scale if they presented it properly.

Mapping the entire waterfront out to the pierhead line as a public park would have the added benefit of protecting the easement in perpetuity. Federal highway beautification funds could be used for eligible improvements. My memo included a hand-drawn map of the esplanade, piers, and underwater property with a dashed line out at the pierhead line, and I suggested it be mapped as parkland from Battery Park City to 42nd Street.[30] My proposal created a major conflict because it prohibited in-water development, but we would not have to pay back the feds, and the public park would not have to be funded by commercial development, in the river.

By the time the Mohonk retreat had wrapped up, the only section of the roadway where plans were not finalized was adjacent to Battery Park City. When the transportation committee proposed options ranging up to $315 million for that grade separation, it pushed the cost of the highway above the $811 million in state and federal funds available, which was more than we had the ability to recommend.[31]

Task force members received a revised draft of our recommendations on December 1, and they included the esplanade.[32] However, Mayor Koch later decided project costs had to be cut and on December 5, 1986, the task force was informed that the mayor and the governor had removed public funding for the esplanade. Our last meeting was scheduled to get feedback on the draft recommendations.[33] The demand for public funding of the esplanade was heard loud and clear from environmental, civic, and community organizations.[34] Public planning is a cumbersome process, but it informs designs and engenders broader support for good ideas.

The city and state then proposed using federal funds for a bicycle and pedestrian path, which they agreed was transportation, but not for the esplanade. That was called landscaping and would be funded by "others."

Scenic Area Designation

I had met Mark Baker in 1983 when he answered the Neighborhood Open Space Coalition's ad seeking a pro bono attorney in the Council of New York Law Associates newsletter. Baker, a Columbia Law School graduate, was a young associate at Dewey, Ballantine, Bushby, Palmer and Wood, a prestigious New York City law firm. He and his wife Diane, an investment banker at Salomon Brothers, lived in a brownstone on State Street in Brooklyn Heights. A Buffalo native and avid gardener, Mark wanted to contribute to his adopted city.

At that time, the coalition was assisting the Brooklyn Heights Association in its fight to stop a Port Authority from building three thousand units of housing on Brooklyn Piers 1 through 6 below the Brooklyn Heights Promenade. We helped organize the Brooklyn Bridge Park Coalition; I became a founding co-chair and Mark agreed to help in that effort.[35] I asked him if Dewey might also help determine if federal highway funds could be used to preserve scenic areas and pay for landscape improvements on the West Side.

Dewey attorneys met with an assistant secretary at the U.S. Department of Transportation in Washington who said that the department's regulations typically encouraged the types of expenditures we were describing. If the state submitted a request to the Federal Highway Administration to fund a scenic easement and landscape the esplanade, the official added, it could be considered an allowable transportation expenditure.

"Indeed, the applicable federal highway regulations promulgated by the Department of Transportation state that highway aesthetics is the most important consideration in the federal-aid program. Highways must . . . blend with our natural social and cultural environment," their December 1986 memo said, adding, "The preservation of valuable adjacent scenic lands is a necessary component of highway development."[36] In other words, state Department of Transportation officials lied to the task force. Spending federal dollars on scenic preservation and landscaping was an allowable use of federal highway funds.

Our final task force meeting was very well attended.[37] After various presentations describing our thoughts regarding land use and roadway design, Roberta asked to speak "on the record," stating she was not convinced the roadway needed to be so elaborate and urging the task force to undertake further studies. I stated "on the record" that the cost of grade separations should be funded by adjacent real estate developments, and any available public funding should be used for the esplanade. If public funding was limited to the bicycle and pedestrian path, the rest of the waterfront would be a wasteland—which is exactly what the pro-development forces wanted to justify development in the river.

My follow-up memo described the benefits of the esplanade, which protected the roadway from flooding, wind, and glare from the river and reduced air and noise pollution; these facts were well documented and common planning practice in roadway construction.[38] In other words, the esplanade was not a frill. I also wrote to task force members and copied all ad hoc advisory committee and coalition members asking them to attend the next task force meeting and reinforce the need for public funding of the esplanade. I also conveyed that a new planning entity must ensure meaningful community participation and follow existing Uniform Land Use Review Procedure requirements.[39]

Finalizing the Recommendations

Arthur asked me to consider compromising on the issue of public funding for the esplanade so the task force could issue a report that represented a consensus. "Foxy," he began, "I've supported quite a few things you care about, and we've gotten along well so far. Could you do me a favor and accept the recommendations without public funding for the esplanade?"

"Arthur," I replied, "if I could do it for you, I would. But I'm representing people who don't have a voice in this process, and they want public funding for the esplanade."

He was not happy. However, it seemed insane to spend $315 million on grade separations adjacent to landfill and high-rise development and leave miles of public property adjacent to the Hudson River barren and undeveloped—especially since the price tag for the esplanade was only estimated at $81 million.[40]

The biggest selling point for the defunct Westway plan was new parks and waterfront access. However, the mayor had scuttled public funding for the esplanade, and Sandy Frucher had agreed.[41] On December 22, a memorandum from the corporation counsel of Battery Park City Authority proposed a revised version of the new entity to continue our work. "In particular," it stated, "you will note that the draft reflects an 'agreement to disagree' with respect to several issues."[42] Sandy was doubling down and no doubt speaking for the governor.

A compromise seemed increasingly unlikely. As the endgame neared, Ann Buttenweiser was in our World Trade Center office, busy writing the task force's final report. A co-founder of the Parks Council who had worked at City Planning when she joined the task force, she was one of us. I told her that I could not approve the report unless it included public funding for the esplanade. I said, "I'll probably never be appointed to another commission as long as I live." She turned to me with her reading glasses poised on the tip of her nose, looked me in the eye, and replied, "You can bet on that!"

The debate raged until the eleventh hour.[43] Arthur stated his "feeling that the environment is so poisoned by the controversy from Westway that it's made the task of development infinitely more difficult. Only with a unified recommendation do I think we have any expectations of making this waterfront what the city really deserves. I think in the absence of that we will be mired in controversy for the next ten years."[44]

Arthur had promised the governor and mayor recommendations for a Westway alternative by the year's end, and he was already a week late. He wanted a consensus agreement, but that consensus required herding cats. The governor and mayor realized that building the esplanade would seriously diminish opportunities for development in the water by providing public access to the Hudson River. There is a reason that critical decisions are left to the last possible moment in negotiations. By then, the level of trust developed is as high as it will ever be, and everyone wants to close the deal.

Frucher often told me he just wanted to expand Battery Park City landfill to extend to Canal Street. It was only sixty-five acres; he argued that he would leave half of it as public open space and finance the entire esplanade with the money generated by development on the other half. Sandy and I were on opposite sides of almost every argument, but I respected him. He was direct, experienced, and committed to the success of whatever he put his talents to—a worthy adversary.

All the task force members had agreed to leave the fate of the underwater property to a subsequent entity and recommend an urban boulevard with at-grade crossings. Three citizen members, however, refused to endorse the final report unless it called for public funding for the esplanade.[45]

Arthur returned from Christmas vacation desperate to reach consensus. He suggested a face-to-face meeting with principals on both sides to resolve the issue of esplanade funding. We met the night before the task force report was scheduled for release. Roberta Gratz, Bob Trentlyon, and I had spoken earlier and agreed to maintain our position. Roberta drafted our dissent.[46]

Opposing us was the crème de la crème of the city's development advocates. Deputy Mayor Bob Esnard attended the meeting with Herb Sturz, Jim Stuckey, and several lawyers and technicians from their respective agencies. Other attendees included Borough President Dinkins and Nathan Leventhal, a former deputy mayor and, at this point, president of Lincoln Center.

Our suite in the Vista Hotel had a bedroom and living room. Chairman Levitt ordered a dozen hot fudge sundaes from room service; waiting for the meeting to begin while chasing maraschino cherries around parfait glasses definitely broke the ice. However, Sandy Frucher, who had attended the governor's State of the State address in Albany, had not arrived yet. He would occasionally join the meeting by car phone while whizzing down the New York State Thruway and demanded that no final decision be made until he arrived. He insisted that the governor would not agree to public funding for an esplanade.

The bottom line was best articulated by David Dinkins: "If Gratz, Trentlyon, and Fox have a dissenting opinion, I'll join them. Frucher will write his own dissenting opinion and we're back to square one. We can't leave this room until we have consensus." Sandy arrived around nine o'clock as Leventhal practiced shuttle diplomacy, carrying offers and counteroffers back and forth between the two opposing camps who were caucusing in separate rooms.

The meeting ended around eleven o'clock, and Ann Buttenweiser left to insert our compromise into the final report, stating that the task force agreed that the roadway, the esplanade, and the bicycle path was one public project, and that public funding for the esplanade was appropriate.[47]

At our last task force meeting, at 7:30 A.M. as usual, Arthur announced that we had reached consensus and recommended that the city and state build a new urban boulevard with a bicycle path and waterfront esplanade on Manhattan's West Side. It was ironic that an urban boulevard was the arterial alternative included in the initial Westway Environmental Impact Statement twelve years earlier.

I asked some task force members to sign my copy of the final recommendations, which I keep in my office. One of the most meaningful comments was from Lillian Liburdi, the director of the Port Authority's Management and Budget Division, "Tom—You helped us understand what 'public involvement' can really mean to everyone," she wrote. "Thank you and congratulations."[48]

I felt an overwhelming gratitude toward my fellow citizen members, and especially to Arthur and Curt Berger, for shepherding this diverse group to a consensus. I also developed a deep respect for opponents like Tommy Maguire and Sandy Frucher; public servants like David Dinkins, Ross Sandler, and Lillian Liberti who were talented, fair, and hard-working; and skilled negotiators like Nat Leventhal.

4

The Letdown
(1987–1988)

● ● ● ● ● ● ● ● ● ● ● ● ● ●

The public and press greeted the task force recommendations with surprise in January 1987.[1] Task force members were praised, both for including public funding for the esplanade—"masterstroke of common sense"[2]—and for reaching a compromise that many had thought impossible.[3] Even the local Greenwich Village newspaper said that the task force accomplished "what some thought was impossible," as they emphasized the importance of including local community boards in the process moving forward.[4]

Our recommendations were described as representing a promising path forward, and there was shared optimism about the future of the West Side. Chairman Levitt hoped that the work of the task force marked the beginning of a new era of government and community cooperation. The failure to recommend that the esplanade be mapped parkland disappointed some, but the recommendations were widely seen as a "praiseworthy compromise" according to a *New York Times* editorial.[5] The following month, Arthur wrote a letter to the *New York Times*, stating, "Our experience suggests that combining community participation with a willingness to reach consensus and open decision-making can produce results we will live to see."[6] The reality would prove much more complicated.

As Sandy Frucher, president of the Battery Park City Authority, predicted, less than two hours after our recommendations were released, Governor

Cuomo objected to public funding for the esplanade.[7] In his State of the State speech, he emphasized fiscal restraint; however, public funding for the esplanade was not consistent with that message. Cuomo complained there was not enough money remaining for mass transit, which seemed strange after he rejected the 1983 recommendation that he trade in Westway funds to support mass transit.

While most people thought that Arthur had crafted a consensus that few believed possible, Cuomo failed to thank him for the six months he had dedicated to the effort. I was sure the major objection was that a publicly funded esplanade would impede proposed or imagined in-water development projects such as the Hudson River Center supported by Sandy Frucher, Deputy Mayor Bob Esnard, and the pro-development lobby. The silence from City Hall was deafening.

As the liberal *Village Voice* editorial put it, "What we have here is a failure to conciliate. The governor purposely excluded premier Westway opponents Marcy Benstock and Gene Russianoff from the West Side Task Force, possibly hoping that those appointed would be more pliant. By approving such a costly road, perhaps they were. But in fighting the landfill advocates to a standstill and advocating a guaranteed esplanade, they were not."[8]

I thanked Governor Cuomo for the opportunity to serve, commended Arthur's dedication and vision, and mentioned that the Neighborhood Open Space Coalition agreed that the roadway was too expensive. The coalition urged removing the roadway's grade separations and using federal funds for the esplanade. The coalition also extolled the boulevard's role in absorbing storm water and reducing air and noise pollution.[9] I wrote again in February explaining the benefits of the esplanade and mapping the waterfront as a park—but to no avail.[10]

The creation of the Hudson River Park has ebbed and flowed like its namesake river. The release of the task force's recommendations and public acceptance of our compromise constituted the peak of an incoming tide. But the tide soon turned because Governor Cuomo and Mayor Koch had not expected the compromise that we had reached. As in nature, the momentum to create the park remains a cycle of ebb and flow.

Staying Involved

After our recommendations were released, Arthur wanted to recognize my hard work and willingness to compromise, and he asked if I ever considered working for Goldman Sachs. However, I thought I would be a poor fit and said that "learning how the sausage is made"—and the future of city determined—was its own reward.

Arthur was a board member of the Norman and Rosita Winston Foundation, so I asked if they might consider a grant to support the Coalition's Brooklyn/Queens Greenway project. Greenways were being used to expand urban recreation opportunities in the 1980s. We had recently completed a feasibility study for a forty-mile bicycle and pedestrian path that ran from the Atlantic Ocean at Coney Island in Brooklyn to Fort Totten at the northeastern tip of Queens on the Long Island Sound. The path linked thirteen public parks.[11]

City Parks Commissioner Henry Stern and Transportation Commissioner Ross Sandler had voiced support for the project, but to move forward, we needed a more detailed design study to address problematic locations along the route.[12] Several months later, the Winston Foundation announced a $30,000 grant to support the completion of a design study.[13] In 1990, the project was featured in a new book on greenways[14] and in an article in *National Geographic*.[15] It also received a merit award from the Municipal Arts Society and was a silver medalist in the Rudy Bruner Award for Urban Excellence that recognizes transformative projects in the urban environment.[16]

In addition, I had asked Arthur for an opportunity to speak with David Rockefeller, a major Westway supporter, to explain our alternative plan to redevelop the West Side waterfront with an urban boulevard and a world-class waterfront park. Several weeks later, we met for lunch in a private dining room at the legendary University Club on Fifth Avenue and 54th Street.

Mr. Rockefeller was joined by George Fox (no relation), president of Grow Tunneling Corporation. Fox was then chairman of Cooper Union's School of Engineering and wielded significant influence in the New York Building Congress and the General Contractors Association. The luncheon was cordial; Rockefeller and Fox spoke about the benefits of Westway and lamented the loss to the city's economy, especially to Lower Manhattan—a matter of particular interest to Rockefeller.

I suggested that a tree-lined urban boulevard would help the city comply with federal air quality regulations and that building a world-class waterfront park would enhance the city's quality of life and its image as a place to live, work, and visit. The park would support tourism and spur real estate development in adjacent neighborhoods. Rockefeller listened politely and then replied, "That's a nice idea, but it will never happen."

I realized the meeting was over and as Arthur lingered to speak with Rockefeller, Fox and I rode the elevator down together. George had a car and driver and was headed downtown to Cooper Union, so he offered me a ride. During the trip, he praised the wisdom of the Westway project and bemoaned the mistake we had made in defeating it.

I listened for twenty minutes as we threaded our way through Midtown traffic, and his arguments were cogent and passionate. As we neared Cooper Union, George confessed surprise that I had not challenged him. "I didn't have to," I replied. "We won." He got out at Cooper Union, thanked me for conversation, and asked his driver to take me to my office.

Apparently, quite a few Westway supporters had significant knowledge of the city and how things work. They believed that they were advocating for the betterment for the city, but as often happens, it was in their own self-interest as well. The lesson that adversaries are not necessarily enemies is important to remember. It came in handy because I would soon realize that several of my former friends and colleagues were about to become my adversaries.

Roaming the Waterfront

While serving on the task force, I had met many local community, environmental, and civic activists involved in various issues affecting West Side neighborhoods. I knew open-space advocates but not the local community leaders. And so, I reached out to individuals I had met during the process who worked on, or lived near, the waterfront. Advocates should seek out the issues and concerns of local communities because a better understanding of the environment they are working in makes them much more relevant and credible.

Our Neighborhood Open Space Coalition office was on Reade Street in Tribeca—five blocks from the waterfront. I rode my bike along the waterfront between my apartment on Bank Street and my office almost every day. This was not easy because the waterfront side of the roadway was fenced off with parking lots and tow pounds, filled with potholes, and littered with discarded auto parts, broken glass, and trash.

Some Tribeca residents had adopted portions of the water's edge north of Chambers Street. At Pier 26, Cathy Drew, an oceanographer with a passion for the Hudson, was live-trapping fish and operating a small aquarium showcasing aquatic life in the river. Her fledgling nonprofit organization, called The River Project, provided simple yet effective environmental education

Dog on a Jersey barrier, at Pier 49 on Bank Street in Greenwich Village. (Tom Fox)

programs introducing anyone she could to the wonders of the estuary—on a waterfront crammed with parking lots, trash, and tow pounds.

I had served ashore in Vietnam, but I was a sailor. Afterward, I spent a year and a half as a mount captain of a 3-inch/50-caliber automatic gun aboard the *USS Raleigh* out of Little Creek, Virginia. [17] We were part of a seven-ship amphibious ready group and practiced invading various Caribbean islands at a time when the Cold War was hot and Cuba was a concern. Having lived along the rivers in Vietnam and spending time at sea, I was drawn to the waterfront.

I was familiar with Greenwich Village and knew that several of my neighbors and others were allies in the fight against Westway. The Village waterfront was wide open and had no parking lots, and residents used several existing piers. Other than sunning, fishing, picnics, and the occasional art project, many activities of a sexual nature took place in and on the piers—primarily at night.

Village residents were the most concerned about change. Some, like history buff Bill Hine, were passionate but reasonable and helpful. Others were not. That group included my Bank Street neighbor Bill Bowser, Margaret "Bunny" Gabel of Friends of the Earth, and the crew that ran the Federation to Preserve the Greenwich Village Waterfront and Great Port (quite a mouthful). To them, everyone's intentions were suspect, and conspiracies to build on landfill and platforms in the river lurked behind every decision.

The government, stung by the loss of Westway, continued to express contempt for community residents. The state Department of Transportation announced that it would tear down Pier 54, the last of the Cunard White Star Terminals, where the *RMS Lusitania* had departed on her ill-fated voyage in 1915 and the *RMS Carpathia* had deposited the survivors of the *Titanic*'s sinking ship in 1912.[18] Many *Titanic* survivors had stayed in the Hotel Riverview, which is still located a few blocks south at the corner of Jane Street.

Despite objections from Community Board 2, the Greenwich Village Society for Historic Preservation, and a raft of historians, officials from the State Historic Preservation Office agreed that the structure could be demolished. The only thing they said was not to be removed was the iconic head house arch, which was eventually included in the park's design.

Things were slightly different in the neighborhoods to the north. In Chelsea, south of 23rd Street, most residents lived east of Tenth Avenue. From 23rd to 42nd Streets, the area along Route 9A was occupied by warehouses, truck parking, the Long Island Railroad Yards, a Greyhound bus garage, and the Javits Convention Center. Bob Trentlyon, a fellow task force member and publisher of the *Chelsea-Clinton News* and *The Westsider* (two community newspapers), was advocating for a waterfront park at West 23rd Street. He introduced me to his colleagues at the Chelsea Waterside Park Association.

The northern boundary of the new boulevard was 59th Street in Hell's Kitchen, but the planned esplanade still ended at 43rd Street. Except for the Intrepid Sea Air & Space Museum, the entire waterfront north of 42nd Street was devoted to commercial maritime activity, including passenger ship terminals at Piers 88–94, a Department of Sanitation garage at Pier 97, a Con Ed refueling facility at Pier 98, and a marine transfer station for household garbage at Pier 99.

Although the entire area from 14th to 59th Streets fell within the boundaries of Community Board 4, Hell's Kitchen residents had not been particularly involved in initial deliberations until the northern boundary of our project was extended.

Chaos Increases

As the ink dried on the task force recommendations, various organizations and individuals weighed in. In January of 1987, the Regional Plan Association, which supported Westway, released a document titled "The Region's Agenda," which called for the entire waterfront from Chambers Street north

Walking north on Route 9A past the MTA bus garage on Pier 57 in Chelsea. (Tom Fox)

to West 36th Street, where the Hudson River Center was planned to be built, to become a recreation area.[19] They wrote to Cuomo and Koch, asking that the waterfront be dedicated to recreational uses.[20]

U.S. Senator Daniel Patrick Moynihan, a staunch Westway supporter, was a member of the Senate Finance committee and was key to federal decision-making regarding many issues that had an impact on the city. Marcy Ben-stock urged him to amend the next rewrite of the federal highway bill and eliminate the need to pay back the federal government for the purchase of the Westway right-of-way.[21] Her letter was hand-delivered and co-signed by nine other environmental, river protection, and transportation groups, includ-ing the Neighborhood Open Space Coalition. Moynihan, as expected, was unresponsive.

Although most of my former colleagues supported the esplanade, hard-core Westway opponents deemed the new roadway and the esplanade too expensive and favored spending as much money as possible on mass transit. Since neither Westway supporters nor opponents were particularly happy about our recommendations, I assumed that the task force had struck an appropriate balance.

While advocating for the expansion of public park space beyond the espla-nade, I suffered the slings and arrows of my colleagues, especially Marcy, who denounced me as a sellout. We presented our opposing visions for the waterfront at the Council of Planning Librarians Conference that April.[22] Her outspoken criticism probably increased my credibility with pro-development advocates, but they were still wary of my intentions.

The design for the roadway was not set in stone, and the high cost of the project was a result of the grade separations. Citizen members had opposed the grade separations during the task force meetings, but we realized that the Lincoln Tunnel was below the West Side Highway between 42nd and 32nd Streets and would thus preclude a tunnel there. In addition, the Hol-land Tunnel and Port Authority Trans-Hudson tunnels severely restricted that option downtown. The length and intensity of the debate over grade sep-arations that could not be built seemed insane.

Just because government agencies propose something, do not assume that they have done their homework and have all the relevant information. Never accept anything as fact until you have personally investigated it yourself.

In the absence of political leadership, the situation devolved into a free-for-all. The city's Public Development Corporation had been designated to oversee all issues involving the use of city waterfront. The corporation desig-nated a development group to build Hudson River Center, which was a twelve-acre platform supporting three hotels with 1,560 rooms, two residential buildings with 850 apartments, a six-hundred-car garage, a performing arts center, restaurants, a new city tow pound, and a waterfront esplanade.[23]

Agencies with jurisdiction over various segments of the waterfront made their plans despite the task force recommendations. For example, the Port Authority proposed building new emergency access and escape routes from the Port Authority Trans-Hudson tunnels in Greenwich Village right in the middle of the proposed esplanade. However, Senate Minority Leader Fred Ohrenstein argued that the Port Authority's proposal would become a bottleneck in the future esplanade.[24]

Esplanade Finally Approved

In August, Mayor Koch and Governor Cuomo announced that they would embrace the task force recommendations but were reluctant to provide public funding of the esplanade. In an editorial, *New York Newsday* urged the mayor and governor to expand the public space beyond the esplanade to include the underwater property. They suggested that the entire area west of the roadway be mapped as a park.[25]

Later that month, eight city and state elected officials representing the adjacent neighborhoods then expressed their "delight" at the agreement to build the roadway and esplanade and said that they should be built as one continuous project using public funds. They objected to the esplanade being held hostage to funding from new commercial developments in the river.[26]

Public funding for the esplanade was not embraced until September, when Governor Cuomo finally commended our effort to encourage community participation and work cooperatively with government and business representatives. He reiterated his desire for a less expensive highway south of Chambers Street but said that the other task force recommendations would be the basis for revitalizing the West Side waterfront.[27]

Visions Differ

In September, the Neighborhood Open Space Coalition testified before the New York State Senate Democratic Task Force on Waterfront Development, decrying the designation of the Public Development Corporation as the lead agency for decisions involving the use of land along the waterfront and asking the state legislature to take a bigger role in promoting what we deemed the proper redevelopment of the city's waterfront.[28]

We also worked with the Regional Plan Association and championed the recommendations of the President's Commission on Americans Outdoors that called for $1 billion a year in new park funding nationally to compensate for more than a decade of disinvestment in city, state, and federal parks.[29] The Regional Plan Association wrote the governor and mayor, supporting the acceptance of the task force recommendations and requesting that they reserve the waterfront for recreation, consider tax increment financing to capture revenue from new development in adjacent neighborhoods, extend the waterfront improvements to Riverside Park, and design the replacement roadway to enhance waterfront access.[30]

The Parks Council hired Steve Carr, who had helped advise the task force, to develop a more complete design for the esplanade. Their report was completed in December 1987 but was not released until the following spring. In addition to the esplanade, their design proposed redevelopment of several of the piers, floating restaurants, performance spaces near the Convention Center, ball fields above the highway in Chelsea, markets on Pier 57, a new rooftop recreation facility on Pier 40, and floating swimming pools and marinas in Tribeca.[31] The design also called for extending the proposed esplanade north to West 46th Street.

Avoiding a Federal Payback

The coalition had reached out to New York City Comptroller Harrison "Jay" Goldin as the task force was finalizing its recommendations. He supported our argument that repaying the federal government for the funds used to purchase the in-water property for Westway was not necessary if the area was designated a scenic area. The city comptroller needed to agree to any settlement of the Court of Claims suit between the city and state.

Goldin refused to approve the Court of Claims settlement unless city and state agreed to apply for a payback waiver first. He became our strongest ally in the battle to designate the underwater property as a scenic area and request a waiver of the federal payback. Goldin was planning to run against Koch in the next Democratic mayoral primary and championing the designation of a scenic area gave him environmental creds.

I have learned that when making requests, it is important to subtly empha-size benefits to the person you are pitching for assistance, but not state the obvious. His reluctance to agree to a settlement stalled the federal payback for three more years.

Difficult Times

By January 1988, city and state officials realized that the comptroller would not agree to their compromise and halted plans to establish a new entity. Instead, they directed their efforts to the design of the roadway thinking that public pressure would eventually force Goldin to change his position.[32] The Municipal Art Society had finished judging the four hundred entries from its December design contest, "Wanted: A Waterfront for New York." The group exhibited twenty of the finalists at the Urban Center for a month, culminating with a forum on West Side waterfront redevelopment.[33] The Parks Council report was released as well.

Both sides were looking for an advantage. State Assembly members Dick Gottfried, Bill Passannante, and Jerry Nadler co-sponsored two bills in the Assembly to complement the bills that Fred Ohrenstein and several of his colleagues introduced in the Senate. They proposed amending the state environmental conservation law to prohibit landfill and commercial devel-opment in designated portions of the Hudson River (i.e., lower Manhat-tan) and designating the lands along the Hudson River waterfront a state park.[34]

Marcy Benstock issued an action alert and requested that recipients sup-port the proposed bills, urge their legislators to sign on as co-sponsors, and participate in a lobbying day in Albany. Marcy was a terrific organizer, and it was amazing how much information she could fit on her one-page action alerts. She asked recipients to encourage people who are concerned with public access to the waterway to fight encroachment by floating prisons and a phalanx of luxury towers on costly platforms and heavily subsidized landfill.[35]

Marcy also pointed out that most of the designs that had won prizes in the Municipal Art Society's competition encouraged landfill and/or plat-forms and included a quote from City Planning Commission Chairwoman Sylvia Deutsch, who said that while there might be new commercial devel-opment between the roadway and the river, she was not prepared to speak to any specific redevelopment plans.

The state transportation department had released a "request for propos-als" for the design of the replacement roadway and again selected Vollmer Associates, a well-respected engineering firm that had worked on many of Robert Moses's parkways. Although Vollmer project managers thought that the esplanade and the roadway should be planned together, the state refused to include the esplanade in Vollmer's contract, insisting again that the road-way be designed independent of the esplanade.[36] Spring was coming, and everyone stepped up their activity. My March op-ed in *New York Newsday* restated the case for the esplanade and warned that excluding it from the plan-ning process would lead to the continuation of a long and bitter fight.[37]

Later in the month, Sandy Frucher and Bob Esnard, the persistent pro-development duo, complained about *New York Newsday*'s coverage in a let-ter to the editor.[38] In it, they agreed that the task force provided an important starting point for West Side redevelopment but claimed that the design of the esplanade was inextricably linked to land-use decisions. They argued that the cost and funding for the esplanade were unclear, and things were proceed-ing as intended. They gratuitously claimed that the esplanade was the glue of the task force consensus and would guide the way forward.

Borough President Dinkins responded with his own letter committing to the task force's vision and suggested the city and state should pay as much attention to the esplanade as the roadway. He warned that a delay in support-ing public funding of the esplanade was undercutting Frucher and Esnard's optimism.[39]

My former task force colleague Tom Maguire had been encouraging the mayor and governor to move forward ever since our recommendations were released. He was joined by Frank McArdle and Gerry Newman of the Gen-eral Contractors Association of New York and Lou Coletti of the New York Building Congress, and they formed a powerful construction industry group supporting the esplanade.

They exemplified enlightened industry leaders advocating a compromise that the civic, environmental, and local community supported and that ben-efited their industry. Their advocacy was a welcome change. In late March, the New York Building Congress honored Arthur Levitt Jr. as a "New York Leader" at its annual luncheon; this strengthened the bonds between park advocates and the construction industry.[40]

In April, the city and state were said to be close to an agreement to move forward and end their tug-of-war as to who would control project planning.[41] As the legislative session proceeded, attention began to focus on the Hudson River Protection Act, which prohibited landfill or platforms adjacent to the planned esplanade and designated the entire waterfront as a park. Frucher's letter to the *New York Times* condemned the proposed restrictions and urged "exploring" all the possibilities for the West Side waterfront to ensure that future development was environmentally and economically sound.[42]

Noting that it would take three to four years to complete the necessary environmental and engineering studies, two years to conduct the required public review, and three to six years to build the actual highway, an article in the *New York Times* in May stated that no new West Side roadway would be built for the next decade.[43] It was a sobering assessment of the dilemma we faced.

By June, all hell broke loose. The *New York Observer* speculated that there would be new attempts to resurrect Westway-style development while editorials poured forth attacking proposed legislative restrictions: the *New York Times*'s "Know-Nothings on the Waterfront,"[44] the *New York Post*'s "Fish Tales in Albany,"[45] and the *Daily News*'s "Dumb, Dumber and Dumbest."[46]

More than forty organizations had formed a group called Citizens for Hudson River Esplanade and planned a rally on June 27 on the steps of City Hall. The participants presented Deputy Mayor Esnard with laurel branches. However, he refused to make a no-development pledge on behalf of the city.[47]

The day before that rally, news broke that earlier in the year, Sandy Frucher had applied for a permit from the U.S. Army Corps of Engineers to build the final piece of Battery Park City's esplanade. He planned to build a 50-foot-by-500-foot platform in the river north of Stuyvesant High School, a project that had been delayed awaiting the approval of Westway.

However, in late April he had begun construction without the permit, which was discovered when a division chief of the Army Corps of Engineers, looking out a window from the World Trade Center during a break from a conference, noticed heavy equipment working on the waterfront. Battery Park City was forced to halt the project—a move that only heightened environmentalists' concerns about platforms over the river.[48]

Doubling down, the city announced that it was relocating a prison barge to Pier 40 in Greenwich Village. The *Bibby Venture*, a British troop barge that had been used in the Falklands War, was to be converted into a floating prison to ease overcrowding at Rikers Island. Marcy asked supporters to speak out against approval of the city's Public Development Corporation's budget unless all development in the Hudson was prohibited.[49]

The prison barge raised the alarm to incredible levels. More than eight hundred residents packed the public hearing at Our Lady of Pompeii Church on Carmine Street to object.[50] In October, the Board of Estimate approved the plan to dock the barge at Pier 40 the following spring.[51]

Family Picnic in Tribeca at Debrosse Street with prison barge at Pier 40 in background. (Tom Fox)

Apparently, the mayor and governor had reached an agreement to move the project forward in May but did not make it public until August, when they announced the formation of the West Side Waterfront Panel to continue land-use and waterfront planning for Route 9A reconstruction. They established shared responsibility for future planning and for the cost of repaying the Federal Highway Administration for the purchase of the Westway right-of-way.[52] Its charter was to develop design guidelines and a financing plan for the esplanade, make land-use recommendations for the piers and underwater property, and coordinate its efforts with roadway planning.

Dewey Ballantine's opinion stated that the preservation of scenic areas and landscaping was an allowable use of federal highway funds, but neither the city nor the state wanted to pay the federal funds back for fear of undercutting the possibility of future in-water development projects by declaring the waterfront a scenic area.

It had taken a year and a half of mounting public criticism until the two men finally acted. The momentum and initial sense of trust developed by the task force's consensus recommendations had been squandered. Once again, suspicion and mistrust ruled the day.

5

The West Side
Waterfront Panel
(1988–1990)

● ● ● ● ● ● ● ● ● ● ● ● ● ●

In July 1988, when Governor Cuomo asked me to serve as a citizen representative on the West Side Waterfront Panel, I was stunned. He and I had never
spoken. I had fought for public funding of the esplanade, and the Neighborhood Open Space Coalition had advocated for the West Side Task Force's
recommendations to rebuild Route 9A as a boulevard with a waterfront
esplanade as one publicly funded project. In addition, as cochair of the
Brooklyn Bridge Park Coalition, I was fighting the Port Authority's plans
for commercial development on the Brooklyn waterfront.[1] However, hopeful that Cuomo's opposition to a park on Manhattan's West Side waterfront
was waning, I accepted.

The state and the city would each appoint three people to the panel. West
Side elected officials approved of the governor's appointment of me; Orin
Lehman, commissioner of the state Office of Parks, Recreation, and Historic
Preservation; and, as chair of the panel, Michael Del Giudice, the governor's
former chief of staff and a man known as an experienced and accomplished
servant.[2]

The mayor, however, was slammed for his appointments, namely Deputy
Mayor Bob Esnard, City Planning Commission Chair Sylvia Deutsch, and

Roger Altman, chairman of the city's Public Development Corporation.[3] All were pro-development advocates. Borough President Dinkins, for his part, appointed Barbara Fife, a knowledgeable park advocate and trusted staff member. All told, the panel had three members in favor of development and three in favor of a park, with Michael as the swing vote. Maybe the good guys finally had equal footing.

At the time, my wife, Gretchen Ferenz—an environmental horticulturist and community educator with Cornell University Cooperative Extension— and I, were living with our three-year-old son, Michael, in a one-bedroom apartment on Bank Street. We needed more room. Although reluctant to leave the Village, we bought a ramshackle century-old Victorian in Flatbush, "the old neighborhood."

It was a hectic time for me. I was running the Neighborhood Open Space Coalition, which now had 120 member organizations, four staff members, and three interns. I had received a Loeb Fellowship in Advanced Environmental Studies at Harvard University's Graduate School of Design and was scheduled to spend a year in Cambridge starting in September—just two months away.[4] But the West Side waterfront had gotten into my blood, and the juice was flowing.

The Panel Assembles

When our work began in earnest that September, members of the panel and the state Department of Transportation worked closely together. The department's Route 9A project team occupied the entire sixth floor of a handsome pre-war office building on Fifth Avenue at 21st Street, and the panel moved into a light and airy space on the building's tenth floor.

Chairman Del Giudice supported community participation, and our space was big enough to accommodate public meetings and design workshops for both the panel and the Route 9A team. The public was encouraged to attend panel meetings and meet with staff and board members. In addition, twenty citizens representing civic, environmental, and community interests, along with labor, real estate, and construction industries were asked to join our civic advisory committee.

Planning for Route 9A had been proceeding for months, and the panel quickly developed a great working relationship with the Route 9A team. Maryann Monte was our office manager, and her husband, Pat, was an engineer with Vollmer Associates, Route 9A's transportation consultants. We also engaged former task force consultants Gary Hack and Lex Lalli.

Chairman Del Giudice had held executive positions with former New York State Assembly Speaker Steingut and Governor Hugh Carey before becoming Cuomo's chief of staff. He had an incredible command of how government worked (or did not), knew everyone, and had a good sense of humor.[5]

When he met people he did not know, he would sometimes say by way of breaking the ice, "I've been working in government for a long time. When I started, I was six feet two and had a full head of hair." That always put listeners at ease because he had a receding hairline and was about five feet seven. Michael was director of municipal investments at Lazard Freres, and because public funding was at the heart of many of our pending issues, he was well equipped for the job.

Orin Lehman was a reserved and dedicated public servant from a prominent New York family. Paralyzed from the waist down, Orin walked with leg braces and crutches, which never stopped him from attending panel meetings, briefings, tours, and public events. I had assumed that he contracted polio as a child. However, one evening over a glass of wine, he told me he had been a B-29 copilot and was shot down and wounded during the Battle of the Bulge. Being a modest man, he failed to mention that he had been awarded a Distinguished Flying Cross.[6]

Lehman was ably assisted by Elizabeth Goldstein, a "parkie" who had been director of planning at the city's Department of Parks and Recreation before becoming the regional director at the state parks office. She was knowledgeable, experienced, participated in most committee and community meetings, and advised Orin at board meetings.

Neither Altman nor Deutsch were people I knew. Roger was the chairman of the Public Development Corporation, yet Koch appointed him as his citizen representative—a move that was not well received. Wanting to know more about the panel members, I visited Sylvia at the city planning department. As I entered her office, she was pacing with her granddaughter in her arms. We sat at her desk, and I started talking about my hopes for the panel. Sylvia was quiet and smiling as I spoke but was not saying anything. She seemed to agree with me, so I asked if she did. "Not really," she replied, "but please keep talking, I've been trying to get my granddaughter to sleep all day, and if you stop, I'm afraid she'll wake up."

I had worked with Bob Esnard when he was Deputy Queens Borough President, he supported the coalition's Brooklyn/Queens Greenway, and we worked well together. After becoming deputy mayor, however, he became a serious pro-development advocate, as I learned during the task force deliberations. I viewed him as Darth Vader serving Emperor Koch.

Unlikely Allies

Tommy Maguire, a critical ally, was not convinced that building a park helped his union members much until I explained the project in a way that made sense to him. I call it speaking in your opponent's language. "The heavy construction industry should really support a West Side waterfront park," I said over lunch one day. "Commercial office and residential development primarily benefit the carpenters, plumbers, electricians, and steamfitters. A landscaped esplanade and rebuilt bulkheads and piers mean most of the work is for heavy equipment operators, dock builders, laborers, and teamsters. And a park will get the roadway built quicker."

"You know, you're not as dumb as you look," Maguire replied.

Maguire is one of the park's founding fathers. He called Cuomo, Koch, Moynihan, D'Amato, and other government officials, personally stressing the industry's support for the project. His lobbyists met with executive staff and agency representatives in Albany and City Hall. A talented, relentless, and resilient man, he recruited construction industry leaders to support the project and gave us credibility where we had trouble developing it.

Coordinating with Route 9A

Although the state transportation department had jurisdiction over the entire right-of-way including the roadway, waterfront property, piers, and underwater property purchased for Westway, the Route 9A team was told to focus solely on designs for the urban boulevard recommended by the task force. The panel would address the waterfront.

The type, scale, and location of outboard developments were critical to roadway design, especially given the range of options still on the table. Route 9A's grade separations, the width of traffic lanes and inboard sidewalks, the median, the location of turning lanes, and pedestrian access to the waterfront were important issues affecting the esplanade.

We all knew that the roadway and outboard development were interdependent. As director of the Neighborhood Open Space Coalition, I had an opportunity to comment on plans for Route 9A at public meetings and, as a panel member, I worked with Route 9A engineers and landscape architects in a less formal and more creative setting. It was great to learn more about the various disciplines involved in such a complicated project.

While policy makers wanted to exploit the Hudson, transportation professionals were focused on safe and efficient transport. Their emphasis reinforced my belief that many public servants often have the best of intentions, despite political directives that do not allow them to exercise their judgment. Transportation engineers planned the roadway but knew the importance of the panel's work and understood the need to maximize public open space to make their roadway designs more acceptable to the public.

The Route 9A team members who creatively interpreted federal highway regulations and made things happen were Dick Maitino (Route 9A's executive director in Albany) and Bob Ronayne (the director of design and development in New York City). Heather Sporn, an associate landscape architect, was responsible for roadway design elements that were important to open-space advocates.

The task force's preliminary traffic study had shown that 85 to 90 percent of Route 9A drivers were traveling to and from the Central or Lower Manhattan business districts, so there were more places to make southbound turns in those locations and fewer in residential neighborhoods. There was concern about southbound traffic leaving Route 9A and using local streets to avoid congestion. To keep traffic moving, those turning options were strictly limited, and traffic lights were carefully timed.

Greenwich Village residents were vociferous Westway opponents—eager to preserve the historic quality of their neighborhood and worried about increased traffic on their narrow streets. So, in the Route 9A plan, almost all southbound turns into the Village below 14th Street were eliminated. The only left turn was three-quarters of a mile farther south at Clarkson Street, just above Houston. Below Houston, southbound turns were limited in Tribeca but more plentiful below Chambers Street in the Lower Manhattan business district.

All design decisions had to be approved by the Federal Highway Administration, and the Route 9A team negotiated with the agency to interpret the relevant federal regulations. The state transportation department was building an urban boulevard but negotiating with federal highway officials, and while sometimes the state's arguments won the day, sometimes they did not. For example, the feds initially wanted a concrete median with what is known as a Jersey barrier in the middle of the roadway to separate lanes of traffic.

But park advocates wanted a median with adequate space for a double row of trees and landscaping. Heather successfully argued for a landscaped median.[7]

The overall width of the roadway depended on the widths of the median, the traffic lanes, the shoulders, and the inboard sidewalk. The standard federal highway lane is twelve feet wide but could vary according to location, type of roadway, and speed of the traffic. The 9A team won federal approval to make the traffic lanes no more than eleven feet wide and to eliminate shoulders.

A narrower roadway was easier for pedestrians to cross, made the roadway feel more like the urban boulevard the task force envisioned, and created more space for bicycle and pedestrian paths and the esplanade. The narrowed lanes also made it possible to add more than five acres to the public open space on the waterfront. In addition, the feds approved a strip of greenery twenty-eight to thirty-six feet wide on the river side of the road that would separate the bike path from the roadway, with additional landscaping, and a walkway.[8]

Several of us advocated for a wide bike path, particularly because rollerblading was becoming popular, and bladers required more space. We were not successful, however, and the overall bike path remained fifteen feet wide. With eighteen-inch drainage areas on either side, the bicycling surface was reduced to twelve feet.

There was concern about the interaction of pedestrians, bicyclists, and vehicles at locations where vehicles crossed both paths to access outboard activities. That issue was not adequately addressed in the initial designs and remains a major safety problem.

The state transportation department allowed the location and configuration of pedestrian path to be determined during the design of the future esplanade, which knit the roadway and park more closely together and provided an opportunity to use federal funding for elements of the waterfront esplanade, where the roadway came close to the water.

Even though the 9A team and Vollmer Associates were focused solely on the roadway, the first elements of the future park were funded with transportation dollars. It is important to remember to leave no stone unturned when approaching project funding, especially in tight financial times. Sometimes funding sources to support your project may not be obvious, and many times, it depends on your timing and how you frame your ask. Advocates need to be creative and flexible and remember that every little bit helps.

The State Department of Transportation Creates Parks

West Street, which later became Route 9A, originally ran along the water-front between Gansevoort Peninsula and 23rd Street. But in the 1840s, the city extended the land in that area hundreds of feet out into the Hudson by selling individual parcels to enterprising citizens who filled them in with trash and other debris—creating Thirteenth Avenue.[9]

By the end of the nineteenth century, the transatlantic passenger ships of the Cunard and White Star Lines were making regular trips to and from Europe. Longer piers were needed keep the ships from protruding into navigable waters, and in 1907, construction began on a new West Side pier complex. The area that had been filled was dredged, Thirteenth Avenue between Bloomfield Street and 23rd Streets was eliminated, and West Street was diverted inboard.

The state-of-the art Chelsea Piers, a row of pink granite-clad structures, was designed by the architecture firm Warren and Wetmore at the same time they were designing Grand Central Terminal in Midtown.[10] The relocation of the West Side Highway had resulted in tight turns at the northern and southern ends of the piers as the roadway jogged inboard, and the state transportation department had to straighten those curves to meet federal highway safety standards. Thomas F. Smith Park, between 22nd and 23rd Streets, though small, stood in the way of the realignment, and federal regulations required that the state both replace and expand parkland taken for highway construction.[11]

Bob Trentlyon and his neighbors wanted the inboard part of their proposed Chelsea Waterside Park connected with adjacent Piers 62, 63, and 64 on the outboard side of Route 9A. The 9A team was sympathetic to community's needs but dead set against anything that required permits from the Army Corps of Engineers. Piers 62 and 64 both jutted out into the Hudson, and if they were included as mitigation for the taking of a portion of Thomas F. Smith Park, such permits would be required. Members of the park association met with Congressman Ted Weiss and advocated for the Corps of Engineers to agree to a permit.[12] The 9A team subsequently wrote to the panel objecting to any mitigation extending beyond the bulkhead.[13]

The 9A team then suggested eliminating 23rd Street between 11th Avenue and Route 9A as the mitigation for reducing the size of Thomas F. Smith Park. It was a great solution, and the secondary benefit was even better. As a result, northbound traffic would be diverted up 11th Avenue, to turn left on 24th Street to enter Route 9A northbound.[14] That required widening

24th Street into a two-way thoroughfare, which allowed the state transportation department to take the entire block.

There was, however, one glitch. The Gambino family owned a small building on the block, and their namesake patriarch, Carlo, known as the "boss of bosses," was once the reputed head of The Commission, the American Mafia's first governing body.[15] Although Carlo died in 1976, some people voiced concern about that condemnation. Fortunately, his son, Thomas, now managed the family business, and since the condemnation required the state to pay fair market value for the property, he took the offer.

The block between 23rd and 24th Streets from 11th Avenue to Route 9A now contains a soccer field, basketball court, playground, gardens, and landscaping. Although the 9A team refused to build out on the piers, they delivered for the community. It was a great example of adaptive and creative use of transportation resources to meet community needs and reinforced my belief that government agencies can be both flexible and creative—when they want to be.

There were several smaller bits of property on the inboard side of Route 9A that were not needed for the highway. Spaces at 14th and Canal Streets were converted into small parks. At 14th Street, Heather worked with the landscape architect Donna Walcavage to design the space. It was built to city Parks Department specifications, which called for a standard six-foot wrought iron fence around the perimeter. Donna suggested adding a small swirl of metal at regular intervals near the top of the fence to give it some authenticity. The swirls were painted seafoam green and really popped against the black wrought iron, giving the fence a charming, whimsical look.

Adjacent to Route 9A at 14th Street there stood a three-story motel that rented rooms by the hour.[16] The realignment of Route 9A on the south end of Chelsea Piers required that the building be demolished, and Bob Ronayne met with its owners to inform them of this. I was told that they did not take the news well, telling Bob that if their building were demolished, his life might become more difficult. It is best not to attend contentious meetings alone.

Unlike what happened at 23rd Street, Route 9A's right-of-way was somehow shifted, ever so slightly, toward the Hudson in that location, and what is now the Liberty Inn remained. The unfortunate result was that the adjacent waterfront became the narrowest part of the future Hudson River Park.

Back in the 1980s and early 90s, the West Side was still the Wild West, and the quirkiest property acquired by the state transportation department was a building housing a club known as The Vault, in Greenwich Village. The Vault hosted different sexual activities on each of the club's five floors, with the S&M floor featuring whipping posts and cages hanging from the ceiling.[17] The building was leased, and the state Department of Transportation was required to reimburse the club owners for permanent improvements made during their lease.

The state's initial payout offer was $229,000, but the owners contested it. They bolted every whipping post and cage into the floor, wall, or ceiling and got their own appraisal, claiming that the improvements were permanent. They eventually received $1.8 million for the various sex toys that were probably worth little more than the amount initially offered.

Continuing Meaningful Community Participation

The task force found community participation critical to developing consensus, and Michael Del Giudice made this participation a major focus of the panel's work. Gary Hack and Kathryn Madden from Carr, Lynch, Hack and Sandel worked well with community residents, elected officials, business and labor leaders, and civic and environmental organizations, and where possible, integrated their ideas into our plans. Doing this engendered significant public buy-in and provided critical information that enhanced the plans for the esplanade, roadway, and outboard development areas.

The project required planners to participate in innumerable meetings with members of community boards, civic and neighborhood associations, and panel subcommittees and conduct briefings for the public, elected officials, and the press. Our emphasis on public participation helped rebuild our partnership with the public, enhanced our credibility, and increased the relevance and efficiency of our designs, which reflected ideas from many, in addition to those of the consultants, highway engineers, and public officials involved.

Meaningful public participation can be a pain in the neck, and it is not always pretty, nor are the results perfect. The process takes time and patience. Although it may go without saying, listening to all stakeholders and integrating others' ideas into your plans is well worth the effort. The plans become their plans, and the public often supports plans they help to create.

All the panel's consultants did a superlative job of involving the community in planning—as did Vollmer Associates and the 9A team. Another lesson: make sure to stress the importance of meaningful public involvement across the board when you solicit consultants. They will rarely complain because public meetings are billable hours.

In September of 1988, my Loeb Fellowship, which offered a unique mid-career learning opportunity for planning and design professionals, began. Eight to ten individuals are appointed Harvard faculty members for a year, and the architects, filmmaker, journalists, transportation experts, naturalist, and commercial and nonprofit developers in my class broadened my view of urban design. The only requirement was that we each deliver a thirty-minute presentation describing our work.

Most Loeb Fellows attend Harvard full-time, but given my workload and family commitments, I received permission to attend part-time and flew back and forth to Boston each week. I took full advantage of the three days a week I spent in Cambridge—taking courses at the Graduate School of Design, Harvard University, and the Kennedy School while exploring Boston on my bicycle and taking photographs. We all shared our real-world experience with students at the School of Design who were striving to become alchemists, turning blank paper into designs for a variety of projects in diverse settings.

Everything Comes to a Halt

In January 1989, Governor Cuomo suddenly announced that he was suspending the panel's work, claiming that planning while the right-of-way litigation with the city was pending was "contrary to the State's interest."[18] Cuomo and Koch had quietly agreed that, without the landfill and planned development, the underwater property the state acquired for Westway was worth what they had paid. The city agreed to drop its claim for more money, and the state agreed to share the responsibility for planning and developing the waterfront property—as well as any future revenue generated.

That agreement increased the pressure on Comptroller Goldin to approve the settlement so that the project could move forward. Thankfully, we had gotten to Goldin early, and he understood the value of public support for the park. It was a city election year, and he was running against Koch—as was David Dinkins. Park proponents wanted to protect the waterfront property and eliminate the need to repay the feds for the money used to acquire the underwater property, but the pro-development forces were hard at work.

That same month, a *WPIX* editorial touted a new city Public Development Corporation study regarding the proposed Hudson River Center. The study supposedly established that, far from harming marine life, platforms might improve the aquatic environment.[19] A February editorial in the *New York*

Times encouraged Goldin to agree to the settlement or face the loss of both the boulevard and what was left of the trade-in money.[20]

In March, Cuomo wrote to Koch suggesting that precluding development in portions of the waterway might be a constructive approach.[21] Park enthusiasts were thrilled at the change of heart but concerned about the term *portions*. Cuomo argued that the state should not make decisions independently; they should be made by the panel, which had equal city/state representation.

The stalemate continued as Goldin insisted that the West Side Waterfront Panel finalize its recommendations before he would agree to the settlement, and Cuomo would not allow the panel to resume planning unless Goldin agreed to settle.[22] Another *New York Times* editorial complained about the delay, asserting that "not only what is desirable but what is feasible" should be considered, while chiding Cuomo and the state legislature asking, "How much waterfront park can the city and state afford, for example?" They proclaimed it was "none of Albany's business to tell the city where it can or cannot develop its own land."[23]

Morton Street Ventilation Shafts

Several months before the panel's work was suspended, widespread objections were raised about the Port Authority's proposed construction project at Morton Street. The Port Authority Trans-Hudson system ran from New Jersey to Christopher Street in Greenwich Village, and up Avenue of the Americas to 34th Street. They proposed building vent shafts, which were also emergency exits, in the middle of the future esplanade, and they were determined to build the simplest, cheapest structure possible. Not surprisingly, their initial design looked like a bunker.

Bill Hine, the Village historian I held in high regard, requested that the panel ask the Port Authority to build the facility below grade. The state had agreed to erect two historic markers there commemorating the launch of the steam-powered *Claremont* and the role of the Village piers as a disembarkation point for immigrants arriving from Ellis Island. With the panel suspended, the Neighborhood Open Space Coalition presented testimony to the City Planning Commission, stating that the Port Authority's plans were not consistent with the task force recommendations. We requested that the facility be built underground or, if not, that the design be modified to reflect the future esplanade.[24]

While bicycling around Cambridge, I had photographed a structure that looked like a town house but obviously was not. Ann Hershfang, vice chair of the Massachusetts Turnpike Authority and a Loeb classmate, told me it was a ventilation shaft. The Massachusetts Bay Transportation Authority had responded to neighborhood concerns while designing vent shafts along the new Southwest Corridor rail line. Some looked like town houses and others were completely underground.

Ken Kruckemeyer, a former Loeb Fellow who managed that project and focused on the marriage of form and function, sent me images of the different shaft designs, and Chairman Del Giudice sent them to the Port Authority, requesting a meeting to discuss the issue. When he was in Albany, Michael had worked with Stephen Berger, the executive director of the Port Authority. He described Berger as a financier, dedicated public servant, and nice guy and said that they had a good relationship.

Steve agreed to meet with us to review the project, and I accompanied Michael to the World Trade Center meeting sometime around Halloween of 1989. I had not met Steve before, and I was not prepared when we knocked on his office door and were greeted by a wizard in purple satin robes with a matching conical hat and a huge unlit cigar sticking out of his mouth. "We're having a little costume party after work," Steve explained. "So I thought I'd dress up and give you guys a little surprise."

Steve supported a redesign of the vent shafts, invited five architects to submit alternative design proposals, and allowed us to join in the selection process. We selected a design by Stanton Eckstut—two granite-clad vent shafts surrounded by a lighted tree-lined plaza with seating. The structure became the first new public space built in the future park. Although it was aboveground, it was cheaper for the Port Authority to do than building underground, and the decision represented an early victory and example for interagency cooperation.

Park Coalition Expands

A year earlier, park proponents, led by the Parks Council, created an organization called Citizens for a Hudson River Esplanade. Members of NYPIRG, NYC Audubon, the City Club of New York, the Neighborhood Open Space Coalition, and the Regional Plan Association now served on the steering committee along with representatives of sixty-five civic, community, and environmental organizations; all the local elected officials; and

PATH ventilation and emergency access shafts at Morton Street in Greenwich Village. (Tom Fox)

representatives of Community Boards 1, 2, 4, and 7—the Manhattan community boards adjacent to the River.[25]

In March, hoping to increase public pressure to build the esplanade, the organization planned a Hudson River Rally and Festival in support of a park on the Greenwich Village waterfront to be held in June.[26] We met weekly to develop plans for the rally and applied for a permit to hang silk-screened banners along the waterfront to promote the event. Miriam Tuchman, a research associate for the Open Space Coalition who was fresh out of college, coordinated our participation. One of her first jobs was raising money by soliciting sponsorship for each of the banners. The requested donation was $100 per banner, and $150 got the sponsor's name appliquéd at the bottom.

The state transportation department issued a permit for the rally, and the city approved the installation of fifty banners, which were to be hung on light poles along the waterfront for three months. The bright green three-foot-by-five-foot strips of cloth with the words "Let's Build a Hudson River Waterfront Park" in blue letters were sponsored by local businesses, elected officials, and political candidates whose names were embroidered on the bottom.[27]

However, the panel was in limbo, and concerns about the delay were growing. Federal highway funds were losing value due to inflation, trade-in funds

Aerial view of June 10 Hudson River Rally and Festival on the Greenwich Village waterfront. (Citizens for a Hudson River Esplanade)

were due to expire in 1992, and the shortened timeframe had forced the state transportation department to compress its environmental review from forty-eight to thirty months. Park advocates were calling for the highway and esplanade to be built as a single project. Pro-development forces responded by claiming that there was no public money available for such an undertaking and that reasonable, well-planned outboard development should fund the esplanade.[28]

On June 10, thousands of community residents, park advocates, and members of labor unions, along with civic, environmental, and political organizations, converged on the Greenwich Village waterfront. Pier 45, at Christopher Street, was the epicenter of the event—the place where speeches were made and musicians entertained the crowd. The future esplanade was filled with food trucks, farm stands, face painters, mimes, and costumed characters. Environmental organizations staffed informational exhibits, the Hudson River Sloop Clearwater offered sails on the Hudson, and kayakers prowled the waterway with signs supporting the park.

Although the work of the panel was suspended, our staff displayed a huge map of the waterfront at the rally and asked visitors about activities they wanted in the park. The Route 9A team had a similar map of the proposed roadway and requested public input on issues ranging from landscaping to

Community planning at the June 10 Hudson River Rally and Festival on Pier 45.
(Citizens for a Hudson River Esplanade)

the locations of crosswalks and turning lanes. The rally showed the solidarity, creativity, and tenacity of local communities and environmental and park advocates, as well as the potential for public use of the waterfront.

Apparently, the rally had the desired effect; Cuomo and Koch reinstated the panel[29] and agreed to consider banning development along the waterfront so that a park might be built there.[30] Landfill in the Hudson was still the boogeyman that had killed previous development plans, and the task force had successfully kicked that can down the road, but it was time to decide about landfill—one way or another.

In a bold move, one of the first actions of the reinstated panel was to rule out landfill along the entire waterfront. "The objective," Del Giudice said, "is to move from contention and litigation to some level of reality. What we're saying is: Forget it. Ain't no way it's going to happen. It's legally and technically impossible."[31]

During the panel's suspension, the Neighborhood Open Space Coalition asked Citizens for Hudson River Esplanade to work with the panel to craft a scenic easement application and copied the panel members.[32] The application could negate the need to repay the federal government for the underwater property taken for Westway. The preservation and enhancement property, out to the ends of the piers, would be considered part of Route 9A, and the purchase would be considered an allowable use of federal funds. That would also be a disincentive to future development in the river, or on the outboard, side of the roadway, as building in the area would require repaying the federal government.

However, the idea of platforms over the water was still on the table, and opponents of development in the river were skeptical about the government's intentions. The panel agreed to expedite an application to declare the entire waterfront a scenic area to avoid repaying the feds, declared that new landfill would not be considered, asked the state transportation department to share all information about proposals under consideration, and declared support for what it described as "interim uses" along the waterfront before construction of the roadway began. We then outlined fifteen planning principles that became the foundation of our final recommendations.[33]

Dinkins Wins Democratic Primary

In September of 1989, David Dinkins won the Democratic nomination for mayor while Rudolph Giuliani, the United States attorney for the Southern District—which includes Manhattan, the Bronx, and six counties north of New York City—received the Republican nod.[34] Koch and Goldin vowed to support Dinkins, and Andrew Cuomo, the governor's son, became a Dinkins campaign advisor. Dinkins squeaked by Giuliani in the November general election, and Ruth Messinger, an ally, was elected Manhattan borough president.[35] With Dinkins and Messinger poised to appoint new panel members and new leadership at city agencies and authorities, there was a renewed sense of optimism about the future of the waterfront.

A Preliminary Plan

In an attempt to change the direction of the public conversation, the panel released a preliminary plan in late October 1989.[36] The plan, which encompassed only the upland area from Chambers to 43rd Streets, designated community coves, or basins, protecting about 20 percent of the overall waterfront.[37] It was the first step, and, despite criticism, it is often wise to move slowly if you are trying to bring a big crowd along with you. The basins were small because Koch was still mayor and objected to anything larger.

Outboard development options were debated internally, but attention was focusing on existing piers at three different locations.[38] However, other than the designated the basins, the remainder of the waterfront was labeled "possible active-use zones." Opponents as well as mainstream environmental, park, and community organizations envisioned platforms on that remaining property and slammed the plan.[39]

It did not help that the Public Development Corporation was still championing Hudson River Center. Their original proposal had shrunk to a single forty-story 1,500-room hotel atop the 5.5-acre tow pound at Pier 76 where the agency proposed replacing the wooden piles with concrete and steel to support new construction. At a December hearing sponsored by Community Board 4, the developers suggested that the revenue generated by the project could fund the esplanade.

The corporation claimed that the project would be a "cash cow," generating as much as $250 million in public funding over a twenty-year period. Ross Graham, a member of Community Board 4, objected, stating, "Our waterfront is to be milked as a cash cow and trashed as a garbage scow."[40] Pro-development forces consistently presented outboard development as critical to providing funding for the esplanade.

Marcy Benstock led the small group of vociferous anti-park activists who wanted all federal highway funds that remained after a simple roadway and a basic esplanade were built to be used for mass transit and wanted the piers to be left alone.[41] She insisted that aquatic life would be enhanced by letting the waterfront deteriorate. However, she ignored over 100,000 people living on Manhattan's Lower West Side who needed recreation, open space, and access to the Hudson. Her perspective seemed confusing—and the fact that she had community allies was even more so. However, vocal public objections, especially unreasonable ones, often help advocates working with the government to reach a compromise.

Citizens Advisory Committee

To ensure transparency and participation, the panel established both a public officials committee and a citizens advisory committee to advise us in our planning. The committees provided significant benefit to the process and the product. Michael Del Giudice noted Arthur Levitt Jr.'s success with community participation and was committed to continuing the process.

The expertise of the members of the citizens advisory committee was particularly valuable. They supplemented the knowledge of the panel members and participated in staff discussions. Managing the group was like herding cats, but they gave us credibility with their constituents and helped counterbalance those fighting against the project.

The twenty citizens advisory committee members included representatives from Community Boards 1, 2, 4, and 7; civic leaders and park advocates from the Municipal Arts Society, the Parks Council, the City Club, the Regional Plan Association, and New York University; environmental advocates from the Hudson River Foundation, The River Project, the Environmental Defense Fund, and NYC Audubon; construction industry representatives from Local 15 of the International Union of Operating Engineers, the New York Building Congress, and General Contractors Association; and representatives from the Real Estate Board of New York and the Association for a Better New York.

In December, members were assigned to one of three separate subcommittees focused on the esplanade, land use, and financing.[42] They reviewed preliminary cost estimates, pier conditions, and existing land-use maps prepared by our consultants.[43]

That month, the panel was informed that our report was scheduled to be released the next April. We then developed an ambitious schedule of meetings, public forums, editorial board briefings, and research products needed to reach our deadline.[44] Although the roadway recommendations went to 59th Street, the panel's city appointees refused to recommend uses for their property north of 42nd Street.

As 1989 ended, Congressman Ted Weiss, along with local elected officials representing West Side communities, the heads of many environmental organizations, and even Marcy signed a letter to Michael Del Giudice, chairman of the panel, expressing strong support for the creation of the Chelsea Waterside Park and for developing Piers 62, 63, and 64 as open recreational platforms without commercial uses.[45]

6

New Park Proposed
(1990–1992)

● ● ● ● ● ● ● ● ● ● ● ● ● ●

After struggling for months to move the project forward, many park proponents were increasingly frustrated. We hoped that Mayor Dinkins's new appointees to the panel would support both the esplanade and what would eventually become Hudson River Park.

One of his most trusted advisors, Barbara Fife, was appointed deputy mayor and remained on the panel. Richard Schaeffer, the new chairman of the City Planning Commission, and Curt Berger, who had returned to teaching law at Columbia after directing the task force, rounded out the new mayor's team. Curt was familiar with the project, he was focused and fair, and he was an avid birder. His continued participation in the project was welcome.

But we were shocked and surprised when, almost immediately after his inauguration, Dinkins indicated his support for repaying the Federal Highway Administration funds used to purchase the underwater property, and he supported the construction of Hudson River Center.[1] The resulting uproar from community and park advocates, however, persuaded him to reverse course, and in February of 1990, he and Cuomo each pledged $100 million to be used to build the proposed esplanade adjacent to Route 9A and make public use of some of the piers possible.[2]

Cuomo proposed what was called the Twenty-First Century Environmental Quality Bond Act, which included $100 million for the project,[3] and

Mayor Dinkins put an additional $100 million for the project into the city's ten-year capital plan.[4]

With the support of the Dinkins administration, the panel presented a new plan for the waterfront park—one whose northern boundary extended all the way up to 59th Street.[5] The four sections of open water designated for public use, however, ended at 34th Street, and all the remaining property along the waterfront was still designated as available for other uses even though the panel was considering public use of several of those piers.

The city's Department of Ports and Terminals proposed converting Pier 94 at 54th Street into a helicopter repair and STOL (short take-off and landing) facility, and the city's Public Development Corporation proposed relocating the Pier 76 tow pound to Pier 94 to allow more space for Hudson River Center. Community Board 4 stressed the fact that Chelsea and Clinton had a disproportionate number of municipal facilities in their neighborhoods and that Pier 94 should be dedicated to public recreation.[6]

The estimated cost of the park was $331 million, which was $70 million more than was available.[7] Michael Del Giudice, the panel chair, suggested several options, ranging from scaling down our plan to identifying new funding sources. He also wanted to find money to support park maintenance and operation for five to ten years. Noting that the park would increase the value of adjacent real estate values and hence city tax revenue, I suggested that the city increase its financial commitment to the project.

Some Trivia

The numbering of Manhattan's West Side piers is a mystery to many. When Manhattan's street grid was established, a different Pier 40 was at Houston Street, where the new street numbering system began. The West Village predated the grid, and streets there were already named. But above 14th Street, as you travel north on the waterfront, just add forty to the number of the street across Route 9A and you will know what the pier is. For example, Pier 57 is at 17th Street, while Pier 94 is at 54th Street.

Similarly, you cannot get lost in Central Park if you know what to look for. Central Park's light poles have a four-digit identification plaque for maintenance. If you are lost, just look at the nearest light pole. The plaque's first two digits are the number of the street to the south of you. If the second two digits are even, you are on the east side, and if they are odd, you are on the west side. So, if you are near lamppost 6811, you are between 68th and 69th Streets on the west side.

Increasing Adjacent Property Values

During my Loeb Fellowship, I explored public financing concepts that had been discussed during my time on the mayor's Open Space Task Force. While browsing through historic records in the library at the Graduate School of Design, I thought I found the precedent. Frederick Law Olmsted's 1875 Report to the Board of Commissioners of the city's Department of Public Works, noted that the public investment in Central Park increased property values in the three "wards" surrounding it, as compared to all the others in the city.

The report covered the design, acquisition, and construction of the park from 1856 through 1873.[8] The park's southern border is at 59th Street, but at the time, most Manhattan development ended at 34th Street. According to the report, the revenue generated "an excess of the increase of tax over the interest on the cost of the land and improvements to build the park" of $4,411,140 in 1873 dollars.[9] Olmsted used this argument to garner municipal investment in parks in cities across the country, and his report became the basis for my research on how parks and open space increase adjacent real estate values and municipal tax revenue.

I shared the information in my monograph on the subject, which was at the printer and was released by the Neighborhood Open Space Coalition a few months later in 1990.[10] The West Side Waterfront Panel needed a viable financial plan for the proposed waterfront park if our recommendations were going to be taken seriously. We had a $200 million commitment if the governor's proposed bond act passed, but getting additional capital or long-term funds for operation and maintenance seemed out of the question. To address this issue, Michael agreed that our financial plan should analyze the potential effect of park construction on adjacent real estate values and a source of capital funding and maintenance and operations.

An Opportunity Lost

Al Appleton, a colleague from NYC Audubon, had been appointed Dinkins's commissioner of the city's Department of Environmental Protection, and Genie Flatow, a member of the Neighborhood Open Space

Coalition board, was director of a group known as the Coalition for the Bight. As we reviewed the panel's preliminary plan and discussed additional sources of public funding, Genie saw an opportunity to enhance the funding for the project while also solving a vexing problem affecting water quality—a plan that involved installing a system to capture combined sewer overflow.

The New York Bight (the word comes from the old English term meaning corner) is a geological phenomenon that encompasses a valuable ecosystem just off the shore of New Jersey and Long Island where the Hudson empties into the Atlantic Ocean.[11] Over the years, the bight had been subject to incredible human destruction, receiving up to two billion gallons of untreated sewage a day before the passage of the Clean Water Act in 1972, which forced the city to spend billions of dollars on wastewater treatment plants.

However, our city's combined sewer system mixes household and commercial wastewater with stormwater before sending it to the appropriate wastewater treatment plant. When more than three-quarters of an inch of rain falls, to keep wastewater treatment plants from being overwhelmed, the combined sewage is released directly into local waterways. There are thirty-three of these combined sewer outfalls that terminate at the bulkhead in the Hudson River Park.

To protect Jamaica Bay, the city Department of Environmental Protection had built one of the nation's first stormwater holding facilities at Spring Creek near Starrett City. The facility held twenty million gallons of combined sewage during periods of heavy rain, which was slowly released into the sewage treatment plant after the initial storm surge.

To address the issue, the department's chief engineer suggested that installing a sewer main forty-eight inches in diameter along the length of the park could collect the combined wastewater, store it, and slowly route it to the appropriate wastewater treatment plant after the storm. Thanks to the storage capacity of the pipe, the flow of sewage into the Hudson could be stopped. The department estimated that the project could cost up to $750 million.[12]

This was a unique point in time. The entire waterfront was being rebuilt, and the Department of Environmental Protection did not require city capital funding for infrastructure projects, but instead, they issued bonds. The agency had the third-best bond rating in the country for municipal infrastructure at the time and had included bicycle paths and landscaping atop previous sewer projects. We suggested locating the large sewer main under the state transportation department's planned bicycle and pedestrian paths and land-scaped area outboard of the roadway.

City Environmental Commissioner Appleton thought that it might even be possible to fund part of the bulkhead reconstruction to protect the new infrastructure in areas where the pipe ran near the water's edge. That might save the panel some of the $50 million (in 1989 dollars) that we were budgeting for bulkhead stabilization.

My May memo suggested that the panel consider West Side redevelopment more holistically. Hudson River Boulevard would cost $500 million to $800 million, a storm water system would cost $600 million to $800 million, and the proposed West Side waterfront park would cost $450 million to $600 million. My memo also advocated for rezoning the adjacent neighborhoods for residential and commercial office redevelopment. My July memo to Del Giudice argued for the inclusion of the combined sewer overflow project, proposed an investment of $2 billion to $2.5 billion to reconstruct the entire waterfront, and recommended a follow-up entity to ensure our recommendations were implemented.[13]

Unfortunately, given the time pressure the panel was under, members deemed the storm water system impractical to include in our recommendation. The uncertainties made it risky, and the timing just did not work. We had a bird in the hand.

In the late 1990s, the city's Department of Environmental Protection initiated an environmental review for a similar facility in Paerdegat Basin that, combined with a holding tank, now captures fifty million gallons of sewage during a heavy rainfall and 1.2 billion gallons annually.[14] Unfortunately, the combined stormwater outfalls in the park continue to release raw sewage into Hudson River Park during heavy rainfalls to this day.

Interim Improvements

After the establishment of task force but prior to the panel, the Neighborhood Open Space Coalition's landscape architecture intern from Cornell University worked with Community Board 2, community residents, and park advocates—to develop a plan for an interim esplanade on the Greenwich Village waterfront. When I joined the panel, I described the coalition's effort and the benefits of interim improvements to show some progress on the waterfront and suggested that we consider building an interim esplanade in Greenwich Village.[15] The panel agreed that interim improvements would show our intent, encourage residents to visit the waterfront, and develop a sense of ownership and momentum.

In 1990, the state Office of Parks, Recreation, and Historic Preservation reviewed our proposed plans for a temporary two-acre esplanade and bicycle path between Christopher and West 12th Streets in Greenwich Village and determined that the project did not require an environmental impact statement.[16] When the plan was presented to Community Board 2, they rejected the proposal, even though they had helped develop it, but the panel felt that it was important.

Given Community Board 2's opposition to our plans, the panel members appreciated the fact that the board's district manager had stated in an article regarding open space needs in Lower Manhattan that our plans for a waterfront park had been applauded by the affected community boards and would be "a breath of fresh air."[17]

Scenic Easement Application

Preparing for our April meeting, panel members reviewed the state Department of Transportation's application to the Federal Highway Administration to designate much of the property west of the roadway as a scenic area and waive the requirement to repay the federal government.[18]

The feds quickly denied the state's request because of "restaurants, museums, marinas and fisheries that may block the views," and by August, they requested that the state repay the federal funds used to buy the right-of-way almost a decade earlier. However, the state had until 1995 to appeal that decision.[19]

By May, the panel proposed limiting commercial activities outboard to the three development nodes and the Public Development Corporation's Hudson River Center. The city and state agreed to restrict new buildings on the remaining 70 percent of the outboard property south of 34th Street.[20] Doing so would require state legislation, and several West Side legislators who had sponsored the Hudson River protection bills supported the initiative.

Planning Continues

During 1990, panel members, staff, consultants, and citizen advisory committee members worked together to craft the plan for a revitalized West Side waterfront. Our goals were to preserve, enhance, and provide public access to the Hudson River; celebrate history, the maritime industry, and the environment; meet the recreational needs of adjacent neighborhoods; and enhance the quality of life and the image of the city. We also wanted a roadway that would enhance mobility, minimize the impact on local neighborhoods, and maximize access to the waterfront.

With these goals in mind, there were numerous community board meetings, design workshops, and discussions with civic and environmental organizations, labor unions, developers, and business associations. We toured the waterfront by land and water and developed concepts that were presented at public meetings. It was easier to reach consensus without the influence of the pro-development forces that had driven the conversation since 1974. However, we knew that our recommendations had to be financially viable.

In September, we presented our draft recommendations, and more than seventy individuals and organizations provided comments. We included public open space on six piers and used the term *park* instead of esplanade. There were mixed reviews.[21] Residents of adjacent neighborhoods supported the waterfront park and access to the Hudson but were concerned about the designated development areas and the Hudson River Center.

"Only in New York," Gene Russianoff said, "would people say that a park is something that includes 2,000 to 3,000 units of residential housing and a forty-story hotel." Lou Coletti of the New York Building Congress countered, "There have to be reasons for them to come there, besides open space." Some people questioned the viability of our financial plan. "It is not compelling and it's fraught with difficulties," concluded Dick Anderson of the Regional Plan Association.[22] I thought we were on the right track because nobody seemed happy.

We integrated public comments into our final recommendations. The state transportation department agreed to continue the landscaping and bicycle and pedestrian paths to the southern terminus of Route 9A at Battery Park. The panel showed this half-mile "tail" as part of the park, even though we had no jurisdiction over it.

It was estimated that our final recommendations would cost $500 million.[23] We had a $200 million city/state commitment and a preliminary commitment of $65 million from Route 9A for the bicycle and pedestrian paths and landscaping on the outboard side of the roadway.[24] The panel needed a plausible financial plan, not only to build the park, but to support long-term maintenance and operation if the park was going to be successful.

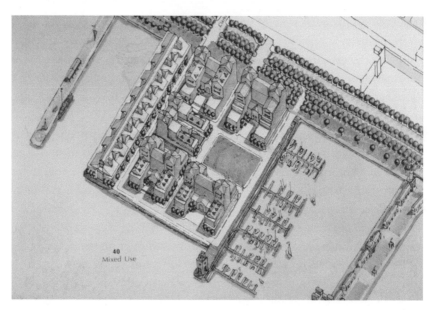

West Side Waterfront Panel's Pier 40 maximum development option. (West Side Waterfront Panel)

We limited outboard development to three "development nodes" where existing piers contained more than four million square feet of space that could be redeveloped.

Considerations other than revenue generation guided our selection of designated development areas. Large structures already blocked the views of the river, we needed attractions to make the park proposal more relevant to the entire region and broaden political support, and the attractions would draw visitors north and south along the waterfront.

The three nodes were the 15-acre Pier 40 at Houston Street, the 1.2-million-square-foot Chelsea Piers complex (Piers 59, 60, and 61), and what we called the Midtown Maritime District (Piers 81, 83, and 84). Responding to significant pro-development interests and the need to support maintenance and operation, we included a broad range of activities—from residential, retail, and offices to new maritime, recreational, and entertainment uses—that would generate revenue and enhance public use of the park.

That proposal held the interest of the real estate industry and building trades who supported the park—if it generated jobs. We had used that technique during the task force deliberations, and the moral is this: always try to keep options open and ensure that everyone has a voice in the discussions so that everyone stays at the table until the final decisions are made.

We set limits on the ratio between height and floor area at each node to make sure the development would not be excessive.[25] We proposed that revenues generated in the park be retained by a successor entity and be dedicated to the planning, construction, operation, and maintenance of the park. This approach contradicted existing city and state legislation requiring that revenues generated in public parks be sent to the general fund.

The panel suggested that funds from a wide variety of city, state, and federal programs—from waterfront redevelopment to environmental protection and habitat restoration—be used to build the park and that private donations be solicited for specific projects. The panel requested that our consultant explore the potential for inboard revenue.

Using growth projection from the Regional Plan Association, we analyzed tax data from adjacent properties, existing values, and the potential for future revenue. We projected potential revenue generation in 1998, 2008, and 2018 using various applicable mechanisms, and the results were significant.[26] We recommended creating three possible mechanisms to capture the increase in real estate values and taxes stimulated by creation of the park, in an area up to 1,500 feet from the roadway.[27]

We suggested tax increment financing which would reduce future funding for other city services or an impact fee to offset the demands that new development would have on the limited recreation space in the area. Some people felt that an impact fee might deter new development during difficult economic times, and others warned that the mechanism might lead to overdevelopment to generate funding for the park. Another suggestion was a special assessment district, which require a small fee over and above normal property taxes. Establishing the district would require both state and city approvals. An appendix of our recommendations spelled out our assumptions regarding potential revenue generation from each mechanism.[28]

After a decade of drastic budget cuts that had decimated city services, ensuring an independent source of revenue to contribute to construction and long-term maintenance and operating costs seemed reasonable. We believed that combining revenue generated in the park; revenue from inboard real estate appreciation; city, state, and federal funding; and private fundraising could make the park "self-sufficient."

In November of 1990, the West Side Waterfront Panel recommended that a four-mile world-class waterfront park, with continuous bicycle and pedestrian paths, be built on all the upland property from Chambers to 59th Streets, including thirteen public piers with more than twenty acres of public open space and a greenway connecting to Battery Park. The waterfront planning principles developed during the two-year public planning process defined the character of the future waterfront we envisioned.[29]

We embraced recreation, education, and water-dependent activities in Tribeca and recommended that nature and the environment be emphasized there, with native plantings, ecological exhibits, and research involving the estuary. Active-play areas from open lawns to playgrounds and hard surface ball courts would add diversity and meet existing recreational needs; community boat houses would be encouraged.[30]

In Greenwich Village, we emphasized the neighborhood's historic character and the community's desires for landscaped open space and unobstructed views of the river. Piers 42, 45, 46, and 51 would be preserved as public piers, and a playground would serve neighborhood children.

The panel supported the Chelsea Waterside Park Association's proposal for a major park at 23rd Street with a grassy esplanade along an open stretch of water between 30th and 34th Streets, the relocation of the heliport, and making Pier 79 a public pier. Pier 76 was not included in our plan, but we recommended that Hudson River Center be designed to minimize its impact on the park. At 42nd Street, we suggested building a large plaza to support the Circle Line and the Intrepid—the only existing maritime attractions on the West Side waterfront—and that Piers 81, 83, and 84 host year-round entertainment attractions such as their popular summer open-air concerts.

During our outreach, we had met with John Bowers, president of the International Longshoremen's Union, and learned the importance of retaining the working waterfront. We recommended maintaining commercial maritime activities from 41st to 59th Streets, and we suggested a creative reuse of several of the passenger ship terminals.

We also recommended that Piers 95 and 96 be removed to create the Clinton Waterfront Park, with Pier 94 accommodating year-round public recreation as well as limited maritime and commercial activity. In addition, we suggested making Pier 97 a public pier. In areas such as the Chelsea Piers and the passenger ship terminals, where it was not possible to build a water's-edge esplanade, we recommended maximizing the space between the roadway and the pier sheds for public use.

The panel recommended creating a new entity to make sure that the plans it recommended were carried out in a timely manner. Also, the panel urged that phased construction begin as soon as money was available and Route 9A was completed in a particular area. We encouraged the successor entity to embrace all the lessons that the panel had learned.[31] The task force had built the foundation, and the panel had drawn the blueprints for Hudson River

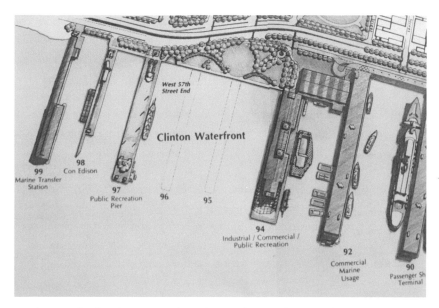

Panel's vision for the Clinton Waterfront. (West Side Waterfront Panel)

Park. Incredibly, after five years of planning and debate, it was starting to look as if there was going to be a waterfront park on Manhattan's West Side.

Things Change Quickly

The panel's final recommendations received mixed reviews. Most people were happy with the idea of eliminating landfill, preserving 70 percent of waterfront to protect views, and requesting a federal payback waiver. But park advocates were concerned about the possible scale of commercial development at the three development areas and at Hudson River Center.

Panel members believed that we had provided an exciting vision for the waterfront, but five days after the release of the panel's recommendations, our financial plan sprang a leak when the governor's environmental bond act was defeated.[32] Now we had a park plan but without the $100 million in state funds needed to match the city's commitment.[33] This sad situation only increased suspicions regarding outboard development and provided ammunition for Marcy and her park opponents.

As 1991 began, the American Forestry Association described the findings of the real estate study I had done at Harvard and reinforced the importance of open space in enhancing home values, business, and tourism.[34] After the panel's recommendations were released, the city and state established a West Side Waterfront Office to oversee the transition between the panel and whatever new entity would oversee future park development.

I continued to work in a semi-official capacity with Michael Del Giudice and promoted the park to anyone who would listen. By May, we had developed a proposed work program for what we were still calling the *entity*.[35] We relied on our consultants to address planning and design, community participation, and legal and engineering issues with a $100,000 budget for the transition work. My primary contacts in Albany were David Nocenti, assistant general counsel to the governor and no fan of environmentalists, and Mary Ann Crotty, the director of State Operations and Policy, who was often sympathetic to our cause. The state proposed the first draft memorandum of understanding, but serious negotiations did not begin until December.[36]

The Outboard Property

The senior state transportation department decision-makers in Albany were chief engineer Mike Cuddy and assistant commissioner for legal affairs John Clemente. Both men seemed bitter about Westway's defeat and local West Side community activism. The Route 9A team was completing the final roadway design and, until the new entity was established, the state transportation department managed the entire right-of-way, including the piers and underwater property taken for Westway.

There were quite a few municipal uses on the waterfront. Cars towed from Midtown were initially brought to Pier 76. If they were not retrieved in thirty days, they were moved to Pier 61 in the Chelsea Piers. If the cars remained unclaimed, they were auctioned from Pier 26 in Tribeca.

They were not too fond of environmentalists either. *E–The Environmental Magazine* featured Barry Benepe's Greenmarkets, the Open Space Coalition's Brooklyn Queens Greenway initiative, and Cathy Drew's pioneering work with The River Project as examples of the city's growing environmental movement.[37] That did little to change their perception.

However, the state transportation department tolerated the river rats in Tribeca who had managed to get a toehold on the waterfront at Piers 25 and 26.[38] Jim Wetteroth, who had started The Downtown Boathouse as a program of The River Project, began operating from a container on Pier 26.[39] By 1990, however, Pier 26 was dilapidated, condemned, and cleared of

The River Project on Pier 26 in Tribeca. (Tom Fox)

vehicles. The panel supported The River Project and The Downtown Boat-house moving to Pier 25—a decision unanimously supported by Community Board 1.[40]

You had to be bold, patient, and creative to get a small boat in the Hudson in those days. Wetteroth worked with Rick Muller, a volunteer who initially dragged a Klepper kayak he stored on 17th Street down to the Hudson. With a certified marine engineer providing guidance, Jim and Rick replaced enough of the deteriorated pile tops under the apron of Pier 26 to support pedestrian access, which allowed both The River Project and The Downtown Boathouse to return.

Pier 25 was the first pier north of Battery Park City. In 1990, Jimmy Gallagher brought the 140-foot *Yankee*, the last of the Ellis Island ferries, to the north side of Pier 25. The *Yankee* had started life as the *Machigonne*, which was launched in 1907.[41] Jimmy was a pied piper who restored *Yankee* with volunteers from Tribeca, including Julie Nadel, who eventually became a board member of the Hudson River Park Trust.

In the spring of 1991, David Pearlman, an itinerant musician with the nom de guerre "Poppa Neutrino," arrived in the harbor with his family. The Floating Neutrinos, as they were known, had built two makeshift vessels with discarded wood that were kept afloat with huge amounts of recycled Styrofoam in the hulls. They moored between Battery Park City and Pier 25, homeschooled their two daughters aboard, and shuttled back and forth to Pier 25 in a dinghy.[42]

However, the state transportation department came under pressure to increase the revenue generated by the property it acquired for Westway and reduce its liabilities. In 1989, the state inspector general had issued a report asserting that the department was not keeping track of land it owned, and that this was costing the state money.[43]

A new "beach club" called the Amazon Village was launched at Pier 25. Amazon Village was the state Department of Transportation's first experience with a commercial food and beverage operation on the waterfront. It was a seasonal attraction—created by a Philadelphia restaurateur and his brother—with the preservation of the Amazon rainforests as the nominal theme for the "club," which had two bars, a volleyball court, a small beach, a large cage filled with parrots, and valet parking.[44] Efforts to save the rainforest were secondary to making money from this novel attraction, and Amazon Village was an immediate hit. By the end of its first season, however, residents of Independence Plaza, a complex of three high-rise residential buildings directly across Route 9A, complained about the noisy, late-night goings-on.

Local entrepreneurs and preservationists were working inboard of Route 9A as well. Peter Obletz, a dance company manager, train buff, former Community Board 4 chair, and chair of their transportation committee, lived in a concrete-block building at West 28th Street under the elevated railway tracks known as the High Line with two railroad cars he had restored in the 1970s.[45]

Conrail auctioned the two-mile section of the abandoned rail line, stretching from Bank Street to the Javits Convention Center, and Peter, who offered $10 and was the sole bidder, won the auction. He started the West Side Rail Line Development Foundation to pursue his dream of running a railroad locomotive and a few railroad cars on the High Line as a tourist attraction. However, the city and adjacent landowners sued to kill the deal. Peter was unable to raise the needed capital, and eventually the city took control of the elevated rail line.

Issues with Route 9A

The task force had envisioned a grand urban boulevard like Park Avenue, and members of the 9A team were sympathetic and flexible. They did a lot of things right—but not everything. For example, the roadway surface was a disaster. NASA had introduced safety grooving on its runways to increase traction and reduce hydroplaning, and their longitudinal safety grooves were carefully cut with specialized machinery.[46] The state transportation department incorporated the concept of safety grooving on the roadway but did not do it correctly. Instead of being cut longitudinal by machine, after the concrete cured, workers manually scored the concrete with perpendicular groves by pulling a rake across the roadway surface as the concrete was curing.

The width and depth of the grooves were inconsistent and created a washboard effect that increased roadway noise. Longitudinal grooves, scored by machine with a specific spacing and depth, would have dampened it.[47] The median had shortcomings too. Although the state transportation department developed a special soil mix, their contractors failed to follow the specifications and deposited soil containing a lot of stone and very little organic material.[48] And because the lead engineer Mike Cuddy objected to installing irrigation in the median, quite a few new trees died and had to be replaced.

In addition, the median was planted solely with beach rose (*Rosa rugosa*). Beach rose is a salt-tolerant plant and was appropriate given the estuary's brackish water and prevailing westerly winds. In addition, roses are perennials and native to the city's shorelines. Their sharp thorns deterred individuals from cutting across the median. But the unintended consequence was that the beach rose plants caught every scrap of plastic, paper, and debris that blew across the median, and the trash was particularly hard to extract because there was no path on the median to allow gardeners to maintain the landscape. After the fact, a footpath was finally added to the middle of the median, along with irrigation.

Delay Heightens Concerns

Failure to establish the successor entity increased the concern of park advocates. In October, key members of Community Board 4's waterfront committee supported the establishment of a park corporation "with clout," if the corporation had certain controls.[49] They were surprised that State Assemblymember Nadler and City Council member Freed agreed while Assemblymember Glick, a vocal opponent of the project, was noticeably silent.

Most people felt that Republicans, who controlled the state Senate, would block any new legislation establishing a successor entity. Seeing no other alternative, Community Board 4 was preparing a resolution endorsing the panel's recommendation, supporting a strong corporation with limitations and community participation, and agreeing to the new entity's oversight and management of both the state and city property. By November, although the roadway was moving forward and the state had proposed a memo of understanding, Dinkins had not engaged in negotiations to create the successor entity.

Bob Laird, the opinion editor of the *Daily News*, praised the panel's plan and the progress being made on the roadway but urged that Dinkins get the city government moving to capture this once-in-a-lifetime opportunity.[50] The value of the available funding was losing about 5 percent to inflation annually. *The Downtown Express* lamented the lack of progress, questioned the wisdom of setting up another authority, and suggested that existing agencies carry out the recommendations. I agreed that the situation was unfortunate but argued that a new authority would be the best way to move the project forward because existing city and state agencies lacked the staff, resources, and ability to direct other agencies to implement the plan.

While agreeing that we all experienced problems with quasi-public authorities, I thought that the Task Force and the Panel showed that with citizens on the board and strong community participation the authority could be kept from running amok.[51] It was hard to believe that I had become a salesman for a new public authority, but by now, I was desperate to get this project going.

Strengthening Relationships with Labor

In December of 1991, Tommy Maguire asked me to speak at a rally in City Hall Park. Given the recession, many large-scale public works projects were on hold, which meant fewer construction jobs and higher industry unemployment. The delay in the planning and construction of the Hudson River Park was an example.

In the largest labor rally in the city since the 1930s, some fifty thousand construction workers from more than two hundred unions marched across the Brooklyn Bridge, chanting and waving flags and banners.[52] Addressing a tough audience, I said that civic and environmental advocates had much more in common with them than they thought.

Our priorities are clean air, clean water, and public open space, all of which ensured a better life for union members and their families. Environmentalists depend on the construction workers because we cannot build parks, sewage treatment plants, museums, and cultural institutions, or restore wetlands and waterways—they do. We would never achieve our goals without the support and involvement of the building trades and construction industry.

I explained my belief that the government pits us against one another to create confrontation so that it does not have to move projects forward. I suggested that by working together and speaking in one voice regarding major projects like the Hudson River Park, we would all benefit. The message was well received, strengthened the bond Tommy and I had begun building, and increased support for the park. Dinkins agreed to a "Rebuilding New York Summit Meeting" the next month.[53]

Maguire then asked me to speak at the International Union of Operating Engineers general executive board meeting in Bal Harbour, Florida, attended by 240 union leaders from throughout the United States and Canada.[54] It introduced me to another group that wondered why an environmentalist was addressing a union convention. My message was the same and so was their reception.[55]

Addressing people with respect, and listening, can help you find common ground with almost anyone. We agreed to disagree on many issues, but building and strengthening relationships is a key to success—and so is turning your enemies into allies.

Clearing the Chelsea Piers

With the panel's recommendations in hand and a desire to increase revenues generated by its property, I worked with the state transportation department and moved forward on our first "node of development," the Chelsea Piers. The initial challenge was relocating municipal facilities. The city's transportation department tow pound, the city's sanitation department garage, an MTA bus garage and maintenance facility, and police department barricade storage occupied a majority of the three-pier 1.2 million-square-foot complex.

When these agencies were informed that they needed to clear the piers, they claimed that they could not relocate without somewhere to go, an approved environmental impact statement, and funding to pay for the relocation. At the same time, the state transportation department was periodically sending marine engineers to monitor the condition of the piers along the right-of-way—and a recent report indicated that the piers could collapse at any moment and should be condemned.

Mike Franchese, the state transportation department's regional director for New York City and an experienced old-school transportation engineer, scheduled a meeting with the affected agencies in his Long Island City office. Although I had butted heads with Mike over several issues, we were now on the same side, and it was a pleasure to watch him at work.

More than twenty administrators, lawyers, and operations directors from four agencies reiterated that they could not possibly vacate the piers. Mike explained the seriousness of the situation and patiently explained that the piers had been condemned and had to be cleared. Finally, one lawyer slapped his palm on the table, expressed that they could not move without their conditions being met, and announced, "This meeting is effectively over."

Mike calmly asked the fellow's name, and when asked for a reason, stated, "When the first person dies on those piers, I want to be able to tell their spouse who's responsible. Oh, by the way, you're right, this meeting is over, and you have thirty days to vacate the piers." Within a month, the entire Chelsea Piers complex was emptied. Where did they go? Who knows? Was there an environmental impact statement? Not a chance. Who paid for the relocation? I have no idea, but the money probably came from the agencies' existing budgets.

The three final bidders for the pier's redevelopment were Hirschfeld Properties, World Yachts, and the Chelsea Piers Partnership. The Piers Partnership had initially approached the state transportation department asking to lease one hundred thousand square feet of Pier 61 for ice skating. Sky Rink, a rooftop rink at 450 West 33rd Street, was closing, and the daughter of a Piers Partnership principal trained there. The group was not happy that they now had to redevelop the entire Chelsea Piers complex, but they gave it a shot.

The Chelsea Piers complex was the perfect place to begin outboard development. The need for parking was critical in any outboard development, and the first floor of each pier contained parking. Our first recreation and commercial development area was underway.

7

Things Finally Start Happening (1992–1993)

● ● ● ● ● ● ● ● ● ● ● ● ● ●

After six years of research, debate, and planning, we were finally focused on the structure and function of the new entity. Many of us had high hopes that things would move more quickly if the city and state agreed. However, it took seven months for the city to respond to the state's initial draft memorandum of understanding, which was issued at the end of 1991. After reviewing the city's response, I wrote to Mary Ann Crotty, the state director of operations, and Michael Del Giudice, our chair, saying that anyone who wanted to see the park envisioned by the West Side Waterfront Panel built would be very disappointed.

The state had proposed establishing a Hudson River Park Corporation to plan, build, operate, finance, and maintain a new park. However, the city seemed focused on meeting the perceived needs and interests of every operating, regulatory, and budgetary division in city government. Their proposal substantially limited the powers of the successor entity envisioned by the panel and, if executed, redevelopment on the West Side would have been set back a decade.[1]

As a member of the task force and the panel, I found that under Koch, the city's Public Development Corporation had consistently supported development on the waterfront. The Army Corps of Engineers had ruled that the steel and concrete caissons proposed by the Public Development Corporation to support Hudson River Center were analogous to landfill. That project was in jeopardy. They had several other waterfront projects, including Brooklyn Army Terminal and South Street Seaport, and were working with the Port Authority to develop Brooklyn Piers 1–6.[2]

When Dinkins expanded and rebranded the agency as the Economic Development Corporation in 1991, Carl Weisbrod, who had worked at the agency during the Koch administration, was appointed the first president. Apparently, the corporation played a significant role in crafting the city's draft response because it contained proposals that were contrary to recommendations that Dinkins had already agreed to.

My five-page memo critiquing the city's draft highlighted the major issues:

- The city wanted the waterfront divided into a city-controlled northern section extending from 35th Street north to 59th Street and a southern section extending from the Battery north to 35th Street that would be controlled jointly by the city and state.
- They eliminated the new entity's ability to make short- and long-term decisions about land use in the city's section, removed all revenues generated in that section, and limited capital investments there to contributions from private developers.
- The city would not transfer their property to the new entity and would not issue short-term leases or assume responsibility for property management until after decisions were made about land use. Revenue generated in the park would not go to the new entity, and their annual budget would be decided by the mayor and governor.
- Municipal facilities in the southern parcel would remain until the new entity recommended by the panel could develop a financing plan for their relocation.
- If established as a subsidiary of the state Urban Development Corporation, the new entity would be exempt from public review of land-use proposals in the jointly owned southern area, and the city Economic Development Corporation would make all decisions about long-term land use in the northern section and be exempt from the requirement mandating public review.

I also wrote to Gary Deane, Deputy Mayor Barbara Fife's right-hand man on the waterfront, reiterating my concerns.[3] I noted that the park was on the construction industry's list of delayed projects and without Route 9A, the redevelopment of inboard real estate and Riverside South were in jeopardy. I thought that we all understood how these projects were interconnected and the need to jump-start the city's sluggish economy and stimulate long-term redevelopment of the West Side.

Quite a few drafts were exchanged over the next three months. In April, final drafts were circulated, and we outlined a plan to hit the ground running—including external briefings with elected officials, community boards, and the press; developing responses to Marcy's objections to the park; and leaking the plan to the *New York Times* the day before the official announcement. We prepared briefing materials for future appointees, proposed interim improvements, and scheduled interagency briefings with ten city, state, and federal agencies and authorities.[4]

The new entity was rebranded the Hudson River Park Conservancy to better describe our intentions. On May 17, 1992, the memo of understanding was signed, and the conservancy was established as a subsidiary of the Urban Development Corporation. It was to be governed by a nine-member board appointed by the governor, the mayor, the borough president—who were required to appoint the city and state park commissioners—and several private citizens. Revenues generated in the park would be retained by the new entity.[5]

Many of us were wary of establishing another public authority, but there were major concerns as to when public financing would be available and whether the panel's recommendation for additional revenue from the appreciation of inboard property could be implemented. Elected officials are reluctant to share any increased tax revenue and jealously guarded their prerogative to make decisions about budget expenditures. That was why the panel recommendation for a special assessment district or impact fee to support park financing in addition to municipal taxes was referred to in several sections of the memorandum of understanding.[6]

An article published in the *New York Times* the day before the final memorandum of understanding was released stated that "the new corporation would also be empowered to coordinate development plans for the two-block corridor directly east of the highway, which is known as Route 9A."[7] I wished that were true. Unfortunately, it was not.

Starting Strong

This time, I was not surprised—given the time and energy I had put into the project—when Cuomo appointed me the first president and chief executive officer of the conservancy. I looked forward to finalizing and implementing the plans for the park. Most park supporters thought that the conservancy being a subsidiary of the Urban Development Corporation was the least desirable but most practical route forward. For my part, I was thrilled by the opportunity to make the concept of the park a reality but not happy about some of the choices I needed to make.

We would work with state Department of Transportation to design a greenway with bicycle and pedestrian paths that they would build along the waterfront next to the boulevard. The conservancy would convert the remainder of the land, piers, and underwater property into a world-class maritime park.

There would be a water's edge esplanade with landscaping, passive recreation, and active recreation on the land along the water's edge, and sports at locations such as Pier 40 and/or the Gansevoort Peninsula. Access to the water would be a priority with human-powered boating and environmental research and education in the waterway. Thirteen of the open piers would become public recreation spaces while the commercial maritime industry in Hell's Kitchen was preserved. Clusters of piers were connected to create larger sections of the park in Chelsea and in Hell's Kitchen.

But I had to work for political operatives like Vincent Tese, chairman of the Urban Development Corporation and Cuomo's close confidant. When I met with Tese's assistant to discuss my appointment, he began by saying, "The governor would like to appoint you president of the conservancy, but if you want the job, you've got to get off his back in Brooklyn."

I had spent most of my adult life fighting government inaction, inefficiency, or chicanery. On both the task force and the panel, I was an independent citizen. I had worked for government, in the military, and at Gateway National Recreation Area, and I hated the bureaucracy. I knew that working for the government would limit my flexibility, but I tried not to dwell on that fact. So I resigned from the Neighborhood Open Space Coalition and as cochair of the Brooklyn Bridge Park Coalition.

Michael Del Giudice approved our list of actions needed to jump-start the conservancy's efforts.[8] Just establishing the conservancy was seen as a major accomplishment by many in the nonprofit, public, and private sector, and the governor was hopeful that this new approach would work. "What makes this more likely is that you have a plan that has community support," said Mary Ann Crotty. "Their concerns seem to be more over the process and the mechanism than the plan itself. But the mechanism and the process will make that plan work."[9]

Predictably, there were vociferous opponents to this approach—among them, Marcy Benstock, Gene Russianoff, John Mylod of Clearwater, the New York Chapter of the Sierra Club, Friends of the Earth, and the Greenwich Village naysayers. However, the three citywide newspapers that had followed the project closely responded positively. The *New York Times* expressed support for the agreement, underscored the importance of combining the park with limited commercial development, and described critics' concern about the involvement of the Urban Development Corporation, but countered that "the compromise can recapture the river."[10] A long follow-up article spoke to the possibilities, described the conservancy's plan, and envisioned the future waterfront.[11]

New York Newsday recognized that plans for the park were neither perfect nor complete and expressed concern about the possibility of outboard residential development but stated that the effort deserved the benefit of the doubt.[12] The *Daily News* noted that the conservancy had the benefit of starting with a "splendid" report released by the panel while affirming that the weak link was funding. The paper called for extensive public participation and complemented Michael and me on being community-minded and pro-park.[13] Both Ernest Tollerson, editor of *New York Newsday*'s editorial pages, and Bob Laird, who was the chief editorial writer of the *Daily News* before becoming the paper's op-ed editor, supported the park and had published my opinion pieces.

The response in the community press was mixed. *The Villager*, true to that neighborhood's continued skepticism, voiced concern that Pier 40 could become another Battery Park City and the entire park might consist only of a bike path from the Battery to 59th Street and otherwise become a receptacle for trash.[14] But the paper acknowledged that parts of the plan had merit and called for a constructive give-and-take.

The *Chelsea Clinton News* was hopeful, stating that the effort to build the park was back on track.[15] Bob Trentlyon, the paper's owner and publisher and my fellow task force member, lamented the fact that the city had not managed to reclaim its waterfront as other cities had, but he noted that Gary Hack, the panel's planning consultant, had listened and incorporated ideas from the community. He declared that with Michael and other park supporters appointed as leaders of the conservancy, the park was in safe hands.

After becoming president of the conservancy, I expressed confidence that the waterfront would become a world-class waterfront park as envisioned by the panel. But even early on, there was resistance to the conservancy being a subsidiary of the Urban Development Corporation. Community

Board 1 passed a resolution condemning the conservancy's very existence. I stressed my past fifteen years advocating for public parks—a record that failed to impress State Assemblymember Deborah Glick. "All Tom Fox has said to us," she complained, "is, 'You can trust me.' That's not enough, given U.D.C.'s track record working with communities."[16] Glick was right to be concerned, and the opposition helped lead to more transparency at the conservancy.

The greatest resistance to the park came from my environmental colleagues, who were concerned about outboard development. When asked if the vagueness of our plans for the development areas made opponents nervous, I admitted that it did. But I said that the arrangement also gave us flexibility, adding that we were a new type of authority with the power to make things happen and ensure public accountability.[17] I believed that we were on the right path, and I wanted to hit the ground running.

Chelsea Piers Lease

Among the major issues facing the conservancy was redeveloping the Chelsea Piers Complex. As the first of the three development nodes expected to generate funding for the park, this issue required immediate attention. By May of 1992, the state Department of Transportation had received nine responses to their request for proposals, but only three were deemed acceptable for final review. The conservancy would play a leading role in the final selection process, which was scheduled for June.[18]

The bidder who had worked the longest on their proposal was Chelsea Piers Partnership, led by Roland Betts, Tom Bernstein, and David Tewksbury. Local elected officials and community representatives were impressed with Betts's pedigree. His father was an attorney for Vincent Astor, and he was a Yale alum, a successful businessman, and a lead investor in both the Texas Rangers and Silver Screen Studios.

The firm's principals were motivated, creative, and well connected, and they rose to the occasion, expanding their initial proposal for an ice-skating rink into a comprehensive plan for a sports and entertainment complex containing a wide range of attractions. On Pier 62, the partnership would work with the local community to create a public pier as part of the Chelsea Waterside Park. Pier 61 would have two Olympic-size ice-skating rinks operating twenty-four hours a day, 365 days a year, with seating for 1,600 spectators and quality amenities.

On Pier 60, there would be a summer games training facility with a quarter-mile jogging track, an eighth-of-a-mile competition track, basketball courts, an Olympic-quality gymnastic facility, a sports medicine center, a rock climbing wall, and eventually a pool. They proposed a golf club with a high-tech, four-level, net-enclosed driving range with a 200-yard fairway, along with putting greens, a pro shop, a golf academy, and a waterfront grill adjacent to a marina on Pier 59.

Silver Screen Studios, which had already bankrolled several successful Disney films, proposed a state-of-the-art film and television studio, expanding the studios where "Law and Order" was being filmed with twelve soundstages and production and support facilities on the second floor of the headhouse, spanning three piers.[19] Several restaurants and food vendors would be scattered throughout the complex, and berthing for yachts would surround the piers.

The state Department of Transportation still had jurisdiction of the state property but was now working at the conservancy's direction regarding all the property west of the roadway. We required a continuous public walkway around the piers, and the Department of Transportation planned to build bicycle and pedestrian paths between Route 9A and the pier's headhouse.

By July, we had approved a ten-year lease for the entire Chelsea Piers Complex with a ten-year renewal if the partnership met certain criteria, including "appropriateness of Lessee's use of the Premises with respect to the long-term uses proposed in the publication 'A Vision for a Hudson River Waterfront Park' and the rebuilding and improvements of Route 9A."[20] In other words—their activities would be consistent with the panel's park plan.

My Guardian and the Team

Given my lack of experience working inside the government and a propensity to shoot from the hip (or lip), I quickly learned another lesson about working within the government when Michael Del Giudice informed me that Dinkins would be appointing a second-in-command. I was asked to meet with Margaret Tobin, a city Economic Development Corporation staffer who often worked with City Hall and would join the conservancy as executive vice president. Margaret was enthusiastic, trusted by the city administration, and confident, and she had a master's degree in business administration from Stanford.

She made it clear that one of her tasks would be to keep her eye on me, and although I never had a "guardian," she was bright, direct, and a good sounding board. I was happy to work with someone who added talent to the team instead of a political hack who brought nothing to the table.

Our nine-member board included two private citizens and the city and state parks commissioners. I was grateful that Dinkins had insisted that the Manhattan borough president be able to appoint a member of the conservancy. Ruth Messinger appointed Libby Moroff, a seasoned political hand, and a potential swing vote on contentious issues.

At this point in time, a broad range of initial challenges were facing the conservancy—specifically, building a solid team with the skills to move the project forward; enhancing our credibility with government agencies, local community boards, elected officials, advocacy organizations, the media, and the real estate, building, and construction trades; completing the public design process for the park and finalizing the plans; coordinating our plans and designs with the plans for Route 9A; and finalizing a credible financing plan and securing initial funding.

As it related to the property, we needed to manage various tenants and city, state, and federal agencies already in the park; remove noncompliant municipal and commercial uses; initiate interim improvements to show progress; support individuals and organizations trying to help us carry out our mission; and initiate the required environmental review and granting of permits. Most important, however, was managing our relationship with the governor and mayor.

The Route 9A team had moved to the sixth floor of the building at 21st Street and Fifth Avenue, and we took over the entire tenth floor. It was a great location because it was accessible by mass transit, it was in the middle of the future park, and it had a large space for public gatherings and design meetings for the conservancy and Route 9A. Our space was comfortable and easy to get to, which encouraged community participation in the process—and we took community participation very seriously.

Assembling a quality team was a priority. We needed someone to manage the tenants, municipal agencies, and everyone trying to grab a piece of the waterfront. That person had to understand property management, have good people skills, and be able to work with the government. And I had someone in mind—a friend named Vince McGowan.

I had kept Vince up to date on the project and had invited him to attend the final review of the three bids for the Chelsea Piers because I thought that he would find the event interesting and that it might help convince him to join our team. Vince was a successful businessman—active in his Upper West Side co-op, his block association, Community Board 7, and the New York Republican County Committee, and he was president of Manhattan Chapter 126 of the Vietnam Veterans of America. His family operated a bar on Broadway and West 76th Street. He owned and managed several retail and residential properties, but he had not worked for anyone since leaving the Marine Corps.

I introduced him to the Route 9A team leaders and prepared a memo for Michael explaining the importance of Vince's participation.[21] He passed muster, and Margaret became chief financial officer while Vince was vice president of management and operations. Together we became an effective leadership trio. We had diverse skills, we knew how to play our respective games, and we were not easily intimidated, which was important, given the formidable cast of characters we had to manage.

Our initial team was small but talented and dedicated to our mission. Mary Ann Monte became my executive assistant and our office manager. Mary Ann knew everyone working on the project, both inside and outside the government, she had great rapport with community members, and she made sure that the conservancy's office was a welcoming place for board members, staff, and visitors.

Arne Abramowitz, the first administrator of Flushing Meadows Corona Park, became our landscape architect and park planner. Arne had just completed restoring the Unisphere twenty-eight years after the 1964 World's Fair.[22] Abby Jo Sigal came aboard to coordinate our summer youth program and help with community outreach, planning, and anything else we could think of. The following year, Noreen Doyle, an enthusiastic young Community Board 4 staffer, was hired as our community liaison; bringing aboard someone familiar with the workings of the community boards was very important. Michael Bradley joined the team as McGowan's property manager.

We selected Quennell Rothschild Associates, a respected landscape architecture firm that was experienced in community participation and had an office in Chelsea, to oversee the planning process. Peter Rothschild, working with Andy Moore and Signe Nielsen, led their design team. Our lawyer was David Paget of Sive, Paget & Riesel, and Lex Lalli was back as community liaison. Although I had been working on the project informally since the panel recommendations were released, there was a tremendous amount of work to be done. Our team spent most of that fall and winter planning to make a splash the following spring.

Encouraging Community Participation

Nurturing our relationships with local communities, advocacy groups, and business interests was critical. We frequently used our large meeting room for design charettes, community meetings, land-use discussions, and public presentations.

The conservancy prepared a list of architects and/or planners and allowed each community board to select one to advise them about their segment of the park during the design process. One important design criterion suggested by Elizabeth Goldstein from the state Office of Parks, Recreation and Historic Preservation was placing the lights to illuminate the water's edge walkway behind the benches rather than along the railing where they would impede visitors' views of the Hudson and the night sky.

All public meetings were held in the conservancy's large meeting room to better accommodate public review of plans and proposals and receive feedback.[23] The Quennell Rothschild team frequently used our meeting space, and large aerial photographs of the park were hung around the room so participants could reference specific places or features while working with

Conservancy staff at a public information tent at the Union Square Greenmarket. (Tom Fox)

the planners and designers. Park plans were regularly updated and posted directly under the photographs to show the progress of the designs. We established a citizens advisory board with three cochairs—from Community Boards 1, 2, and 4—as well as topic-based subcommittees consisting of knowledgeable people who cared about the issues.

We kept the public informed about the park's progress via a quarterly newsletter, encouraging public participation. Conservancy staff attended block parties and street fairs and manned information booths in pop-up tents in locations like the Union Square Greenmarket and Riverside Park to solicit input and attract volunteers. I had hoped that we would continue building the new model for public participation in the design, management, and implementation of public works projects, although time would temper my optimism.

In 1993, Margaret even volunteered to support The River Project by swimming in the Hudson—notoriously polluted in the nineteenth century but much cleaner now. She was a strong swimmer and wore goggles with a nose guard, ear plugs, and a bathing cap to protect herself, but she felt a little the worse for wear afterward. Several years later, Cathy Drew, founder of The River Project, had a visiting photographer on hand and needed people swimming off Pier 26, so I took the plunge.

I discovered that you are not pulled out into the river's current because wakes from ferries and windblown swells push you gently toward the bulkhead, and the water tasted sweeter than I had imagined. It is strange bobbing around in the Hudson because everything else looks huge—especially the piers. The most daunting task was climbing up the ladder to the pier deck and hoping that you did not scrape the barnacles and mussels on the pier piles on the way up.

I learned that when you are working on a controversial project, people you know, and respect, can turn against you. Because I had been appointed to the task force, the panel, and now the conservancy, anti-park advocates were convinced that I had gone over to "the dark side." Opponents like Marcy Benstock called me a sellout, telling the *New York Times*, "Tom Fox was never an environmentalist."[24] At first, those attacks hurt. When you follow your convictions, you are often ignored or abused, but I was not used to being condemned by my fellow environmentalists.

Some Greenwich Village residents joined the chorus. I had worked with my Bank Street neighbor Bill Bowser on our block association's beautification committee. Our neighbors would clean up the block during work parties and plant and prune street trees. When I was appointed to the conservancy, however, he wrote to Cuomo stating, "I know Tom Fox and I wouldn't trust him to sweep sidewalks." It was sad but ironic because I literally had swept Bill's sidewalk, and he had not complained that my work was substandard.

In August, the Greenwich Village fight against the park plan was in full swing. However, in a letter to the *New York Times*, one Village resident noted that those fighting against the park had cited huge development schemes in the river, with access restricted to the wealthy, as justification for their fears, while in fact, the waterfront at that point was a wasteland filled with crumbling docks, shattered glass, and rotting litter.[25] The author envisioned dockside restaurants and shops along a restored waterfront and feared that, without activities that made the waterfront attractive, it would be taken over by the people who would return the waterfront to a dangerous place whether you planted trees or not.

Despite the general resistance, there were creative suggestions coming from Village residents. For example, the flower market located on Sixth Avenue in Chelsea was being forced to move. The panel had entertained the idea of relocating the market to the Chelsea Piers, but their bid for those piers was rejected. The Port Authority began transferring its property to the conservancy, and Village preservationists suggested the flower market might relocate farther south to Pier 40.[26]

The Tale of the Tail

It was a simple sleight of hand that ensured that the Route 9A right-of-way stretching all the way to the Battery became part of the park. Gary Deane had been the director of planning for Battery Park City Authority, which was battling bicyclists who were overwhelming pedestrians on their waterfront esplanade, and he knew that the Route 9A bicycle path would provide an alternative that could draw cyclists away. We wanted the Route 9A bicycle and pedestrian paths to extend from 59th Street to Battery Park at the southern tip of Manhattan, so that the paths could link up with other bicycle and pedestrian infrastructure.

We agreed those paths should be built along the length of the roadway and remain public open space—we called the stretch of park from Chambers Street to Battery Place *the tail*. Gary and I had included that stretch in the boundaries of the future park in the memorandum of understanding.

A few years later, I visited David Emil, then president of the Battery Park City Authority, after being told that he planned to erect a new building, with Public School 234 at its base, in the Route 9A right-of-way and outside the authority's existing property line. I informed him that Route 9A and the conservancy currently had jurisdiction over that property and would be building bicycle and pedestrian paths there, that the area was part of the park, and that his new building would have to adhere to the authority's existing setback from the roadway.

Emil did not believe me, and he did not want the bicycle path. After declaring there would be no bicycle path in front of Battery Park City, he suggested a wager. Whoever lost would buy lunch at The Four Seasons, a celebrated restaurant in the historic Seagram Building on Park Avenue and East 52nd Street, where the city's movers and shakers lunched. When I agreed, he wrote down the wager and asked me to sign it. Emil countersigned the document and put it in his safe.

I won the bet but held off collecting for two reasons. First, I enjoyed David's reminding me whenever we met at one event or another that he owed me lunch. Second, we did not really get along, and neither one of us would have enjoyed lunch together. In any case, I waited too long. The Four Seasons closed in 2019.

Amazon Village Is Closed

In 1992, the median of the temporary Route 9A roadway was a single Jersey barrier separating northbound and southbound traffic. The crosswalk was several blocks away from Pier 25, at Laight Street, and late-night Amazon Village patrons thought it quicker to stagger across the roadway and climb over the median to get home—sometimes still holding their drinks.

The conservancy asked the state transportation department to install a chain-link fence atop the Jersey barrier to prevent certain catastrophes, and the four-foot chain-link fence put a stop to those late-night dashes. However, the noise emanating from Pier 25 kept residents of Tribeca's Independence Plaza up at night, especially those who slept with their windows open on summer nights to catch the cool breezes coming off the Hudson. Members of Community Board 1 complained, and the proprietor, Shimon Bokovza, promised to buy an air conditioner for anyone in Independence Towers who was bothered by the noise.

It was an empty promise, and when the club opened for the 1993 season, noise complaints from Tribeca residents poured in. Perhaps buoyed by the success of his bluster, Shimon later added insult to injury by placing a crane on Pier 25 with its boom extended over the river and charging people $25 a pop to bungee jump.[27]

McGowan and I arrived on a Friday afternoon in July and saw someone jump from the crane and plunge into the Hudson, landing upside down with their head hitting the water. At the time, the Hudson was filled with flotsam and jetsam and even floating wooden piles and beams that could maim or kill someone plunging headfirst into the water. The conservancy complained to the state transportation department, and Amazon Village was closed—never to reopen.

Marking the Turf

By 1993, our team was assembled, and board, staff, and citizen advisors were working well together. We really wanted to create a recognizable brand for the park and establish our presence on the waterfront. Leslie Kameny, a talented graphic designer I had worked with since my Green Guerilla days, developed a logo for the conservancy. We wanted something simple but elegant that would say "waterfront park," and she designed a beautiful logo that was quickly approved by the board. It was a stylized green tree above three wavy blue lines in broad brushstrokes and conveyed the movement of the waves in the water and wind in the future trees.

Remembering the success of the banners at our 1989 rally, the conservancy printed more than a hundred three-foot-by-six-foot banners and hung them on the light poles along the outboard side of Route 9A from the Battery to 59th Street. None of the tenants, maritime operators, government workers, or vendors who sold stuffed animals, hot dogs, and fruit from trucks, old school buses, and makeshift booths along the waterfront had any idea what the Hudson River Park Conservancy was. But once the banners were up, everyone knew where it was.

Showing Progress on the Waterfront

It was important to demonstrate the waterfront's potential, and we exploited the opportunity to meet pent-up demand for public access. For starters, we began a summer youth employment program and hired and trained local young people who helped carry out various interim recreational programs.

Our first effort created a funky but functional recreation area on Pier 62 that was designed to become part of Chelsea Waterside Park. Parked cars were removed, and street sweepers cleaned the pier while participants in the youth

Hudson River Park Conservancy banner in Chelsea. (Tom Fox)

program measured and painted a volleyball court and three basketball courts for which we had bought nets and portable backboards. The young people placed picnic tables at various locations and set up a roller-skating area and pop-up tents with benches and bowls of water for dog walkers. We also started a fishing program.

People constantly dumped all sorts of stuff in the "sewers" on the pier. They were not actually sewers but drains to clear the pier of water accumulation during heavy rain or firefighting. The drains went straight into the Hudson River. Few people purposely throw garbage into our waterways, so in an effort to educate the public, our summer youth interns stenciled painted logos with large fish and text near the drains, informing visitors that anything dumped in those "sewers" went directly into the Hudson and could harm the fish and other wildlife.

These interim activities strengthened the bond between the conservancy and the public and helped the public view us as a more open and transparent public agency. They also gave residents a taste of what was to come.

Our most ambitious interim improvement was a combined bicycle and pedestrian path along the water's edge extending from the Gansevoort

Opening of the interim park at Pier 62 in Chelsea. (Tom Fox)

Peninsula at Little West 12th Street and south to Chambers Street. There were challenges—not the least of which was that the state transportation department did not want any part of the project—and we needed their money to build it. Department officials argued that they would lose revenue from the parking lots lining the waterfront. They argued further that the paths would be neither visible nor accessible and no one would use the path during the reconstruction of Route 9A and create public safety issues in Greenwich Village and Tribeca.

It helped, however, to be working for the governor. State transportation department officials proposed the project to the Federal Highway Administration as an "interim public safety area adjacent to a federally aided highway under construction" and received permission to build a simple path. One advantage of our regular public meetings was that we could propose an initiative and see how it flew. Ideally, a project will be well received. In the case of the path along the water's edge, members of local communities supported the project as did advocates for cyclists and pedestrians.

I spoke with Ernest Tollerson at *New York Newsday* about the project and the support we were getting. In an editorial, *Newsday* supported the initiative, pointing out that highway construction would cause the area to be ripped up for nearly a decade but that adjacent neighborhoods desperately needed open space and the path could be built quickly and cheaply.

The editorial also noted that the path, combined with the new lease for the Chelsea Piers Complex, would show progress toward building the waterfront park and could help allay fears that, as a subsidiary of the Urban Development Corporation, the conservancy was primarily interested in development along the waterfront. "The best way to do this," the editorial said, "is by providing something fast that most West Siders want and need: open space and access to the river."[28] As I had learned many times in the past, support from the media is the best form of advertising and advocacy.

After our plan was approved, I walked the waterfront and spoke with many parking lot operators in Tribeca. I informed them that they would have to move twenty-five feet away from the river's edge so the path could be built. In most cases, it did not diminish the permitted area much but, except for Ben Korman and Meir Cohen of C&K Properties, they all complained and told me it was not possible. But Ben and Meir just asked when they had to move. Their reaction was a pleasant surprise, and C&K Properties developed a good working relationship with the conservancy and community over the years.

We then invited six landscape architects to a charrette to design the path and a new railing to replace the deteriorating chain-link fences along the water's edge. And the results were worth it: a beautiful new bicycle and pedestrian path along the waterfront would be installed in spring of 1994.

Pier 34

In addition to Pier 40, the Port Authority of New York and New Jersey had a large presence on the West Side waterfront that included the Midtown passenger ship terminals, the 30th Street Heliport, the Holland and Lincoln Tunnels, and Port Authority Trans-Hudson subway tunnels and vents. Other than the Morton Street Vent Shafts, the Port Authority had not proposed new initiatives for the West Side. The Holland Tunnel ventilation shaft in Manhattan is located about nine hundred feet out in the river at Canal Street, and the Port Authority proposed rebuilding a portion of Pier 34 in 1993.

I have mentioned that the Holland Tunnel was the first air-ventilated tunnel in the world, and there were four large ventilation shafts along its length—one on land and another in the water in both New York and New Jersey. Pier 34 straddled the tunnel tubes that ran under it and provided some protection where they rose closer to the surface. Commercial vessels navigating this section of the river could lose power or steering.

The original Pier 34 was abandoned and deteriorating, but it had become an offbeat art gallery of sorts by 1983 before it was demolished in 1985.[29] Only the wooden piles and the concrete platform surrounding the vent shaft itself remained. The ventilation shaft provided emergency access and egress in emergencies. The Port Authority also needed access to the shaft for maintenance, and the pier had to be restored.

When the conservancy was established in 1992, only thirty-seven of the original ninety-nine West Side piers remained along the four miles of waterfront between Battery Park City and 59th Street. Many of them were in various stages of disrepair, but the repairs were critical when it came to our goal of enhancing public recreation and access to the Hudson. The panel's plan recommended that a majority of Pier 34 be built as a public pier with a dedicated 14-foot right-of-way on the north side to allow for the Port Authority's use.[30]

Although the underwater property was still under the jurisdiction of the state Department of Transportation, the conservancy was developing the final plan for the park and would eventually have property jurisdiction. Local communities were clamoring for open space, and this could be an opportunity to build the first new recreational pier in the park with someone else's money. The conservancy initially requested that the Port Authority rebuild the pier as recommended by the panel to protect the Holland Tunnel tubes, enable access to the vent shaft, and provide public recreation.

However, just as with the design of the Morton Street vent shafts, the Port Authority balked at spending more than what was necessary to restore basic infrastructure. They proposed rebuilding the north and south pile fields to protect the tunnel tubes but only capping the north one with a 14-foot-wide deck that could accommodate emergency vehicles. If Pier 34 was not going to be rebuilt completely, we wanted wider decks on both the north and south side of the tunnel that we could eventually link together. Community Boards 1 and 2, who rarely agreed on anything, agreed with us.

The Port Authority's major new concern was terrorism. The first bombing of the World Trade Center had occurred that February, and Bill Goldstein, director of capital programs for the Port Authority, believed that opening Pier 34 to the public would allow terrorists to blow up the Holland Tunnel.

Concerned, I toured the vent shaft and invited Bill Hine, the engineer who focused on historic preservation from Community Board 2, to join me. We entered through the tunnel, and traffic had to be stopped for us to access the vent shaft. It was obvious that maintenance access at the surface was needed to avoid disrupting trans-Hudson traffic. However, the outboard vent shaft was nine hundred feet from the bulkhead and surrounded by a wide moat with a curved twelve-foot-high steel fence topped with spikes. The tunnel's tubes were thirty feet below the surface. The landside ventilation shaft on Washington Street offered a more likely target.

In doing some research, I had learned that in the crash of Avianca Flight 52 on Long Island in 1990, the loss of lives was exacerbated because there was only a narrow one-lane roadway that provided access to the crash site. Ambulances carrying away injured passengers were blocked from leaving, and emergency vehicles trying to reach the crash site were impeded.[31] Emergency vehicles might be blocked if the piers were too narrow or there was only one pier deck.

The Port Authority agreed to deck the piles protecting both sides of the tunnel but held firm to a fourteen-foot width and would not allow public access. To resolve the issue, conservancy chairman Del Giudice arranged a meeting with Stanley Brezenoff, Koch's former first deputy mayor who was now executive director of the Port Authority. However, he and I did not get along very well, and this time our meeting at the Port Authority was not particularly pleasant.

The Port Authority eventually agreed to widen the decks to eighteen feet, but discussions regarding access became heated when we insisted on public access to both piers. I knew that during the recent World Trade Center bombing, Stan and two other guys had carried his wheelchair-bound secretary down sixty-seven floors in the darkness.[32] Being a Vietnam veteran, I knew post-traumatic stress when I saw it, and I realized that there was no way Brezenoff would change his mind.

At one point, Stan—who is a big man—stood and held up his right hand with his palm facing towards him and his index and middle fingers extended in a "V." "Tom," he said, "you keep pushing us, and you're not going to get two finger piers." Then he lowered his index finger, kept his middle finger erect, and said, "You'll only get one." The room fell silent. "That's an appropriate finger, Stan," I finally replied, "given what you're trying to do to the public." Unsurprisingly, the meeting ended abruptly.

The Port Authority eventually agreed that the southern pier deck could be open to the public and equipped with lighting, benches, a sidewalk, and a roadway. The north finger pier, however, would be for their exclusive use and remain closed to the public with no amenities. The vent shaft was Port Authority property, but Pier 34 was on state transportation department property

Reconstructed South side of Pier 34 at Canal Street. (Tom Fox)

and would become part of the park, so we appealed to its commissioner, John Regan. He approved the Port Authority's exclusive use of the north finger pier for a five-year period, after which he would no longer be the commissioner and the conservancy could revisit the issue.

The redesigned Pier 34 opened in 1996 with a major public event on the south finger pier and images projected on the vent shaft every evening after sundown for a week.[33] However, there were no accommodations to allow a connection of both sides to rebuild most of the pier for public recreation. As of fall 2023, the north finger pier is still closed to the public.

The conservancy had hit the ground running with a quality team, and we were communicating openly and frequently with the adjacent communities, elected and appointed officials, our advisors, and the press. Some of the city and state agencies with jurisdiction in the future park were helping us implement interim improvements that gave the public a little taste of what was to come. At the same time, we were continuing the community design process that began with the West Side Task Force and refining the park design. We felt comfortable that we were headed in the right direction and beginning to develop credibility and the momentum needed to pull this off.

8

Completing the Plan and Change at the Top (1994–1995)

● ● ● ● ● ● ● ● ● ● ● ● ● ●

The conservancy hit its stride, and by 1994, and there were tangible changes on the waterfront. However, our most important task was completing the design of the proposed park and recommending the appropriate strategy for the public financing. But in November 1994, George Pataki was elected governor, and the situation changed rapidly.

Route 9A Alternatives

The first public meeting to discuss the scope for the environmental review for Route 9A was held in November of 1988.[1] Five years later, in 1993, the state Department of Transportation released five alternative plans for Route 9A for public review, ranging from rebuilding the road in place for $370 million to a $965 million highway with elevated viaducts. Department officials claimed that the roadway itself would not noticeably affect nearby development but noted that parks traditionally increased the desirability of adjacent real estate. This reinforced the panel's recommendation that the park should get some of the value it generated from adjacent development.[2]

Public meetings offered a chance for the conservancy's board, staff, consultants, and the media to hear firsthand the concerns of residents and opponents, and the meetings often increased our leverage on the inside. The park and outboard development were not included in the Route 9A alternatives, although predictably, Marcy Benstock—who continued to oppose both the roadway and park—attacked the plans, claiming that they would spur future outboard development.

In this case, however, her fears were warranted, and I continued to have my own doubts about what the state was proposing. The Hudson River Park Conservancy still had an option to develop Pier 40 with up to 1,700 units of housing and 240,000 square feet of commercial space in eight-story buildings. I believed that most commercial and residential real estate development should be located inboard, and that the increased inboard real estate value should generate funding to build and maintain the park.

By 1993, the entire Route 9A corridor sprung to life. Chelsea Piers Management completed its environmental impact statement and scheduled construction to begin that fall. The Port Authority's lease for the passenger ship terminals was about to expire in 1996, and twelve operators responded to a Request for Expression of Interest in the facility. The Port also applied for permits to build the two finger piers at Pier 34.

Thanks to the conservancy's interim improvements at Pier 62, the summer began with basketball and volleyball courts on the site, along with a picnic area, a dog run, a play area with sprinklers, and space for roller skating. We were also awaiting bids for building the interim bicycle and pedestrian path the following spring. The city planning department was completing new waterfront zoning regulations, which increased constraints on in-water development, and the city Economic Development Corporation's plan to build Hudson River Center at Pier 76 appeared to be dead.

"Kelly's Collar"

I am a big fan of the history of the West Side, and I wanted to preserve the remaining maritime hardware—much of which was falling into the river—and integrate it into the new park. Cleats and bollards are maritime hardware used to secure vessels to the West Side piers. I had a good working relationship with David Dunlap, a *New York Times* reporter who covered Westway and the unfolding West Side redevelopment saga. I pitched him a story about preserving the maritime hardware, but his editor did not think it was newsworthy.

Several weeks later, I got a call from Cathy Drew, founder of The River Project, who lived in an apartment on Vestry Street—which overlooked Pier 26—and she was quite upset. She had seen two men in a barge with a crane removing the short vertical posts known as bollards from the pier, and she had called the police to report the theft. At the time, Ray Kelly, Dinkins' new police commissioner, was taking his inaugural tour of the waterfront with the department's Harbor Unit, and the group was passing Pier 26 when the call came over the radio. Kelly demanded that the police "arrest those men"—and so began what insiders in the police department dubbed "Kelly's Collar."

The culprits were tracked down at the nearby Ear Inn on Spring Street, a small bar on the first floor of one of the area's oldest buildings that is still one of the legendary spots in the city. The structure was built before 1800 by one James Brown, who was said to have been a freed slave, and the area became part of the city in 1817 when New York annexed what was then called the "Upper West Side" and eventually became known as Greenwich Village.[3]

Because the building had settled over the past two centuries, the floor was tilted in various directions. Walking across the room felt like you were aboard a ship. The walls and ceiling were covered with dusty maritime artifacts, ceramic jugs, photos, pennants, signs, and newspaper articles from bygone eras. Amenities included a tiny kitchen with four tables next to the bar and eight in the rear. The place was beloved by all who visited.

Captain Rip Hayman, the building's owner, was one of the guys who had been removing bollards from Pier 26 along with George Petescola (also known as "Captain Pepsi"), a dock builder from New Jersey who owned a small barge with a crane. When the police arrived, the bollards were in a pickup truck in front of the Ear Inn, and Rip and Pepsi were sitting at a table in the back. When the police asked about the bollards, both men claimed that they had been, as they put it, "rescuing" them.

Unfortunately, the police found some pot in Rip's pocket, and the pair were carted off to spend the night in a holding cell at the First Precinct. The next morning, they were transported to the Tombs, the notorious jail in Lower Manhattan. It was rumored that one of the "Earregulars," as the bar's regulars were known, had managed to remove the controlled substance from the First Precinct's evidence room.

Cathy asked if I could help get Rip released. I called a friend who had a contact at the district attorney's office and told him that Rip had a solid reputation (as per Cathy). I suggested that the conservancy would be grateful if the culprits were released pending dismissal of the charges if they salvaged the remaining bollards on Pier 26 for preservation. In what may be the only occasion when a punishment involved continuing to commit the crime, Rip and Pepsi were freed. Several weeks later, they removed the remaining bollards, which the conservancy put in storage.

This event had other positive outcomes: the "Ballad of the Bollard" became local folklore,[4] Pepsi was hired to salvage artifacts from other parts part of the park, and David Dunlap called to say, "I can't believe you had two guys steal bollards off a pier so I would write that story."[5] About a month later, officers from the First Precinct asked Rip to remove the bollards from the sidewalk in front of the precinct where they had been deposited as evidence. He demurred, and to this day, no one is quite sure where they went, although Rip swears that the bollards now outside the Ear Inn sprouted from the sidewalk.

The Village Halloween Parade

Because Greenwich Village residents were always suspicious of the conservancy's agenda and worried about the impacts on their neighborhood, we planned a staff outing to show our true colors—an event that involved marching in the celebrated Greenwich Village Halloween Parade.

Ralph Lee, a local puppeteer, had started a parade of puppets in 1973. Costumed revelers, huge puppets, and choreographed groups paraded along local streets, marching from Westbeth, the artists' cooperative on Bank Street and the West Side Highway, to Washington Square Park. By 1993, the parade drew a crowd of some 250,000 marchers and viewers. Bands and floats had been added to the parade, which now began at Spring Street and headed up Sixth Avenue to 14th Street.[6] That year, the conservancy fielded a diverse group of celebratory marchers.

Senior staff chipped in to buy about sixty four-foot-by-eight-foot sheets of cardboard and rolls of twine and tape from a shipping company, along with glitter and watercolor paints from a local art supply store and three boxes of blinking reflectors from the bicycle store down the block. Cathy Drew created small cutouts of various aquatic creatures that are native to the Hudson, such as seahorses, striped bass, crabs, and sturgeon. On the afternoon of the parade, conservancy staff and a half dozen park supporters gathered in our large conference room to make their costumes.

A spotlight illumined Cathy's silhouettes so they cast larger shadows on the sheets of cardboard. Each participant traced a five- to six-foot fish, crab, or seahorse out of a sheet of cardboard. The "fish" were painted and sprinkled with glitter and then hung from each shoulder. Half the creatures had googly eyes made of red bicycle reflectors that flashed in random patterns.

Our office manager, Maryann Monte, found a group of skimpily clad mermen to follow, and about two dozen conservancy "fish" danced up Sixth Avenue to music from a boom box behind a seven-foot seahorse holding a Hudson River Park Conservancy banner. Our group was featured on Manhattan's new cable channel *NY1*, which started in 1992, and our appearance sent the message that we were a different kind of public authority—one that might relate to the communities we served. Street theater proved to be a great way to send a message, build comradery, and have fun doing it.

Giuliani Elected Mayor

In November of 1993, Rudy Giuliani was elected mayor by the same slim margin by which Dinkins had beaten him in 1989.[7] I had briefed Rudy during the campaign and received an invitation to his inauguration, which I attended with Vince McGowan, a self-described level-headed Republican.

Fran Reiter, who was chair of the Independent Party and served as Giuliani's deputy campaign manager, was appointed deputy mayor and vice chair of the conservancy. New appointees joined the board—among them, Henry Stern, who was the city's returning parks and recreation commissioner and an eccentric but brilliant colleague and dedicated public servant.

During the transition period, Tommy Maguire, president of the Operating Engineers Local 15, was yet again a major asset. He had an incredible Rolodex, and his close ties with the new mayor allowed him to call Giuliani directly without going through gatekeepers. If we had a request that Tommy thought made sense, he would ask me to fax him a short note, and he would call the mayor and relay the message on behalf of the construction and building trades. He would also ask his lobbyist and colleagues in Albany to stay on top of our issues—a move that built awareness among state decision-makers and increased the conservancy's credibility.

One key decision that was not viewed as being in the interest of the building and construction trades, or of his union, was prohibiting residential, office, and hotel development at the three development nodes and limiting commercial uses in the park to maritime, recreational, and entertainment activities. However, Tommy understood that it was important to get support from local communities and that the park would help get the roadway built and create jobs for the heavy construction unions while spurring future inboard real estate development regardless of what was built.

That prohibition helped reduce community and environmental opposition while increasing support from inboard property owners. They understood that the park enhanced the desirability and value of their property and would not compete for residential, hotel, and commercial office development. We also minimized plans for restaurants in the park, so as not to compete with restaurants, cafes, and bars across Route 9A—a decision that helped garner support from local retail businesses.

Chelsea Piers Groundbreaking

It took Chelsea Piers Management two years to refine their designs for what was now the Chelsea Piers Sports and Entertainment Complex and to get the approximately twenty city, state, and federal permits that were needed.[8] At the groundbreaking ceremony held on July 12, 1994, Dennis Connor, the 1987 America's Cup victor, sailed across the harbor, accompanied by several television reporters. Inspiring speeches were delivered, and New York Rangers goalie Mike Richter handed out commemorative hockey sticks and autographed pucks to dignitaries from the worlds of sports, entertainment, and

Chelsea Piers Sports and Entertainment Complex under construction. (Tom Fox)

politics, as well as members of the local community. The first phase of what became a $100 million privately financed facility was completed in just over a year, and parts of it opened in stages beginning in August 1995.

About five years later, while walking down Fifth Avenue, I saw Abe and Elie Hirschfeld, who had lost the bid for the piers. When Abe had lost the bid for the piers, he told me that I would have hair on the palms of my hands before Chelsea Piers became a recreation complex. He seemed pleased to be recognized but confused when I held out both hands with my palms up and said, "Look, Mr. Hirschfeld—no hair." Abe eventually went to prison for paying someone $75,000 to hire a hit man to murder Stanley Stahl, another bidder for the piers. I later learned that Stahl had been Abe's longtime business partner—never a dull moment on the West Side waterfront.[9]

Port Imperial and Ferries

Arthur Imperatore Sr.—a bright, successful, and demanding businessman—had asked me to join him for lunch in New Jersey to discuss an issue of importance, although the exact issue escapes me now. In the early 1980s, Arthur had bought 350 acres of land along the waterfront of New Jersey towns Weehawken and West New York from the bankrupt Penn Central Railroad for $7.5 million in cash. He hoped to develop the property as a privately managed $5 billion "Venetian city."[10]

Arthur also acquired Pier 78, where the railroad barges once landed, and in 1986, he pioneered the return of trans-Hudson ferries with the launch of the Port Imperial Ferry Company, which he used to develop a waterborne transportation plan and market his planned real estate empire.[11] The company was rebranded "NY Waterway" several years later.

I arrived at his one-room Pier 78 ferry terminal, where a ticket was waiting for me, and I boarded the next ferry to Weehawken. Arthur greeted me warmly, and we walked to Arthur's Landing, his restaurant adjacent to the ferry terminal. There we headed to the second floor, where a single table stood next to floor-to-ceiling windows that overlooked the Manhattan skyline. Arthur made his request during lunch and then asked if I wanted to tour his property.

On our way back to the ferry, he drove into an abandoned railroad shed toward a brick building and said, "I want to show you something." I followed him up a narrow dimly lit staircase to a large metal door at the top of the stairs.

Arthur pulled a key from his pocket, opened the big padlock, and shouldered his way through. I was stunned to enter an apartment with marble floors, a canopied bed, upholstered chairs, and tapestries lining the walls—a space that was flooded with natural light and offered a panoramic view of the Manhattan skyline. "This is where I take the ladies," Arthur said.

I later learned that we had entered through the back door of his apartment; the front door led to the NY Waterway offices in an adjoining structure. We could have entered through his office, but he probably thought that a dramatic entrance would get my attention—that it did.

I cannot remember what Arthur wanted, but I could not agree to whatever it was. A few weeks later, he called the conservancy chairman Michael Del Giudice asking if he was willing to meet. Michael asked me to accompany him, and Arthur appeared annoyed when the two of us arrived at Pier 78 where he was waiting to accompany Michael across the river. As the ferry pulled away, we stood alone on the bow of the vessel where the public was not allowed to ride. Michael said to Arthur, "I bet you'd like to throw Fox right off this ferry." Arthur looked at me, looked at the river, looked back at Michael and said, "It's not deep enough yet."

Michael could not accommodate Arthur's request either, and I realized we had made a powerful enemy on the waterfront.

Water's edge in Tribeca before interim bicycle and pedestrian path installation. (Tom Fox)

Interim Bicycle/Pedestrian Path Opens

We selected the winning bidder for the interim bicycle and pedestrian path and began buying and fabricating various components in the winter of 1993–1994. The railing was designed in eight-foot sections so it could be moved to other areas of the park once the permanent railing was installed. It was made of galvanized steel with mesh panels and a strip of steel that mimicked a wave in a gap under the top rail to represent the river.

The design of the top rail was based on the bar rail in the Blarney Rose, a local bar on Reade Street. Ours was made from Ipe, a dense wood that at the time was considered sustainable. The top and bottom of the rail had smooth wide surfaces, and they were gently rounded to accommodate arms resting against it. It proved perfect for the waterfront because it was comfortable to lean against and almost impossible to climb over. Anyone who tried to sit on top of the rail immediately slid toward the land. All in all, the design was simple, functional, and elegant.

We painted a faux median green to suggest grass on a thin layer of asphalt we laid atop the path that helped direct cyclists to travel on the inboard side of the path and pedestrians to the outboard side. Every other block, we installed two benches on the median with four-foot mooring buoys—which are used to indicate the location of mooring anchors for ships—painted white,

Water's edge in Tribeca after interim bicycle and pedestrian path installation. (Tom Fox)

on either side of the benches. They helped delineate the shoreline pedestrian walkway from the cycling path while protecting errant cyclists from running into the benches.

The path quickly filled with cyclists, pedestrians, roller bladers, parents pushing strollers, readers, and sunbathers. We featured before and after pictures of the change in the water's edge in the fall issue of *VIEWS,* the conservancy's quarterly newsletter, to describe our progress and encourage public involvement.[12] We also described the summer youth program, the Pier 62 interim park, and the groundbreaking for Chelsea Piers. We told of a demonstration on the steps of City Hall supporting the Hudson River Waterfront Park Planning and the Development Act that state legislators were proposing to protect the future park and limit development in the river.

A *New York Times* editorial on the path commented, "It is a modest path, but there are times, and this is one of them, when small is beautiful."[13] But of course no good deed goes unpunished. Stu Waldman of the Federation to Preserve the Greenwich Village Waterfront and Great Port wrote a letter to the editor stating that although the path might be simple, the conservancy was an Urban Development Corporation subsidiary proposing a "grandiose and ill-conceived scheme for the Hudson River waterfront" with "shopping malls, high rises, and commercial development while blocking the river for the rest of us."[14]

Eight years later, when the highway was complete and the park was under construction, the interim path was still heavily used. As for the fence and railing, twenty years later, it would be recycled to serve as a railing around the perimeter of Governors Island's Pier 101.

Clearwater's Annual Meeting

John Mylod, executive director of the Hudson River Sloop Clearwater, was a rabid "nothing can happen on Manhattan's West Side waterfront except what I think should happen even though I live somewhere else" type of person. He fought Westway and seemed to be misinforming his organization about our plans in an effort to continue his fight—this time against the park. Clearwater was a plaintiff in a lawsuit seeking to disband the conservancy—as were the Clean Air Campaign and NYPIRG.

As a member and former volunteer at Clearwater, I knew that some of the group's members were confused by Clearwater's position, especially since landfill and platforms had been eliminated from the project. Michael Mann, a board member, suggested that I attend the group's annual meeting in Pough-keepsie, some eighty-five miles north of the city. Vince McGowan and I arrived forty-five minutes early and parked our white van, with a Hudson River Park Conservancy logo prominently displayed on the front, sides, and back (always reinforce your brand), in front of the building where the meeting was taking place.

Michael was the first person I saw when we arrived. He and I had worked together on the Environmental Education Advisory Council in 1975, and he was cub master of the legendary Cub Scout Pack 8 (the 8-Balls), my son Michael's pack, which was in Flatbush, where we both lived.[15] I was warmly welcomed by Michael and his wife, Marcia Kaplan-Mann, and they introduced me to the legendary folk singer Pete Seeger, who had stopped by to greet board members before the meeting.

I had met Pete on a blustery day in 1978 when he performed at the dedication of a forty-kilowatt windmill erected at the Bronx Frontier Development composting site in the South Bronx. I had also met him and his wife, Toshi, while volunteering to provide security at the Annual Clearwater Festival in Croton-on-Hudson for several years in the early eighties. Pete remembered our meeting and asked, "So, what are you up to?"

I told him I was heading a conservancy that was planning a world-class waterfront park and that we would be prohibiting landfill and platforms along the old Westway right-of-way. "That's wonderful," Pete replied. But I added that there was a significant problem because Clearwater was suing us.

"We are?" he replied.

We had a productive ten-minute discussion with Pete and any of the Clearwater members, now filtering into the building, who would listen. Meanwhile, Vince placed brochures on the information table. But we had not come to cause a scene—just to make a point—so as the meeting start time approached, we prepared to leave. As we were leaving, Marcia, who was president of the Brooklyn Friends of Clearwater, pointed to a T-shirt. "That's a great T-shirt," she said. "How much are they?" "It's yours for free," I told her.

As we walked to the van, John Mylod was just entering, and his jaw dropped as he asked what we were doing there. I told him that as a longtime Clearwater member, I was sharing information about the conservancy. Being a member of an organization objecting to your project gives you access to their alerts, newsletters, and meetings to better understand and address their issues.

With the Chelsea Piers under construction, several other piers cleared of undesirable uses, a successful community participation process in place, interim improvements opening along the waterfront, and the conservancy gaining credibility, we redoubled our efforts to complete what was known as the Concept and Financial Plan for the park.

Route 9A Construction Approved

In August of 1994, twenty years after that car came crashing through the elevated West Side Highway, state and federal officials agreed that Route 9A would be rebuilt as an urban boulevard. The urban boulevard would be a $380 million project, and the funds were available for the first three years of construction, which was expected to take seven years.[16]

Fortunately, Doug Currey, a Route 9A engineer, ensured that utility conduits for electricity and other services were placed under the highway to accommodate whatever the bicycle path might need or what future smart traffic devices might need. He insured that "all of the infrastructure work that's costed out and included in the project is utility work necessitated by the roadway."[17] He also included feeder lines for irrigation in the median but not the system. That was a brave decision because chief engineer, Mike Cuddy, had told the 9A team that if any irrigation was put in the median, he would fire the person who approved it.[18]

The Route 9A team embraced public participation in their planning process, and there was consensus that the plan would make it through the final permit approval. The planning of the park was still contentious, especially in Hell's Kitchen, where Community Board 4 wanted Pier 94 removed from any passenger ship terminals development plans and designated—like Pier 84—as a public pier.[19] Giuliani then announced that he wanted to remove the terminal piers from the park altogether, which would reduce the park's footprint and eliminate a potential revenue stream to support the park.

U.S.S. *Guadalcanal*

There was consensus on one issue: everyone wanted the 30th Street Heliport removed from the future park. One day, Zach Fisher, founder and chairman of the Intrepid Sea Air & Space Museum, said to me, "Did you know they're about to decommission the U.S.S. *Guadalcanal*?" Apparently the Intrepid's president had seen her on a list of U.S. Navy ships scheduled for decommissioning.

Fisher suggested that the *Guad*, as the ship was known, might become an addition to the Intrepid Museum's collection and the new heliport for

Midtown. The conservancy's board agreed the idea was great. Zach called the Secretary of the Navy, and the next thing you know, we were flying to Norfolk Naval Air Station on his private jet. He invited City Comptroller Alan G. Hevesi hoping to leverage city support for the project, and I invited Al Trenk, the operator of the 30th Street Heliport.

When we landed, a car sporting the two-star flag of a rear admiral picked us up on the runway and drove us to the *Guad.* By coincidence, she was docked at the Naval Amphibious Base Little Creek, Virginia, where I had been stationed twenty-five years earlier.

Al Trenk was blown away. "It comes with all those guys in the white hats, right?" he asked. After a tour, Zach told the Navy that he was interested, and they offered to sell her to the Intrepid Museum for a dollar. The Intrepid hosted an annual Fleet Week event in New York Harbor, and Zach asked if the Navy would include the *Guad* in that year's parade of ships so we could promote the project. They agreed, and the *Guad* led a parade of some ten U.S. Navy warships into the harbor that year.

Our proposal to relocate the heliport to the USS *Guadalcanal* was well received, but an unanticipated problem arose when we could not agree on where the vessel should be berthed. Zach wanted it next to the *Intrepid,* oriented north/south on the tip of Pier 86. However, she was five stories tall at the flight deck and would block the view down West 45th, 46th, and 47th Streets.

We thought she should be placed on the south side of Pier 76 near the existing heliport and across from Convention Center or at the remnants of Pier 72, which could be rebuilt. Both locations would allow an east/west orientation. Neither location blocked view corridors, and there was not an adjacent residential community. Although Pier 86 was not the perfect solution, Community Board 4 said they would reluctantly agree to the Pier 86 location. As Ross Graham, the board's chair, put it, "It gets the helicopters further away from the people. And the best part is we get the old site for a park."[20] Views of the river were precious, however, and Community Board 4 now had two projects blocking their views: the *Guad* at Pier 86 and the Chelsea Piers, where the head houses blocked the river-view street corridors.[21]

Concept and Financial Plan Completed

The close of 1994 brought two major events that affected the park. After almost ninety meetings with various constituencies, the conservancy finished two years of public planning, completing a process first begun by the task force. Also, George Pataki was elected governor. After reaching a consensus on most of the contentious redevelopment issues, the conservancy had established relationships of trust with many elected officials and members of the local, business, and environmental communities. It had also developed an exciting and achievable vision for the future.

Several issues remained unresolved, notably the location of the U.S.S. *Guadalcanal* and the future of the Gansevoort Peninsula and Piers 79, 92, and 94. But the conservancy's staff and board wanted to release a plan, and Deputy Mayor and Conservancy Vice Chair Fran Reiter agreed to produce the final Concept and Financial Plan presenting the entire waterfront as a park. She insisted, however, that unresolved issues and existing uses at Gansevoort, Pier 79, and the Passenger Ship Terminal be indicated as well.

Our plan showed three possible locations for the *Guad*, but the community's strong objections to blocking their views prevailed. The Pier 86 site was rejected, and Zach declined to provide financial support for the project. The *Guad* joined the Naval Reserve Fleet and was expended as a target in 2005.

Our senior staff and design consultants focused on preparing a plan that we hoped would guide the next stage of park development and provide the basis for the required environmental impact statement. We did so despite any indication that Pataki would support the conservancy and our mission to create the park, but we were determined to stay the course.

After the election, there was a fear that the governor might disband the conservancy. State Senator Franz Leichter and Assemblyman Richard Gottfried renewed their push for the Hudson River Waterfront Park Bill. John Bowers, however, objected to the legislation, contending that it did not recognize the existing commercial maritime and passenger ship uses.[22]

Bowers was the president of both the International Longshoremen's Association's Local 824 on the West Side and the entire union, which covered all ports on the Atlantic and Gulf Coasts, the Great Lakes, major United States rivers, Puerto Rico, and eastern Canada.[23] Leichter, Gottfried, and I met with him and tried to ease his concern, noting that the bill acknowledged and permitted continuing commercial maritime activity.[24] But by June, the two legislators realized that their bill would not pass during the 1994 legislative session.[25]

Getting Whacked

When George Pataki was inaugurated in January of 1995, Republicans rejoiced. He announced that allies like Senator Alphonse "Al" D'Amato should feel at home in Albany.[26] With Giuliani as mayor, Republicans had brought about a complete change of command at the city and state, and they now controlled the conservancy because it was a state Urban Development Corporation subsidiary.

However, I had been appointed to my third West Side entity, was a recognized park professional with a few successes under my belt, and had quite a few Republican friends, several of whom were influential. I thought that if anything changed, nothing would happen until the spring because it usually takes a while for newly elected officials to make appointments, and the conservancy probably was not a high priority.

From 1992 to 1995, opponents had fought against the conservancy, but we had prevailed in the court of public opinion. On January 12, 1995, we defeated the latest round of litigation, but while the judge praised our efforts, she halted further decisions on the project until our environmental impact statement was completed.[27]

We anticipated that the Concept and Financial Plan could be released later that spring, and we could then begin the environmental review process, which would take about a year and a half to complete. Construction at Chelsea Piers was well underway and was not affected by the court decision. However, a new problem arose when Chelsea Piers Management proposed a forty-thousand-square-foot Herman's sporting goods store in the complex—a move that ignited strong community opposition and was eventually defeated.[28]

The day after our court victory, Margaret, Vince, and I took the staff to lunch to celebrate. We headed to Lofland's, a restaurant and bar down the block on 21st Street and the preferred lunch and after-work hangout for both us and the Route 9A team. Lunch ended at about 2:30, and we gave the staff the afternoon off. Margaret returned to the office to wrap up some financial details before the weekend, and I arrived about half an hour later to pick up some work for the weekend.

When I got there, Margaret greeted me with a strange look on her face. "I can't tell you what I was just told on the phone," she said. "You have to call Joe Branca and hear what he has to say for yourself." Branca was the chief financial officer at the Urban Development Corporation, and the new governor had been inaugurated a week earlier. I called right away.

"Tom," Joe said, "your services are no longer needed. Put your ID card and keys on the desk with an address where you'd like your personal effects sent and be out of the office by five o'clock."

I was stunned. I had worked on the project for ten years with Cuomo and Koch and survived the transition to Giuliani. The conservancy had just completed an extensive public design process for the park and was about to release its plans. We had defeated yet another lawsuit challenging our existence, were overseeing the construction at Chelsea Piers, had cleared the waterfront, and implemented major interim improvements that were hugely popular. Surely there was some mistake.

I was not involved in politics and believed that my experience as a park professional and coalition builder underpinned my appointments. However, the appointments were, in fact, political. I had just never experienced the other edge of the sword. Landfill and platforms had been prohibited in the Hudson, and we had eliminated residential, hotel, and commercial offices from the park's development areas. There were few in-water development opportunities for Pataki's friends, donors, and future supporters, and those that existed were primarily on the other side of Route 9A.

However, I am basically a street kid from Flatbush. "I don't work for you, Joe," I said on the phone. "I work for the conservancy's board of directors, and I'll poll them between now and five. If they tell me to leave, I'll be gone by the end of the day. If not, I'll be here on Monday, and if you want me out, send the state police."

Joe was taken aback. "Don't get upset with me," he said. "I'm just the messenger."

"Then tell them that's the message," I replied.

Going Down Swinging

After hanging up the phone, I called Del Giudice and Reiter. There was a lot at stake. We were all worried that the new governor might not support the park or provide the state's matching $100 million. He could disband the conservancy altogether.

What had dramatically changed the picture was the appointment of Charles Gargano as president and chief operating officer of the Urban Development Corporation. Gargano had been ambassador to Trinidad and Tobago during the Reagan Administration and preferred that title; he was also one of Pataki's most prolific fundraisers, and he was strongly pro-development.

Our board and staff had invested significant time and energy developing the park plans, and Pataki had failed to announce my replacement. I suggested to the conservancy board that the lack of a replacement would make it easier for the governor to fold up shop and reallocate the

remaining Port Authority funds—which constituted our entire budget—
to other projects, effectively consigning our project to more confrontation
and litigation.

Thankfully, the board would not agree to my termination unless a replacement was named. So I started gathering support from a broad range of
colleagues and friends to convince the governor that I was an asset, not a
political hack, and to contact Ambassador Gargano directly to plead my
case. We all understood that it was in the public's interest to release the plans
for the park, so the staff raced against the clock to finish.

My first call was to Peter Stanford, founder of the South Street Seaport
Museum and Pataki's neighbor in Poughkeepsie, in upstate New York. A half-
hour later, Peter sent the governor a telegram urging him to reconsider my
dismissal, noting that I had significant support, had attracted private funding for development, had instituted improvements like the bike path, and was
a "can-do guy."[29] He also wrote a follow-up letter, as president of the National
Maritime Historical Society.

I thought that hearing from a broad range of individuals and organizations
who supported our progress might convince the governor that he had the best
man for the job and should continue state support for the park. By the end
of the next day, letters began arriving.

Tommy Maguire wrote, "Tom Fox has built a bridge among labor, business, environmental interests. Our industry trusts Tom and so do the community groups and environmentalists. . . . With Tom as president of the
Conservancy, this project has moved more in the past two years then all
the talk, rhetoric, and plans in the past 20 years."[30]

Manhattan Community Board 1 passed a resolution stating that the park's
planning process was a "noble attempt to involve all parties," voicing concern
about my sudden dismissal and urging the governor and Ambassador Gargano to continue the planning and construction of the park.[31] Community
Board 4 passed a similar resolution.

Kent Barwick, president of the Municipal Arts Society, wrote, "Although
I have had disagreements with the president, Tom Fox, I think he has done
an extraordinary job of keeping this improbable coalition together, and I hon-
estly doubt that anyone else could've done it."[32]

Ed Cleary, president of the 2.3-million-member New York State AFL-CIO,
wrote, "Tom can be credited for the Conservancy spending $5 million in
public funds which has leveraged $100 million dollars in private invest-
ment now and the construction in the park. This is truly a remarkable
achievement."[33]

Sam Pryor, writing on behalf of the 65,000-member Appalachian Mountain Club, said, "Tom is well known to me and many of our staff. We consider him to be an unusually able and dedicated person. We assume the Governor and Ambassador Charles Gargano are well briefed on Tom's role in the planning of the redevelopment of the west side. We would be very concerned if he was replaced for political reasons."[34]

Many calls were made, and letters sent. I am thankful that such a diverse group of individuals and organizations, including major Republican donors and fundraisers ranging from the chairman of Grace Industries and the Whitestone Republican Club to Arthur Levitt Jr. (then chair of the Securities and Exchange Commission), spoke on my behalf.[35] A *Chelsea Clinton News* editorial, "Fox Fire Misguided," and *The Villager*'s, "Repeat After Me: The Waterfront Needs Leadership" soon followed.[36]

I wrote to Gargano describing the progress we had made and noted that after almost three years of work, we still had $600,000 of the initial $2.8 million in Port Authority funding we had received. I requested an opportunity to brief him.[37] He never responded.

Our next board meeting was scheduled for early February. Michael was an old hand at state politics and was not certain that the new governor would continue to support the conservancy. When I asked about my tenure, his answer was, "You know the way the game is played." I sent Michael a memo describing what I thought were suitable terms for my resignation but found out that was not the way these things work.

My actions were a bit naïve and disrespectful given that Michael was the primary reason why the panel and conservancy had been successful. He had direct access to the second floor, was committed to the park, and understood the importance of a robust public planning process. He was, as we say in New York City, my "rabbi," someone who valued my experience and tenacity, protected me from political harm, and paved the way for our success.

I am sure Pataki did not appreciate the public hassle, but Del Giudice remained conservancy chair—a wise move as Michael's dedication to the project was widely respected, and his presence gave comfort to local elected officials, community organizations, and park advocates.

Cuomo's appointees had no incentive to support my removal while awaiting their own. Fran did not want to see the project fail, and the city appointees would not support the termination until the governor named a replacement.[38] As the writing on the wall became much clearer, I asked Fran if my replacement needed to be a competent park professional. "Not really," she replied. "Just a replacement."

At the February 1995 board meeting, my termination was not mentioned, and the staff continued to work on producing the Concept and Financial Plan. We prepared a schedule for the final release with a series of briefings for elected officials and community boards. The release was scheduled for Fleet Week in June, when Pataki planned to announce a new "Empire State Waterway" project.[39] My memo to the governor's staff described the many events planned along the waterfront during the spring and summer and outlined capital projects underway and media events Pataki might attend.[40] That was not answered either.

My early April memo to Michael and Fran complained about the Urban Development Corporation's increasingly intrusive role in the day-to-day work of the conservancy, described the negative impact of the governor's indecision on the overall project, and detailed the challenges to financial planning, management, and operations going forward.[41] They knew what was happening and could not do anything about it either.

The staff and consultants worked like crazy to complete the plans for the park, and copies were printed and stored in the office. However, with no options left, I resigned the day before the meeting so that I would not be fired, which I had been assured would happen.[42] The next day, Pataki appointed as my replacement Peter Keough, a corporate real estate manager at a Grumman Aircraft subsidiary with zero public park experience. Apparently, his bona fides were that his son had married the daughter of incoming state Parks Commissioner Bernadette Castro, and Keough needed a job. Politics again.

I had been fired for the first time in my life. At the board meeting, I thanked the individuals and organizations who had supported me and introduced my successor.[43] I said I was confident the appointment indicated that Pataki would not abandon the project and would support our plans, although that proved to be wishful thinking. Marcy Benstock's response to the whole matter was predictable: she said she saw no difference between Mr. Keough and me.

By contrast, an article in the *New York Times* stated, "Many proponents of the Conservancy's plan for the riverfront, which ranges from developing a midtown maritime district to transforming some abandoned piers into islands for wildlife, lamented the loss of Mr. Fox," adding, "He had widely been credited with charting a middle course between the frequently conflicting interests of environmentalists, West Side residents, and the business community."[44] Compromise may be the key to achieve a consensus, I reluctantly concluded, but apparently not the key to keeping your job.

The support was gratifying, but I was devastated. Do not give up until you absolutely have to, and go down swinging when you do—that has always been my motto. The park had a better chance of survival because of the broad-based coalition and public plan that we had established. Many people had shaped the park, felt an ownership of the project, and would fight for it. That is a major benefit of meaningful community participation.

9

A New Approach
(1995–1997)

● ● ● ● ● ● ● ● ● ● ● ● ● ● ●

In May of 1995, having been summarily ousted from my position as the Hudson River Park Conservancy's president, I began consulting on urban park and waterfront projects and producing special events. Vince McGowan, the conservancy's chief of operations, had played the lead role in helping to revive the United War Veterans Council and city's Veterans Day parade. Participation and attendance at the parade had been slowly declining, and the council became my first client.[1]

The U.S. Department of Defense requested that New York City host the closing ceremony of America's fiftieth anniversary celebration of victory in World War II, and the November 11th Veterans Day parade was rebranded the "Nation's Parade." For this event, the military came through big-time with nine aircraft, including a B-1 bomber providing a spectacular flyover of the parade route and the skies of Manhattan. Also, the 10th Mountain Division provided several 105-mm howitzers that were placed in Central Park to render a twenty-one-gun salute during the parade.

Although many people were skeptical about whether we would succeed in pulling off this event, the entire veteran community supported the effort, and by early November, there were forty marching bands, twenty floats, and thirty thousand marchers registered for the event.[2]

I initially accepted a six-month assignment to produce the parade because Zach Fisher, chairman of the Intrepid Sea, Air & Space Museum, asked me to step in and contributed $100,000 to support the event. But the remaining $600,000 that was needed was hard to come by. By August, the United War Veterans Council had $1.71 in the bank, but fortunately, I convinced Donald Trump, then a prominent real estate developer, to contribute $350,000. The event proved a great success.[3]

On November 11, as dignitaries gathered on Fifth Avenue at 44th Street to begin the march uptown to 86th Street, I noticed Governor Pataki standing alone. I approached him and mentioned that the veterans community had him to thank for this incredible event. Pataki stood a little taller and looked at me quizzically but smiled as I added, "I'm Tom Fox. After you fired me from the Hudson River Park Conservancy, the veterans community asked me to produce this parade, so it couldn't have happened without you."

His smile faded as I turned and left without waiting for a response.

News of the Nation's Parade made the front page of the *New York Times* and was broadcast around the nation and the world.[4] My wife, Gretchen, was in Moscow as part of a college faculty leadership program and saw the parade on television. Most important, World War II veterans received much-deserved thanks, and the Veterans Day parade had been rejuvenated. The United War Veterans Council still hosts what continues to be known as the Nation's Parade, America's largest Veterans Day parade, every year.

Ominous Signs

Starting from the time he joined the state government in 1995, Ambassador Gargano accumulated quite a few titles. In addition to being chairman and chief executive of the New York State Urban Development Corporation, he became commissioner of the state Department of Economic Development and vice chairman of the Port Authority.[5] Accumulating multiple titles was a source of his power and influence. Gargano's stated priority was building a better business climate and downsizing state agencies and authorities. To that end, he immediately embargoed the release of our Concept and Financial Plan, a move that gave Pataki more time to decide whether he supported the project.

My removal heightened concern that the project might be abandoned, especially given Gargano's proclamations about downsizing. In early May, the

Chelsea Clinton News warned that changing course on the park would, as the newspaper put it, "relegate what could have been a park similar to Central Park to nondescript patches of greenery between nodules of commercial development."[6]

That year, Gargano and Peter Keogh, the new head of the Hudson River Park Conservancy, toured Chelsea Piers, which were under construction. Roland Betts, a principal in the Chelsea Piers Partnership, thought they were excited about that project, suggesting the Pataki would not shut the park project down altogether.[7] Two ice-skating rinks on the second deck of Pier 61 had opened in July.

No one knew how Gargano would advise the governor regarding the park. The terms of the existing conservancy board members expired in June and, although Michael Del Giudice was still chairman of the conservancy, it was just a matter of time before Pataki appointed his replacement—that is, if he intended to move forward on the park (a big "if," given that the state was not flush with cash).

Apparently, Gargano was considering new residential development on the waterfront. In July, he asked Vince McGowan to meet with him and Larry Silverstein, a real estate developer who owned property opposite the park just south of 42nd Street. They met on the waterfront, and Silverstein asked if the Circle Line and World Yachts leases at Piers 81 and 83 could be terminated to allow residential development there. Vince said that residential development was prohibited in the future park.[8]

The debate about whether to declare the park a scenic area and apply for a federal repayment waiver had stalled that decision for eight years, but the 1995 final Federal Highway Administration repayment deadline was fast approaching. City Comptroller Alan Hevesi sued Pataki, demanding he seek a federal waiver. Pataki responded that a 1987 law Moynihan had sponsored allowed the state to repay the money, which would then be returned to the state for other transportation projects.

Moynihan had indeed inserted that caveat—quietly. In September 1995, the state Department of Transportation did not spend $80 million in Federal Highway Administration funds it had been allotted for approved projects and received that same amount of funding from the feds the next month when the new federal fiscal year started.[9] The fact that there were now no safeguards against development in the future park heightened concerns that the state was about to run amok on the waterfront.

Interim Pier 25 Opens

The conservancy's staff continued expanding interim uses along the water-front, reopening Pier 25 in Tribeca—where there was already considerable activity—as a public recreation pier. Vince McGowan and Margaret Tobin at the conservancy drafted the $2,000-a-month lease for the pier while Arne Abramowitz, the conservancy's landscape architect, oversaw the design of the interim improvements. They spent about $67,000 converting the pier into what was called "Manhattan Beach," a funky neighborhood that included three beach volleyball courts, a café, a children's recreation area with sprinklers, ping-pong and picnic tables, the historic ferry *Yankee*, and sculptures made from recycled materials.[10]

Pier 25 was leased to Manhattan Youth Recreation and Resources, a non-profit organization that operated various after-school, weekend, and summer recreation programs for young people and was led by Bob Townley. Townley's team consisted of his assistant Dubbie, Jimmy Gallagher, who was restoring the *Yankee,* and Veso Buntic, a talented welder who operated the beach volleyball facilities and assembled a sculpture garden on the pier. Like the Amazon Village, Manhattan Beach became a popular destination for residents of Tribeca and Lower Manhattan.

Concert at interim Pier 25 in Tribeca. (Hudson River Park Conservancy)

A New Player Arrives

I had been the spokesperson for the conservancy, and Margaret Tobin, the chief financial officer, was reluctant to speak publicly about the project for fear that both she and the project might be terminated. She warned the environmental community that the waterfront could have a new roadway without a park if they did not step up their involvement. Traditional environmental groups were not willing to challenge Pataki, and park opponents like the Clean Air Campaign and the New York Public Interest Research Group (NYPIRG) wanted the Hudson River Park Conservancy disbanded.[11]

Albert K. Butzel, an accomplished environmental attorney who had been a leader in the Westway litigation, offered to help. Before Westway, he had worked on the Storm King litigation, a landmark victory that stopped Con Edison's planned hydroelectric plant and led to the passage of the National Environmental Policy Act of 1969, legislation that gave citizens the right to bring environmental lawsuits in court.[12]

Al was a founder of the law firm Berle, Butzel and Kass and had worked with the Clean Air Campaign as the lead attorney in the Westway fight since 1977, but he had resigned a year before Judge Griesa's final Westway decision in 1985,[13] withdrawing to his Park Avenue apartment to write novels and recuperate from the burnout that afflicts many a public advocate. He continued to advise Mitch Bernard, who became the opponents' lead attorney after Al's departure.[14] Margaret Tobin was happy that someone familiar with the issue—if not the park—was willing to speak to the press.

Butzel had been away from the debate over the future of West Side for more than a decade, but he quickly became a de facto spokesperson for the park. When reporters called Margaret, she would brief them off the record and then refer them to Al for a suitable quote.[15]

A Slow and Steady Assault on the Park

The wait for the governor to embrace the park continued into 1996 as speculation grew.[16] Keough, the conservancy's president, was ineffective, and Margaret and Vince ran the conservancy even as Giuliani and Pataki played a greater role in day-to-day decision-making. Although Vince was a Republican, Margaret was a Dinkins appointee whose position was precarious, and she could not push back against their demands. The staff described her leadership at this time as demanding, and some began to move on.

Other public agencies saw the situation as an opportunity. The Port Authority began to release some of the property it controlled on the West Side, transferring ownership of the 15-acre Pier 40 to the conservancy. However, they had stopped providing power to the pier's cathodic protection system years before. Without it, electrolysis created by interaction between the saltwater and the steel accelerated pile deterioration and shoddy roof repair leaked large amounts of water into the building. Their lease required the tenant pay rent—but not maintain the pier—and the structure was neglected.

At the time, the cruise industry was in decline and had not yet made its dramatic recovery, so the Port did not want to operate the passenger ship terminals at Piers 88, 90, 92 and 94. Only Piers 88 and 90 were required to maintain cruise ship activity in Midtown, so the West Side Waterfront Panel had reduced the size of the terminals by recommending that half the Pier 94 headhouse be removed to create public parkland on the water and the pier itself become an indoor recreation space to expand year-round recreation opportunities in the Clinton waterfront.[17] The conservancy's Concept and Financial Plan went even further and removed the entire Pier 94 headhouse to create "Clinton Cove" and proposed tennis courts on the roof of Pier 92, but an option for continued use of the piers as passenger ship terminals was also included at the Giuliani administration's insistence.[18]

The properties were in the city-owned section of the park, and Giuliani insisted they be transferred to the city Economic Development Corporation. The passenger ship terminals were removed from the park plan, which reduced potential revenue for the conservancy and diverted it to the city. The corporation continued operating Piers 88 and 90 for passenger ships, but two northernmost piers, Piers 92 and 94, were put out for bid.

Community Board 4 did not support any of the responses and stated that those piers should draw the public to the water's edge and that the area should contain a continuous bikeway and walkway, consistent with the conservancy's plans.

At the same time, Giuliani removed the 5.5-acre Pier 76, which housed the city's largest tow pound, from the park altogether and made a play for building a new Yankee Stadium over the Long Island Railroad Yards. Traffic concerns, and the prohibitive cost of building a platform to accommodate a stadium, eventually killed that proposal.[19]

Roadway Construction Begins

By 1996, anticipation about the construction of Route 9A had reached a peak.[20] Proponents focused on the benefits for Lower Manhattan. As Richard Anderson, then president of the New York Building Congress, put it, "The need for this project has been recognized for two generations by decision-makers who talk about how difficult it is to get their employees to Lower Manhattan." Carl Weisbrod, now president of the Alliance for Downtown New York, added, "The demise of Westway and the failure to build a major arterial road to Lower Manhattan were major factors undermining the downtown economy."

On April 1, the state Department of Transportation broke ground on the first thirteen-block segment of the highway, which extended from Clarkson to Horatio Streets in Greenwich Village. Tommy Maguire, president of the Operating Engineers Union Local 15, stood next to Governor Pataki—shovel in hand—at the groundbreaking.[21] That September, I received a gold shovel encased in a Lucite obelisk with a plaque reading "Son of Westway—At Last" from Maguire and Frank McArdle, the head of the General Contractors Association.[22]

Route 9A's first segment under construction in Greenwich Village. Note interim bicycle and pedestrian path. (Tom Fox)

Renewing Advocacy Efforts

A year after my termination from the conservancy, I ended my self-imposed silence and began advocating publicly for the park. I wrote to Pataki and spoke with Joyce Purnick, a *New York Times* reporter who was writing an article after the groundbreaking for the roadway. I lamented the fact that we would have made more progress on the park before Pataki's election if it were not for the opponent's litigation, to which Marcy replied, "That's a straight lie. Character assassination."[23]

Over the next few months, I submitted op-ed articles and wrote letters to the editor supporting the park. My letter to the *New York Times* addressed the need for creative financing and suggested that the park would anchor the future Hudson River Greenway.[24] An op-ed in *The Villager*, which followed several days later, countered opponents' claims that New York could not afford a park and cited Olmstead's Central Park study.[25] The op-ed in the *Daily News* stressed the fact that enhancing the environment and quality of life was important as New York competed with other world capitals for resources, adding that we could not afford not to build the park.[26]

When the panel released their recommendations in 1990, I had encouraged mainstream environmental organizations to support the planned park, but none engaged in the struggle.[27] I was not well known in that world and did not feel accepted there primarily because I was from the "street" and not a member of the environmental "elite."

By contrast, Butzel was well educated and had a historied environmental record and strong relationships with mainstream environmental leaders— among them, Paul Elston (the chairman of the New York League of Conservation Voters) and John Adams of the Natural Resources Defense Council.

In the spring of 1996, hoping to garner greater support, Al Butzel, Bob Trentlyon, and I formed a group we called Citizens for a Hudson River Park, with Bob as the president, and applied for nonprofit status that June.[28] Park plans had progressed, and Al was able to recruit ten environmental and civic organizations to support the effort that dispelled the perception that environmentalists opposed the park. Our first initiative was an advocacy campaign that generated more than two thousand postcards asking Governor Pataki—Senate majority leader and Assembly Speaker—to dedicate $100 million of state funding to the park. By October, we drew up a budget for the following year and planned a conference, newsletter, and research project focused on Pier 64.[29]

Concept and Financial Plan Released

In June, I called Douglas Martin, another *New York Times* reporter with whom I had developed a working relationship, and told him that the Concept and Financial Plan was finalized, printed, and sitting in boxes at the conservancy's office. Doug was writing about the state's failure to release the plan and called the ambassador for a comment. Gargano said the governor had not decided what to do yet but asked when the article would be published. "Tomorrow," Martin replied. Gargano said the plan was released, adding that Martin could get a copy from the conservancy.

Doug's inquiry apparently forced the ambassador's hand and got the park project rolling again.[30] After a year of admonishment and encouragement from the community, park and environmental organizations, the building and construction trades, and the media, the plans were released and eventually became what was known as the General Project Plan for the park's environmental impact statement.

With a few exceptions, the plans were almost exactly like the one we had produced a year earlier. The introductory letter, signed by Del Giudice and Reiter, was still dated May 1995, when the conservancy had initially completed the plan.[31] I was grateful that the staff acknowledged what they described as my "enlightened leadership in the early, critical years."[32] Landfill and platforms were prohibited, along with residential, hotel, and commercial offices.

However, some of the financial assumptions had been changed, and the park's cost estimate was reduced to $330 million. There was no mention of securing park funding from inboard property appreciation—a proposal opposed by Giuliani—yet the plans claimed that the park would now be self-sufficient simply by retaining the revenue generated in the park.[33]

After the release of the Concept and Financial Plan, Pataki was urged to state his intentions regarding the park.[34] Gargano said that the governor had to be convinced that the park was "really something the community wants." There had been nothing but twenty years of lawsuits against government plans on the West Side, so it was another delaying tactic.

Later in the month, the ambassador responded to what he described as my "informative" April letter to Pataki and urged that I continue to participate in the public process.[35] In other words, "We do not need your advice, and you will get three minutes to talk at public hearings like everyone else." He had new letterhead because Pataki had rebranded the Urban Development Corporation as the Empire State Development Corporation, perhaps to appeal to his upstate constituents.

It is important to maintain good relationships with the press and remember that their currency is information. Understand there is no formal quid pro quo, but realize that helping journalists can be useful. Once, while pitching for support of the park at a meeting of the full board of Community Board 1, I was undergoing a withering third degree from Ann Compaccia, their tough-as-nails chairperson, when Madelyn Wils, a member of their Waterfront and Parks Committee, came to my defense. "This man's trying to build a park in our neighborhood," she said. "Why are we giving him a hard time?" It put things in perspective and ended my grilling.

When Douglas Martin was profiling interesting New Yorkers and asked me if I could think of anyone, I had a chance to return a favor by suggesting Madelyn's husband, Steve Wils, the last of the "butter-and-egg men" in Manhattan. Steve had helped pioneering new restaurants get established in Tribeca, where his business was located, and had broadened his offerings beyond butter and eggs. Doug got a good story, and Steve was recognized for his contribution to the city's restaurant industry.[36] That was a twofer.

New Chelsea Piers Deal

In the absence of leadership, everyone scrambled for a piece of the waterfront. Among this group was Roland Betts, a principal partner in Chelsea Piers Management. He was a well-connected Republican and had been a fraternity brother of the future President George H. W. Bush at Yale. Betts owned a major stake in the Texas Rangers, made Bush the Rangers' general manager and a partner in Silver Screen Studios, and contributed to Bush's political campaigns.[37] He also had a good working relationship with Gargano and Pataki, another Yale graduate.

The Chelsea Piers Partnership was having financial problems because their preliminary 1992 budget of $25 million had swelled to $100 million by 1996. They were having trouble refinancing $55 million in high-interest short-term debt because their lease term was twenty years, maximum.[38] Betts and company lobbied for a forty-nine-year lease to replace their ten-year lease with a ten-year renewal option.

The longer-term lease allowed Chelsea Piers to refinance the junk bonds they used to complete the complex. In addition, the state deferred rent payments for five years with low-interest repayment afterward. Community residents and elected officials objected to both the lease modification and the changes to their original plans, but to no avail. The fix was apparently in, and neither the conservancy nor the state Department of Transportation could stop them from making changes in their initial plan, including

- a wider service road in front of the complex that reduced the space available for the public walkway and bike path and created one of the narrowest public spaces in the park,[39]
- removing the interim improvements from Pier 62 and building two private roller-skating rinks on a pier originally planned as part of the Chelsea Waterside Park,
- replacing the large themed murals that highlighted the activities in each of the Piers with commercial advertising, and
- adding a bus stop, taxi stand, and entrance to their expanded frontage road at 23rd Street, which further reduced the size of the future Chelsea Waterside Park and a two-lane exit roadway at 17th Street across the now-diminished bicycle and pedestrian paths.[40]

A small section of the walkway around the complex at the southern end of Pier 59 was unbuilt. That restricted public access to the mile-long public promenade surrounding the complex unless visitors walked through the parking garage in the headhouse of Pier 59. However, their tenant at Pier 59 installed a marina without securing the required U.S. Army Corps permit. They were fined $200,000 and had to build the missing section of walkway as mitigation.[41]

Even then, Michael Bradley, the conservancy's property manager, had to remove encroachments in the public walkway. For example, the brewery in Pier 59 placed tables and chairs in the public space where a twelve-foot walkway was required to ensure public passage. Vince McGowan had provided his field staff with Polaroid cameras to document issues needing to be addressed. Bradley was seen laying a tape measure on the deck and taking a photograph documenting the lack of the required twelve-foot clear public space there.

Starting a New Gig

With little to show financially after twenty years in the nonprofit world, I owed it to my family to try a new approach. As my wife, Gretchen, said, "If you don't get a real job soon, we're going to be in trouble." I took her words to heart and decided to do good and do well by creating a viable business. In 1996, I started New York Water Taxi to connect attractions in the future park with other parks, cultural attractions, and neighborhoods in Manhattan and Downtown Brooklyn.

Water taxis were included in the park's plan to enhance access to and within the park. While at the conservancy, I had found that none of the existing commercial maritime operators were interested. So I ran with the idea. Within a year, I had completed a business plan, secured landing rights at eight properties, received the necessary city, state, and federal permits to install docks, and identified docking facilities and available vessels while raising the initial capital. I am sure that my job was made easier because most government officials knew me as a missionary rather than a mercenary—plus most of them liked the water taxi concept.

I met Jim Fuchs that September on a chartered Boeing 737 flying to Andrews Air Force Base in Washington, DC, for Zach Fisher's birthday party. He was a wealthy resident of Park Avenue, and he was interested in the water taxi. He was an accomplished Olympic athlete who won bronze medals in 1948 and 1952. His Olympic-winning shot sat behind the bar at the 21 Club, where we met often to discuss his participation in the undertaking.

I proposed leasing equipment and operating from Memorial Day to Labor Day in the first year to test the viability of the concept. I estimated that doing this would require $1.2 million. Jim agreed that if there was any shortfall in equity the company needed, he would cover that investment. He agreed to become chairman of New York Water Taxi. By year's end, even State Assemblywoman Deborah Glick, who had objected to any commercialization of the waterfront, said that the undertaking was "not necessarily a bad idea" adding, "In fact, it might be a good one."[42]

The Pataki Team Takes Ownership

In September, Michael Del Giudice resigned from the Hudson River Park Conservancy, and James Ortenzio, a Republican fundraiser, was appointed conservancy chair. Ortenzio, who owned Long Island Beef, a meat wholesaler in the Meatpacking District, was known as "Mr. Meat." But he was not your usual meat purveyor.[43]

James fancied himself a Renaissance man, spoke in verse and riddles, and quoted Copernicus, Nietzsche, and himself. His intentions were opaque, and he operated more like Machiavelli than Leonardo, the "park" name given to him by the city parks commissioner Henry Stern, who bestowed names on city park supporters.[44] Tommy Maguire congratulated Ortenzio on his appointment and reiterated the construction industry's support for the park.[45]

Pataki had proposed a new $1.75 billion Clean Water/Clean Air Bond Act to be on the November ballot—an initiative supported by a broad range of environmental organizations.[46] The act was passed, making new state money available for environmental projects, including $20 million to $30 million for the park.

The governor embraced his new mantle of environmental champion.[47] He could now brand the park as his own. Mayor Rudy Giuliani, however, wanted to control both the project and the city property in the park.

By the end of 1996, opposition to the Hudson River Park Conservancy and the park plan softened, and Al Butzel now had a dozen mainstream civic and environmental organizations supporting the conservancy and our plan.[48] Peter Keough resigned as president of the conservancy in January of 1997 to take a month-long vacation, reinforcing speculation that he had been appointed simply as a caretaker. His tenure had been unremarkable and his departure the same. The only progress made on his watch was the release of the Concept and Financial Plan, which had been completed before he arrived.

The *Downtown Express* noted, "As was characteristic of his two-year tenure, Keough did not say much in announcing his resignation."[49] Pataki had yet to commit the state's $100 million for the park. The draft environmental impact statement, which was based on the Concept and Financial Plan, was undergoing review. But Giuliani still had not signed off on the plan, which meant that the project was basically in limbo, and no replacement for Keough had been named.

Gaming Washes Ashore

The next assault on the park followed a court decision allowing vessels traveling beyond the three-mile limit (that is three miles from the shore) to gamble, and in response, maritime operators initiated what they described as "cruises to nowhere."[50] Giuliani did not like gaming. He wanted to quell concerns about safety and organized crime involvement, and he set a significant application fee for an operating license. Local Law 57 was passed, requiring all maritime gaming operators be licensed by the New York City Business Integrity Commission.[51]

After an unsuccessful court challenge to the law, daylong "cruises to nowhere" operating from Circle Line's Midtown piers were proposed, but the logistics of onboard gaming proved daunting, and casinos and gambling were soon added to the list of activities prohibited in the park.[52]

The Launch of the New York Water Taxi

In February of 1997, an article in the *Daily News* described the plans for the launch of the water taxi.[53] A subsequent editorial stated, "If Tom Fox gets his way—and he should—aquatic cabs will transform Hudson and East River into a Venetian spectacle. All that's needed is approval from officials. They should get those rubber stamps ready."[54] Articles in several publications followed, agreeing that the service could enhance public access to the waterfront.

I had met with Bob Bekoff, who ran the successful Fort Lauderdale Water Taxi. Bob did not want to be a partner, but he said he would provide three forty-nine-passenger vessels with crew during the summer, which was his slow season. He assured me that the vessels could be transported by trailer to the city and provide the planned service starting on Memorial Day. And so, I was floored in April when I tried to finalize the initial equity investment required and Jim Fuchs said, "Tom, I'm sorry, but I have a little tax problem and won't be able to participate at all."

But by then, the docks and vessels were on their way. New York Water Taxi began service on Memorial Day weekend and docked in the future park at Piers 84, 62, 45, and 25, along with Battery Park City and Fulton Ferry. The press and public liked the service, and we attracted over seven thousand customers in our first few weeks of operation. However, I did not have adequate operating capital, and construction blocked access to docks at the Battery and South Street Seaport—two very popular attractions. Worse, the boats did not have enough power to maintain the schedules we had developed, and Bekoff threatened to stop the service unless he received the next payment under the lease.

I did the hardest thing I had done since returning for my second tour in Vietnam. I pulled the plug.[55] The *New York Times* wanted a photo to accompany their article about the water taxi's demise, and I sat on our dock at Circle Line looking forlornly out toward the Hudson. My wife's reaction was, "How could you let them take a photograph of you looking like that?" I told her that I wanted everyone to know how devastated I was by my failure.

However, you always learn from failure. Enthusiasm and passion are great, but I had been foolish to depend on people I had just met. Stung by the defeat, I was determined that New York Water Taxi would sail again. I slowly dusted myself off and started anew.

Hudson River Park Alliance

After the Environmental Bond Act passed in November 1996, the distribution of the money it generated quickly became controversial. My *Daily News* op-ed article of January 1997 argued that the tug of war over the funds should be straightforward. Upstate counties had voted against the measure by a three-to-two margin, and city voters had approved it by a three-to-one margin. Nonetheless, downstate counties would be repaying 75 percent of the debt, and I argued that most of the money should be spent on downstate projects like building Hudson River and Brooklyn Bridge Parks and closing the Fresh Kills Landfill.[56]

Marcy and I then wrote dueling op-eds in the *Daily News*. I argued we had the right plan that had finally been endorsed by mainstream environmental organizations. She argued that "what bloated, all powerful, unaccountable authorities do best is suck in limited public resources, including environmental Bond Act funds, waste the money, cut deals for bad plans, and then once they gain control over a site make those bad plans worse."[57] Obviously, her position had not softened.

In April 1997, Pataki committed the state's $100 million to the park, and the next day, the Greenwich Village Little League sued, claiming that their request for playing fields on Pier 40 had been denied.[58] The lawsuit was settled when the conservancy agreed to build a soccer field on the roof of Pier 40, which opened in 1998.

Citizens for a Hudson River Park had been incorporated as a nonprofit organization to advocate for the park the year before, so Bob Trentlyon and I were surprised when Al Butzel created a new organization to be called the "Hudson River Park Alliance" with the environmental organizations that he had persuaded to support the park, and we were not invited to join. Al became the chairman and the alliance operated from the Environmental Defense Fund and eventually grew to include more than thirty organizations.

The alliance roared to life in 1997 when the initial seventeen member organizations issued four major goals for park legislation. They focused on protecting the estuary and the priceless marine habitat in the future park; ensuring that the park was protected in perpetuity and that all the revenue generated in the park was used for maintenance, operations, and improvements; and creating an independent authority to build and operate the park.[59]

A seven-page meeting notice was sent to more than twenty organizations that highlighted the alliance's plans, asked for suggestions from organizations that might get involved in their work, described a June rally planned to support park legislation, and announced funding commitments from founding organizations. The alliance praised the governor's $100 million commitment but raised several other issues involving the park.[60]

Al failed to ask the Neighborhood Open Space Coalition, which had played a leading role advocating for the park, to join his new group. He also failed to send Bob or me information regarding the alliance's agenda and meetings. I was persona non grata with Pataki. I was starting my water taxi business and happy that someone was continuing the fight for the park. But it was clear that I was being excluded from the effort.

Legislative Negotiations

State Senator Franz Leichter and Assemblyman Dick Gottfried led the charge for new legislation in Albany. Assemblywoman Deborah Glick, whose district included the park, was a major opponent. She resisted any commercial development in the park and was allied closely with opponents like Benstock, Gene Russianoff, and Community Board 2. Deborah's objections made it difficult to get the support of Assembly Speaker Sheldon Silver. Legislative leaders usually respect the position of members who represent the district where a project is located and often use their dissension as a rationale to stall projects.

Attempts to pass the legislation fizzled—although not the passion of the bill's lead sponsors. A new legislative initiative began in 1998, and the alliance distributed a detailed twelve-page memo reviewing issues involving land use, traffic, transit, and habitat protection that had been cited in the draft environmental impact statement.[61]

Giuliani had been reelected by a wide margin in the 1997, there had been no substantive progress made on the park, and his attempt to control the project was running up against state opposition. After the election, Giuliani was castigated in the press for failing to take a leadership role in creating the park and urged to support an independent city/state entity to oversee the project or risk jeopardizing the opportunity.[62]

Many of us were concerned about the new entity controlling the property, and Dick Gottfried proposed that the title to the property be transferred to the new entity only if it was consistent with the park plan as reviewed after a State Environmental Quality Review and certificated by the governor and the mayor.[63] I had discussed this issue with both city and state park agencies and argued that the best protection was officially designating the waterfront as city parkland. Doing that would offer the greatest protection against using any of the property for anything other than a public park.

The city owned the property from 36th to 59th Streets outright, and the Court of Claims settlement regarding the federal payback requirement gave the city 50 percent ownership of the rest of the park. So the city actually controlled 56 percent of the park property. I suggested that designating the property as city parkland would make sense, while planning, financing, construction, management, and operations could still be a joint city/state responsibility, as it had been since 1985.

By the December, Al apologized for "inadvertently" deleting me from the alliance's mailing list. I followed up with a memo suggesting issues that the alliance should consider—and among the most critical was protecting the property.[64] Many people had worked long and hard to assemble this property, and it was critical that any new legislation contain the most stringent protections against future commercial exploitation.

I commented on the proposed legislation and objected to reusing Pier 76 as the heliport, asked why eight acres of new platforms and floating structures should be allowed, and voiced a major concern about insurance. If the park were mapped city parkland, the new entity would not pay for insurance because the city was self-insured, and their attorneys would fight any litigation. I doubted a new entity could secure, or afford, liability insurance.

Although the in-water uses allowed in the draft legislation were appropriate, the term "water-related" allowed too much wiggle room, so I suggested "water-dependent" as more appropriate. I suggested that working committees might give alliance members a greater role in decision-making and ended with a plea that the alliance respect decisions made during the multi-year public planning process.

Butzel incorporated several suggestions in the alliance's proposed legislative platform,[65] but he did not establish subcommittees to help with the workload. He was a brilliant litigator and strategist, but he was also a prickly and impatient fellow who wanted things done his way. I am sure he saw my participation as an unwelcome distraction. Within the alliance, several members complained that the leadership was not interested in opinions that differed from theirs. Tensions grew regarding how to best protect the aquatic habitat, which was all the underwater property from Chambers Street north to 59th Street.

The initial draft of their proposed legislation failed to gain traction, and objections were raised by Scenic Hudson, The River Project, NY/NJ Baykeeper, and Environmental Advocates—groups that wanted the strongest possible habitat protections. In December, Scenic Hudson wrote to alliance members, stressing the importance of protecting the estuary and calling for the park to be designated an estuarine sanctuary, with preservation entrusted to the state Department of Environmental Conservation.[66] That position was strongly supported by other members of the alliance who were concerned about habitat protection. In the end, the solidarity of the environmental movement held.

The alliance received significant financial support for its efforts and raised over $165,000 during its 1997 calendar year and had $62,000 remaining at the end of the year.[67] Our 1998 fiscal year budget was $310,000, as we anticipated a strong push for the legislation that year. We included $57,000 for legislative consultants, $50,000 for an economic study, and $30,000 to support grassroots mailings and calls to action.[68] We were determined to get park legislation passed in the new state legislative session.

10

Hudson River Park
Act (1998–2000)

● ● ● ● ● ● ● ● ● ● ● ● ● ●

January of 1998 brought a burst of activity as the Hudson River Park Alliance reviewed drafts of new legislation, discussed the future of Pier 40, and critiqued the draft of the environmental impact statement issued by the Hudson River Park Conservancy, all as part of the effort to craft new legislation governing the park. Members of the Hudson River Park Alliance worked closely with State Assemblymember Richard Gottfried and State Senator Franz Leichter to produce a bill that would garner a broad base of support.[1]

The alliance also established a legislative committee, chaired by Rich Kassel of the Natural Resources Defense Council, to coordinate various aspects of the alliance's legislative initiative.[2] New organizations were invited to join the alliance—among them, the Neighborhood Open Space Coalition, the Architectural League, and the Public Art Fund.[3]

Assemblymember Gottfried shared a draft of a possible bill, and Al Butzel, chairman of the alliance, incorporated alliance member feedback. The term "water-related" became "water-dependent," the open-view corridors from neighborhood streets to the Hudson were protected, and the in-water property was designated as what is known as an estuarine sanctuary—a preservation, research, and restoration area where scientists could study marine life.[4] We made some overall comments on the legislation, along with specific ones.[5]

We recommended that four deteriorating piers be designated as wildlife piers, that a dozen others with their associated upland property be designated for park use only, that Pier 76 and the passenger ship terminals be returned to the park, and that Pier 40 be designated for "predominantly" public use. We wanted to prohibit a heliport in the park—including at Pier 76—as well as high-cost, large-scale sports or recreation facilities in park-use areas while recommending that all municipal uses be removed from the park by December 31, 2003.

We wanted the in-water section of the park to be included in the state's Estuarine Sanctuary Program. We also wanted city and state to retain the ownership of their respective portions of the park and put the property under the jurisdiction of their respective park agencies with roles narrowly defined because we did not want to impede the transfer of design, construction, and management responsibilities to the new entity. We recommended that all revenues from commercial activities in the park be used solely for the park with no transfers to the city or state general fund.

The *New York Times* increasingly supported the park, and an article that appeared in the paper in February urged the governor and mayor to endorse the park as a city/state venture.[6] Giuliani, however, opposed the idea of any state legislation and asserted that the city would not cede any land or jurisdiction to either the state or a new entity. A *Times* editorial that appeared a week later urged the mayor to take a more proactive stance, to stop nibbling away at the park, to commit to removing municipal facilities from the future park, and to compromise with the governor.[7]

Although both Governor George Pataki and Ambassador Charles Gargano, chairman of the Empire State Development Corporation, insisted that new legislation to create the park was not necessary, efforts to pass legislation rose to a fever pitch that spring. At a press conference on Pier 84 in March, Assemblymember Gottfried and State Senator Leichter announced the introduction of the bills in the Assembly and Senate that would create the park, protect the estuary, and ensure meaningful public participation in the process.[8]

The event was well attended, and a number of elected officials and leaders of organizations advocating for the park spoke in support of the proposed bills.[9] Marcy and her cohorts, who opposed the legislation, arrived carrying signs and shouting protest slogans. Park-related theatrics on the West Side were once more attracting attention.[10]

Yet another *Times* editorial criticized the mayor's reluctance to embrace the plan, described his attempts to negotiate each issue in the legislation separately as a recipe for delay, and encouraged Community Board 2 to support both the plan and the proposed legislation.[11] Ironically, Pier 84, where the press conference had been held, was closed the following month because its piles were infested with marine borers—aquatic "termites" that eat wood.[12] The city estimated that pile repair would take several months and cost $300,000.[13]

After the formal introduction of the bills, the stampede began. With the passage of Pataki's Environmental Quality Bond Act in 1996, the "Second Floor" wanted to position the governor as an environmental champion in preparation for his 1998 reelection bid. Alliance members traveled to Albany to advocate for the bill's passage. And once Assembly Speaker Sheldon "Shelly" Silver signed on, negotiations moved quickly.

Concerns about Leadership and Design

The conservancy staff was significantly diminished when Arne Abramowitz was appointed park commissioner of White Plains in April and, shortly thereafter, Margaret Tobin left to begin a career in real estate. Peter Keough had yet to be replaced, and the conservancy's advisory board passed a unanimous resolution urging the conservancy to recruit strong leadership to fill executive vacancies.[14]

At this point, the conservancy's advisory board weighed in on a design of the Greenwich Village segment, the first to be designed and built. The Concept and Financial Plan was the result of years of extensive community input and would shape the identity of the park, along with the Design Guidelines Master Plan.[15] The design of each segment, however, was influenced by the adjacent community board, and because the Village segment was first up, Community Board 2 would establish a precedent for the entire park.[16]

The advisory board expressed concerns about common elements proposed by the community board's design advisors. They requested that their own design consultant review the common elements and expressed doubt that a design could be completed by the June 18 deadline.[17]

The Working Waterfront Association, which consisted of organizations focused on preserving active maritime uses on the waterfront, also expressed concerns about the design. They questioned whether the design consultants understood the concept of a water-based park and noted that the proposed design discouraged water-dependent activities. They described the impact of the proposed designs on construction, maintenance, and maritime use of the bulkhead and piers.[18]

The association recommended installing a protective system on all the park piers. The system is called "fendering" and is used to prevent boats, ships, and other vessels from colliding against the piers. They suggested restoring marine hardware such as bollards and cleats to their original locations on the piers and bulkhead. The association also wanted removable railings installed to allow for emergency access, and they wanted ladders along the bulkhead and piers spaced as far as a person could swim in the winter if someone fell into the water. They advocated for the conservancy to provide fresh water, the removal of wastewater, and electrical utilities on the piers to support boating and other maritime uses.

In short, association members complained that these elements did not appear in the plans and suggested that the proposed design would both set a dangerous precedent for the rest of the park and fail to comply with various federal, state, and local laws.

Hudson River Park Act Passed

Negotiations continued for three months, and the bills that had been drafted were constantly redrafted. Pataki and Giuliani finally agreed that a new public benefit corporation, under the jurisdiction of the newly rebranded Empire State Development Corporation, would be responsible for governing the park, even though Ambassador Gargano said of the park, "It should be run by the Parks Department. Empire State should not be in the business of running parks."[19] Almost everyone agreed with him, but a new entity seemed to be the mechanism most likely to move the project forward.

As always, you win some and lose some. The Hudson River Park Act established the Hudson River Park Trust to complete the work of the Hudson River Park Conservancy, with an expanded thirteen-member board.[20] The park included all the piers and in-water property from Chambers to 59th Streets and the property along marginal way in front of Battery Park City.

The act had some clear shortcomings. The land in question was not officially designated as parkland, although the city and state each kept control of their respective properties. While all the revenue generated in the park would be dedicated to the new trust, there was no provision for financial contributions from the appreciation of inboard property. However, language stating that the park would be self-sufficient was tempered with the phrase "to the extent practicable," adding that city, state, federal, and private funding "may" be needed to build and maintain the park.

Unfortunately, Giuliani prevailed. Piers 76 and the passenger ship terminals were removed from the park, and Gansevoort Peninsula was designated a city sanitation department facility. The wildlife piers were also removed, but all the in-water property became part of the state's Estuarine Sanctuary Program. Except for the tow pound at Pier 76 and the marine transfer station at Pier 99, municipal facilities were given until December 31, 2003, to relocate.

Importantly, however, the meaningful public participation that had created the park was required to continue. There was also a requirement that an advisory council continue the work of the advisory board. Finally, restrictions were imposed on the new trust's ability to issue bonds or override city zoning regulations, and the trust had to follow the City Environmental Quality Review process. The legislation was passed in the late-night hours of June 19, 1998, thereupon to await the governor's signature.

The request from the *New York Times* for an interview surprised me, given my resignation from the conservancy and the failure of my plan for a water taxi. A Public Lives profile recognized my park advocacy and the decade I had spent pushing for the project and included a predictable dig from Marcy, who described the park as "twice as bad as Westway."[21]

A few days later, while waiting on Fifth Avenue for Vince McGowan, the conservancy's vice president of operations, to join me for lunch, I saw John Adams walking toward me. Adams, the founder of the Natural Resources Defense Council, seemed upset. He berated me for the praise I had received from the *Times*. "We want the governor to get all the credit for the Park," Adams complained. I responded by saying that if the *New York Times* thought that Pataki deserved all the credit, they probably would have said so.

During a meeting of the alliance shortly afterward, Paul Elston claimed he had been the first person to suggest legislation to establish the park in 1997 and spoke derisively about the *Times* article, as if it had been written about the bill and not a fourteen-year struggle to forge the consensus plan that made the legislation possible.[22] When Elston said Pataki deserved all the credit, I reminded him that Pataki had yet to sign the bill and that Gottfried and Leichter had introduced a Hudson River Protection Act—that had gone nowhere—back in 1990.

However, I was becoming increasingly aware of the fact that I did not really fit in the mainstream environmental world, and for the first time during the long struggle over the park, I realized that some people were trying to rewrite history.

A *Daily News* editorial soon encouraged the real estate developer Donald Trump to ensure public passage in his planned development between 59th and 72nd Streets and connect the park with Riverside Park, which would create another link in the future Hudson River Greenway.[23] Later in June, the Army Corps of Engineers announced a public hearing on the conservancy's environmental impact statement.[24]

Andy Darrell, the executive director, presented the alliance's testimony on behalf of the membership at the Army Corps hearings.[25] Individual alliance members testified in favor of the permit, as did organizations that had not participated in the alliance. It was unusual that the preponderance of comments at an Army Corps public hearing supported a project.

There was, and is, a natural tension between public use of the waterway and preserving the aquatic habitat. Public use of the Hudson is benign compared to the two centuries of abuse that the estuary received from industry and from careless, clueless, and/or corrupt corporate and government officials. The challenge of balancing habitat protection with the human needs for recreation, navigation and connecting with nature continues here and elsewhere in the nation.

Time to Celebrate

In July, the conservancy hosted a party at Pier 40 celebrating the passage of the legislation officially creating the park.[26] It's important for advocates, elected officials, community members, and even members of the press to celebrate victories. Major victories are few and far between, and it is good to revel in a successful, hard-fought campaign to build a shared sense of accomplishment, community, and purpose.

Nonetheless, obstacles still lie ahead. Opponents of the park requested a more detailed environmental review under the National Environmental Policy Act and urged the governor to veto the bill. Most important, proponents charged that the state was trying to make the park cheaper to build, and opponents said that no one knew where the funding for the park would come from. But this was nonetheless a momentous occasion—one that those of us who had struggled to create the park thought we would never see. The conservancy's invitation to the party was in the form of a birth announcement, stating that the baby's "gestation period had been 14 years."[27]

An editorial in the *New York Times* the next day began by affirming proponents' right to celebrate after fourteen years of hard work.[28] The editorial also cautioned that the city and state needed to secure the necessary funding and appoint talented people to leadership positions in the new trust rather than "political hacks," urging that appointees have "energy, focus and vision" lest "an inept or inattentive board err on the side of inappropriate development." Unfortunately, those words would prove prescient.

That moment was probably one of the last times there would be recognition of the struggle that had paved the way for the legislation. The alliance leadership wanted Pataki to take all the credit, as did Ambassador Gargano and the governor's staff. The future trust leadership would celebrate the 1998 act as the birth of the park, ignoring the hard work of untold New Yorkers who made it possible.

For me personally, there was a damper on the festive mood with the death—just a month later—of Curt Berger, one of the unsung heroes of this West Side story.[29] As the task force's executive director, he had successfully pushed the park's northern boundary from 42nd to 59th Streets, he was an involved and effective board member of both the panel and the conservancy, and he had become a friend.

A Busy Summer

Several months after complaining to conservancy chairman James Ortenzio, the advisory board had its design consultant, who considered their concerns regarding the design of the Greenwich Village segment of the park. They wanted more priority given to the park's history and less use of stainless steel, a material that reflected the state's directive to cut costs.

The advisory board presented its concerns to the conservancy regarding materials, structures, and furniture, including the light poles, benches, trash receptacles, and bollards. They encouraged integrating sculpture and art in the park over time, enlarging the planned playground, considering a nautical theme and signage, and installing a coordinated system of identifying symbols to give visitors a better park experience.[30]

For better or worse, the park's design had been the result of significant public participation in terms of both function and aesthetics. Subsequently, the design of the Greenwich Village segment of the park was modified to include more granite, individual paving blocks rather than a stamped concrete surface, and other details that enriched the park's design. In August, an interim Pier 84 reopened to the public after a significant investment by the city.[31] My hope was that the cost and immediacy of the emergency repairs to that pier would dampen Mayor Giuliani's desire to control everything north of 36th Street.

I realized that Pataki was making the Hudson River Park "his" project by vacillating on approving it while the public clamored for his support. With the passage of the 1996 Bond Act and the Hudson River Park Act, he would head for reelection wearing the mantle of environmental champion. Throughout the summer, Pataki increasingly used the park as a site for announcements that would burnish his environmental creds. In mid-August, the alliance priorities were park funding, the state and federal permit processes, traffic, and public access at Chelsea Piers and other locations.[32]

The alliance did not get involved in design issues. Members were told to prepare for a bill-signing ceremony and were asked to help by ensuring a large turnout. In late August, Paul Elston, vice chair of the alliance, invited members of the environmental community to a press conference at which the League of Conservation Voters would announce its endorsement of Pataki for reelection. The event was held on Pier 25 in Hudson River Park, and Paul stated that the event would give us a chance to show Pataki our appreciation. He also confirmed my suspicions that some of the alliance leaders had a political agenda.[33]

But opponents fought back. Judith Enck, from the Green Party of New York, encouraged Greens members to disrupt and/or protest at the bill-signing ceremony, perhaps dressing as fish heads to emphasize their point. Her email inviting people to the event included an overview by John Mylod—formerly Clearwater's executive director, who emphasized the impact the park would have on the aquatic habitat—and the letters from federal agencies voicing objections to the environmental permits.[34] The alliance sent urgent requests that members write to Pataki to offset letters being sent by park opponents.[35, 36]

Because much of the waterfront was zoned for manufacturing, it had to be rezoned to allow the construction of features like recreational fields. But although the City Council played a critical role in approving zoning changes, the council had not been invited to participate in negotiations. Feeling ignored, council members balked at any zoning change.[37]

We had allies on the City Council—among them, Kathryn Freed, a long-time park advocate. Kathryn represented Lower Manhattan and had cosponsored City Council restrictions regulating billboards within two hundred feet of a highway. The outdoor advertising industry had begun to exploit the proposed roadway and park with billboards sprouting up on the inboard side of Route 9A. The new regulations forced the removal of the billboards, enhanced roadway safety, and minimized visual pollution along the waterfront.

Pataki finally signed the bill into law on September 8 on Pier 25.[38] A week later, Pataki was back in the park to open the soccer field atop Pier 40.[39] On my way to the opening, I stopped at the Ear Inn to speak with Captain Rip Hayman, who owned the building and complained that a sewer line for Route 9A that was being installed on Spring Street was threatening the stability of his building. He feared that the historic structure could collapse. I mentioned that the governor would be at Pier 40—several blocks away—an hour later and, I suggested that he join me at the opening and speak to Pataki directly.

Rip came along, and after the ceremony, he approached Pataki, told him of the Ear's history and his concern, and asked for his intervention. Soon afterward, the state Department of Transportation reinforced the first floor of the Ear with steel beams.

After the bill signing, some leaders of the alliance mentioned that they had not participated in creating the park plans and might have a slightly different vision—for example, suggesting relocating the Circle Line. Several community leaders pushed back, saying that the park plan had a life of its own and that introducing another vision would be counterproductive and diminish the role of the community boards. Others were concerned that changing the plans could trigger a new environmental review, thus delaying the park. The consensus was to stay the course.

State and city funds were available to move the park forward, and Route 9A was under construction, but delays establishing the new trust reduced the opportunity to achieve economies of scale that might have been possible by coordinating both projects. Even worse, the value of the available funding diminished daily with millions lost to inflation and rising construction costs.

My next *Daily News* op-ed article focused on funding, criticizing efforts to scale back the park or reduce the quality of its components, and arguing once again for additional funding to ensure that the park reached its full potential.[40] Options included a special assessment district, a park improvement district, impact fees on new commercial and residential development adjacent to the park, corporate sponsorship, and public funding from specific sources for discrete park projects.

Pataki won reelection handily in November, and park supporters thought that the city and state would finally move forward quickly.[41] We were wrong. As the governor had waited to sign the act, Community Board 2 was working with the Van Alen Institute on a redevelopment plan for Pier 40 that attracted 144 entries. A week after the election, Community Board 2 selected winning proposals, to be announced in January of 1999. But it soon became public knowledge that the Guggenheim Museum was working with the architect Frank Gehry on plans to build a new branch of the museum at Pier 40.[42]

Tensions Increase

As Route 9A was being built, commercial tenants like Chelsea Piers and the Circle Line were negotiating directly with the state transportation department to increase vehicle access to their facilities.[43] In addition, the City Council was not the only legislative body frustrated by Pataki's actions. The governor's failure to move the project forward in 1998 meant that only $4 million of the $20 million in state funding previously approved for the park was spent, so the State Senate balked at approving Pataki's $28 million request in the state's budget for the 2000 fiscal year, which was being finalized in spring of 1999.[44]

Park supporters complained about the delay while opponents continued to demand that the Army Corps undertake a full National Environmental Policy Act review. The alliance claimed that a more detailed review was unnecessary, given the state's stringent environmental review, which caused significant friction. Several alliance members were uncomfortable because they had always championed an open public process—including environmental review—and defected from the group.[45]

An alliance letter in January claiming that the review would needlessly delay the project was signed by only twenty-three of the over thirty member organizations.[46] There was also growing concern about closed-door decision-making; Al Butzel, the alliance chairman, was now consulting for the trust on the environmental review and attending meetings with the Army Corps as the trust's attorney.

As the public outcry increased, the city blamed the state for delaying the project by failing to appoint trust board members.[47] However, the state's park and environmental conservation commissioners were required to be appointed to the board, and they were already serving in the Pataki administration, so there were few other appointments for the state to make. There still was no construction manager for the Greenwich Village segment of the park or designs for any other segment; the Army Corps was considering a full review under the National Environmental Policy Act, which would delay the project for another two years; and the available funding was losing value every day.[48] Things were not getting off to a strong start.

Manhattan Borough President C. Virginia Fields had announced her three appointees to the trust, all of whom were park enthusiasts. Former State Senator Franz Leichter had retired in December, leaving on a high note as a cosponsor of the Hudson River Park Act. Franz lived in Community Board 7 on the Upper West Side, and the other two appointees were members of Community Board 1. Madelyn Wils was a former chair of the conservancy's advisory board, and Julie Nadel was a founding member of the North River Historic Ship Society. It was notable that Virginia Fields failed to appoint a representative from Community Board 2 in Greenwich Village, which was still fighting creation of the park.

Six months after Pataki signed the legislation, the city and state finally announced their appointments to the trust board.[49] James Ortenzio, now a major fundraiser for both the governor and the mayor, transitioned to be chairman of the trust. He expressed doubt that there had been a significant break in momentum or that coordinating park construction with Route 9A would result in savings, but he promised to run a cost-efficient operation.[50]

As vice chairman Giuliani appointed Randy Levine, deputy mayor for economic development and planning. Levine's title betrayed what Giuliani saw as the goal of the park—economic development, not public park development. That city attitude toward the park has continued ever since. Giuliani also appointed to the board Georgette Mosbacher, a businesswoman, author, and top Republican fundraiser; Richard Schwartz, who had led the Parks Department's capital division and was recently Giuliani's senior advisor; and the city official whose appointment was required by the act, Parks Commissioner Henry J. Stern.[51]

The governor's appointments included Teddy Roosevelt IV, a conservationist with whom I had worked on the Brooklyn Bridge Park Coalition; Diana Taylor, a former assistant secretary to Pataki who was a vice president at Keyspan Energy; and the two state officials required by the act: state Environmental Conservation Commissioner John Cahill and state Parks Commissioner Bernadette Castro.

Stumbling Out of the Gate

Meanwhile, the trust staff kept working. Vince McGowan helped the Intrepid Museum relocate parking for school buses from Pier 86 to minimize the museum's impact on the park. There was a vacant lot across Route 9A, which was the site of a former coal gas tank that had once supplied neighborhood streetlamps with fuel. Con Edison took a hard line in the negotiations until significant amounts of mercury were identified in the soil.

Vince reached a deal that allowed the state to condemn the property in exchange for a modest payment and a longer-term lease for Con Edison at Pier 98—where their diesel fuel barges moored to supply the generators at the massive steam power plant designed by McKim, Mead & White across Route 9A. The mercury-laced soil was covered with eight feet of fill and topped with asphalt, and the state built a $12 million bridge connecting the new parking facility with the Intrepid.[52]

Chairman Ortenzio was a hands-on guy and quickly took control, becoming a ubiquitous presence as he rode around the waterfront in his Mercedes, often wearing a fedora. Under the guise of frugality, he relocated the trust office from Fifth Avenue, where there had been ample room for community design meetings and public presentations, to a fifty-foot construction trailer at the northern end of Battery Park City.[53]

The move was a smoke screen for limiting transparency and public participation. The trailer was hard to find, uncomfortable in both summer and winter, and had no room for public gatherings. By June, the Pataki/Giuliani takeover was almost complete. Rob Balachandran, a Pataki attorney who had worked on the act, was appointed president and chief operating officer, and Connie Fishman, a City Hall staffer who had represented Giuliani on the conservancy board, became executive vice president.[54]

At the same time, McGowan requested a leave of absence to run for the State Assembly. Vince got things done. He had extensive knowledge of the park and the major players, important institutional memory, and a good relationship with the community and the tenants. His request was granted, and he ran as a Republican in the heavily Democratic district but, as expected, lost to Jerry Nadler.

When he asked to return to the trust, Chairman Ortenzio, a member of the Manhattan Republican County Committee which had backed McGowan, informed him that the trust no longer needed his services. Vince's termination completed Ortenzio's control of the trust. He was much more comfortable with yes-men like Balachandran, who would not question his intentions or directions.

Rethinking Park Financing

Ortenzio and Gargano teamed up to reinforce the myth that the park was required to be self-sufficient and that long-term maintenance and operations must be supported solely by revenue generated within the park. I began to rue my "eureka" moment in the Loeb Library and my proposing the concept of a self-sufficient park.

The West Side Waterfront Panel had agreed to the concept because no one would support a $500 million park in an era of fiscal austerity without a creative financing plan. Chairman Del Giudice was a municipal finance expert, and he thought the concept made sense. Capturing the funds generated in the park was an important precedent for funding the park. But without additional funding from the inboard properties, the revenue was inadequate to ensure long-term self-sufficiency and would eventually lead to commercial exploitation of the park.

Despite strong opposition, for over ten years I had worked primarily with like-minded New Yorkers who helped craft a vision of a world-class waterfront park. Although we had little actual power, we were persuasive, and the vision was powerful. After my departure, the paradigm shifted, with the governor and mayor taking greater control. I had come to believe that the strength of the vision and the public support would ensure that the initial vision would endure. I was wrong.

I had been naïve, and now I was paying the price. The design of the park was being dumbed down, the concept of self-sufficiency was being bastardized, and the governor and mayor were more interested in other projects. Slowly, the original vision began to atrophy. The new staff and board of the trust proclaimed the need for self-sufficiency, yet the governor and mayor refused to develop a mechanism to capture any revenue from inboard properties, and they allocated all the increasing tax revenues to their pet projects.

Park Construction Begins

Construction on the part of the park in Greenwich Village had begun in early 1999. We hoped that building the first segment there would show Village residents the benefits of the park and help silence their constant criticism. In addition, the Village waterfront was unobstructed, no commercial permits or leases had to be terminated, and the adjacent segment of Route 9A was nearing completion.

By September, portions of the park in the Village were nearing completion, but the plans had been scaled back. Various maritime and historic elements of the park were eliminated, and the designs had been modified to meet a shrinking budget. And the reconstruction of the piers could not proceed until the Army Corps issued a permit.

Marcy continued to threaten litigation, using the same technique we had used in our final push to stop Westway. She got out-of-state U.S. Senators John Kerry and Ted Kennedy of Massachusetts to pressure the Army Corps for a review of the project under the National Environmental Policy Act, claiming that it would affect fishing in Massachusetts. New York Senators Moynihan and the newly elected Chuck Schumer took umbrage at this out-of-state interference.

Park supporters were fortunate that Joe Seebode, chief of the Army Corps Regulatory Branch in New York, and Jim Haggerty, their Eastern Permit administrator, were reviewing the application. They were professional, fair, and above politics.

Same Strategy and Tactics, Different City

That spring, Justine Liff, park commissioner of Boston and a former Loeb Fellow, asked me to speak about New York City's experience building coalitions and expanding public open space. The audience included a delegation from San Francisco. I was told that their park system was deteriorating, and Mayor Willie Brown wanted to turn the situation around.

A few months later, I agreed to be a consultant for the mayor and proposed a public campaign to revitalize the city's park system.[55] I worked with Elizabeth Goldstein as I had in the earlier years of Hudson River Park when she was the regional director of the state Office of Parks, Recreation and Historic Preservation. Elizabeth had moved to San Francisco and was appointed to a senior position in the San Francisco Recreation and Parks Department to coordinate the city side of the campaign, an initiative that was not necessarily welcomed within the department.

Naturally, the local park community had to spearhead the effort, so we reached out to the Neighborhood Parks Council. They in turn established a powerful broad-based coalition that included schools, civic groups, and sports leagues to advocate for structural changes in the agency and new funding for public open space. Working with the coalition and the Board of Supervisors, we crafted City and County Propositions A (a $100 million bond to fund capital improvements to the park system) and C (a 20-year extension of a real estate transfer tax that funded the system and was scheduled to end the next year).

Both initiatives were on the March 2000 ballot and were overwhelmingly approved by San Francisco voters.[56] This legislation changed the planning and construction of recreation and park projects and helped generate more than $300 million in new funding over the next twenty years.[57]

Enlightened politicians, strong community leadership, and the public's affinity for parks and open space reshaped Manhattan's West Side waterfront with the creation of the park. The same strategy and tactics worked in San Francisco, a city with a similar problem but a unique physical, social, and political environment. Over two years, I had spent two weeks a month in each city and stayed involved in both the Hudson River Park Alliance and a new organization that formed in 1998 called Friends of Hudson River Park. Acknowledging her major contribution to the effort, Mayor Brown appointed Elizabeth as the general manager of the revitalized Recreation and Parks Department.

Friends of Hudson River Park

Unlike the leadership of the alliance, the leadership of Friends of Hudson River Park was composed primarily of West Siders, many of whom had been involved in planning the park for years. The group's founder and chairman, Captain John Doswell, was a mariner and leader in Friends of Pier 84. The board was diverse and included community residents, park tenants, businesspeople, mariners, former West Side political operatives, and real estate developers as well as Al Butzel, Vince McGowan, and me.

At one of the initial Friends board meetings, the only person in the room whom I did not know sat across from me. He seemed familiar, and when I introduced myself after the meeting, it turned out that he was Douglas Durst, Seymour's son. We had originally met in 1994 at an exhibit of photography by William H. "Holly" White that Seymour Durst sponsored. Holly was a journalist, a former U.S. Marine, and a fantastic urban observer who inspired and mentored many activists ranging from Jane Jacobs to Fred Kent, founder of the Project for Public Spaces.[58] Douglas had long hair and a beard, and he and his wife, Susanne, were keen on organic farming.

Six years after I had met him, he was still into organic farming and a partner in McEnroe Farm, but he was also the clean-shaven copresident of the Durst Organization, his family's real estate business. Real estate developers who are organic farmers are few and far between, and I was happy that Douglas shared his father's interest in sensible West Side redevelopment.

Several months later, a colleague who worked for the North Brooklyn Development Corporation mentioned that two large parcels on the Greenpoint waterfront had what he described as "development potential." The community, he confided, was looking for a developer with good manners and common sense, adding that they might be willing to trade additional density for amenities and affordable housing.

Douglas, the only developer I knew, seemed to have both good manners and common sense. We drove to Greenpoint to see the two sites, and he expressed interest. It turned out that neither site was available. But if the ride out to Brooklyn proved futile, the ride back was anything but. I was explaining my difficulties finding investors to relaunch New York Water Taxi, when Douglas asked if I had a business plan and how much money I needed. I told him I did indeed have a plan and needed approximately $4 million. Douglas suggested that we meet the following week to discuss the matter.

When we met, Douglas was accompanied by his attorney, Gary Rosenberg, and his daughter Helena, who was an intern with the trust. Douglas agreed to take what he called the "second half" of the equity if I found the first. I was elated, knowing that a $2 million commitment from Douglas Durst made it much easier to find the "first" half. And so I started hunting again in earnest.

Pier Reconstruction Begins

Meanwhile, the Army Corps permit for limited in-water construction was issued on May 31, 2000.[59] This time, Al Butzel, chairman of the alliance, was the subject of a *Times* Public Lives profile, and none of the "environmentalists" complained.[60] It was great that work on the park piers was finally beginning, but the trust's insistence on frugality resulted in the removal of Pier 42's two acres of public open space from the Greenwich Village waterfront. Pier 46 was rebuilt to less than half its original length, and Pier 49 was left as a pile field that we hoped to find funding to rebuild and deck in the future.

At the same time, two new fifteen-story residential towers by the celebrated architect Richard Meier on Perry Street across from the park hit the market.[61] Apparently, the moneyed folks knew what was happening and realized that the park would add value to the inboard property—what better proof than Calvin Klein and Martha Stewart placing deposits on multimillion-dollar apartments and restaurateur Jean-Georges Vongerichten planning to open one of his celebrated restaurants in the buildings.

As predicted by the Working Waterfront Association, the trust failed to include many elements necessary for maritime use of the Greenwich Village piers. They installed a timber protection, called a fendering system, around the three rebuilt piers, but there was no dredging to deepen the water, no maritime hardware installed on the piers, and no gates on the fences. These shortcomings effectively precluded maritime use in the Village, and it is a flaw that still plagues the park.

But the trust claimed that the local community did not want any vessels docking at the Greenwich Village piers. The leadership of the Federation for the Preservation of the Greenwich Village Waterfront and Great Port had been so focused on opposing the park that they missed an opportunity to rebuild the Greenwich Village waterfront with the elements required to dock vessels. But they responded creatively by shortening their name and removing the reference to the Great Port.

**West Side
Waterfront
Transformation**

● ● ● ● ● ● ● ● ● ● ● ● ● ●

Hell's Kitchen's in 1988. West 59th to 52nd Streets including Piers 99, 98, 97, 96, 95, and 94. The elevated West Side, or Miller, Highway is closed to traffic, and traffic comes down to grade at 57th Street. On the waterfront are the Department of Sanitation marine transfer station under construction at Pier 99, the Con Edison diesel refueling facility at Pier 98, the Department of Sanitation's garbage barges and trucks at Pier 97, a bow notch, vacant Pier 96 with its headhouse demolished, and abandoned Pier 95 with Pier 94 at the beginning of the Midtown passenger ship terminals. Across the West Side Highway are the Con Edison steam power plant between 58th and 59th Streets and low-rise warehouse and manufacturing buildings, including Artkraft Strauss and De Witt Clinton Park with its worn-out ball fields between 52nd and 54th Streets. (Credit Tom Fox)

Clinton Cove Park in 2021. West 59th to 52nd Streets including Piers 99, 98, 97, 96, 95, and 94. On the waterfront are the rebuilt marine transfer station at Piers 99, Con Edison water cooling facility at Pier 98, Pier 97 (after a $16 million pier rebuild and awaiting $38 million in landscape and park improvements), the bow notch, Pier 96 boathouse, Clinton Cove Park, and Pier 94 awaiting redevelopment on the waterfront. Across Route 9A are GT Development's One Waterline Square, Con Edison's steam power plant, and the Durst Organization's VIA 57 West, with The Helena behind it. Across 57th Street is TD Cornerstone's The Max behind the Department of Sanitation garage built to relocate garbage trucks from Pier 97. The ball fields at De Witt Clinton Park are in much better shape. (Credit Tom Fox)

West 42nd Street in 1986. On the waterfront are the Intrepid Sea, Air & Space Museum at Pier 86, a vacant Pier 84, and Circle Line at Pier 83 on the waterfront. The elevated West Side, or Miller, Highway terminates abruptly at 43rd Street, and West Street continues at grade. On the other side of Route 9A parking at the former Con Edison gas site, low-scale manufacturing, the UPS building, the Sheridan Hotel at 42nd Street, a whole block parking facility between 41st and 42nd Streets, and the Metropolitan Transit Association's Mike Quill bus garage. (Credit Tom Fox)

West 42nd Street in 2021. On the waterfront are the Intrepid Sea, Air & Space Museum at Pier 86, concessions, restrooms, a fountain, playground, boathouse and open lawns at Pier 84, and Circle Line and New York Cruise Lines at Piers 83 and 81 on the waterfront. Across Route 9A are a bridge from the parking lot on the former Con Edison gas site to the Intrepid Museum, a low-rise storage facility, the UPS building, the Chinese Consulate General in the converted Sheraton hotel at 42nd Street, Silverstein Properties residential development between 41st and 42nd Streets, and the Metropolitan Transit Association's Mike Quill bus garage. (Credit Tom Fox)

Chelsea with Thomas Smith Park in 1986. On the waterfront are auto body and glass shops and rooftop parking in Pier 63 with parking at a vacant Pier 62. World Yacht dinner cruise boats are docked there and at Pier 61 in the Chelsea Piers. West Street snakes around the Chelsea Piers and through Thomas Smith Park. This section of West Street needed to be realigned to meet federal highway standards when Route 9A was reconstructed. Across the roadway is a heavily trafficked West 23rd Street with warehouse and manufacturing buildings to the north and Thomas Smith Park to the south. Low-rise manufacturing and warehouse buildings line 11th Avenue between 21st and 24th Streets. (Credit Tom Fox)

Chelsea Waterside Park in 2021. On the waterfront, the tree-lined Pier 64 rises as it gets farther from the shore with stunning vistas at the tip. A stone sculpture garden, skate park, and gardens ring the lawn with sunbathers on the former Pier 63. In addition to the gardens and skate park, Pier 62 has a carousel under a shade structure with a green roof. Classic Harbor Lines and City Experience vessels dock at Pier 61 in the restored Chelsea Piers Complex. Route 9A has been realigned. Across Route 9A, a new U.S. Postal Service garage was constructed between 24th and 25th Streets, 24th Street was designated a two-way street and widened, 23rd Street was eliminated, and Thomas Smith Park was expanded with a playground, dog run, athletic fields, and restrooms to create the upland portion of Chelsea Waterside Park between 22nd and 24th Streets. New high-rise residential buildings are on 11th Avenue between 21st and 24th Streets. (Credit Tom Fox)

Lower Chelsea/Meatpacking District in 1986. On the waterfront are the municipal bus garage at Pier 57, vacant Pier 56, Pier 54 (last of the Cunard-White Star Piers), and the Department of Sanitation Destructor Plant on the Gansevoort Peninsula with the city Fire Department's Marine 1 firehouse "Tiltin' Hilton" at Pier 53. Across the West Side Highway, the National Biscuit Company is between 15th and 16th Streets and the entire block to 10th Avenue. There is a vacant block with parking backed by the High Line which continues through buildings to Bank Street. The Liberty Inn is the triangular building south of 14th Street with various low-rise meat processing buildings between 14th and Gansevoort Streets to the south. (Credit Tom Fox)

Lower Chelsea/Meatpacking District in 2021. On the waterfront are Pier 57 with Google offices, a circumferential promenade and rooftop park, Little Island, and a widened esplanade. Natural shoreline restoration, boat launch, a beach, and ball fields are under construction on the 5.5-acre Gansevoort Peninsula. A rebuilt Fire Department Marine 1 firehouse and dock at Pier 53 just out of sight. Across Route 9A are the Chelsea Market between 15th and 16th Streets and a small park created by NYS Department of Transportation with the transformed High Line behind it. The Liberty Inn is the triangular building south of 14th Street with new buildings, like the Standard Hotel at 13th Street, displacing the low-rise meatpacking buildings, which gave the district its name. The new Whitney Museum of American Art is at Gansevoort Street. (Credit Tom Fox)

Greenwich Village in 1988. On the waterfront are vacant Piers 46, 45, and 42, and car and truck parking on the 15-acre Pier 40. The area between Route 9A and the water is vacant. Across Rout 9A is historic Greenwich Village with low-rise commercial and residential buildings, between Perry and Clarkson Streets. The Federal Building on Christopher takes up an entire city block, and St. John's Terminal just south of Clarkson Street was built by New York Central Railroad as the terminus of the High Line. (Credit Tom Fox)

Greenwich Village in 2021. On the waterfront is a truncated Pier 46, a bow notch, restrooms, and a fountain at the foot of Christopher Street on the esplanade. Pier 45 is crowded with sunbathers; the remnant piles of Pier 42 can be seen just below the water. Pier 40 has parking but with multiple ball fields in the center court, and the building hosts support facilities, Hornblower Cruises, and the headquarters of the Hudson River Park Trust. There is a richly landscaped area between the esplanade and the bicycle path next to the roadway, with the PATH vent shafts at Morton Street. Across Route 9A are three Richard Meier buildings between Charles and Perry Streets, the Archive Building on Christopher Street, and converted low-rise and new high-rise residential buildings lining Route 9A. The vacant block south of Clarkson Street is awaiting a new residential high-rise. Google occupies the modified St. John's Terminal building south of Houston Street, which is now open to the sky. (Credit Tom Fox)

Tribeca in 1994. On the waterfront is vacant Pier 26 with The River Project conducting research in the concrete block building. A vacant Pier 25 has the former Ellis Island ferry *Yankee* and tug *Pegasus* on the north side with The Flying Neutrinos floating home in the embayment on the south side. The newly constructed interim bicycle and pedestrian path is at the water's edge. A recently opened American Express office complex is across the West Side Highway between Hubert and N. Moore Streets. The Borough of Manhattan Community College faces the highway, with Independence Plaza's high-rise residential buildings immediately behind it. (Credit Tom Fox)

Tribeca in 2021. On the waterfront, Pier 26 with the Downtown Boathouse and novice kayakers exploring the embayment between Piers 26 and Pier 34 along with natural vegetation and engineered wetland at the tip of the pier interrupted by a children's play area surrounded by a bright blue fence that separates both natural areas. The City Vineyard restaurant with an empty space, where the new playground and estuarium will be built, is between Piers 25 and 26. Pier 25's historic vessel docks include the U.S. Coast Guard steam-powered buoy tender *Lilac* close to shore and the visiting former fireboats *Governor Alfred E. Smith* and *John D. McKean* on the north side. On the south side of the pier are the *Sherman Zwicker*, a Canadian schooner housing a restaurant, a town dock supporting moored sailboats in the embayment, and Citigroup's private water taxi dock next to the children's playground. Pier 25 has miniature golf, beach volleyball, and an open lawn with spectacular vistas from the viewing area at the tip. The esplanade has a skate park, dog run, and basketball courts. Across Route 9A, there are new and redeveloped residential buildings north of Citigroup's headquarters, with Borough of Manhattan Community College and Independence Plaza's residential towers behind it. (Credit Tom Fox)

11

The World Changes (2001–2003)

● ● ● ● ● ● ● ● ● ● ● ● ● ●

As the new century rolled in, the park and the roadway began taking shape, and the public's response was encouraging. However, the unprecedented terrorist attack on the World Trade Center shook the city and the nation to its core, and the West Side waterfront contributed to our response and recovery from the tragic events of 9/11. Meanwhile, the governor continued cost-cutting measures to reduce the public investment in the park, and a new mayor began to rezone the entire West Side without providing any additional funding for the park.

As part of the Hudson River Park Trust's cost-cutting measures, president Rob Balachandran proposed selling the USCGC *Tamaroa* (WMEC-166), a United States Coast Guard cutter with a fabled past. The *Tamaroa* had served in the Pacific during World War II, was transferred to the United States Coast Guard after the war, and was the first rescue vessel to arrive upon the sinking of the *Andrea Doria* in 1956. The *Tamaroa* was best known, however, for the depiction of her in *The Perfect Storm*, a book and later a movie that tells the story of how she rescued four of the five crew members of a downed National Guard helicopter that had crash-landed after a failed attempt at a dangerous rescue during a terrible storm at sea.[1]

The *Tamaroa* had been donated to the Intrepid Sea, Air & Space Museum, and the conservancy provided a mooring at Pier 40. We hoped that, as outlined in the park's General Project Plan, the *Tamaroa* would eventually join other historic ships to tell the story of the waterfront's maritime past. However, because of the failure to conduct adequate historical research, the vessel was denied its proper historic designation. She was eventually sold to a Virginia foundation that hoped to restore her, but they were not successful, and in 2017, she was scuttled off Cape May, New Jersey.[2]

The loss of the *Tamaroa* revealed the trust's lack of commitment to historic vessels and to interpreting the waterfront's storied maritime past. The old joke is that "boat" stands for "break out another thousand," and historic preservation is not cheap. Rather than solicit public or private support for the vessel's preservation, the trust continued to reduce its investment in the park and to scale back its plans. In addition, power struggles between Pataki and Giuliani continued to delay decision-making, not surprisingly, since the governor and mayor are traditionally competitive and routinely engage in unproductive rivalries.[3]

Friends Plays a Bigger Role

For Friends of Hudson River Park, the group generally known simply as "Friends," the year 2001 began as 2000 had ended, with the organization trying to get the city to reconsider the removal of Pier 94 from Clinton Cove Park. The city's Economic Development Corporation had already selected a developer who planned to operate an exhibition center on Pier 94.

The name of that park, by the way, has an interesting history. The West Side neighborhood directly north of Chelsea, which extends from West 42nd to West 59th Street between Seventh Avenue in the Hudson, was traditionally known as Hell's Kitchen—a tip of the hat to its rough and rowdy past, largely courtesy of the docks that lined the adjacent waterfront. However, in the 1960s (there is some debate about the exact date), the neighborhood was rebranded as Clinton—real estate developers marketing new residential buildings in the area thinking that the name Hell's Kitchen lacked a certain cachet.

Perhaps fittingly, the park's namesake, DeWitt Clinton, who served as mayor, U.S. senator, and governor at the end of the eighteenth century, was also a naturalist.[4] In addition, he championed the building of the Erie Canal, which transformed the economies of the city and state in the early nineteenth century.

In February, the Friends board discussed Pier 94. The conservancy's plan had removed its headhouse and included it as a year-round recreation area in Clinton Cove Park. The proposed reuse of the headhouse and commercial redevelopment in the pier significantly reduced park and recreational space in Clinton, and we considered our options to oppose the pier's commercial use.[5]

In May, Al Butzel, now a Friends board member, sent a memo indicating that some board members were reluctant to take a strong position in the negotiations. He pointed out that we had taken a strong position in our initial letter to the city's Economic Development Corporation, and if they did not believe we would fight, they would have no reason to strike a better deal for the community. Al was ready to engage.[6]

The state transportation department did many things right while rebuilding Route 9A. However, my *Daily News* op-ed article in April highlighted some elements that I thought had cheapened the boulevard and diminished the park experience. Cost-cutting had resulted in a road that fell short of the tree-lined urban boulevard originally imagined as an amenity to complement the park.[7] A decorative fence in the middle of the median, proposed to keep pedestrians from crossing between designated crosswalks, was eliminated. Instead, the median was heavily planted with beach roses (*Rosa rugosa),* which were native plants but caught plastic bags and windblown garbage, creating a trashy aesthetic. Moreover, without irrigation, many trees in the median struggled and died.

As mentioned earlier, the grooves in the road's surface to enhance drainage lay perpendicular to the flow of traffic rather than parallel and thus increased noise levels. The large barriers surrounding the median were being struck and damaged, as were the vehicles hitting them. And the proposed bridge over the widest part of the roadway connecting DeWitt Clinton Park to the waterfront was scrapped. The transportation department ignored suggestions about changing the things that could be changed— for example, building the bridge from DeWitt Clinton Park, ripping out the roses, and creating a more diverse landscape in the median that was easy to maintain. Eventually, however, they got around to installing irrigation.

Later that month, Noreen Doyle and Michael Bradley, the last two senior staff members of the original conservancy, resigned. Noreen took a position at Alee King Rosen and Fleming, the trust's environmental consultants, while Michael joined the Riverside South Planning Corporation to oversee the design and construction of their waterfront park. At their final trust board meeting, Noreen and Michael announced their engagement, eliciting an audible gasp from a surprised audience.

September 11

The terrorist attacks of September 11, 2001, devastated the nation, the city, the Lower West Side of Manhattan, and the Hudson River Park. Battery Park City and the park became important escape routes for traumatized people fleeing Ground Zero. Every boat afloat raced to evacuate people in Lower Manhattan by water, transporting some one hundred thousand stunned victims from Ground Zero alone and more than a million people from Manhattan ferry terminals.[8]

The maritime evacuation exposed the shortcomings of a waterfront design that failed to accommodate vessels. The concrete bulkhead of Battery Park City had no fenders, and the waterfront railing had no gates. Panicked evacuees had to climb or be dragged over a railing that was designed to keep people from doing just that. The undertaking was the largest maritime evacuation since British and French forces fled Dunkirk in 1940 and a tribute to the bravery, compassion, and quick thinking of mariners throughout the harbor under extraordinary difficult conditions.[9]

On the day of the attack, the historic fireboat *John J. Harvey* was being restored at Pier 63 Maritime by the river rats who had banded together to buy her at auction. Because subway service was halted and vehicles were not allowed to travel south of 14th Street, the only way to get in and out of Lower Manhattan that tumultuous day was by water. The maritime response was spontaneous and cacophonous yet quite successful. *Harvey* quickly sailed to Lower Manhattan to assist where she was needed more than anyone had anticipated. Lower Manhattan water mains were damaged when the towers fell, and *Harvey* was one of the only sources of water, which came from the river and was used to supply the fire hoses.

Initially, the flow of water went to the vessel's cannons, and the cutoff valves were not working yet. Crew members tried plugging the cannons to redirect the water to the fire hoses. Plastic water bottles did not work for this purpose, but tennis balls did, enabling *Harvey* to act as a pumping station, supplying the hoses used to put out fires and douse smoldering debris. Without mooring hardware to hold the ship against the bulkhead, *Harvey* was initially tied to trees on the esplanade. Those trees, however, could easily be ripped out, so an offshore sea anchor was positioned to stabilize the vessel.[10]

It is fortunate that Vince McGowan, the trust's former vice president of management and operations, was now the chief operating officer of Battery Park City. He remained on-site for weeks during and after the attack to help emergency responders and direct support on land for the maritime evacuation. The right man in the right place at the right time, Vince was one of twelve New Yorkers awarded the 9–11 Medal from the United States Department of Transportation for "extraordinary service to the citizens of the United States."[11] Unfortunately, like so many other first responders, Vince continues to suffer the effects of that horrendous atrocity over twenty years later.

Within minutes of the attack, normal life in the city and the park came to a screeching halt. The Brooklyn Bridge, Brooklyn Battery Tunnel, and Holland Tunnel were closed to all but emergency vehicles, and no one could travel to Lower Manhattan. The falling towers had destroyed that section of Route 9A, and the roadway was closed south of Canal Street. The Federal Emergency Management Agency turned Pier 40 into a storage and distribution center for relief supplies, emergency equipment, and support for volunteer search-and-rescue units from across America.

The park played an important role in the recovery effort. Pier 57 housed law enforcement and other emergency vehicles, and Pier 92 hosted the U.S. Navy hospital ship *Comfort*, which sailed into the harbor to help provide care for the wounded. The underwater area between Battery Park City and Pier 25 was dredged to allow tugs, cranes, and barges to moor and offload construction equipment. The debris from Ground Zero, trucked up Route 9A for months, was dumped into hopper barges destined for the Fresh Kills Landfill on Staten Island. In the first two weeks after the disaster, workers removed one hundred thousand of the 1.8 million tons of debris that were eventually cleared away from the area.

Community Board 1 and its chairwoman, Madelyn Wils, were important in the recovery and redevelopment efforts. The Lower Manhattan Development Corporation was created to coordinate the redevelopment of downtown, and Roland Betts, the chairman of Chelsea Piers and a close friend of then President George W. Bush, was appointed to that board.[12]

In the immediate aftermath of the attacks, Douglas Durst and I agreed that creating an intracity waterborne transportation service would help the recovery while enhancing access to the park. We officially became partners, and the Durst family committed the entire $4 million required to restart New York Water Taxi.

Douglas assigned Richard Kohlbrecher, a building engineer, to help with that effort. Richard, a lifelong fisher and boater, was a knowledgeable and trusted advisor. Working with a naval architect and shipyard, we designed and built six seventy-four-passenger water taxis that could travel at 23 knots. They were painted yellow and accented by a black-and-white checkered stripe—an image that quickly became a New York icon.

As environmentalists, Douglas and I wanted to minimize the boats' impact on park infrastructure, marine life, and recreational boaters. They were designed with energy-efficient engines, hospital-grade mufflers, and hulls that reduce the wakes produced by the vessel. They were also the first handicap-accessible small passenger vessels in the United States.

In November of 2001, just two months after the terrorist attacks, Michael Bloomberg was elected mayor of New York City, replacing Rudy Giuliani.[13] Everyone's focus was on the recovery at Ground Zero, but Bloomberg also envisioned expanded development in other parts of the city.

He appointed Dan Doctoroff as deputy mayor for economic development and recovery. I had met with Dan when I was soliciting investors for New York Water Taxi, and although he did not invest, he saw the potential of waterborne transportation. Bloomberg's new park commissioner, Adrian Benepe, joined the trust's board, and his predecessor, Henry Stern, remained as a citizen representative.

Friends Finds Its Footing

Late in 2001, Friends of Hudson River Park reviewed the plans for Pier 94 and prepared comments on the Pier 94 study that Community Board 4 had requested from Dattner Architects.[14] Friends was dealing with several pressing issues. The reduction of Clinton Cove Park was at the top of the list, as was the future of Pier 40 and the need to continue funding park construction at a time when the organization itself was struggling to find its footing.

Members of the group's board were dedicated to the creation and protection of the park, but they approached advocacy in different ways. Some, including several tenants, community board members, and businesspeople, had a more reserved approach to advocacy—one that I would describe as passive aggressive. They favored extensive negotiations, presenting testimony to the Hudson River Park Trust, speaking at meetings of agencies and community boards, and responding to press inquiries.

Others favored proactive tactics like staging rallies and demonstrations, requesting information under the Freedom of Information Act, carrying out independent analyses of plans, leaking stories to the press, threatening litigation when negotiations floundered, and using the courts as a last resort.

Friends' primary role was providing support and assistance to the trust in planning, programming, fundraising, and volunteer programs. We therefore needed to present cogent arguments that were both constructive and supported by the public. We also needed to be strong enough to act independently if the trust charted what we considered the wrong course. Discussions about strategy and tactics distracted board members and reduced our effectiveness. That was about to change.

One of Friends' biggest assets was Douglas Durst. Although responsible for managing and expanding the almost eight million square feet of commercial real estate that his family owned, he was a lifelong environmentalist who lived in Hell's Kitchen, two blocks from the park, and dedicated significant time and energy to Friends. Douglas was a philanthropist and a major player in the real estate industry with experience in politics, finance, construction, planning, litigation, and public relations. His father had been a Westway opponent, and Douglas shared Seymour's vision of an open Hudson waterfront and thought that all new real estate development should take place inboard. He was very active in both board and committee meetings.

The Durst family provided general support for Friends and hired engineers, architects, urban planners, and lawyers to advance our planning and decision-making. Douglas also used his connections to leverage support from individuals and organizations, such as the Real Estate Board of New York, that might not have been receptive to the park if he had not been involved.

Douglas brought an understated gravitas to our efforts and was elected cochairman of Friends board of directors in 2002—a change that brought renewed energy to our efforts.[15] At the same time, Al Butzel stepped down from the board and became president of Friends, and the group's more proactive board members began playing a greater role in charting our agenda.

In January of 2002, Friends leadership met Deputy Mayor Doctoroff to discuss Pier 94. We had petitioned Bloomberg and his new deputy mayor to revisit the decision to develop Pier 94 and hoped that Doctoroff, with his keen interest in the West Side, might be more helpful than his predecessor, Randy Levine, had been. Although separated in age by about eighteen years, both Butzel and Doctoroff had grown up in the Detroit suburb of Birmingham. Al thought the two men might have a natural connection.

At the meeting, Doctoroff expressed his support for a public waterfront and announced that he did not care much for the planned exhibition space but added that he was not excited about the alternative plan developed with

Dattner Associates.[16] In the end, Doctoroff was no more helpful, and the development of exhibition space on Pier 94 moved forward. It was one of our first losses, but unfortunately neither the biggest nor the last.

The Tide Heads Out

One noticeable change in the post-9/11 world was that the trust seemed less committed to public participation than the conservancy had been. Decisions were being made without community consultation, and projects were increasingly planned behind closed doors.

For example, two-hundred-foot-high smokestacks at the Gansevoort Destructor Plant, which had been preserved in the park's General Project Plan, were demolished.[17] That facility was once part of the city's solid waste disposal system and burned 1,500 tons of trash every day, with the cinders carted away to landfills by barge.[18]

We had thought that preserving the smokestacks as beacons on the shore for mariners and as industrial artifacts would help interpret the park's maritime industrial past. The inspiration was the abandoned steel mills in Germany's Ruhr Valley that were being converted into recreational facilities and concert halls. But they may have interrupted the view from the property of trust chairman James (Leonardo) Ortenzio, which was across Route 9A. The trust began demolishing the smokestacks with no community review and no public announcement that they would be torn down. Members of Community Board 2 learned about the demolition in *The Villager*, a community newspaper.

Pier 57, a few blocks away at West 17th Street, could also be seen from Ortenzio's property, which might have been why the trust, again without public input, painted the entire pier even though it housed a municipal bus garage and maintenance was the responsibility of the Metropolitan Transportation Authority. The trust's opacity seemed to grow, and concerns about Ortenzio's stewardship grew as well.

Al Butzel and I sent a memo to the Friends board describing trust efforts that undercut the park citing the lack of professional management, inadequate funding, slow progress, and reduced community involvement.[19] In addition, Community Board 4 sent a second memo to trust president Balachandran in January of 2002 requesting a public planning process for redeveloping Pier 57.[20] That is when news broke that the trust was negotiating with a radio station for a twelve-concert summer series.[21]

All in all, decisions were obviously being made behind closed doors.

New Ferry Terminals

I had joined NYC2008, a group Dan Doctoroff assembled in 1999 to advocate for New York's hosting the 2008 Summer Games. Beijing ultimately won the honor. But Dan, undaunted, focused on hosting the 2012 Summer Olympics. I served on the environmental committee of NYC2012, and our bid was submitted to the International Olympic Committee in June of 2001.[22]

Our plans placed athletic venues throughout the city that were connected by subway and waterborne transportation, which in turn was supported by new ferry terminals planned for Midtown Manhattan and Long Island City, Queens. But the proposal to build an Olympic Stadium on a platform above the MTA's rail yards on Manhattan's West Side presented the same air pollution and traffic issues that killed the previous proposal to build Yankee Stadium there.

In April, Bloomberg announced an expansion of public ferry terminals. Although municipal funding was tight, the events of 9/11 highlighted the importance of ferries in emergency evacuation. City Hall announced that the Department of Transportation would rebuild the Whitehall Ferry Terminal, make major improvements to the St. George Terminal on Staten Island, and build a new terminal for West Midtown at Pier 79. The Port Authority announced its plans for a new ferry terminal at the World Trade Center and in Weehawken, New Jersey, where NY Waterway was based.

Although park supporters suggested using Pier 76, which could accommodate passenger pickup and drop-off on the Pier, the new terminal was planned on Pier 79—wrapped around the Lincoln Tunnel Vent Shaft. The location seemed strange because the Lincoln Tunnel is critical infrastructure, and could increase security concerns as thousands of commuters would pass through daily. If terrorists targeted the terminal, they might disable both the terminal and the tunnel below. Moreover, the property in front of the terminal was part of the park, quite narrow, and planned for the esplanade. The trust, was firmly controlled by the city and the state, ignored public concerns, and allowed this temporary taking of public parkland—which is still being disputed.[23]

The Relaunch of New York Water Taxi

In the summer of 2002, New York Water Taxi received three of its six state-of-the-art vessels. They were named for unsung heroes of the harbor; the first was christened the "Mickey Murphy," in honor of a recently deceased octogenarian whose real name was Mary Ellen Murphy and who had been a leader in the fight to preserve the historic Fulton Ferry Landing in Downtown Brooklyn.[24]

In September, we held a launch party on Pier 25 at N. Moore Street with hundreds of guests from the tour and travel trade, the maritime industry, the government, and local communities. Everyone feasted on Brother Jimmy's barbecue, danced to the music of a ten-piece Brazilian band, and watched a city fireboat streaming plumes of red, white, and blue water from its cannons as it led our first three bright-yellow water taxis down the river. When darkness fell, fireworks filled the sky.

As I watched the fireworks from an abandoned golf driving range on the pier with my family, Gary Rosenberg—Douglas Durst's attorney and friend—turned to me and said, "I never thought you would pull this off." Gary had been skeptical of the whole idea. Better than most, he knew that we had undertaken a Herculean task that would never have come to fruition without persistence and significant financial support.

Water Taxi billboard at 4 Times Square. (Tom Fox)

A Major Setback

Mayor Giuliani and City Planning Commissioner Joe Rose had released a plan to rezone "Far West Midtown from 24th to 42nd Streets shorty before leaving office.[25] An editorial in *City Journal* encouraged Bloomberg to embrace the plan and extend it south to 14th Street.[26] Many of the park advocates saw the rezoning as an opportunity to generate a critical new funding stream for the park that had yet to be secured. As Doctoroff stated, "The West Side presents the best opportunity for the city to invest in its future and grow."[27] It soon became apparent that Bloomberg had plans for the entire West Side.

Local community boards and elected officials objected to much of the rezoning. Nevertheless, over the next decade, City Hall undertook what became the most comprehensive rezoning in West Side history. They rezoned properties from warehousing, manufacturing, and transportation to residential and commercial offices and increased building density along four miles of Route 9A from North Moore Street in Tribeca to West 59th Street in Hell's Kitchen.

With a few exceptions, including historic districts championed by the Greenwich Village Society for Historic Preservation and the West Chelsea Historic District, the strip was transformed from low-rise manufacturing, warehousing, and commercial transportation uses into higher-density residential and commercial office development.

Doctoroff was appointed vice chairman of the trust and Diana Taylor was a trust board member. With two individuals close to the mayor serving on the trust board, Bloomberg was certainly aware of the challenges facing the park in terms of financing its completion and long-term care. I hoped that Bloomberg would finally create the last critical public financing element needed to support the park.

Bloomberg was a creative businessman and could have structured a rezoning plan that included a creative funding mechanism to support the park and set a precedent for self-sufficient parks throughout the country. Instead, he ignored the panel's recommendation to secure support from the increased value of inboard real estate or leverage significant private funding and deprived the park of critical resources for its long-term viability.

Both Friends and the Hudson River Park Alliance were increasingly concerned about inadequate funding and encouraged the city and state to identify new revenue sources to supplement the public funding previously committed. Balachandran declared that the governor and mayor regarded the park as a once-in-a-lifetime opportunity, while a trust spokesperson proclaimed that Bloomberg "has given every indication that he understands how important this project is to the city."[28] Nonetheless, nothing happened.

The city simply amplified Pataki's false claim that the park was required to be self-sufficient and funded solely by private donations and commercial revenues generated in the park. Simply put, both city and state offloaded their responsibility to provide public support for the park and instead played to pro-development interests. As a result, more densely developed inboard neighborhoods would place increasing demands on the park without providing any new support. In addition, development pressure within the park increased as the trust focused on commercialization of the park itself.

Bloomberg eventually invested over $700 million in city tax revenue on the construction of other park projects that could be branded as "his"—The High Line, Brooklyn Bridge Park, and Governors Island. In effect, the model proposed for a self-financing park was bastardized and used to justify commercial development in future parks, while the significant economic value that the parks generate was conveniently ignored.

Trying to Redevelop Pier 40

The permits held by C&K Properties, a property management and development group, to operate Pier 40 expired in December of 2003, and the trust released a Request for an Expression of Interest at the beginning of 2002. The document asked bidders to increase parking from 2,000 to 2,900 vehicles. Pier 40, located at Houston Street, was one of the park's three areas designated for park-related commercial development and expected to contribute to the park's self-sufficiency.

Chelsea Piers, another of those areas, was already developed, and commercial maritime uses occupied the entire Midtown Maritime District. The third designated area included the passenger ship terminals that had been removed by the Giuliani administration. So the long-term economic viability of the park's largest structure was critical to the trust's financial future.

The redevelopment options for Pier 40 were limited because residential, commercial offices, and hotels were prohibited by the act. Moreover, the act required that Pier 40 provide significant open space for public use because it was one of the few piers that had enough space to accommodate baseball, soccer, and football fields. Tobi Bergman—a member of Community Board 2, a former employee of the city's Department of Parks and Recreation and a Friends board member—had helped establish an organization called Pier, Park & Playground to advocate for active recreation at Pier 40.

In May, the trust leadership asked State Assembly members Dick Gottfried and Deborah Glick to support an amendment to the act allowing the existing lease at Pier 40 to continue operating on a month-to-month basis, without a fixed term, but they failed to make their request public. When the Assembly members informed Friends and the alliance of the request, both strenuously objected.[29] It was the first of several attempts by the trust to amend the act. This one failed, and at their June meeting, the trust board announced that any future amendments to the act would require their approval.[30]

The trust had released a Request for Expression of Interest and by the summer of 2002, the responses were made public.[31] Proposals ranged from big-box stores to an aquarium and exposition center, but they all contained varying amounts of retail activity. Because a primary concern of Community Board 2 was traffic, proposals such as the one from Forest City Ratner, which included three big-box stores, generated strong community resistance.

Also, although proposal drawings and renderings were displayed in the lobby of Pier 40, the specifics of each proposal could only be viewed at the trust's small trailer about a mile away in Battery Park City. The arrangement of separating the proposal drawings from the information needed to assess their benefits and impact sent a clear message about the agency's receptiveness to public participation. The trust began to operate Pier 40, which was generating more than $7 million per year, but none of that money was spent to maintain the pier.

FedEx was already a major tenant at Pier 40, and C&K teamed up with the Durst Organization to compete for the lease. FedEx wanted to build a new sorting and delivery facility at the pier and transport packages that arrived daily at Newark Airport to Manhattan by water. However, after the initial submission, FedEx decided that waterborne transportation was prohibitively expensive, which forced C&K/Durst to modify their proposal to include a Home Depot—a use allowed under the existing zoning because Pier 40 was in a manufacturing zone where hardware stores are allowed.

Of the four competing respondents, Community Board 2 objected most to Forest City Ratner's plan for three big-box stores.[32] The final choice came down to C&K/Durst versus the Oceanarium, a proposal for a five-acre multistory aquarium. That proposal, however, included offices, which were prohibited, and did not include the full-size athletic fields that were important to the community. Eventually, Community Board 2 announced its support for the C&K/Durst proposal.[33]

However, in June, trust chairman Ortenzio inexplicably withdrew the Request for Expression of Interest and announced that the trust was hiring a marketing team to help determine the best use of the pier. The stock market had recently experienced one of its cyclical downturns and the trust decided it would only allow interim recreational improvements until the economic climate improved. That decision set the entire project back to square one.

The Greenwich Village Segment Opens

A grand celebration was held in June of 2003 to open the first segment of the park on Pier 45 at Christopher Street.[34] The guest list included Pataki, Bloomberg, Borough President C. Virginia Fields, trust board members and staff, local elected officials, and community, environmental, and civic leaders. It was gratifying to see a celebration of a mutual accomplishment. It was even sweeter for those who actually made it happen.

The community's designs for Greenwich Village were primarily focused on passive recreation like picnicking, sunning, and strolling. The rebuilt Pier 45 and half of Pier 46 were large open lawns with clusters of trees, shade structures, walkways around the perimeters, and seating. The remnant 160-foot section of Pier 51 became a popular water playground for young children, and the esplanade was edged with lawns and landscaped gardens. There were restrooms at Piers 45 and 51 and a decorative fountain at Christopher Street, the primary Village portal into the park, but there were few recreation areas for particular uses—like the Leroy Street dog park—in this first segment of the park.

When the task force was considering the future of the West Side, Marcy Benstock advocated for painting the waterfront green and letting the piers fall into the river so nature could reclaim the estuary. Her priority was the fish, not the hundreds of thousands of people who lived adjacent to the park. Most park proponents wanted to benefit both, and the Village segment proved that this was possible. Large open-water areas and the piles that once held up now-missing decks on Piers 42 and 49 remained to support the aquatic habitat, while the landscaped esplanade, public piers, and playground were filled with people enjoying themselves, each other, and the wonders of the Hudson.

But although the metamorphosis of the Village waterfront was spectacular, signs soon emerged that the trust viewed recreation in the park more

Pier 45 at Christopher Street with the Richard Meier buildings in the background, 2006. (Tom Fox)

commercially. That fall, Red Bull hosted an event called "Flugtag" on Pier 45 in which human-powered craft were pushed off an elevated platform to see how long they could stay aloft before crashing into the Hudson. Banners and loudspeakers promoted the event with a roar, and food trucks parked along the esplanade.[35] Across Route 9A, two residential towers between Charles and Perry Streets—and designed by Richard Meier—had recently opened, presenting an ominous picture of things to come.[36]

Toward the end of that year, the trust issued a Request for Proposals for commercial redevelopment at Pier 57. By then, it appeared that commercial development was the trust's priority and the creation of a grand public space on the waterfront less so. In addition, to accommodate new real estate development, the city relocated the city's mounted police stables from their longtime home on West 42nd Street to Pier 63.[37]

Frying Pan and Pier 63 Maritime

One of the few public spaces along the Chelsea waterfront was Pier 63 Maritime at 23rd Street. Its main attraction was a pair of historic vessels: the *Frying*

Pan, a lightship that once illuminated Frying Pan Shoals in South Carolina, and the *John J. Harvey,* the fireboat being restored by a team of river rats.

The free-spirited Captain John Krevey had raised *Frying Pan* from the mud, installed a diesel truck engine, and sailed her up to the New York in 1989. The vessel then moved from pier to pier, guided by John's creative genius and tenacity. In 1995, he restored a historic railroad car float (barge) originally built for the Delaware–Lackawanna–Western Railroad, and the conservancy had given him a permit to moor at Pier 63.[38] John was a Renaissance man—electrician, welder, entrepreneur, restaurateur, maritime historian, and a founding member of both the North River Historic Ship Society and Friends of Hudson River Park.

He attracted like-minded individuals, and the barge provided important public access to the Hudson. With kayak storage and a launch, a bar, a small restaurant, a stage with a dance floor, and public restrooms, Pier 63 Maritime became a local hangout and gathering place for a growing cadre of urban mariners. As the park became more developed, Krevey and other maritime advocates worried that the pioneers who had opened the waterfront might be displaced by more commercially oriented development.[39]

They had some cause for concern because Ortenzio had hired Archibald Robinson, his former law school professor, to help Balachandran with legal advice regarding tenants. On arrival, Robinson made it clear that he was the new sheriff in town and told tenants that the trust was going to get stricter with both events and tenant oversights. However, Robertson's tenure was short-lived. He overindulged at an awards luau at Pier 63 Maritime sponsored by New York Outrigger, and he was seen staggering down the pier and urinating in a garbage can in front of three guests, who reported the incident to Balachandran. Robertson left the trust, and Ortenzio apologized for his actions.[40]

Friends of the High Line

A nearby abandoned structure that held the promise of adding public open space to the Chelsea neighborhood was the abandoned elevated rail line known as the High Line that Peter Obletz had purchased for $10 and attempted to save in the late 1980s.[41] Giuliani wanted to demolish the structure but in 1999, but Joshua David and Robert Hammond formed a group called Friends of the High Line to advocate for adaptive reuse of the mile and a half portion of the High Line that ran south from the Javits Convention Center through Chelsea, ending at Gansevoort Street.

In 2002, Bloomberg sought permission from the U.S. Department of Transportation to allow the right-of-way to be used as a trail that complemented his planned Olympic Stadium.[42] Chelsea, once a working-class neighborhood, was at this point a rapidly gentrifying area—its development driven by art galleries that had been priced out of Soho. Many of the new neighbors, like the fashion designer Diane von Furstenberg, championed the High Line cause, and in late 2002, Friends of the High Line issued a "Call for Ideas" that received a wide range of entries from around the world, followed eventually by a design competition.

The concept was an adaptation of Coulée Verte René-Dumont, a tree-lined park built atop an unused rail line in Paris that had opened in 1993.[43] The project was innovative, the design ideas were captivating, and the repurposing of the High Line as a public space was a brilliant idea that garnered broad community support and resources.[44]

The property beneath and adjacent to the High Line had multiple private owners who supported Giuliani's efforts to tear it down so they could develop their land. The city created transferable development rights for these properties and rezoned parts of the surrounding area to increase density so those property owners could sell their air rights.[45] It was frustrating that Bloomberg and City Planning chairperson Amanda Burden used creative mechanisms here but seemed unwilling to use them to support the Hudson River Park.

As post-9/11 plans for Lower Manhattan took shape, State Assembly Speaker Shelley Silver supported the trust's $70 million request that Lower Manhattan Development Corporation complete the Tribeca segment of the park, which was damaged by the 9/11 terrorist attack.[46]

But the trust's obfuscation continued, as was demonstrated by their proposal to build an ice-skating rink south of Pier 40 on the same site where tennis courts had recently been built. At their fall board meeting, Balachandran announced that additional money would be used to convert the tennis courts to a covered ice-skating rink, and he stated that Pataki had been thinking about the project for months. A permanent structure was required to keep the ice cold in the summer and protect skaters from the wicked winter northwest wind whipping off the Hudson.[47] However, Rob had not bothered to inform Community Board 2 or the Advisory Council, and the trust board had not even been told about it. No one was pleased with the surprise.

The next month, as I lamented the trust's growing lack of public involvement,[48] the Neighborhood Open Space Coalition warned its member organizations about the increasing commercialization in the park.[49] Thankfully, Balachandran resigned from the trust in December.[50]

12

Hope Renewed, Problems Continue (2004–2008)

● ● ● ● ● ● ● ● ● ● ● ● ● ●

Twenty years after the defeat of Westway, the public was beginning to see the metamorphosis of the waterfront in Greenwich Village. However, the park budget began to suffer from reductions in state and city funding, and there were continuing leadership changes at the trust.

In the fall of 2003, Governor Pataki nominated James Ortenzio as chair of the Manhattan Republican County Committee; he accepted and resigned as chairman of Hudson River Park Trust. Charles E. "Trip" Dorkey III, another Republican fundraiser and a partner in Torys LLP, a Canadian law firm with a sizable New York office, replaced him.

Connie Fishman, who represented the Giuliani administration during park planning and the Hudson River Park Act negotiations, was appointed president in January of 2004. Connie had a good relationship with the local community and civic groups and understood the role that community participation played in creating the park. Noreen Doyle returned as a vice president, and together these "veterans" provided continuity, which was welcome and gave park proponents hope that a more proactive and cooperative approach to park planning and development might return.

That January, Arthur Schwartz sued the trust to force the selection of a developer for Pier 40 and prevent interim improvements on the pier. It was not clear who he was representing, but he was opposed by Community Board 2, local elected officials, and many of the sports leagues.[1] His suit never got traction, and the trust proceeded with plans to build sports fields in Pier 40's inner courtyard, which were strongly supported by the local community.[2]

A year after the Greenwich Village segment of the park opened, the impact of the public investment was apparent as the new park captured the interest of real estate developers.[3] However, without the ability to secure new revenue from inboard properties, the trust began to experience major problems funding capital construction.

In July of 2004, Friends increased the pressure on the new trust leadership to secure additional funding. Connie agreed to schedule a meeting with Trip Dorkey, and Al Butzel provided Douglas Durst, who had been unable to attend, with a brief describing a range of options that were discussed. The initially aggressive Dorkey mellowed during the meeting, but Al was sure that he would call Ortenzio afterward and probably regress.[4]

Butzel also sent our funding strategy memo to the Hudson River Park Alliance, and sixteen of the remaining alliance members signed letters imploring Pataki and Bloomberg to identify $170 million in new public funding.[5] I followed with a memo to Butzel and Paul Elston describing various mechanisms used across the country to generate financial support for parks.[6] Friends urged the Lower Manhattan Development Corporation to fund construction of the Tribeca portion of the park, and the trust finally petitioned the federal government for funding.[7]

The Olympic Stadium is Defeated

The Bloomberg administration was finalizing its bid for the 2012 Olympics and had proposed rezoning and platforming over the MTA's West Side railroad yards to build an Olympic/NY Jets Stadium and an expanded convention center while construction of the Midtown West ferry terminal moved forward.[8]

Toward the end of 2004, thousands of construction workers rallied in front of Madison Square Garden to support the proposed stadium and the 2012 Olympic bid.[9] Cablevision owned the Garden and apparently did not want competition, so it opposed both. Several months later, the city submitted its final bid for the 2012 Olympics to the International Olympics Committee. We were competing with London, Madrid, and Moscow.[10] The stadium plan was killed when state legislative leaders refused to support the project in 2005.

During 2004, the park began to receive professional recognition from landscape architects, engineers, archivists, graphic designers, and the Waterfront Center—a national waterfront advocacy organization.[11] The precedent-setting transformation of Manhattan's West Side waterfront was being recognized nationally.

Pier 57 Redevelopment

By January of 2005, the two local organizations that submitted bids to redevelop Pier 57 were eliminated. Two teams remained in the running: Chelsea Piers Management and restaurateur Giuseppe Cipriani. Local activists and politicians were upset that the local bids were eliminated, and some joked that the contest was between two powerful Republicans—Ortenzio versus Roland Betts. Ortenzio, who had resigned at the end of 2003, was quoted as favoring the Cipriani team in early 2004 but denied any personal preference.[12] The Hudson River Park Act precluded commercial offices, hotels, or residential development, so the respondents had to be creative.

Chelsea Piers Management proposed expanding south to Pier 57 with a swim center, a marina, a tennis bubble on the roof, and a variety of cultural activities ranging from dance and art galleries to sound studios for National Public Radio. But their failure to honor their initial agreements at Chelsea Piers apparently raised concerns among the community and elected officials.

In October of 2002, for example, even though retail activities unrelated to the uses of the piers were prohibited, full-page ads in the *New York Times* solicited shoppers to purchase their Christmas gifts aboard a Target holiday boat docked at Chelsea Piers from November 1 to December 15.[13] Target donated 5 percent of their holiday boat proceeds to the trust, which got a little piece of the action. It did not win Chelsea Piers Management many friends, and it never happened again.

The restaurateur Giuseppe Cipriani partnered with the developer Steven C. Witkoff to propose an Italian-themed project dubbed "Leonardo." They proposed installing a branch of an Italian design museum with stores and shops owned and operated by Italian artisans and craftspeople. The major attraction was the city's largest banquet hall and event space, and their plan included a marina and a rooftop park, which appealed to many Chelsea residents and seemed more consistent with the Hudson River Park.[14]

The competition got nasty. Cipriani claimed that Chelsea Piers was supported by Deputy Mayor Dan Doctoroff, who hoped that Roland Betts would influence his friend, President Bush, to support his Olympic bid. Chelsea Piers, in turn, analyzed the impact of Cipriani's banquet hall and event center, which would compete directly with their profitable event spaces at Piers 60 and 61. They claimed that the Cipriani/Witkoff plan would generate unacceptable levels of traffic. Somehow, the trust received letters stating that a mob turncoat's testimony at a John Gotti trial claimed Cipriani paid the Gambino family for union labor peace.[15]

In April, the trust selected the Cipriani team to redevelop the pier.[16] And in July, stating that Pier 57 was a historic site, the state amended the Hudson River Park Act to allow a forty-nine-year lease at Pier 57 but noted that it should be the only pier granted such a long lease.[17]

As supporters hoped, the trust leadership began focusing on public projects in the park. In April, athletic groups celebrated when the interim ball fields were opened on Pier 40.[18] Schwartz had withdrawn his lawsuit, and the trust spent about $3 million placing artificial turf fields in the center courtyard of the pier. The demand for baseball, soccer, football, and other active recreational use was overwhelming, but unfortunately the park's narrow esplanade and piers did not have enough space to accommodate many sports fields.

Spring saw the opening of the first two-acre section of Clinton Cove Park with a new boathouse and access to the river at Pier 96. The opening was quickly followed by an announcement that Lower Manhattan Development Corporation had allocated $70 million from recovery funds to the reconstruction of Piers 25 and 26 in Tribeca.[19] In addition, Congressman Jerry Nadler secured $5 million from the federal Water Resources Development Act to support pier reconstruction and estuary enhancements.[20]

Friends Grows Stronger

Connie Fishman understood the importance of Friends and thanked us for our advocacy with the Lower Manhattan Development Corporation, adding that she looked forward to working with us.[21] A week later, two relevant editorials appeared on the same day in the *New York Times*.[22] The first chided Bloomberg for diverting $300 million of payments in lieu of taxes from real estate projects unrelated to the stadium to the Industrial Development Agency—whose board he controlled—to help finance the proposed stadium. This only magnified my frustration that the mayor would not consider a similar mechanism to capture increased revenue from the inboard real estate for the park.

The second editorial mentioned the buzz about Brooklyn Bridge Park and reminded New Yorkers that the first project to turn the city's attention to waterfront revitalization was Hudson River Park. The editorial mentioned the new funding for the Tribeca waterfront while noting that the completion of the park continued to face hurdles.[23]

The Friends staff was small. Al Butzel was supported by junior staff who helped prepare position papers and testimony for public meetings, grow the membership, and communicate our message, including our occasional newsletter, while supporting fundraising and the annual gala.[24] Most importantly, our board committees met frequently and were quite active, but Butzel had a lot on his plate. So, Friends decided to increase the staff.

That spring, Al hired Matthew Washington, a recent Alfred University graduate with an interest in open space, education, and community participation. He often accompanied Al to Albany and City Hall. Matthew was observant, soft-spoken, and intelligent. He provided much-needed support for Al, put in long hours, and learned quickly. A few months after joining Friends, Matthew was appointed to Community Board 11 in East Harlem where he eventually became chairman.

Walking up the esplanade that spring, Vince McGowan and I noticed new construction behind a building on the Gansevoort Peninsula. The city sanitation department was building a new garage on the Gansevoort Peninsula, which they were required to vacate. We alerted the Friends board. Ross Graham, former chairman of Community Board 4, was now Douglas's cochair, and the organization was beginning to step up its advocacy. We had asked the sanitation department to remove its trucks from Pier 97 a year earlier, after the Hudson River Park Act's December 31, 2003, deadline for their removal, but the request fell on deaf ears.[25]

At that time, Butzel warned the trust that Friends might consider legal action, but City Hall pushed back, claiming that it bought a second property across Route 9A at 57th Street and planned to relocate the garage within three years. Friends demanded that the sanitation department stop construction on Gansevoort, but they refused. It was evident that they were not using "best efforts" to remove the facilities from Gansevoort or Pier 97. It also showed that the trust was unwilling, or unable, to enforce the act.

With a more assertive leadership in place, Friends sued the city, the state, and the trust to force the removal of the garbage trucks and maintenance facilities from the park. We were represented by Danny Alterman of Alterman and Boop, a boutique law firm located in Tribeca. He was a friend of Douglas, a West Side resident, and a successful civil rights attorney.[26] Two advocacy groups from Clinton, concerned about the shrinking Clinton Cove Park, joined the suit.

At Gansevoort, we were joined by local elected officials and members of Community Board 2 who hoped that the landfilled peninsula—one of the few places in the park big enough to accommodate ball fields—would eventually be used for active recreation. We had asked politely and had gotten nowhere. The litigation was Friends' first forceful move against government agencies standing in the way of park development; it could not have happened without the financial support of the Durst family.

Water Taxi Beach

In 2005, New York Water Taxi created a beach on a vacant lot adjacent to our water taxi stop in Long Island City. Residents there wanted weekend service, but no one traveled to Long Island City on the weekend. Mark Baker, who was still on the board of the Brooklyn Bridge Park Coalition, was now Water Taxi's chief business officer. He thought that creating some sort of attraction at our Long Island City location, which was in the middle of a former industrial area, might make that stop more viable. We devised a plan and convinced the Port Authority that developing a "temporary passenger amenity adjacent to a ferry terminal" would increase seasonal traffic and help New York Water Taxi continue the service.

We dumped four hundred tons of sand, erected a volleyball court and a small tent, set up picnic tables, and engaged chef Harry Hawk and his partners to open a funky beach bar and restaurant and manage the facility. Although the beach was on an abandoned stretch of former industrial waterfront, the place was an instant hit. Locals of all ages visited during the day, while evening concerts attracted hundreds of revelers who danced in the light of the moon and often took our water taxi back and forth from Manhattan.

An editorial in the *New York Times* described the effort as "Imagination on the Waterfront."[27] We gave credit to the Port Authority for its flexibility and for giving us the opportunity. To be honest, it is not often that the word "imagination" is used to describe the Port Authority. Publicly thanking those responsible, especially public agencies, builds teamwork. We doubled the size of the beach the following year and helped our fledgling company financially. Our year-to-year lease continued for another five years.

The Tribeca Piers

By the end of 2005, there were positive developments on both sides of Route 9A. Pier 25 was closed and anticipating reconstruction, which was welcomed but bittersweet for many of us.[28] I had spent innumerable hours enjoying Pier 25, one of the few piers open to the public and safe to use. Bob Townley, a gregarious mensch who founded Manhattan Youth, an important Downtown nonprofit organization, ran the place.

The conservancy had issued a permit to Manhattan Youth to operate there early in 1995. Bob offered an eclectic mix of activities—beach volleyball, roller skating, children's play areas, a driftwood-and-flotsam sculpture garden, a miniature golf course made with recycled materials, and ping-pong and picnic tables. Dubbie ran the rebranded Sweet Love Snack Bar and almost always beat me at ping-pong. Veso Buntic, a talented welder, helped build and maintain many of the improvements to the pier and managed the beach volleyball courts. Jimmy Gallagher was restoring the *Yankee*, the last of the Ellis Island ferries, on the north side of the pier. There were barbecues, music, and great nighttime dancing on the pier and aboard the *Yankee* until he sold the vessel.

The Downtown Boathouse operated from containers on the apron between Pier 25, and The River Project was on Pier 26. Pier 25 was a local hangout where Tribeca residents and park proponents gathered to play, dream, and scheme—funky, but a very functional example of what human ingenuity and waterfront access can create. Bob Townley hoped the future Pier 25 would contain a mix of active and passive recreation activities—although we were all sure it would not be quite as funky. The conservancy had incorporated a "funky crab shack" on Pier 25 and it was included in the General Project Plan for the park, along with a town dock, a mooring field, and historic ship berths.

The trust served an eviction notice to the *Yankee* to facilitate the reconstruction of Pier 25. The historic vessel had been bought by a couple who completed the restoration begun by Jimmy Gallagher and upgraded the interior as their home. After they completed the renovation, however, the *Yankee* afforded little interpretive benefit to the public other than as a visual amenity and the occasional home tour. Eventually, the trust changed the locks on Pier 25's entrance, marooning the *Yankee* and generating bitter complaints from its new owners. In due course they sailed off, and the reconstruction went forward as planned.[29]

Court Settlement and Solid Waste Controversy

By November of 2005, Friends reached a settlement that penalized the city $21.5 million for failing to remove its facilities by the deadline set in the Hudson River Park Act. The sanitation department was given until 2012 to remove the garbage trucks from Pier 97 and Gansevoort along with a shed where they stored salt for use in the winter. Consequently, they built two modern sanitation garages across Route 9A with a $250 million six-story garage at 56th Street. A five-story garage on Spring Street with a green roof and an award-winning $21 million salt shed north of Canal Street were both built despite being strongly opposed by neighbors, including James Gandolfini and Lou Reed.[30]

Friends celebrated the victory, and Community Board 4 shared a rendering that its community design consultant had prepared for Pier 97.[31] In six months, Friends had generated new funding for the park and forced the city

Spring Street sanitation garage and salt shed. (Tom Fox)

to comply with the act. Although the trust could not publicly applaud our initiative, they were clearly pleased with the results, and Friends was now taken much more seriously.

The year ended, however, on a strange note. Manhattan District Attorney Cyrus Vance announced that he had received an anonymous letter accusing James Ortenzio of steering the Pier 57 bid to the Cipriani family, one of his business clients.[32]

It suddenly seemed to make sense why the trust might use its limited funds to paint Pier 57 while James was chairman. It would benefit Cipriani, who, perhaps coincidentally, dubbed the proposed project "Leonardo"—the "park name" Henry Stern had given Ortenzio. Cipriani withdrew from the Pier 57 project, and his partner Witcoff carried on alone.

The new year began with concerns about the impact of the city's Solid Waste Management Plan on the park. The city had initially announced their plan in 2002. Two existing marine transfer stations were already in the park. The plan expanded the facility at Pier 99 and changed its focus from paper recycling to household waste while rebuilding the unused facility on Gansevoort Peninsula to process recycled materials.

Another marine transfer station included in the plan was on the Upper East Side, where a lawsuit had blocked implementation of the plan—until now.[33] In 2004, the proposed scope of the project's environmental impact statement was released for public review. Michael Bradley, now at Riverside South Planning Corporation, submitted detailed comments regarding the deficiencies in the characterization of the study area around 59th Street, the draft scope, and possible conflicts with plans to relocate Route 9A inboard in the future.[34] Friends agreed with Bradley's concerns, but our requests were ignored, which was another precursor to our successful suit.[35]

The city insisted Gansevoort Peninsula could accommodate recreation and a recycling facility but declared that the Hudson River Park Act might have to be amended to allow for their plan's execution. Many environmental advocates were determined to ensure equitable distribution of solid-waste facilities throughout the city, and this issue pitted environmental groups against one another.

Although sympathetic to distributing the solid waste disposal burden equitably, local elected officials, community organizations, and park advocates—including Friends—objected to siting two marine transfer stations in the park.[36] The New York League of Conservation Voters and the Environmental Defense Fund supported the city, and in 2008, the act was amended to allow a recycling station—with environmental education—at Gansevoort.[37]

Twenty Years after Westway

In the spring of 2006, the trust was developing a code of ethics, as required by the 2005 Public Authorities Accountability Act. Board members were surprised at their April meeting by proposed text that read, "Trust directors, officers and employees shall avoid any unauthorized *ex parte* communications concerning a pending matter and avoid comment about such a matter outside the trust director's, officer's, and employee's official duties." Several members objected strongly to what they considered an infringement of their First Amendment rights, and that language was eliminated.[38]

Apparently, it was not enough that the governor and mayor chose the board members; they wanted to gag them too. It was a far cry from where we started, and it was ironic because it was the twentieth anniversary of the withdrawal of Westway and the initiation of the public planning process that created the park.[39]

Concerned about inadequate long-term park funding, Friends began a multiyear research effort to document the impact that the park's first completed segment, in Greenwich Village, had on adjacent real estate values and to suggest mechanisms to capture some of that value for the park. The Durst family was our primary patron, and Douglas served on the board of the Regional Plan Association, which had advised on the panel's 1990 study, and the Real Estate Board of New York. He convinced both organizations to join the project steering committee.

Design and Construction Problems Continue

Park construction funding was scarce, and as several newly built elements of the park began to fail, the impact of reduced construction budgets and inexperienced staff became clearer. Pavers on Pier 45 were beginning to crack just a year after installation, and the new fields at Pier 40 were flooding.[40] The trust debated whether the problems were poor design, substandard materials, or improper installation, but other park elements were showing wear as well. The problems were exacerbated by a shortage of money for maintenance and the fact that most contractors refused to work with the trust's design and construction team after their initial interaction because they were difficult to work with and did not want constructive feedback—even if it improved a project.

The failures should have been investigated, and the source of problems should have identified and corrected prior to any future park construction. But the same pavers were still used on Pier 84 in Midtown, which opened in 2006, and throughout the park. They continued to crack and required repair and replacement.

The problem was, and continues to be, the thickness of the pavers. Pavers used in Battery Park City Park and other city parks are 3.5 inches thick, yet—to reduce costs—the trust design and construction team specified two-inch thick pavers. Driving vehicles of almost any size on the piers required plywood to be laid atop the pavers to protect them from cracking. The decorative fountains at Piers 45 and 84 were another disaster. Although working when first installed, they required constant repair.

In a private company, these issues would be addressed, specifications would be modified, and those responsible would presumably be let go. The cost of correcting repeated mistakes would be unacceptable. Unfortunately, the trust's vice president of design and construction did not seem to understand that concept. How he oversaw hundreds of millions of dollars in park construction for so long is a mystery to many.

Most projects are designed by professional architects, landscape architects, and engineers. The projects are reviewed and implemented under the direction of the trust, which develops, or approves, specifications for components such as pavers, railings, lighting, benches, maritime elements, and water features. I have heard of numerous complaints from construction professionals, contractors, engineers, mariners, and tenants about substandard designs, shoddy materials, poor installation, and inadequate construction oversight.

The trust's chief engineer seemingly compounded problems. He was a licensed professional engineer and diver but not a design engineer. He joined the trust in 2001 and is responsible for many substandard elements in the park, particularly in-water construction. For example, the floats he specified at Piers 25 and 66 were poorly chosen and reinstalled improperly. They were parallel to the river instead of perpendicular, and the impact of wind-blown swells and ferry wakes required their constant repair until replacements were installed properly.

His preferred concrete piles were precast with holes in the top to accept rebar. When not immediately filled with rebar or grout, rainwater collected there and, if temperatures dropped, the water expanded and shattered the pile tops.

Park Professionals and Financing

Hudson River Park is the largest park built in Manhattan since Central Park. Would Frederick Law Olmsted tolerate this quality of design and construction in Central Park, or would the Central Park Conservancy allow it in restoration and operation? Robert Moses could not have created his incredible park legacy without talented architects, landscape architects, engineers, sculptors, masons, arborists, and the like.

The Hudson River Park is a high-profile public work viewed as a national model for urban waterfront revitalization. You would think the trust would have had its pick of the finest design and construction professionals in the public realm. These days, however, politics often get in the way of sound decision-making.

Entities, or authorities, with politically appointed boards are increasingly overseeing the creation of new public parks. Those projects are often planned and managed by political appointees and not experienced park professionals. Decisions are often made by inexperienced leadership responding to political pressure rather than the quality of their performance, public participation, the product, and professional peer review.

I have great respect and appreciation for park and recreation professionals who plan, operate, and maintain our public patrimony creatively and responsibly. They are dedicated and doing the best they can, often in the face of reduced budgets and political interference. These caring professionals are critical to the future of America's parks and recreation heritage. I would encourage young professionals to pursue a fulfilling career in public parks. As you explore and embrace nature, you can teach the children and involve people in its protection and care. You experience the best of both worlds.

Unreasonable demands for self-sufficiency often result in overcommercialization allowing real estate development and management staff to play an outsized role in planning and operations. You need competent real estate and property management professionals to get the best deal possible if there is any commercial development in public parks and to keep an eye on the store.

But every public works project has unique goals and physical, social, and financial parameters. In the Hudson River Park, public funds were hard to come by. There was a significant amount of built space on the waterfront, preserving existing commercial maritime activity was important, and the adjacent neighborhoods were ripe for rezoning and lightly populated, which minimized gentrification.

In this unique situation, limited commercial development in the park was one element in a three-legged stool proposed to insure self-sufficiency. Every new park has positive impacts on surrounding real estate and the local economy. Public funding and capturing revenue from inboard property appreciation were the other two. However, I may have unwittingly contributed to the myth of a self-sufficient Hudson River Park by believing that elected officials would commit some funding from inboard real estate appreciation to the long-term needs of the park as proposed in our initial financing recommendations, or in any other form.

Another Request for Proposals for Pier 40

The trust issued a second Request for Proposals for Pier 40, and two responses were under review as 2007 rolled in. Big-box retail had been ruled out, and the respondents had very different visions for the pier's future.[41]

A joint venture, called "Pier 40 PAC," among the Related Companies, Cirque du Soleil, and the Tribeca Film Festival proposed building a downtown performing arts center that included a two-acre theater for shows, a large restaurant, a club, a movie complex operated by the Tribeca Film Festival, two large private event spaces, and a fifty-slip marina. The plan would cover the pier's center courtyard and move the ball fields to the roof, despite the wicked winter northwesterly winds.

The People's Pier was proposed by Urban Dove, a nonprofit organization that uses sports to teach life skills to at-risk teens, and CampGroup, a group of summer camps that teaches students skills that are not learned in the classroom but are thought to be critical for success. Both were founded in 1998, and their proposal focused on athletics and education. They kept the ball fields in the courtyard, expanded the rooftop fields, and included multi-use courts, several swimming pools, a large summer camp, a high school, and a college complex almost double the size of the parking facility. They had the support of Pier, Park, and Playground (P3), whose president, Tobi Bergman, was also a member of Community Board 2.

By April, both respondents had refined their proposals, and Community Board 2, always wary of new development, reviewed both submissions. The neighborhood drums signaled opposition to what was dubbed "Vegas on the Hudson."[42] However popular the People's Pier was, there were serious questions about its economic feasibility and ability to generate the funding the park required. Final presentations were made in May, and debate continued through the year.

Earlier that summer, the groundbreaking ceremony for the reconstruction of Piers 25 and 26 was attended by Governor Pataki, local elected officials, and community members. Missing from the announcement, however, was an initial element—the "estuarium" that was planned to expand the pioneering work of The River Project at Pier 26 to support marine research and environmental education programs in the park.

The Estuarium, Orphaned Again

In 2003, the trust had entered into an agreement with the Beacon Institute to design, build, and operate the estuarium. The institute was created with public funding championed by Governor Pataki in 2000 and was planned to partner with the State University at Stony Brook, which had a robust marine science program.

Many saw the selection of the Beacon Institute and Stony Brook as another attempt to offload public responsibility for building and operating park facilities to minimize design and construction costs and long-term maintenance and operations. Trust chairman Trip Dorkey III, a Pataki appointee, sat on the Beacon Institute's board, but the institute had very little experience, especially in fundraising.

Unfortunately, Beacon was unable to meet its commitments by the time the trust started construction at Piers 25 and 26 and the project was put on hold.[43] Beacon eventually faded from the scene, but it would not be the trust's last failed attempt to offload the construction and operation of the estuarium.

The wider portion of the apron between Piers 25 and 26 closest to the bulkhead included a new Downtown Boathouse and access ramps adjacent to the esplanade. Space was set aside in that area for the estuarium. However, the "funky crab shack" envisioned by the conservancy at Pier 26 became a much larger building than initially planned, with outdoor and rooftop seating. In addition, it was eventually operated by City Winery, a popular Tribeca dinner and entertainment venue. It was another reminder that the trust's priority was generating revenue rather than environmental education and research.

The attention to the park's Tribeca section stimulated the recycling of an old idea when James Gill, chairman of Battery Park City Authority, proposed extending their landfill from Chambers Street to Canal Street and expanding

Battery Park City in October.[44] It was the same proposal Sandy Frucher made in 1986 and seemingly the last gasp of a Pataki appointee trying to influence the future of the West Side before the governor's departure. It went nowhere, and Eliot Spitzer was elected governor of New York State in November.

In December, the trust celebrated the opening of Pier 66 with another boathouse, which eventually housed Hudson River Community Sailing, a nonprofit youth sailing academy that diversified the park's people-powered public boathouses enlivening the waterway. The trust placed a decorative tidal wheel at the pier's tip.[45]

Tragedy on the Bicycle Path

But 2006 ended on a tragic note, revealing a fatal flaw in the bicycle path adjacent to Route 9A. In December, a drunken reveler leaving a holiday party at the Chelsea Piers mistook the bicycle path for Route 9A and drove over a mile south until he struck and killed a twenty-two-year-old named Eric Ng.[46] Eric was an active member of Transportation Alternatives, a bicycle and pedestrian advocacy group.

As an avid bicyclist, I attended Eric's memorial service. A "ghost bike" was placed on the path where he was killed as a memorial to his life and a reminder of the importance of bicycle safety. It was the second fatality on the bicycle path that year. The previous June, a beloved local doctor had been struck and killed by a police department tow truck entering Pier 76 and crossing the path.

These deaths followed a long list of vehicle and bicycle interactions on the path that should never have happened. Surprisingly and tragically, the issues were never addressed. In 2014, another bicyclist was run over by a shuttle bus entering the Pier 79 ferry terminal, and the number of accidents and fatalities continued to grow over the years.[47]

Spitzer Takes the Helm, Briefly

After taking office in January of 2007, Governor Spitzer was less eager than Pataki to take control of the trust. This might have been because he was quickly embroiled in a scandal, was dubbed "Troopergate," and failed to appoint new trust board members.[48] Incoming state park Commissioner

Carol Ash and state Department of Environmental Conservation Commissioner Pete Grannis automatically replaced Pataki's commissioners on the board of the trust in January.

The trust had begun clearing the property between 22nd and 25th Streets to build the outboard segment of Chelsea Waterside Park. The police department stables were relocated from Pier 63 to Pier 76, and Captain John Krevey's historic railroad barge, the *Frying Pan,* and the *John J. Harvey* were relocated to the historic float bridge at Pier 66a. John had bought a historic Lackawanna Railroad caboose and placed it on his barge, demonstrating how trains had once been ferried across the Hudson before the tunnels were built. His ingenuity coupled the park's historic float bridge with a railroad barge and showed how the waterfront worked at the turn of the twentieth century.[49]

Frying Pan continues to be extremely popular and a great example of appropriate economic development in the park. The historic vessels, barge, and railroad caboose celebrated maritime history while providing revenue for the trust—and an attractive destination for park visitors.

In August, Spitzer appointed Diana Taylor as the trust's new chair.[50] Many saw the move as solidifying Bloomberg's control of the project, while others thought Spitzer was trying to mitigate the political damage from Troopergate. Taylor had resigned as the state banking superintendent and was now a managing director at Wolfensohn & Co., a small investment firm.

In any case, I thought that her appointment was a positive sign. Although previously funded park projects were moving forward, a huge funding challenge lay ahead, and two revenue-producing developments, at Piers 40 and 57, were stalled. Maybe someone who had public and private financial experience and was familiar with the park could complete those projects and secure additional public money.

Earlier in the year, Dan Doctoroff had been quoted in a *New York Times* article about three exhibitions opening at various locations around the city that focused on Robert Moses' achievements. Dan crowed that "with the exception of the stadium"—the defeated Olympic/Jets stadium proposal—"there hasn't been a single project we have pushed through that hasn't been approved."[51]

The Hudson River Park did not need help with approvals; it was languishing without adequate capital and maintenance funding. But the park was definitely not getting Bloomberg's attention. I hoped that would change with Diana as chair of the trust and Dan as vice chair. Bloomberg's attention was focused on rezoning the entire west side, and public investment in the park would increase adjacent property values while new land uses and increased density would generate the third source of revenue to build toward self-sufficiency for the park. I thought that Friends' real estate study would verify the initial research and recommendation of the panel and encourage elected officials to finally act. Boy, was I wrong!

Ortenzio Takes a Dive

As Diana Taylor came aboard, James Ortenzio, the first chairman appointed by Pataki, was convicted of tax evasion in an investigation that began with that anonymous letter to the trust regarding Pier 57.[52] Although neither incident resulting in his conviction was proven to occur during his tenure as trust chair, both incidents involved trust tenants.

Apparently, shortly after leaving the trust, Ortenzio became an arbitrator in a disagreement between the heliport operator at West 30th Street and his tenant who operated tourist flights and was accused of skimming money from their partnership. The heliport operator disputed Ortenzio's arbitration ruling, sued, and lost because the arbitration was binding. They appealed, claiming that there was not an arbitration because Ortenzio had not held a single hearing, or collected any evidence, as required in binding arbitration. The appeals court ruled in the operator's favor, and the next week, the tenant paid the operator approximately $5 million to settle.[53]

Ortenzio failed to claim the $80,000 arbitration fee he received in his 2005 federal tax returns. He also failed to report a $100,000 consulting fee he received from Fisher Brothers Management after leaving the trust. Although neither party was willing to share information regarding the subject of that consultation, it was rumored that he had helped the Intrepid acquire the Con Edison site across Route 9A for parking and secure the state funding to build a pedestrian bridge to the museum in 1999 when he was the trust chair. For falsifying his federal tax returns for 2004 and 2005 and violating state financial disclosure laws, he was sentenced to five years' probation. And in June of 2008, Ortenzio sold his property in the Meatpacking District for $40 million.[54]

Friends' Transition and Real Estate Study

The end of 2007 brought a series of changes affecting the future of the park. In October, the Friends board asked Al Butzel to step down as president and join the board. Al seemed increasingly unhappy with a stronger board leadership providing direction, and internal tensions were growing. He wound down his employment as Friends searched to fill a position that we now call "executive director."

Dan Doctoroff resigned as deputy mayor and as the trust vice chairman to join Bloomberg LP as president.[55] The Hell's Kitchen Neighborhood Association sued to block the rezoning of Hudson Yards.[56] And a Greenwich Village parent group, the Pier 40 Partnership, presented a third bid for Pier 40. The parents proposed creating a nonprofit conservancy to redevelop the pier for athletics, the arts, and a school—a proposal that was well received by the community.[57]

By January 2008, Pier 57's redevelopment was still in limbo.[58] The city Department of Investigation had not approved Stephen Witcoff's background clearance that was required of all businesses working with the trust. Apparently, they were concerned by reports that Witcoff bribed former NYPD Commissioner Bernard Kerik with an apartment in 2001.

Julie Nadel, a trust board member focused on protecting the public's interest, objected to Witcoff's continued involvement in Pier 57, and Taylor voiced concern as well.[59] By the end of the month, Witcoff withdrew his bid.[60]

Then there was a bizarre proposal by Spitzer to rename the park for Governor Pataki. Some people thought that Spitzer was still trying to mend fences with state Republicans after Troopergate. That soon proved to be the least of his worries.[61] In a shocking turn of events, Governor Spitzer resigned two days after it became known that he had frequented a high-priced prostitution ring and used state money for his transportation.[62] Lieutenant Governor David Paterson, the son of Harlem political leader and labor lawyer Basil Paterson, stepped up to be the state's fifty-fifth governor.

As the debate over Pier 40 was reaching a crescendo, just before the trust board's decision-making meeting, Pier 40 Partnership, which had received the support of Community Board 2, held a rally. In March, the trust rejected the bid from the Related Companies.[63]

In April, Friends was fortunate to hire A. J. Pietrantone as our new executive director. Pietrantone had fundraising experience, appreciated the board's passion and our mission, and worked well with the board and with Matthew Washington, who had become a valued staff member. A. J. jumped right in and helped coordinate the Greenwich Village real estate value project that we were finalizing.

In September, after two years of focused and intense research and analysis supported by the Durst family and the J. M. Kaplan Fund, we released our study. The report showed that a $75 million public investment in the construction of the Greenwich Village segment of the park had generated more than $200 million in increased real estate value in properties within three blocks of the park.[64]

The study recommended formation of a neighborhood improvement district, modeled on a tradition of the city's business improvement districts. The first of these had been the Union Square Business Improvement District, formed in 1984 to support the restoration and long-term maintenance of that deteriorating city park.

A business improvement district is a defined area in which property owners and commercial tenants promote and fund business development, quality-of-life improvements, and supplement city services like sanitation and public safety. They also provide visitors' services, improve street furniture, and support landscaping and tree plantings. Their work is funded by an assessment on all property owners in the district.

Friends called our effort a "neighborhood improvement district" because we included both commercial and residential property owners. Land use on the Far West Side was shifting from manufacturing, warehousing, and transportation services to commercial office and residential development. Each individual condominium owner was a property owner within our proposed district. We hoped that by creating such a district, we would include residential real estate, which is not included in a traditional business improvement district.

The report clearly described the positive impact that the park was having on adjacent real estate values to elected officials, business leaders, and the general public. We were certain that creating such an entity would provide the final critical element of park financing initially proposed in 1990 and allow the project to become as self-sufficient as possible. It could also reduce political involvement in decision-making by introducing a third independent party to the discussions.

13

Going from Bad to Worse (2009–2012)

● ● ● ● ● ● ● ● ● ● ● ● ● ●

The year began with an incredible feat of aviation and maritime rescue adjacent to the Hudson River Park. It was a bitterly cold January 15, and I was in my office in Red Hook, Brooklyn, from where our water taxis operated. One of New York Water Taxi's deckhands raised an alarm that a plane had ditched in the Hudson. Every now and then, a helicopter or small private plane plunges into the Hudson, so I did not think it unusual—until I heard it was an airliner.[1]

The U.S. Coast Guard called all available vessels to aid US Airways Flight 1549, which had crashed with 155 passengers and crew onboard.[2] The disaster became known around the world as the "Miracle on the Hudson" due to the steely professionalism of Captain Chesley "Sully" Sullenberger and the rapid response of our maritime community. We raced upriver with three water taxis, although as it turned out, our help was not needed because other vessels were already surrounding the downed aircraft.

NY Waterway's ferry fleet was warming up at the Weehawken, New Jersey, homeport, just south of where the plane splash landed; they were fueled, crewed, and preparing for the evening rush hour when the plane landed nearby.[3] NY Waterway, Circle Line, and other mariners were on the scene in minutes as the plane slowly submerged while being pushed along by the river.

If Sully had landed the plane five miles farther south, in the Lower New York Harbor, there would have been serious injury and fatalities.

Mariners are required to aid others in distress at sea, and it is as much a personal commitment as a legal obligation.[4] Just as on 9/11, the harbor's mariners showed their quick response, bravery, and selflessness by helping people in imminent danger and thus saving lives.

The rescue reinforced the importance of preserving an active maritime industry and having piers capable of accommodating vessels.

A Circle Line captain once complained that newly built piers often lacked fendering, marine hardware, and gates in the railings, which make it difficult to respond to emergencies. Previously, the captain could call 911 and coordinate a rendezvous with an ambulance at a mutually agreed upon pier to help a passenger in distress.[5] Unfortunately, these shortcomings continue in many new piers being constructed in the harbor.

Neighborhood Improvement District

In spring of 2009, Friends of Hudson River Park hired Brendan Sexton, the founding president of the Times Square Business Improvement District, to assist in our implementing the Neighborhood Improvement District proposal to generate park funding from the adjacent real estate. Friends established a steering committee to guide our advocacy, and Brendan helped develop a strategy, timeline, and budget for our campaign, advising us to start with an informal process and test reactions.[6]

Getting our proposal reviewed and approved involved overcoming significant procedural hurdles over several years. We began by briefing the Hudson River Park Trust board at the office of The Durst Organization, and although board members voiced support, they basically said, "Make it happen." Unfortunately, that is about all they did to support the effort. The one exception was a former journalist named Pamela Frederick, appointed to the trust board by the borough president, who followed up matters under consideration, provided contacts for local outreach, and attended community meetings.

Developing a relationship with the city's Department of Small Business Services, the agency responsible for the creation and oversight of the city's business improvement districts, was critical.[7] There were forty-five such districts when Bloomberg took office in 2002. He introduced new initiatives to support them and he created nineteen new districts by 2008, bringing the citywide total to sixty-four.[8]

After our initial meeting with the trust board, we briefed local elected officials, community boards, neighborhood organizations, and nonprofit organizations from adjacent neighborhoods to describe the park's funding needs and our proposal for a neighborhood improvement district. A major concern was that it might increase gentrification. Anticipating the problem, we excluded all publicly supported housing and small businesses in our proposed three-block-deep improvement district adjacent to the park so they would not have to pay the annual assessment to the new entity.

Existing residents in our proposed district had by now seen an increase in their taxes. Their property value had increased as well, but they would not realize the benefit of increased values until the property was sold. Residents in new residential developments near the park felt that they had paid a premium purchase price for their property because of the park's proximity. Both groups used and appreciated the park but believed that their taxes were already providing support. It did not help matters when the *Wall Street Journal* called the proposal a "special tax."[9]

In 1990, the West Side Waterfront Panel had recommended that a mechanism be developed to capture revenue increasing the value of adjacent real estate before the park was built. However, neither the city nor the state included any such mechanisms in the 1998 Hudson River Park Act. The entire West Side was rezoned by Bloomberg, yet the panel's recommendation to secure additional revenues from inboard real estate was ignored, and the park was having real financial troubles.[10] The neighborhood improvement district was our Hail Mary pass, a last-ditch effort to find an alternative source of funding to support the park without destroying it by commercialization.

Although the proposed High Line Business Improvement District failed, other such districts were formed in areas fronting the park. Carl Weisbrod, the former president of the city's Economic Development Corporation, established a Hudson Square Business Improvement District when he led the effort to rezone, and rebrand, Trinity Church's commercial properties as Hudson Square. Dan Biederman created the Chelsea Improvement District. Both were within our proposed district, and they benefited from proximity to the park, yet neither provided annual support for the park.

The response to our proposal for the improvement district from elected officials was mixed. Assemblyman member Dick Gottfried supported the initiative, but Assemblymember Deborah Glick opposed it, as did City Council Speaker Christine Quinn, who represented an adjacent council district. Community Board 4 complained that it was already supporting segments of the park downtown with revenue from commercial use in their Midtown segment, and Community Board 2 objected to almost everything related to the park. Thankfully, Community Board 1 initially supported the proposed district.

All in all, most local politicians, community boards, and existing business improvement districts objected to the neighborhood improvement district, and support from the trust was lackluster. But Friends was undeterred, and, more importantly, the Durst family was steadfast in its support. We soldiered on, understanding that the park was in big trouble without an additional revenue stream. Momentum was moving toward commercial exploitation of the park itself with the trust courting new development, even though failed requests for proposals at Piers 40 and 57 indicated that the trust was not too adept at it—which was a good thing.

A New Proposal for Pier 57

The trust received responses to their second Request for Proposals for Pier 57 by October of 2008.[11] Bidders included the Related Companies, the Durst Organization/C&K Properties team, and Youngwoo & Associates.

This time, Helena Durst, Douglas's youngest daughter, represented the Durst Organization and worked with Ben Korman, a principal in C&K Properties, to craft their submission. They understood that, given the limited uses allowed by the Hudson River Park Act, any redevelopment would not be profitable in the short term. Developing Pier 57 would require a large capital investment, and permanent improvements would belong to the trust, but with the new forty-nine-year lease term, there was the potential for long-term profitability.[12] They proposed revenue sharing to minimize their initial risk while the trust shared in the future upside.

In August of 2009, the trust selected Youngwoo & Associates as the winning bidder. Their initial plan called for a four-acre public market with affordable space for artisans and small businesses. Part of the market would be housed in recycled shipping containers. The ground floor would be home to a 98,000-square-foot Contemporary Culture Center with a mix of auction space, galleries, cafés, and performance space.

The landscaped roof would feature a permanent outdoor entertainment space run by the Tribeca Film Festival, along with park improvements. A large restaurant would be located at the tip of the pier with a vast Underwater Discovery Center in one of the pier's caissons. Seasonal docks would be installed for kayaks, canoes, and other craft.[13]

New Zoning for Hudson Yards Approved

The International Olympic Committee had chosen London to host the 2012 Summer Games in July 2005, but the Bloomberg administration's interest in developing the area continued. In December 2009, the City Council approved the final phase of Hudson Yards, the largest of Mayor Bloomberg's Far West Side rezoning proposals.[14] Although there was no stadium, the Hudson Yards Special District was incredibly dense. The initial project included some twenty-six million square feet of commercial office development, twenty thousand housing units, two million square feet of retail space, and three million square feet of hotels.

The plan also included building six new blocks of Manhattan covering the twenty-six-acre rail yards, a development that would include amenities such as a new north-south roadway, between Tenth and Eleventh Avenues; cultural facilities; a public school; a twelve-acre park over the rail yards and smaller public spaces elsewhere within Hudson Yards; a link to the High Line along its southern and western borders; and the extension of the No. 7 subway line from Times Square to 33rd Street and Eleventh Avenue.

The entire $25 billion complex was scheduled for completion 2024, and this vastly out-of-scale redevelopment project reminded me of Dubai—on the Hudson.[15]

The first phase of Hudson Yards under construction, 2018. (Tom Fox)

Progress Keeps Hope Alive

Chelsea Waterside Park, the park's largest public space, was a green open space. Pier 64, the first pier rebuilt in Chelsea Waterside Park, opened in 2009. It was like the public piers in Greenwich Village and featured an open design with expansive lawns flanked by English oaks and a plaza at the tip.[16] The pier's deck gradually rose from the bulkhead to the tip which made for great view up and down the river.

In May of 2010, Piers 62 and 63 opened. The area that formerly housed the Pier 63 headhouse was shaped like a bowl with a large open lawn for sunning, picnicking, and yoga that also could accommodate various informal activities like small pick-up ball games. The area surrounding the "bowl" had a wonderful collection of small gardens to the south and a stone sculpture garden to the north. The landscaping was beautiful and looked like it would mature well.

Pier 62 also had a skate park and public restrooms as well as a carousel featuring aquatic creatures found in the Hudson and a unicorn to tantalize (and perhaps confuse) children's fantasies.[17] Unlike the Village waterfront, however, the remainder of the Chelsea waterfront between 29th and 42nd Streets remained unfinished and was occupied by the heliport, the Pier 76 tow pound, and ferry terminal bus parking at Pier 79.

The 1998 Hudson River Park Act had banned tourist or recreational flights from using the adjacent heliport, but the ban was not being enforced.[18] There was speculation that the trust ignored the ban to generate increased revenue. Whatever the reason, Friends' 2007 suit to stop the tourist flights at the heliport was settled by March of 2010, which in turn reduced chopper noise in the park significantly. A. J. Pietratone's op-ed article in the *The Villager* announced our victory, and once again, the Durst family's support allowed Friends to prevail in our second lawsuit to ensure compliance with the act.[19]

That fall, Pier 25 and the upland portion of Pier 26 in Tribeca opened after five years of reconstruction. These were the piers that had been funky favorites during the 1990s, and we worried that they would lose that neighborhood feel. However, the community design process created a wonderfully diverse mix of uses on Pier 25 that included space for both active and passive recreation. Marine activity was a major component of these piers, with moorings and a town dock on the south side and the necessary maritime hardware like bollards and gates in the railing to support historic ship berthing along the north side—just as it had been for the *Yankee* and the *Pegasus* back in the day.

Beach volleyball at Pier 25 with historic lightship in the background. (Tom Fox)

The following summer, the last of the U.S. Coast Guard's steam-powered buoy tender, *Lilac*, which had made its maiden voyage in 1933, became the first historic vessel to dock at the pier.[20] Buoy tenders maintain navigational aids to assist commercial and recreational maritime traffic, and *Lilac* provided educational programs, beginning with an exhibit of Shelley Seccombe's wonderful photographs of the 1970s West Side waterfront.[21] Shelley was a talented photographer who lived in the affordable artist housing at Westbeth and had documented public use of the abandoned piers in Greenwich Village.

Pier 25 was one of the few piers rebuilt to its original 990-foot length. The pier had room for a wonderful children's playground with an interesting fountain at the entrance, public restrooms, a miniature golf course with a cascading waterfall, and three beach volleyball courts flanked by blue reclining chaises, allowing people waiting to play to catch some rays or socialize. An open lawn surrounded by benches and a generous tree-covered seating area toward the end of the pier and the tip had shade trees and seating that offered majestic views of the Hudson, and like all the piers in the park, this one was ringed by a promenade, a railing, and lighting.[22]

Issues with Construction in the Hudson

Approximately four hundred acres of the park are underwater, and the park plan encouraged a broad range of water-dependent activities like kayaking, rowing, fishing, mooring historic vessels, sailing, and occasionally swimming. The plan also encouraged environmental education and aquatic habitat research and restoration. Although the Hudson is an integral part of the park, building and maintaining the infrastructure in the water to support these activities does not come cheap—not to mention the fact that there are liability issues. Providing adequate funding for in-water infrastructure, maximizing marine safety, and minimizing liability are challenges that most waterfront parks must address.

The trust's design and construction team installed a large wooden fendering system around Pier 25 to support vessel docking and provided additional protection with pneumatic fenders, but they selected the type designed for ocean-going vessels. This prevents many smaller vessels from docking for public events or environmental education programs because their gangways are not long enough to reach the pier.

The trust stipulated that a ship's gangway could not protrude out onto the pier; but that is how gangways function. In addition, the trust failed to provide water, sewer, or electrical hookups for the historic ship berths, and it installed gates that were too narrow to allow gangways to move with the vessels without damaging the pier's railings. The Working Waterfront Association had highlighted these and other issues years earlier, but their advice was ignored.

The North River Historic Ship Society, a group of historic vessel owners, operators and supporters founded aboard *Yankee* in the early 1990s, was led to believe that they would participate in the pier's design review, but the trust limited the review to the Advisory Council and told the society that their members could not participate in the process because they would be bidding for the berths, which was a conflict of interest.

The trust assumed—wrongly—that each berth had to be designed to accommodate a specific vessel. Involving experienced mariners in developing an appropriate generic design would have made it possible to accommodate many different vessels. There was no real conflict of interest, and the trust could have asked any knowledgeable marine professional for advice, but the design and construction team did not embrace public participation, and they were reluctant to listen to the advice of the people they were paid to serve.

Prospective tenants were forced to pay for their own electrical runs from the beginning of the pier to their berthing space, although the trust had been told it was cheaper to wire the entire pier rather than stop at the pier's edge. Most vessels have standard connections that can be plugged into almost any electrical box. The trust also insisted that tenants install their own electric meters, but Con Edison stated that the property owner—the trust—had to request meter installation.

To compound the problem, nonprofit groups that operate historic vessels, or community boating programs for that matter, cannot afford tens of thousands of dollars of permanent infrastructure improvements to public piers. As a result, many mariners could not apply to dock in the park—which may have been what the trust wanted.

The General Project Plan, the blueprint for the future park, was designated in the 1998 Hudson River Park Act. The plan celebrated the rich maritime history of the West Side waterfront and called for historic and visiting vessels at three primary locations: Pier 25 in Tribeca, Pier 54 at the border of Greenwich Village and Chelsea, and Pier 97 in Hell's Kitchen. The original concept was that resident historic vessels would pay $1 a year for rent and get adequate infrastructure in exchange for providing historic and environmental programming for park visitors.

It was envisioned that this public/private partnership would keep the park flexible, interesting, and relevant. But the trust has had trouble providing appropriate site designs and adequate capital improvements to support historic vessels and will not consider dredging. An inexperienced design and construction team and budget cuts have diminished what was intended to be a waterfront park that celebrated the rich maritime history of the New York/New Jersey harbor. Hopefully, that shortcoming can be overcome as the park matures.

Pier 25 included a mooring field on the south side, where the free-spirited Neutrinos had squatted years earlier, and a "town dock" to accommodate access to a mooring field for sailboats. As it did in other areas, the trust installed five sections of steel docks filled with Styrofoam, capped with concrete.

Steel is relatively inexpensive and strong, but it is also rigid. The docks weighed more than forty tons each and were overkill. The river is constantly moving, and rigid steel docks can crack and the piles securing the docks can fail. The docks were relocated but only two sections of the original dock remain.

The General Project Plan also envisioned a range of nonmotorized vessels in the park. Five facilities dedicated to kayaking, rowing, and sailing are located

Kayakers receiving instructions before launch from volunteers at the Pier 26 Downtown Boathouse. (Tom Fox)

along the park's four-mile length. However, the design of these facilities had problems as well. For example, the Downtown Boathouse at nearby Pier 26 provides inexperienced park visitors with an introduction to kayaking, and their free kayak program is one of the largest in the state—if not the nation. In 2022, they recorded their half-millionth kayaker. But the steel dock supporting their kayak access and egress from the Hudson was poorly designed.

Kayak docks are usually flat with a surface about eight inches from the water to support kayak launching and egress. The Downtown Boathouse dock at Pier 26, however, is an eighteen-inch-high dock at its center and tapers down to eight inches on each side to accommodate kayaks. As a result, its sloping deck pitched kayakers toward the water, and the surface became especially dangerous when covered with algae. The trust's failure to provide fresh water to the dock prevented volunteers from removing accumulating algae. In addition, the float's north side was unusable due to swells and vessel wakes washing up on that side—because the facility did not have a breakwater.

Finally, the large garage door of the Downtown Boathouse did not line up with their float. Kayakers need to make a right turn, walk thirty feet carrying their kayak, and turn sharply left to enter the ramp. As a result, the Downtown Boathouse leaves as many as forty kayaks out on their float each night because it is impractical to carry them all up and down at the beginning and end of each day. The area in the front of the boathouse is a public walkway, and many visitors stop to watch novice kayakers attempting to paddle for the first time. Not surprisingly, the walkway gets crowded, which further impedes access to the float.

With the Downtown Boathouse on Pier 26 and historic vessels on Pier 25, the trust failed to build a lay-by space on the side of the Route 9A roadway to accommodate the loading and unloading of supplies, equipment, and trash. However, when the City Vineyard restaurant opened on Pier 26, the trust relocated the bicycle path and eliminated the landscaped area protecting the path from Route 9A traffic and installed a lay-by to make it easier for the restaurant to handle both trash and supplies. Creating such a space, even if modest, sent the unmistakable message that commerce was king in the Hudson River Park.

Lost Heroes, Big Changes

As 2011 began, our maritime community suffered back-to-back blows. In February, the legendary waterfront advocate, entrepreneur, and historic ship owner John Krevey, who had played a central role in opening access to the Hudson, died unexpectedly. John had been a tireless advocate for public use of the waterways and often interpreted the rules broadly as he navigated government oversight, pursued his dreams, and succeeded in getting things done.[23] His motto was that it is easier to ask for forgiveness than for permission. Be bold and pursue your dreams, he advised—you can change the world. April brought the death of Bernard Ente, a talented and generous photographer whose work focused on the ships and maritime activities in New York Harbor.[24]

In October of 2010, Dan Kurtz became chief financial officer and executive vice president of finance and real estate of the trust. Dan was the only executive vice president at the city's Economic Development Corporation in the 1990s, and he was described by colleagues as someone who was always right. He left the corporation in 2002 when Bloomberg installed a new leadership team and then worked for the Bayonne Local Redevelopment Authority.

In November, Andrew Cuomo was elected governor, and new appointees joined the board of the trust in January of 2011. The next month, Connie Fishman resigned as president of the trust and began work at the Greater New York YMCA.[25] Diana Taylor had recently become vice chair of that organization's board and would be named its chair several months later.[26] Connie, who had been at the trust since its inception, had worked well with the community and was seen as someone who listened and believed in the vision for the park. As president, she had been effective, and I love her blue lighting fixtures along the park's railing.

Madelyn Wils, now an executive vice president at the Economic Development Corporation who focused on planning and maritime projects like the failed redevelopment of Atlantic Basin in Brooklyn, was appointed president of the trust. Funding for the park was a major concern, and as the *New York Times* article stated, "Ms. Wils will have to devise ways of increasing revenue from the waterfront property to help pay for the continued development of piers that make up much of the park. A critical question is what to do with Pier 40, which houses a parking garage that provides more than one-third of the trust's annual revenue."[27]

The previous trust leadership had reduced capital and maintenance spending to adjust to limited government support for the park. With Diana Taylor—now a member of Citigroup's board—as chairwoman of the trust and two former executives from the city's Economic Development Corporation in senior leadership positions, the trust ramped up commercial development efforts in the park instead.

Friends Makes a Fateful Choice

At the same time, rapid turnover in individuals responsible for decision-making regarding our application for a neighborhood improvement district slowed that effort because we continually had to bring new appointees up to speed. Not surprisingly, things were not looking too good for the neighborhood improvement district, especially after Madelyn told A. J. Pietrantone that Friends' effort to create the district was all wrong and recommended that we change course.

Friends had begun our final push for the neighborhood improvement district. Bloomberg would be leaving office shortly and had significantly increased the number of the city's business improvement districts.[28] Considering the fact that his extensive inboard rezoning did not generate any new funding for the park and that the chairwoman of the trust and Bloomberg were an established couple, we thought we had a shot. However, when asked to reinforce the need for park funding, Taylor claimed that she did not discuss specific projects with the mayor. That seemed like a convenient but disappointing excuse. But all you can do is move forward.

In 2011, Diana and Madelyn requested that Friends become the park's official fundraising organization and pledged to provide Friends with a $500,000 loan, which would be forgiven if the restructured Friends generated a minimum of $1 million a year in funding, which we had done consistently. The trust indicated that they would establish a competing nonprofit to support the park if we refused their offer. Many board members assumed that the trust wanted to eliminate our pesky proclivity to litigate and release statements that sometimes contradicted their proclamations.

Douglas Durst and Ross Graham agreed to continue leading a restructured Friends, and Ben Korman stayed as the secretary. Susanna Aaron, a Village resident who had recently joined the Friends board, supported the changes, and several other board members agreed stay. We voted to accept the trust's offer, and Friends transitioned to become a fundraising organization with the sole mission of supporting the trust.

The majority of the board members resigned to make way for individuals more capable of fundraising; serving on the reconstituted Friends board required $25,000 "give or get" each year.[29] Friends continued to pursue the neighborhood improvement district during the transition, and I remained on the district's steering committee. Diana and Madelyn became ex-officio Friends board members, and A. J. remained executive director.

Diana and Madelyn purported that the reconstituted Friends could establish the neighborhood improvement district while increasing charitable contributions from the adjacent neighborhoods, where an influx of affluent residents and corporations was changing the demographics.[30] The reconstituted Friends may have been better able to support the park financially, but, without the district, they could not raise the level of funding required for long-term maintenance, operations, and capital replacement in the park. Most importantly, the transition eliminated the independent advocacy group to protect the public interest and leverage city and state support and funding.

Many newer residents seemed more focused on issues that were important to their families rather than the needs of the entire park. Diana wanted a high-powered board, so she and Madelyn began assembling a Friends board more to their liking. The dissolution of our successful, independent, advocacy organization further enabled trust efforts to commercialize the park.

At the close of 2011, Chelsea Piers Management sued the trust for $37.5 million to pay for the maintenance of the piles supporting their complex.[31] By this point, the park was in serious financial trouble as the city and state had rapidly reduced their annual investment in it to $7 million from $42 million in 2008. The trust was responsible for their own defense and hired Randy Mastro, a former deputy mayor under Giuliani, to defend them against the suit. In 2013, the New York State Supreme Court Appellate Division, however, eventually dismissed the suit.[32]

Completing the Takeover

By spring of 2012, budget shortfalls at the trust for 2011 and 2012 heightened concerns about the need for additional financial support for the park. Madelyn formed a twenty-nine-member Hudson River Park Task Force chaired by her former colleague at the city's Economic Development Corporation, Carl Weisbrod (now at HR&A Advisors, a major real estate advisory firm) to examine funding challenges and explore solutions— not that the Friends had not been working on the solution—that is, the neighborhood improvement district, for which plans were almost completed.

As a result, another economic development advocate was put in a prominent role.[33] By June, the task force recommended changes in the Hudson River Park Act to allow the trust to extend lease terms, issue tax-exempt bonds, eliminate restrictions prohibiting residential, hotel, and commercial office development, relinquish the park's tail in front of Battery Park City, eliminate the need for liability insurance, and implement other "minor" changes like modifying Pier 54's footprint.[34]

It was ironic that Community Board 4's letter to elected officials supporting the task force recommendations repeated the trust's position that when the park was created, many feared that the waterfront would be walled off with high-rise condos and commercial office towers, and those prohibitions were critical. However, they believe that since 75 percent of the park was completed and they felt that the trust had an excellent track record as public-minded stewards of the park, the fears were no longer relevant. In other words, the park was ripe for commercial development.

Outboard development walling off the waterfront had been prevented; now, however, Bloomberg's massive rezoning of adjacent West Side neighborhoods increased the height of the building wall on the other side of Route 9A.[35] My September op-ed article in the *The Villager* called for a return to the original park vision and stressed the fact that the creation of the neighborhood improvement district was critical given the failure of both the Hudson River Park Act and Bloomberg's rezoning to provide a consistent source of long-term funding from inboard redevelopment.[36]

The trust's new leadership began using what some called a Balkanization technique. If they did inform the public of a new policy, plan, or project, they limited their presentation to the affected community board. Other stakeholders, such as the Advisory Council, Friends, and sometimes even their own board, were increasingly unaware of deals the trust leadership negotiated. All in all, the trust played to the parochial interests of each individual community board and avoided the Advisory Council and other civic and environmental groups while insisting that they were complying with the public review requirements enshrined in the 1998 act.

In summer of 2012, Madelyn loudly proclaimed that Pier 40 was in danger of collapsing and might have to be closed unless something was done soon. Through the strong and consistent advocacy of youth sports leagues in Greenwich Village and Tribeca, and the support of Community Board 1 and 2, Pier 40 had become a valuable neighborhood recreational facility. A group called Pier 40 Champions was formed by seven local youth sports leagues to respond to the potential loss of the playing fields. Tobi Bergman of Community Board 2 and Daniel Miller—a local parent, past president of the Greenwich Village Little League, and a commercial filmmaker and producer—were the cochairs.

Tobi wanted to "think outside the box" and suggested residential development at Pier 40. He floated the idea to Madelyn. Pier 40 Champions produced four videos describing the importance of Pier 40, the critical financial issue, and their proposal for housing to raise needed funding for the pier.[37] Surprisingly, state Assemblyman Dick Gottfried, a cosponsor of the 1998 act, supported a consideration of housing, and city Park Commissioner Adrian Benepe, a Bloomberg appointee to the trust board, confirmed that the trust's concerns were not exaggerated and needed creative solutions.[38] However, Assemblymember Deborah Glick, whose district included Pier 40, and City Councilman Brad Hoylman objected, as did the chair of the reconstituted Friends—Douglas Durst.

As usual, Durst acted. Although not proposing to redevelop the pier, he and Ben Korman drafted a concept plan to show that Pier 40 could be redeveloped without residential development and that the trust should consider adaptive reuse of the existing structure with commercial offices, parking, recreation, and accessory retail.

The Durst family hired a marine engineer to independently analyze the condition of the 3,600 piles supporting Pier 40. The results were surprising.[39]

Although Madelyn insisted that stabilizing the pier would require a $100 million investment in the piles, the engineering report stated that the trust could spend a third of what the trust was estimating, or $30 million, to stabilize Pier 40 for the five- to seven-year period the trust claimed they needed before redevelopment.

Durst also hired a parking consultant whose analysis suggested the trust underestimated the revenue from retaining parking by about 20 percent, which was more than one million dollars annually.[40] Finally, he retained Dattner Associates to develop an alternative redevelopment plan without housing.[41] Douglas does his homework.

Both plans were scheduled for presentation to Community Board 2 on October 29 and to the Advisory Council on November 7. On October 29, however, an incredible natural disaster overwhelmed the city and the park as Superstorm Sandy charged ashore with a storm surge of more than thirteen feet. The storm surge inundated the region's coastal areas, including my home in Breezy Point on the western tip of the Rockaway Peninsula.[42] The park was suddenly under water, and the city again came to a standstill. The trust estimated that the storm had caused ten million dollars' worth of damage, reinforcing the importance of the neighborhood improvement district to support the future needs of the park.[43]

Frustrated by Madelyn and Diana's manipulation of Friends, Ross had already resigned. Alarmed by their willingness to consider residential development in the park, Douglas Durst and Ben Korman both resigned from the reconstituted Friends board in December.[44] Although the park was hobbled by Superstorm Sandy, Madelyn and Diana were now prepared to exert full control of the waterfront.

14

The Trust Goes over
to the Dark Side
(2013–2014)

● ● ● ● ● ● ● ● ● ● ● ● ●

With new leadership and consultants from the city's Economic Development Corporation, and with Friends of Hudson River Park reconstituted as a fundraising organization rather than an advocate and watchdog, the trust focused on park development working with real estate interests and private philanthropy. Transparency became opaque, decision-making was limited to a privileged few "in the know," and meaningful public participation slowed significantly.

By January of 2013, the takeover of Hudson River Park Friends was complete. The transition was sealed when Mike Novogratz, a principal at Fortress Investment Group and a board member of the Hudson River Park Trust since 2010, stepped down and became chairman of the reconstituted Friends.[1]

Two weeks earlier, Fortress had joined with Atlas Capital and Westbrook Partners to buy a 50.1 percent stake in St. John's Terminal for $250 million.[2] The huge warehouse, which bridged Houston Street and occupied three city blocks, was originally planned as the southern terminus of the High Line, but it now housed back-office and storage space for financial companies like Merrill Lynch and Bloomberg LP. It also sat directly across Route 9A from Pier 40, which the trust desperately wanted redeveloped.

A. J. Pietrantone, who remained as executive director of Friends after the transition, had negotiated the agreement for the park's neighborhood improvement district with the trust and the city's Department of Small Business Services, but Diana Taylor, chairwoman of the trust, did not think that he was the right person to lead Friends in its new role as a major fundraising group.

Pietrantone had done an excellent job leading the original Friends, but given the fact that Diane and Madelyn Wils were determined to set the new agenda for the organization, he had announced his resignation the previous September, effective in the spring of 2013 or when an appropriate replacement was found. Diana and Madelyn would then in effect control both Friends and the trust.

Like virtually everyone else, A. J. had been shocked by Douglas Durst's sudden resignation as Friends chairman in December. He had no allegiance to the incoming chairman of Friends, Mike Novogratz, and was not supported by the leadership of the trust. So he left Friends in March even though his replacement had not been chosen. Meanwhile, Friends recruited new board members and hired an interim management company to move forward.

That February, the trust announced a partnership with an organization called Bowery Presents to relocate summer concerts from Pier 54 to Pier 26 in Tribeca.[3] Pier 26 had been rebuilt but without surface amenities, so it was an open platform that could accommodate various activities in addition to concerts. That decision was not without controversy, however. The Pier 54 concerts had created a series of issues, from noise complaints to pedestrians crossing Route 9A.

Growing Troubles for the Neighborhood Improvement District

Resistance to the neighborhood improvement district had begun to emerge as some residents, primarily in Tribeca, objected to the proposal. The original Friends had sought to ensure that the district's structure and mission supported the park and were relevant to the inboard communities. The district would have an independent board allowing businesses, residential property owners, and other stakeholders in the district inboard of Route 9A to direct the organization and allocate annual revenues.

The proposed mission included improvements to landscape, signage, and street furniture on the major streets leading to the park. The concept harkened back to Frederick Law Olmsted's parkways, which is what he dubbed the thoroughfares that led to his parks. The purpose of these improvements was to allow visitors to begin their experience before they reached the park and to increase the value of properties lining the thoroughfares. This, in turn, had helped generate greater local tax revenue, which helped fund his new parks, which were built primarily in undeveloped sections of the cities where they were located.

In our plan for the neighborhood improvement district, we included support for the maintenance of the landscape, the bicycle path, and the median along Route 9A because the roadway had become the bastard child of West Side redevelopment. The state Department of Transportation had built the project on the cheap; the median, for example, had substandard soil, no initial irrigation, and received only occasional maintenance, and the department was slow to replace the many trees and shrubs that died.

Because the department did not practice quality landscape management, the inboard street trees fared no better than those on the median. The roadway, which had been envisioned as a grand landscaped boulevard, like Park Avenue, needed proper attention to become one, but it was not getting it.

In the beginning of 2013, the steering committee for the neighborhood improvement district refined its talking points[4] and "Frequently Asked Questions" to better educate the public.[5] We had worked hard to develop an annual property assessment that would be reasonable, fair, and provide sufficient financial support for the park. The residential assessment was seven and a half cents per square foot, a calculus that would generate $8 million a year. Someone owning a thousand-square-foot condo across from the park, for example, would pay $75 annually to support the neighborhood improvement district—chump change, as they say.

Some residents, however, objected to this plan, claiming that the assessment was yet another tax, and they wrote letters and opinion pieces to local newspapers opposing what they called "The Hudson River Park Tax." Although Community Board 1 had initially approved the district in December, the rising crescendo of opposition forced some of its members to reconsider. After the board's meeting about the district, my op-ed article in *The Villager* reminded everyone that past attempts to provide adequate funding for the park from the appreciation of inboard real estate had failed.

I also mentioned that the city's Economic Development Corporation had unusual influence on the trust. That was because Robert Steele, the deputy mayor for economic development, was now vice chairman of the trust; Madelyn Wils, the former executive vice president of the corporation, was the trust president; and Dan Kurtz, another former corporation vice president, was over-seeing real estate and finance for the trust.[6] In addition Carl Weisbrod, the founding president of the corporation, was heading a task force that the trust established in 2012 to consider changes to the 1998 Hudson River Park Act.[7]

Seven trust board members responded with their own opinion piece in *The Villager* lauding their task force and its transparency, lamenting opposition to residential development at Pier 40, reiterating the park's dire financial situation, underscoring their hopes for the trust's new fundraising partnership with Friends, and expressing their support for the neighborhood improvement district.[8]

Opponents of the neighborhood improvement district created their own social media site, nohrpnid.blogspot.com, along with a PowerPoint presentation entitled "Hudson River Park NID: A Bad Idea."[9] They argued that the district represented an abuse of the law governing business improvement districts because it included residential property owners. They complained that they had not been properly informed about the plans and questioned the need for the assessment, stating that public taxes should pay for parks.

Opponents further claimed that the boundaries for the district were arbitrary and that the funding would be spent on street vendors, newsstands, and pay phones to increase advertising revenues. They also claimed that the board for the district, which was structured to ensure inclusion in decision-making, was too big. Overall, they were short on accuracy and long on stoking fear.

Nonetheless, they garnered support from the diminishing group of park opponents like the Clean Air Campaign, Friends of the Earth, Sierra Club's NYC Chapter, and two Democratic political clubs. They claimed to represent twelve thousand residents and small business owners—a fraction of the people living in the proposed district. One major objection was that some revenue from the district would be used to improve landscaping along Route 9A, the bicycle path, and some major streets approaching the park. Obviously, including amenities for adjacent neighborhoods to encourage local support for the district was not helpful.

Pier 40 Heats Up

After the hiatus caused by Superstorm Sandy, the debate over the future of Pier 40 grew more urgent. Pier 40 Champions shifted the location of their proposed residential redevelopment from the pier itself to the upland property in the park adjacent to Route 9A.[10] Ben Korman, who worked with Douglas Durst to show the trust that the existing Pier 40 structure could be repurposed, met a cofounder of Newmark, a major commercial real estate advisory firm, at a holiday party in December of 2013.

Korman was told that Newmark had been hired by the trust to determine the best uses for Pier 40 and was working closely with Dan Kurtz to show that office and retail uses were inappropriate and risky and that housing was the safest choice.[11] When Korman met privately to discuss the concept with Diana Taylor at Citigroup Headquarters on East 53rd Street, he was told it had no chance of being considered.

Speaking about the Pier 40 Champions proposal, Madelyn Wils said, "Certainly of all the plans that we've seen, it has the most promise." She said that she was not sure whether residential or commercial office development would be the most financially viable but noted that both would require amending the 1998 act. In addition, she stated that maintaining the pier to support redevelopment would now cost $125 million.[12] However, without knowing what the future redevelopment plan would be, Madelyn could not know if the existing pile configuration would support new development, and many considered her proposed investment in pile restoration a waste of money.

In late April, the conflict over Pier 40's future reached a crescendo as three hundred people gathered to hear trust presentations at the Saatchi and Saatchi building near Pier 40.[13] The Pier 40 Champions' two-towers plan now called for buildings twenty-two stories tall, and Madelyn had commissioned her own financial analysis comparing this with the Durst/Korman concept of adaptive reuse. Just as Ben was told four months earlier, Madelyn's study claimed a residential plan would generate adequate funding for the park, but that adaptive reuse would not generate the revenue projected in the Durst/Korman estimate.[14]

Tobi Bergman was a founder of our original Friends of Hudson River Park but had resigned from Friends to support the Pier 40 Champions plan and, at the Saatchi meeting, his comments regarding the Durst/Korman concept seemed both hostile and misleading. Immediately after the meeting, Bergman congratulated the Pier 40 Champions on their strong showing, organized a demonstration, and urged them to continue their fight.[15]

The Durst Organization has been in the real estate industry for more than a century. It had developed or managed eleven million square feet of Manhattan and was building One World Trade Center, which would contain 3.5 million square feet of space, in partnership with the Port Authority.

Their adaptive reuse concept and estimates were based on real-world experience. Moreover, Douglas was not someone to make unsubstantiated claims. Eventually, several state-elected officials objected to the trust's residential proposals and refused to support legislative changes required to allow it.

Slipping Farther into Darkness

By 2013, the trust's ability to be both evasive and obscure was obvious. Over the next several years, its leadership continued to share their plans and financial information selectively while negotiating privately with developers and real estate interests. They briefed "community" representatives most likely to agree with their plans and continued to Balkanize decision-making, sowing distrust and confusion. They were acting like a full-blown economic development entity, not a public benefit corporation building a park.

The trust began presenting park finances in different ways to different people at different times and, when discussing issues, emphasized whatever suited their purpose at a particular moment. Although the trust was a public entity, it released inaccurate financial information to the public, exaggerated the need for increased commercial development, and stressed the importance of private support even as it failed to press the city and state for adequate public funding. Former city Economic Development Corporation staff in leadership positions on the trust board, assisted by their consultant, Carl Weisbrod, were creating a self-fulfilling prophecy.

The quest for commercial development, both in and next to the park, shifted into overdrive. The trust quietly started implementing several recommendations made by Madelyn's hand-picked task force, but for the most ambitious plans like modifying land-use restrictions and extending the length of commercial lease terms, they needed to amend the 1998 act.

A major initiative that had not been recommended by the task force but was mentioned by opponents of the neighborhood improvement district was the sale of air rights from the park. "Air rights" generally refers to the empty space above a property that allows a certain scale of development, where the zoning defines the type of development allowed. Few of us remembered that twenty years earlier when the city's 1992 Comprehensive Waterfront Plan recommended the transfer of air rights from piers that existed before 1988,[16] which was codified in an amendment to the zoning resolution in 1993.[17] Although the trust would receive money from the sale of air rights, the short-term infusion of capital would not be a reliable way to meet the park's long-term maintenance and operational needs, and it would increase density in the adjacent communities and demands on the park.

In April, trust leadership worked with sympathetic elected officials like Assemblymember Dick Gottfried to modify the act.[18] Changes were proposed without public review or approval and only brought to the Hudson River Park Advisory Council the day before the bill was introduced in Albany during the last week of the legislative session that June.[19]

The trust did not give community boards, the Advisory Council, or any of the community, civic, and environmental stakeholders supporting the park a chance to review and comment publicly on proposed amendments before the bill's introduction, which should have been illegal. Nor were the proposed amendments made public at any trust board meeting. It would not be the first—or last—time that the trust cloaked their actions in secrecy.

The reconstituted Friends had hired a lobbyist even though both Madelyn and Diana Taylor served on the Friends board, ex-officio, and were precluded from lobbying the state. Wils even made a personal financial contribution to Friends to support the lobbying effort.[20] Then, Madelyn Wils and a trust attorney parked themselves in the capitol building in Albany and lobbied anyone and everyone they could. Many of their proposed amendments were pushed through at the end of the last day of the legislative season.

With few exceptions, the amendments to the act favored increased commercial exploitation of the park.[21] The most significant amendment involved transferring unused development rights from the piers to inboard properties across Route 9A. They extended commercial leases at eight piers in the park to ninety-nine years and allowed commercial offices at Pier 57. City zoning regulations could also be ignored on piers with pedestrian walkways around their edges.[22]

"Park use" now included amusement rides, and the definition of allowable "park/retail use" was broadened to include restaurants, broadcast television, and film or media studios. "Commercial recreational use" included commercial amusements, performing arts, and schools and educational facilities. A $2-per-person fee was levied on every passenger boarding commercial maritime businesses operating in the park (excluding ferries). "Water-dependent use" included the development, operation, and maintenance of a non-tourism/nonrecreational heliport located between West 29th and West 32nd Streets which could now be expanded into the Hudson on floating structures.

Some changes had strong community support, such as returning the 5.5-acre Pier 76 to the park, with 50 percent of the pier designated for commercial development and the remainder for public open space, relieving the trust of its responsibility to secure liability insurance and transferring the half-mile of the park below Chambers Street (the tail) to Battery Park City Authority. An amendment that no one thought particularly troubling was allowing Pier 54 to be rebuilt outside its original historic footprint—until several years later, when we realized what they had been planning in secret.

Community Concern Grows

Opposition to the bill came from several quarters. Environmental organizations lobbied Cuomo to veto it. The maritime industry pushed back against the new tax. And preservationists decried the increased density of inboard properties that would result from the transfer of air rights.[23]

It was at this point that Douglas ended his seven-year quest to create the neighborhood improvement district, and in July, the Durst family stopped providing financial support for the effort.[24] Durst understood that increasing the height of buildings next to the waterfront reduced the value of buildings farther inland. He also understood that the transfer of air rights played into the hands of opponents of the neighborhood improvement district yet failed to provide long-term maintenance and operating support for the park.

The governor still had to sign the bill, and public debate began immediately after the legislature's approval. The sudden introduction of air rights transfers seemed to distract public attention from other proposed changes. To generate support for the commercial amendments, the trust amplified its bogus claim that the park was required to be self-sufficient, bemoaned the park's dire financial condition, threatened the closure of the Pier 40 athletic fields, and played to community residents who visited the park during the summer when it was most heavily used.

Try to keep in mind this is all being done by a public benefit corporation established "to operate exclusively for purposes relating to the promotion of the health and social welfare of the people of the state."[25]

Madelyn defended the $2 fee on maritime passengers—an important "piece to the puzzle," which is the term Dan Kurtz used in a PowerPoint presentation sent to A. J. to describe the finances of the park in support of the district. However, Dan's PowerPoint presentation differed from what the trust presented in public and listed contributions from Pier 40 at

$8.5 million—not the $10–12 million the trust stated publicly. He projected revenue from the neighborhood improvement district at $3 million annually, which was nowhere near the $10 million projected by the district's steering committee, and he did not include an annual contribution from Friends.[26] But then again, he was trying to provide rationale for the legislative amendments.

Although the board of the reconstituted Friends professed to soldier on, the campaign for the neighborhood improvement district slowly faded. The leadership of both the trust and Friends probably realized that the district conflicted with their interests. While it would provide critical long-term funding for the park, it would reduce Friends' ability to raise money from the same audience. More important, it would create an independent board making decisions about spending and introduce a third party they did not control to their dance.

Criticism about the eleventh-hour deal to allow the transfer of air rights to nearby property owners grew. The chairman of the reconstituted Friends, Mike Novogratz, was a principal of Fortress Investment, a company that oversaw the funds in the partnership that had bought a majority stake in St. John's Terminal directly across from Pier 40.

Even though the trust and Friends had lobbied for the legislation, Novogratz claimed ignorance about the air rights provision and insisted that he was not involved in the St. John's purchase six months earlier while he was on the trust board. I questioned the appearance of impropriety, and Common Cause agreed that when property owners serving on nonprofit boards potentially benefit from decisions, it "raises red flags immediately."[27]

That is a potential problem with corporate and real estate leaders serving on government entities and nonprofit boards. On government entities, they cannot oppose the position of the elected official who appointed them and can sway government decision-making to their benefit, and as important benefactors, they can influence nonprofits agendas.

In August, the Greenwich Village Society for Historic Preservation spoke out against the potential impact of the air rights transfers on neighborhoods facing the park. However, Tobi Bergman from Community Board 2 dismissed concerns about luxury high-rise development, and a citywide park advocacy group, New Yorkers for Parks, described the strategy as innovative. The trust tried to tamp down the controversy by stating that they would only transfer air rights from the half dozen piers where the Hudson River Park Act allowed development, which represented about 1.6 million square feet of new transferable air rights.[28]

Amendments Finalized

In November, Bill de Blasio was elected mayor in a landslide victory. De Blasio had run on a campaign of empowerment and equity, and everyone expected a change from Mayor Bloomberg. But we had no idea what de Blasio's position regarding the park would be.

Later that month, after Cuomo had approved the amendments to the act, trust board member Paul Ullman wrote in *The Villager*, "This legislation was born out of extensive, exhaustive, and comprehensive discussions hosted by HRPT and included every conceivable slice of the parks various constituencies. And, yes, air rights were discussed."[29] The statement was an absurd description of the public process that had preceded the passage of the legislation.

The transfer of air rights, a possible expansion of the heliport, a $2 fee on maritime tour and travel passengers, and many other changes had not been discussed publicly. Some issues had been discussed at various meetings, but no public review or approvals were requested or provided. Except for a privileged few, no one had reviewed the legislative language, and even elected officials who supported the changes later claimed that they were misled about aspects of the bill.

Unfortunately, the liability insurance waiver only covered the bicycle path, which was already under the jurisdiction of the state transportation department. The trust was still required to buy liability insurance for the park in the private marketplace. Circle Line filed suit against the proposed passenger tax, claiming that they already paid rent to the trust and the new tax had not been included in their lease. As the year ended, Pier 57 was still in limbo, and Youngwoo proposed placing shipping containers on the pier and renting them to artisans for markets and craft shows in what he was calling the "Super Pier."

As 2014 began, controversy over the transfer of air rights reached a fever pitch. At a meeting of the land-use committee of Community Board 2, Madelyn revealed that the legislative amendment created more transferable air rights than she had initially led the community to believe. All the piers in the park, including the twelve public recreation piers, were covered by the provision for the transfer of air rights.[30]

The huge potential for out-of-scale development raised alarms to a much higher level. The estimated 3.5 million square feet of development rights eligible for transfer could be worth as much as $1 billion.[31] The trust indicated, however, that they would initially limit transfers to 1.6 million square feet because they wanted to develop some of the piers themselves. "This will be a very transparent process," Wils promised, astonishingly. "We are here to work with the community."

In March, Mayor de Blasio appointed Carl Weisbrod as chairman of the City Planning Commission and thus director of the City Planning Department. De Blasio stressed that Weisbrod would focus on housing and jobs to address the city's affordability crisis.[32] Carl had led the rezoning of Trinity Church's property in Hudson Square, established their business improvement district, and had recently led the trust's task force. He would be approving any rezoning and the air rights transfer across Route 9A, which were prohibited under current city zoning. Perhaps de Blasio did have plans for the park.

In early May, elected officials and community board members were further shocked to discover that a secret agreement had been signed six months earlier by the governor's office, the trust, and the Atlas Group (an owner of St. John's Terminal) to transfer $100 million worth of air rights from Pier 40. Their plan was to build several residential buildings as well as retail and commercial office space.

The governor proposed using the Empire State Development Corporation's power to avoid the city's land-use review process, which reduced public involvement and shortened the time required to implement the transfer. That proposal seemed to put Cuomo at odds with de Blasio, who had called for a thorough city review, and place Deputy Mayor Alicia Glenn, now vice chairwoman of the trust, in a difficult position.[33] It also made Mike Novogratz's statement that he was unaware of the air rights transfer more difficult to believe.

Later that month, a suit was threatened against the secret agreement, but Madelyn indicated that the deal had been scrapped and that the trust would follow required land-use review procedures and involve the local community.[34] Local elected officials had filed a request under the Freedom of Information Law for the signed secret document but had yet to receive a copy.

For me it was déjà vu all over again, reminiscent of the falsehoods and collusion of the battle over Westway thirty years earlier. I questioned whether the trust could still be trusted given its lack of transparency and the behind-the-scenes deals that were eroding faith in both its leadership and the public process.[35] I warned of a return to the legal and political battles that had stymied West Side development for more than a decade. Due to government reluctance to develop a viable long-term funding mechanism as initially envisioned, the park was still starved for resources, and "spot" zoning was an inappropriate, one-shot approach to the problem.

Susanna Aaron, a Friends board member and local community resident, responded in *The Villager*, defending the trust leadership and asserting that they were trying to find solutions and that no one else was stepping up.[36] But the trust was not involving elected officials, local community boards, or the Advisory Council in its decisions, nor was it pushing the city and state to address public funding shortages. Instead, they were busy creating new commercial development opportunities in the park and in adjacent communities.

Concerts on Pier 97

In August of 2013, problems arose with the concert series at Pier 26 as noise levels disturbed Tribeca residents. The trust announced that the concert series would not return in 2014 and hired an acoustic engineer to propose ways to reduce noise emanating from the park during concerts.[37] In 2014, the trust relocated the concert series that had infuriated Tribeca neighbors to Pier 97.[38] The original Friends lawsuit had forced the relocation of Department of Sanitation parking and maintenance facilities from Pier 97 to a new garage build directly across Route 9A. The trust had spent $16.1million of the settlement funds we generated rebuilding the pier. However, just as at Pier 26, the pier's deck was left as an open concrete slab without any improvements for recreational use and was closed to the public.

The trust was exploiting these open venues for short-term revenue with concerts, photo shoots, and commercials while keeping them closed to the public. It claimed that the concerts were an interim revenue-producing activity that would not affect the Hell's Kitchen neighborhood because the area was primarily industrial. This was not strictly accurate. Even though two adjacent neighbors were the new Department of Sanitation garage and the Con Edison power station, the Durst Organization was building a state-of-the-art "green" residential building just across the street from the pier. Some thought that the trust failed to complete the public amenities on Pier 97 because Douglas had resigned as Friends' chair.

At Pier 97, the trust implemented their sound engineer's recommendation to relocate the stage and point the speakers across the river to reduce noise complaints in the adjacent neighborhood. After the first major concert in 2014, noise complaints from the residents in new condominiums on the Jersey's Hudson shore came pouring in.[39] The concerts ended abruptly that year.

Pier 57 Changes

It became apparent that Youngwoo & Associates' proposed retail and entertainment project at Pier 57 was failing. As a result, in September, the trust announced that RXR Realty would join the Pier 57 development team and that a new plan would be proposed—one that included commercial office space that the original plan lacked.[40] The new plan would retain the market and retail space on the pier's first floor that Youngwoo & Associates had proposed. One might think that a new partnership, a major land-use change, and a now ninety-nine-year lease had changed the financial prospects of the redevelopment project significantly.

The new project was an entirely different project from the one the trust had approved five years earlier. For this reason, they should have issued a new request for proposals to ensure that the public got the biggest bang for its buck. However, the trust had already failed to redevelop Pier 40 twice and Pier 57 once. They were desperate for a win.

It so happened that Scott Rechler, the chairman of RXR, was a friend of Governor Cuomo who had appointed him vice chairman of the Port Authority. RXR's president, Seth Pinsky, who led their negotiating team, had been the president of the city's Economic Development Corporation and was Madelyn Wils' former boss. RXR would now develop between 200,000 and 300,000 square feet of commercial offices on the pier while Youngwoo focused on retail uses and markets on the ground floor.

Pier55 Inc. or Diller's Island

Another surprise announcement from the trust knocked civic leaders, park advocates, environmentalists, kayakers, rowers, and the historic ship community for a loop. Facilitated by new amendments to the Hudson River Park Act, the Diller/von Furstenberg Family Foundation had agreed to donate $130 million to build a new "island" at West 15th Street in Chelsea.[41] Diller and von Furstenberg were generous High Line patrons, and Diller's Gehry-designed, sail-shaped headquarters for IAC, his media conglomerate, was located just a few blocks up Route 9A at 18th Street.

The trust proposed a 2.4-acre theater complex at Pier 55 to replace the historic Pier 54, but this proposal raised serious concerns for several important reasons. For one thing, Pier 54 was the pier from which the *Lusitania* had sailed and the pier where the survivors of the ill-fated *Titanic* disembarked from the *Carpathia* after that historic tragedy. This Cunard-White Star Pier thus had significant importance in terms of maritime history, and the park's General Project Plan had called for the pier to be public, with exhibits and public education about the parks maritime history and hosting historic vessels.

The proposed replacement, Pier 55, would be sixty-six feet high, with no fendering and with only one berth for a barge planned to support three new theaters. Pier 55 was also in an entirely different location and had a different configuration than the historic Pier 54. The planned "island" was about 150 feet offshore and required that more than five hundred new piles be driven into the Hudson.[42] Although the facility would be open to the public, its use and design had not received public input or been subjected to public review.

Moreover, given its location in an officially designated state Department of Environmental Conservation estuarine sanctuary, there should have been a robust environmental review—but there was not. Anything built in the sanctuary was legally required to be water-dependent—but this project was not. The island would contain three performance spaces with extensive landscaping even though such spaces could be built anywhere on the inboard side of Route 9A and did not need to be in the Hudson.

The trust defended the secretive planning process, explaining that the donor would not provide the necessary money unless he controlled the design. In addition, both the trust and the donor made the argument that Pier 54 had been used for concerts since the 1990s and the 2013 amendment allowed performing arts in the park, ignoring the fact that Pier 54 had supported commercial maritime activities since 1910 and had been designated as a historic pier in the park's General Project Plan. Pier 54 had indeed hosted a popular concert series in the late 1990s, but it was widely viewed as an interim use, to be discontinued once the pier was rebuilt to celebrate the maritime history of the West Side waterfront.

It was apparent that Diana and Madelyn had solicited private donations to rebuild the pier and offload the public responsibility to restore it much earlier. They started working with Barry Diller in 2012, but he was not interested in rebuilding Pier 54. He was interested only in building a new "pier" to his specifications. They were told that if his request were to be accommodated, the Diller/von Furstenberg Family Foundation would pay for pier construction and operation for the first twenty years. It was an offer the trust could not refuse.

The project prompted an opinion piece by David Callahan in the *New York Times* questioning the influence of billionaire donors and suggesting that declining public support for public projects provided an opportunity for a new generation of Medici privatizing decision-making in the public realm.[43] Madelyn Wils took offense, stating that she was leveraging public funding and had discussed the public nature of the project with the donors.[44] In reality, she was trading control of public property for private funding.

The arrangement underscored another problem with the involvement of private donors in public spaces. Rather than addressing agreed-upon public needs, these donors often use their philanthropy to celebrate themselves and control public property to meet their own goals. There are exceptions in which patrons support public design and construction. But there are also examples like Pier 55 that raise red flags.

Budget and Contracting Audited

In December 2014, the chair of the trust received a report from the state comptroller with the results of his audit of trust finances between April 2010 and March 2014, the period after Dan Kurtz assumed responsibility for financial oversight.[45] The audit found that despite regularly crying poverty, the trust had been lax in collecting almost $300,000 in rent and had allowed some tenants to deduct capital investments from their rent. That provision was not included in their lease.

The report recommended the trust improve its practices related to revenue collection, purchasing, investments, payroll, and budgeting. According to the report, the trust had awarded or modified $16.9 million in contracts without complete documentation regarding vendor selection and other information.

The report made nineteen recommendations to improve financial management and increase the transparency and competitiveness in contracting at the trust. Key recommendations included strengthening controls regarding revenue contracts and revenue monitoring, following guidelines for the procurement of goods and services consistently, and improving budget procedures to ensure they comply with regulatory requirements.

Apparently, our perception that the trust did not have a good handle on its finances was accurate. As the new year began, questions were raised about the trust's transparency and the activates of the reconstituted Friends.[46]

15

Public Resistance
Builds (2015–2016)

● ● ● ● ● ● ● ● ● ● ● ● ● ●

The 2013 amendments to the Hudson River Park Act had given the trust new tools for commercialization of the park, and they leaned into the opportunity. I was primarily focused on stopping the construction of the theaters on Pier 55 in the estuarine sanctuary.

As 2015 began, the Hudson River Park Trust again tried to offload the cost of building and operating the estuarium, the estuary research and education center that everyone had wanted built since construction of the park began. Clarkson University, located in the upstate New York town of Potsdam, agreed to build and operate the facility, which Clarkson estimated would cost about $50 million. As would eventually become apparent, Clarkson failed to implement its agreement.

However, other projects moved forward, and there were even proposals to repurpose a fabled ship. Later that year, RXR, now the lead developer of Pier 57, proposed docking an ocean liner next to Pier 57 and converting it into a hotel.[1] The previous year, Anheuser-Busch had docked a Norwegian Cruise Line ship at the Manhattan passenger ship terminals to be used as a hotel for the Super Bowl game in nearby Giants Stadium in the New Jersey Meadowlands. Apparently, that idea resonated with the Pier 57 development team.

Sixteen years earlier, New York Cruise Lines, which owned Circle Line and World Yachts, had asked me if the SS *United States* could be converted into a hotel to be docked at Pier 83 at West 43rd Street. The *United States*, at 990 feet in length and a hundred feet longer than *Titanic*, was the world's largest passenger ship. Aluminum had been used in her construction, and that, combined with her powerful engines, made her very fast. On her maiden voyage in 1952, she had crossed the Atlantic at thirty-eight knots (forty-four miles) per hour and was the first American ship in a century to win a coveted Blue Riband for the fastest Atlantic crossing.[2]

Susan L. Gibbs, granddaughter of the ship's designer, had worked tirelessly to preserve the vessel, and RXR Realty expressed interest in repurposing the ship. However, the firm faced the same problem New York Cruise Lines encountered because the ship was longer than the West Side piers and would stick out into the navigable waterway—even though the Chelsea Piers had been cut into the city so that ships of the day could dock there. The plan never came to fruition, but to the developer's credit, RXR continued their effort to preserve and repurpose this storied ship on the Philadelphia waterfront.[3]

Pier 55 Review

The trust requested public comments on its proposal to replace historic Pier 54 with a new Pier 55, which Barry Diller proposed as a theater and entertainment pier. In 2015, I joined more than a hundred elected officials, individuals, and representatives of organizations who weighed in on the issue.[4] Riverkeeper and the NY/NJ Baykeeper, a nonprofit citizen guardian of the New York–New Jersey Harbor Estuary that I hold in high esteem, submitted a detailed thirteen-page list of objections focusing on environmental issues.[5] As expected, the trust denied that any of these issues prevented the project from moving forward.

In February, I received a call from Paul Gallay, the new executive director of Riverkeeper, telling me that the organization was considering filing a lawsuit to stop the project if it did not receive additional environmental review. O'Melveny & Myers, a law firm with more than seven hundred lawyers, agreed to represent Riverkeeper pro bono, and they needed co-plaintiffs with standing, a legal term meaning that the court recognizes a plaintiff's right to sue. They had read my testimony, knew of my historic involvement in the park, and asked if I would help.[6]

I agreed, as did Rob Buchanan, an educator, environmental advocate, and boat builder who operated out of the Village Community Boathouse on Pier 40. Rob taught a course at The New School that included boatbuilding and rowing and emphasized the history, geology, and politics of the harbor. He regarded the harbor as a public space, and he had often voiced concern about commercial exploitation of the waterway.

We met with the attorneys and Riverkeeper staff to discuss strategy for the lawsuit, and the trust caught wind of our intentions. I was told that two of Riverkeeper's major financial supporters who had relationships with members of the trust's leadership threatened to withdraw their support, which represented approximately 7 percent of the organization's $3 million annual budget—if Riverkeeper continued with the suit.

In a shocking about-face, both Robert Kennedy Jr. (a Riverkeeper founder) and John Adams of the Natural Resources Defense Council, two influential members of the Riverkeeper board, objected to the lawsuit. In what Rob Buchanan called "the darkest moment of the whole thing," Riverkeeper withdrew from the suit just three weeks before the filing deadline. Gallay was embarrassed and upset, and their action was a shameful reminder of the disproportionate influence of wealthy donors.[7]

O'Melveny & Myers were willing to continue their representation, but they needed a nonprofit client so they could continue to work pro bono. One problem is that we, and they, were counting on Riverkeeper's legal and technical expertise. At the Metropolitan Waterfront Alliance annual conference and boat trip, which took place two weeks before the deadline, I bumped into Kent Barwick, one of the city's most respected and experienced public advocates, and Clay Hiles of the Hudson River Foundation. When I complained bitterly that the trust might succeed with the project without a challenge, they mentioned that the City Club of New York, which had been reconstituted after a long hiatus, included some accomplished and committed public advocates and lawyers dedicated to protecting the public realm and might assist.

I had initially met Seymour Durst, Douglas's father, at an anti-Westway luncheon hosted by the City Club in 1983. The club had recently stopped the Wilpon family, who owned the New York Mets, from building a shopping mall in the Shea Stadium parking lot, which was public parkland. Kent agreed to contact Michael Gruen, the club president, and ask if they would consider joining the suit. Within a week, they agreed, and our papers were filed the day before the deadline. It is no exaggeration to say that this action shook the trust's world.[8]

Pier 57 Reimagined Again

As 2015 ended, Governor Cuomo approved a modified development plan for Pier 57 that called for half a million square feet of offices, markets, stores, and cultural spaces topped by an 80,000-square-foot rooftop park. Google, which already had five thousand employees working in West Chelsea, was expected to occupy 250,000 square feet of office space there.[9]

Anthony Bourdain, the celebrated television personality, chef, and author, agreed to create a market focused on international food and local offerings on the first floor and part of the mezzanine. The Pier 57 project had received its approvals in 2013, prior to legislation allowing commercial offices on the pier. The governor's press release referenced the park as operating on the premise of self-sufficiency—not that self-sufficiency was required.

Pier 57 had become an interesting mixed-use project, but the trust had manipulated procurement regulations over time, presenting the park purist in me with a dilemma. Our original prohibition against hotels, commercial office space, and residential development had two purposes—reducing commercial development in the park and stimulating redevelopment across Route 9A. But the one thing you can count on is change. Stimulating inboard redevelopment was initially intended to generate capital funding and stable, long-term financial support for maintenance and operation of the park. But those inboard neighborhoods had been rezoned without any new revenue being designated for the park.

The modified plan for Pier 57 ensured the preservation of a historic nine-hundred-foot-long pier that had been built for the Grace Line in 1952 and was listed on the National Register of Historic Places. The public would benefit from a rooftop park and an acre of perimeter walkways that allowed visitors to get closer to the river. The modified plan did not preclude future maritime activity. I would have preferred that Pier 57 be redeveloped with uses that complemented maritime activity and the public use and enjoyment of the waterfront. But after eight years of trying, Youngwoo & Associates had not crafted the right formula to restore the pier and ensure a financial return for the trust.

Restoring a half-million-square-foot historic pier might not be possible if its uses were limited to maritime and recreational activities and entertainment. Remaining true to initial intentions verses maximizing public good may sometimes require a recalibration to reflect changing economic and social realities. No one benefits from a large, empty, deteriorating hulk on the waterfront. In the end, the goal is to maximize public benefit, but the public bidding process should never be corrupted.

As the new year began, I publicly questioned the change in the development team, land use, and the lease term for Pier 57.[10] The plan moving forward was very different from the one the trust had approved eight years earlier. The new uses and a ninety-nine-year lease created the opportunity for a greater financial return for any developer and, hopefully, for the park. I thought that issuing a new request for proposals would draw significant interest from other developers and increase competition for the use of this public asset.

The scope and quality of the environmental review was important too. Pier 55, which would now be built at the same time, was less than two hundred feet away. Considered together, the offices, markets, and multiple performance venues in both projects would generate significant pedestrian traffic across Route 9A, especially in the evening when office workers were leaving, concertgoers were arriving, and shoppers were traveling in both directions. Evening is also the busiest time on the bicycle path.

I thought that the environmental review should assess the cumulative impacts of both projects and that the trust should not be allowed to separate the environmental review of the two projects being built at the same time right next to one another. Both projects were overseen by the trust, but segmenting the environmental reviews ignored the cumulative impacts of these two major projects.

It did not take long to get a response. Diana Taylor wrote a nasty retort insisting that I stop pretending to know anything about the park or care about those in the community who loved it.[11] She further charged that my true goal was to stop a widely supported park project while burnishing my own reputation.

My response was swift. My op-ed article in *The Villager* stated that I was saddened by Ms. Taylor's vituperative and fallacious attack and that I would much rather be cheering on the trust than questioning them.[12] The environmental impact statement for Pier 57 anticipated Pier 54 would become a public pier celebrating the waterfront's maritime history, yet an entirely new Pier 55 was now being proposed right next door.

At the time, the initial Pier 57 environmental review took place. The surrounding neighborhood was primarily meat-packing plants and warehouses and was now adjacent to the Chelsea Market and the upscale Meatpacking District with hotels and boutiques. The cumulative impact of Piers 55 and 57, as now proposed, had not been analyzed. Unsurprisingly, the trust had no response.

The year ended with a *New York Times* editorial regarding the redevelopment of Pier 40 and air rights transfers.[13] It spoke to the park's financial need and the concerns of elected officials and community residents. It also questioned the accuracy of the figures the trust bandied about regarding the costs and value of air rights, especially since the value had been agreed to before an appraisal was even completed.

Elsewhere in the Park

In May 2015, the opening of a new Whitney Museum in the Meatpacking District made it abundantly clear that the West Side waterfront was being transformed. That summer, the trust continued its efforts to commercialize public open space, proposing that a beer garden be allowed on Pier 62 in Chelsea Waterside Park.

Save Chelsea, a broad-based coalition concerned with preserving the integrity of this historic neighborhood, objected to commercial development displacing public space and compared the beer garden to other restaurants opening in public parks throughout the city.[14] Although community opposition killed the project, the proposal represented yet another example of the trust subverting its responsibility to provide for public use and enjoyment of the waterfront.

During the summer of 2015, there were also changes at St. John's Terminal. Fortress Investment Group sold its stake to Westbrook Partners for $200 million.[15] Fortress had brought Westbrook into a deal to buy a majority interest in the 1.1-million-square-foot building three years earlier. In October, Mike Novogratz retired from Fortress where he had overseen $9 billion in assets.[16]

In spring of 2016, the trust signed a lease with the Classic Car Club to occupy about an acre of space on Pier 76 and replace the stables being vacated by the police department's horses. The club had thirty-eight high-end cars, ranging from a Lamborghini Huracan to a McLaren 570S. Members paid monthly dues of $180 and bought points, allowing them to drive the car of their choice for a day.[17]

Although the club planned to open its café in the front of its building—which was adjacent to the bicycle and pedestrian path—to the public, its bar and lounge were for members only. Commercialization had won again, with the trust leasing space to a high-end private car club in a section of the park that had the least amount of public open space. That space could have hosted year-round recreation opportunities for community residents. The following year, the reconstituted Friends hosted a high-stakes casino night at the Classic Car Club with tickets priced at $150 each to raise money for the trust.

The trust continued to monetize the rebuilt piers they had left unadorned and with open surfaces. They hosted a fashion shoot on Pier 26 and concerts on Pier 97. However, by 2016, the Durst Organization's new residential building, the Via, was nearing completion. Douglas had hired acoustic engineers to monitor and record sound levels emanating from the Pier 97 concerts during construction, and it turned out that levels far exceeded those specified in the city's noise code.

Concerned that noise would significantly diminish the quality of life for his future tenants, Durst complained to the trust during the 2015 concert series and threatened to sue if the concerts continued. After many months of rancorous legal back-and-forth, the first concert of the 2016 season proved to be the last.

Pier 55 Suit Moves Forward

By mid-2015, my primary focus became our lawsuit against Pier 55. O'Melvany and Meyers had assigned three lawyers to the case, and Michael Gruen, an attorney and president of the City Club, provided additional advice. Although O'Melvany made it possible for us to file our objections by the deadline, they had clearly expected to be working with Riverkeeper. Through the efforts of Douglas Durst, who continued his involvement in the park, we received the additional assistance of Richard Emery of Emery, Celli, Brinckerhoff, and Abady, an accomplished environmental litigator and a City Club member.

The trust was represented by David Paget of Sive, Paget & Riesel, an experienced environmental litigator who had represented the park when I was president. I knew David as a colleague, but our relationship was quite different now that he was an adversary working for Diana and Madelyn. He was cordial, but he told me he was confident that we would be defeated, adding that he had never lost an environmental litigation in his career.

Douglas objected to the lack of an environmental impact statement and the failure to involve the public in the decision-making, and the Durst family provided financial support to bolster the club's participation in the litigation. By the end of the year, Richard Emery was working with O'Melvany to prepare our case for the state Supreme Court.

With support from the Durst family, we hired Mortimer "Morty" Matz, a nonagenarian public relations wizard, to manage our press strategy. His team drafted press releases, helped shape and pitch stories, hand-held journalists, and provided timely follow-up to press inquiries. Public relations and the media are an important element in advocacy and public persuasion. The press can be a double-edged sword, so you have a better chance of shaping your message if you articulate your purpose clearly when interacting with the press and respond to questions accurately. When dealing with public works projects, earned media coverage can often get the attention of decision-makers at all levels.

In April of 2016, while the state Supreme Court was reviewing our case, the *New York Times* published a long and complimentary article describing the trust's solicitation of the donors for Pier 55.[18] Our opponents had apparently gathered as Superstorm Sandy was washing ashore to review plans for the project.

The article described the objections of Assemblywoman Glick and preservationists like Andrew Berman of the Greenwich Village Society for Historical Preservation but neglected to mention the City Club suit. It discussed the donor's generosity to the High Line and noted that the local community boards supported the project. The article ended with a quote from Tobi Bergman. "It is going to put the park on the map in ways that it's never been before," he said. "It hasn't been a glamorous park. But this is New York City, and what's important in New York is glamour." Who would have thought that a dedicated youth sports director would be advocating for glamour? It is a funny world.

Opponents' Issues

Pier 55 opponents were passionate in our objections. Rob Buchanan was most disturbed about the fact that, without any public review, someone was building a new structure in a protected area of the park that would impede navigation and the public's right of passage on the river. Most landlubbers think that kayakers and rowers just go out, paddle around a bit, and return to where they started.

Many human-powered boaters, however, see themselves as navigators exploring our city's waterways. I have met kayakers from Canarsie's Sebago Canoe Club having lunch with paddlers from Lower Manhattan on the bayside beach at the tip of Breezy Point in Queens, where I live.

Young boatbuilders rowing in gigs between Piers 34 and 40. (Tom Fox)

They were relaxing on the sand while waiting for the tide to turn to help take them home.

New York's waterways are inviting, exciting, therapeutic, alive, fun to explore, and should be accessible to the public. However, New York Harbor has a lot of commercial vessel and ferry traffic, strong currents, wakes, and winds. Human-powered navigators need protected spaces to get out of the current and away from larger motorized vessels. These protected spaces, or coves, are like rest areas along the Hudson River, the state's first natural highway.

Rob Buchanan was a cofounder of the New York City Water Trails Association, and he was representing that constituency as an individual plaintiff in our suit. The trust claimed that members of their staff never saw anyone boating or fishing in that area and that there was no real demand for access to that protected cove between the piers. They argued that navigators could find haven elsewhere in the park.

Rob and I were both concerned about the secretive nature of the planning and the reliance on an environmental assessment rather than on a full environmental impact statement. I was also exercised about the loss of a historic pier, historic ship berthing, and open public space on the waterfront.

The trust and Diller had been secretly planning this vanity project for two years before announcing it to the public, and Madelyn Wils apparently misled the state legislature to get their support. In her deposition, state Assemblymember Deborah Glick, one of the two cosponsors of the 2013 amendments stated, "Ms. Wils' testimony implies that the passage of this amendment was an implicit endorsement of the Pier 55 project. That implication is wrong. At the time the amendment was being considered, the HRPT led myself and other legislators to believe that plan was to make minor changes to then-existing Pier 54."[19]

In issuing its environmental assessment, the trust claimed that because the project would have minimal impact on the environment, there was no need to produce a full environmental impact statement. The trust argued that Pier 55 was simply a replacement for Pier 54, whose redevelopment had been assessed in the original environmental impact statement for the park. But much had changed since that statement had been issued. Adjacent Pier 57 was being redeveloped, and Pier 55 now blocked the "view corridor" along West 15th Street. More important, the adjacent neighborhood of warehouses and meat-processing plants serviced by refrigerated trucks had given way to hotels, shops, and restaurants whose patrons routinely arrived in Ubers and Bentleys.

The Design of Pier 55

Pier 55 was designed by Barry Diller and the landscape architect Thomas Heatherwick, with the landscape designed by Signe Nielsen of Matthews Nielsen. Heatherwick was also designing London Garden Bridge, which was being proposed at the same time.[20] Both of these projects were being presented as "gifts" from wealthy patrons, and each was "floating" over their respective city's signature waterway.

In New York, Pier 55 was endorsed by the mayor, the governor, local elected officials, and the public, who perceived the project as a gift that would provide public entertainment, theater, performances, and apparently a bit of glamor. In London, where the city was contributing $37 million to the Garden Bridge, local vocal opposition claimed that the project would displace green open space in a neighborhood and argued that prohibitions on public use—no bicycles, picnics, public assembly, kites, or musical instruments—were too restrictive. London's mayor questioned the public contribution required, and the project was eventually scrapped.

The 2.4-acre "island" called Pier 55 undulated with richly landscaped hills separating the three performance spaces intended for crowds of different sizes.[21] The overall design was complicated, and the island rose to a height of sixty-six feet. The pile-supported structures were unique. As a result, several marine engineering firms refused to bid on the project, and eventually construction costs escalated to $260 million.

The trust had obviously been waiting for the passage of the legislation before presenting the final design for public review, which they did almost immediately after Cuomo signed the bill. The public comment period was scheduled between Thanksgiving and New Year's Day in an obvious attempt to minimize public participation, although after complaints from the community, the trust extended the comment deadline to mid-January.

Losing in Court

O'Melvany filed our objections to the trust's approval of the project in state court in June 2015, and Regional Director Judith Enck stated that the U.S. Environmental Protection Agency determined that the project may "result in substantial and unacceptable impacts to the aquatic resources of natural importance" and informed the Army Corps that they were undertaking an additional twenty-five-day review of the application.[22] Richard Emery filed a complaint with the Environmental Protection Agency in December questioning the potential impact of the project on an aquatic habitat of significant national importance.[23]

Unfortunately, O'Melvany's argument—that the trust had violated the Public Trust Doctrine—was rejected in April 2016.[24] After that loss, O'Melvany announced that they would no longer represent the City Club, and Richard Emery directed our legal initiative moving forward. We appealed the state court ruling, and, in June 2016, the state Appellate Division issued a preliminary injunction against construction in the Hudson while our appeal was pending.[25] The trust then got New Yorkers for Parks and the New York League of Conservation Voters to file amicus briefs.[26] We tried to solicit Riverkeeper to file an amicus brief and rejoin the fight, but they turned us down.

There is a moratorium against driving piles in the park's estuarine sanctuary between November 1 and April 30 each year.[27] On July 18, the preliminary injunction was modified, allowing nine piles to be installed to support the south "balcony" along the bulkhead. In September, they ruled against us.[28] Less than three weeks later, the trust and Pier55 Inc. proposed driving forty-four piles to support the causeways, arguing that pile-driving had to be completed by November 1 to keep the project on schedule.

We then filed another Article 78 against the trust, Pier55 Inc., and the state Department of Environmental Conservation, which was represented by Attorney General Eric Schneiderman. On January 20, 2017, the state Supreme Court denied that petition, paving the way for the project to proceed in the spring.[29]

The First Air Rights Transfer

Another major effort moving forward was the rezoning of the St. John's Terminal and the transfer of air rights to that site from Pier 40. The project was rebranded St. John's Center, and the air rights transfer and rezoning required a City Environmental Quality Review. Madelyn still insisted that Pier 40 was in danger of falling into the Hudson and that repairs would cost between $100 million and $125 million. In October 2015, the city and the trust had agreed on the transfer of air rights from Pier 40. The trust was allowed to transfer 200,000 square feet of air rights, for which the developer agreed to pay $100 million, and they received permission to demolish the existing building.[30]

By November of 2015, West Side elected officials weighed in, complained that the initial scope of the environmental assessment was inadequate, and questioned the preliminary results, which claimed critical elements of the project could only be determined later in the process.[31] They questioned the impact of the project and voiced concerns about big-box stores, public-school seats, and the claim that all outstanding questions would be addressed by additional study before the certification of the project. Soon afterward, Community Board 2 passed a unanimous resolution agreeing with the elected official's concerns and requesting the air rights transfer be limited to 200,000 square feet.[32]

In April of 2016, the appraisal commissioned by the trust valued the Pier 40 air rights at $75 million—far below the $100 million Atlas and Westbrook Partners had agreed to pay—but the deal proceeded as agreed.[33] The planned development now had five buildings—two of them thirty-six and forty-five stories tall.

That summer, City Planning created a Hudson Special Hudson River Park District to allow 1.5 million square feet of air rights to be transferred to properties directly across Route 9A, stretching four miles from Chambers to 59th Streets. It included the entire Greenwich Village waterfront and was strongly opposed by both Community Board 2 and the Greenwich Village Society for Historic Preservation.[34]

Carl Weisbrod at City Planning and Madelyn Wils at the trust worked both sides of the street, as the economic development crew had finally found a way to facilitate new West Side development projects. They used air rights from the park to increase density in adjacent communities and generate a one-shot revenue source. It was the opposite of what the West Side Waterfront Panel initially proposed, which was using the increased value generated by the park and the rezoning of the adjacent inboard properties to provide reliable maintenance, operating, and capital replacement funding for the trust.

A *DNAinfo* article detailed the Pier 40 air rights deal along with the central role played by the lobbyist Jim Capalino, beginning in 2014 shortly after the amendments were passed.[35] Capalino had been on the board of the original Friends since 2005 and was known to be close to Mayor Bill de Blasio. He had done the right thing and resigned from Friends when he began representing Atlas and Westbrook.

However, his chief operating officer apparently tried to convince the city to skip the required land-use review process and use the state's powers instead. He parroted Wils's claim that Pier 40 was going to collapse, and the trust could not wait the year or two required to complete the review process. The article mentioned numerous meetings and communications with now City Planning Commission chair Weisbrod and Deputy Mayor Alicia Glenn. Apparently, the De Blasio administration was interested in the West Side waterfront.

By October of 2016, after two years of contentious negotiations, the City Planning Department agreed that the St. John's site could be reconfigured as a mixed-use development with 1,586 residential units. Elements like big-box stores, which were most objectionable to the community, were removed from the plan.[36] During subsequent negotiations, the developer reduced the amount of parking and agreed that 30 percent of the residential units would be affordable housing, which was a top priority for the City Council Speaker and the de Blasio administration.

In addition, a new South Village Historic District, encompassing ten blocks and 250 buildings, was created thanks to advocacy by Community Board 2 and the Greenwich Village Society for Historical Preservation. By year's end, the City Council approved the air rights transfer, the developers put $100 million in escrow, the city kicked in another $14 million for Pier 40, and Madelyn made it known that the trust now hoped to develop commercial office space on Pier 40 to generate additional revenues for the park.[37] That would require amending the Hudson River Park Act again. Concurrently, the condo market was softening, and it looked like the St. John's project would not be moving ahead quickly.

Tourist Helicopters in the Park

The 2011 settlement between Air Pegasus/Liberty Helicopter and the Hell's Kitchen Neighborhood Association had banned tourist flights at the 30th Street Heliport. However, Douglas Durst happened to read on a blog that indicated tourist flights might be operating again. Douglas informed the Neighborhood Association and Danny Alterman, the lawyer who had worked with Al Butzel on the earlier suit. Danny, in turn, arranged for his paralegal to make a reservation for a flight—and to bring his camera.

The flight included several other people—tourists—who had their cameras as well. With the transgression documented, the Neighborhood Association filed suit in state Supreme Court and got an injunction to stop the flights. This time the settlement was quick; the heliport operator agreed to pay the group's legal fees and to contribute $50,000 a year to the trust for the next five years.[38] Helicopter noise is a constant problem, and controlling it is like a game of whack-a-mole: the moment you stop one source, another pops up.

Several years later, helicopter flights began leaving from New Jersey to circumvent city restrictions against tourist flights. These choppers flew the same routes prohibited at city heliports and soon began advertising so-called thrill rides during which passengers could take photographs while flying with the chopper doors off, posing yet another challenge for the Hudson River Park and other parks in Manhattan, Brooklyn, and Queens.

16

A Court Battle Ends, and the Governor Delivers (2016–2018)

• • • • • • • • • • • • • •

As the popularity of Hudson River Park increased, so did interactions involving pedestrians, bicycles, and vehicles. Not surprisingly, transportation safety would become an increasingly important issue as the number of accidents grew. In June of 2016, for example, a bicyclist heading south on the Route 9A bike path crossing Chambers Street was killed by a drunk driver.[1] In January of 2017, the Clinton Hell's Kitchen Chelsea Coalition for Pedestrian Safety renewed calls to address serious issues involving bicycle safety in the park.[2]

The waterfront esplanades in both Hudson River Park and Battery Park City are shared public space, and it has always been difficult for bicyclists and pedestrians to coexist in a limited area. In both locations, the Route 9A bike path was designed for cycling, not strolling. Just as bicyclists are asked to walk their bikes on the esplanade, so too should pedestrians avoid the bicycle path. Enforcing that rule is generally a losing battle but one worth fighting. Bicyclists use the esplanade, and people stroll on the bike path. In September of 2017, Community Board 1 asked the city transportation department to modify its official bike map to indicate that the esplanade was a shared space and that bicyclists should use the Route 9A bike path rather than the esplanade.[3]

The bike path below 59th Street is the southern portion of what is known as the Hudson River Greenway, which is part of the 750-mile Empire State Trail that runs from Lower Manhattan to Canada.[4] The 12-mile section on Manhattan's West Side follows the waterfront from the northernmost tip of the island south to the Battery. The segment in the Hudson River Park has been described as the busiest bicycle path in America, and its uses continue to grow.[5] New attractions in the park have begun to draw larger crowds to the waterfront, and the introduction over the years of electric bicycles, skateboards, and scooters have only exacerbated the problem.

Ensuring public safety in the park requires public education, appropriate design and signage, and consistent enforcement. There is a major problem because the bike path falls under the jurisdiction of the state transportation department but is maintained by the Hudson River Park Trust. The divided jurisdiction makes it harder to make safety improvements, install appropriate signage, or enforce regulations governing the bike path in the park because no one is quite sure who is responsible for enforcement.

In October 2017, a terrorist drove a rented pickup truck down the bike path from Pier 40, killing eight people and injuring eleven others before smashing into a school bus near Battery Park City. The assassin leaped from his vehicle, screaming, "Allahu akbar!"—Arabic for "God is Great!" He was shot by a police officer as he ran along Route 9A.[6]

It was the city's worst terrorist attack since 9/11. It drew even greater attention to the serious problems on the bike path that the state transportation department had yet to resolve—more than a decade after Dr. Carl Nacht and Eric Ng had been killed there in 2006.[7] A report issued the following year by the nonprofit group Transportation Alternatives had called for installing bollards to protect cyclists and pedestrians throughout the city, but their recommendation had been ignored.[8]

The state transportation department is responsible for design and capital improvements on the bike path, and the Hudson River Park Trust cannot install signage, let alone bollards. Not surprisingly, the issue of pedestrian and bicycle safety along Route 9A has consistently fallen through the cracks, and since addressing the issue requires time and money, it is a political hot potato and continues to be a challenge.

The state transportation department initially responded to the problem by placing large concrete barricades and highway barriers along the length of the bike path, much to the chagrin of cyclists.[9] The agency subsequently bought and began installing bollards on the bike path, but they were fixed in place and, as I have heard said, designed to "stop a tank."

In September of 2018, prosecutors sought the death penalty for the terrorist.[10] The following month, the surviving victims filed a lawsuit against New York City and the trust for $600 million.[11] The New York City Law Department responded, erroneously, that the bike path was designed and maintained by the trust and that the city had no responsibility. The confusion is typical of issues related to who is responsible for the bicycle path. The bike path is state property.

Special Permit for Piers 92 and 94

In 2017, the city Economic Development Corporation had proposed extending three special permits for the commercial use of Piers 92 and 94. Vornado Realty held the permits and relied on an affiliate, MMPI Piers Inc., to manage the operations and implement public improvements requested by Community Board 4 in 2009 when the permits were issued.

Community Board 4 had initially objected to uses of the pier that were not water-dependent but reluctantly agreed that the project could move forward with one provison: public open space along the north side of the pier would have to be connected to a large public area at the pier's tip, with an extended roof to provide shade and interior space with public restrooms. The board also requested traffic improvements, changes in the city bus route serving the piers, and shuttle buses to reduce pedestrian crossings of Route 9A traffic. After eight years, the developer Vornado Realty Trust had yet to meet its commitment, and the community board insisted those measures be implemented.[12]

"Obnoxious Persistence" at Pier 55

Back in 1978, when I was working in the South Bronx coordinating a national community gardening demonstration project, I met a spirited community activist named Irma Fleck, a sixty-year-old, four-foot-eleven-inch dynamo who was a successful fundraiser. When I asked Irma what her secret was, she replied, "Obnoxious persistence." She added, "I find someone with money, sink my teeth into their ankle, and I don't let go until they donate."

Our effort to defend the estuary was a David vs. Goliath struggle. Pier55 Inc. was supported by the trust, the reconstituted Friends, Barry Diller and Diane von Furstenberg, the donors who proposed the pier's construction, the mayor, the governor, the media, and almost all the local elected officials. We applied Irma's legal version of obnoxious persistence in the hopes of leveling the playing field.

We got beaten up in the press, and we were condemned by the new West Side social set and community activists like Tobi Bergman of Community Board 2 who supported the project. However, our attorney, Richard Emery, was both resourceful and tenacious. And although the City Club, Rob Buchanan, and I were frustrated by our losses, we shared a desire to continue the fight. Most important, the Durst family was committed to seeing the effort through.

We had appealed to the State Court of Appeals, New York State's highest court, but perhaps not surprisingly, the judges in that court refused to hear the case. All seven of them had been appointed by the governor, who strongly supported the project. At the one public court hearing, Barry Diller himself arrived on a bright red Vespa. While the press focused on Mr. Diller's novel entrance, I noticed Marcy Benstock, with whom I had not spoken for over twenty years and who said, "Hi, Tom," as we were leaving the courthouse. I assumed that she approved of our lawsuit, but she had also heard that I was writing this book and offered to fact-check my manuscript.

We had filed a complaint challenging the project's compliance with the Clean Water Act in federal court because the estuarine sanctuary was a "special aquatic site," and the proposed use was not water-dependent. After exhausting our options on the state level, we hit pay dirt on the federal level. In March of 2017, Judge Lorna Schofield ordered the permit be rescinded and construction halted, and the application for a permit reassessed by the Army Corps of Engineers.[13]

When the news hit the press, it unleashed a torrent of criticism from trust chair Diana Taylor and Mike Novogratz of Friends.[14] Novogratz wrote letters to *The Villager*, one of which ran under the headline "Thanks, 'Crusty' Club" and another headlined "Row, Row Your Selfish Boat," castigating the plaintiffs personally. I responded that our objections were not personal and failing to follow the required public review process could be costly in the long run.[15] That is what I had told Sandy Frucher back in 1986—after the defeat of Westway, but he had listened.

The previous September, Barry Diller had voiced his suspicion that Douglas Durst was bankrolling the City Club's legal fight.[16] Douglas finally confirmed his impression,[17] and the unexpected revelation changed the narrative in the press, which began pitching the litigation as a billionaires' battle.[18]

I tried to dispel that perception, explaining that the battle was actually "a struggle between two groups with diametrically opposed views for the future of Hudson River Park." I noted that wealthy donors throughout the country were trying to shape the future of public parks, and citizens were resisting. In this case, a vanity project had been struck down in federal court.[19] But the story in the press remained two billionaires battling each other from then on.

The trust had redesigned the project to circumvent the need for a Clean Water Act permit at the end of 2016, and the Army Corps issued a permit modification allowing construction to continue in May. We filed a second federal complaint in July reiterating our claim that despite the changes in project design, the project was not water-dependent.[20] Barry Diller was concerned that litigation would continue to stall the project, so the trust requested a meeting to discuss a possible settlement in August 2017.

We met with the trust leadership and their attorney at Mr. Diller's InterActiveCorp headquarters to attempt a compromise. The Pier 55 senior team, including artistic director Scott Rudin and their attorneys, were in the conference room. Introductions were made followed by light banter while we all awaited Diller's late arrival.

Once Mr. Diller concluded his monologue, we proposed various compromises, and it seemed as if further discussion might lead to some sort of resolution. We offered to prepare a proposed settlement agreement.[21] Just as the meeting was breaking up, Richard Emery asked if anyone knew why the director of the Whitney Museum of American Art had invited him to a meeting the following day. Everyone at the table, including Madelyn and Diana, shrugged.

Diller Walks

The next day, Richard met with Adam Weinberg at the Whitney and was told they had been working with the trust to install a sculpture by the artist Richard Hammond on the southern shore of the Gansevoort Peninsula. In 1975, the architect Gordon Matta Clark had created a sculpture that involved cutting huge holes in the walls of the abandoned Pier 52, at that location, to highlight the setting sun over the Hudson and encourage public use of the waterfront.[22] *Day's End*, as the piece was known, was popular even though a warrant issued for Matta Clark's arrest forced him to leave the city.

A week later, the City Club plaintiffs joined the Whitney team in a briefing at the museum, complete with a model of the work. The Whitney was committed to meaningful environmental and public review and asked for our feedback. Mr. Hammond's skeletal sculpture evoked the park's maritime past and did not impede recreational reuse of the Gansevoort Peninsula or boating access to the water. If the museum followed a public review process and secured the required approvals and permits, which they committed to doing, we had no objections.[23]

This time, Madelyn's proclivity for secrecy seems to have come back to bite her. Two weeks after we had met to discuss a compromise, Diller suddenly announced he was taking his marbles and going home.[24] Project costs had grown to $260 million, and he was furious that after spending $40 million, he might face another setback—one that might be serious.

Immediately after his announcement, a headline reading, "Diller: Fools Kill Park for No Reason," appeared in the *New York Post*. Someone must have decided that was a little over the top because the online edition read, "Diller Upset He Wasted 'Way More than $40 Million' on Failed Park Plan."[25] Thankfully, a *New York Times* story the next day more accurately described the demise of the project.[26]

Let's Make a Deal

After our victory, Mayor de Blasio called Douglas to suggest that the trust would compete the reconstruction of Pier 97 adjacent to his new building on West 57th Street if Durst withdrew his support for continuing litigation. That pier had been rebuilt, but the project still required over $30 million in surface improvements, which had been delayed by the trust. Douglas declined, and soon afterward, we invited representatives of several environmental organizations to meet at Douglas's office to explore possible settlement agreements and discuss how we might all work together to restore the estuarine sanctuary.

A few days before our meeting, Cuomo called Douglas to ask what it would take for the City Club to withdraw its objections so he could bring Diller back to the bargaining table. Douglas called me to discuss possible options, and we agreed that if the governor committed to fund the completion of the park and protect the estuary against any similar incursions, we should withdraw our objections.

Having invited our colleagues to consider alternatives, we presented the governor's offer at our Friday meeting. Everyone agreed that if Cuomo committed, we should accept the deal since completing the park was our shared goal. The trust had stated that 77 percent of the park was complete, and private funding was committed for both Pier 55 and the rooftop park on Pier 57.[27] According to the trust, the public funding gap to complete the park was $189 million, and the state was required to contribute half.

But the park is over 70 percent water. And to understand what restoring and protecting the estuary entailed, the Hudson River Foundation outlined a research and restoration plan for the estuarine sanctuary.[28] The Hudson River Foundation and The River Project were members of the trust's technical advisory committee for the Estuarine Sanctuary Management Plan and had worked together on other in-water projects in the park. They estimated that research and restoration plans would cost $134 million over ten years.

I doubted that Cuomo would convince the state and city to commit a total of $323 million in new public funding to the park to save the Pier 55 project. But one thing I had learned early on in fundraising and negotiating is that you never know until you try.

On Saturday, Douglas called Cuomo with our proposed terms. I asked him to emphasize that Governor Mario Cuomo had started the park with Mayor Dinkins in 1992 and Andrew could complete his father's legacy. Cuomo said he would speak with Diller. That afternoon, Cuomo confirmed that Diller agreed to return to the table and said that the "Second Floor" was preparing a statement announcing the compromise.[29]

However, we had nothing in writing, and we requested a memorandum of understanding or letter of agreement. Cuomo refused to put anything in writing and said we had to rely on his word. We agreed, and on Tuesday Cuomo announced that he had brokered a compromise allowing work on Pier 55 to proceed.[30]

I have always believed that agreements should be in writing so they are more easily enforced. If the other side balks, it is a warning sign that should not be ignored. In this case, there was no way to enforce this agreement, we had almost settled for less, the time was tight, and the prize was the completion of the park.

After a three-year fight, we had reached a compromise in a week. It is important for advocates to understand how quickly things can move when the person in power wants something to happen and the issue has a lot of press appeal and influential supporters. You have to close the deal and move quickly when the time is right—closing is critical.

The estuary research and restoration plans were sent to the governor's staff, and we began follow-up discussions with a negotiating team of senior staff from the "Second Floor" lead by the governor's Counsel. In addition to the promised funding, we voiced serious concerns about the trust's leadership making backroom deals without appropriate community participation, which became a major theme in our continuing discussions with the "Second Floor" over the next year and a half.

At the same time, we held our breath to see what the governor would include in his budget that spring. Of course, Cuomo had to win a third term to keep his commitment, and we would not know about that until the next November.

An Updated Value Study

In 2017, the reconstituted Friends had released a report on the benefits of the park. The report was compiled by the Regional Plan Association, which had worked on the both the West Side Waterfront Panel's 1990 assessment of potential impact of the park's construction and the original Friends 2008 real estate study.[31] Their report showed that public investments in the park had generated significant dividends for the city and the state beyond increasing property values.

The report emphasized the park's influence on local and regional economies, employment, tourism, development, property taxes, property values, and demographics, and it broadened the understanding of the park's impact from 2000 to 2015. A $720 million public investment in the park had resulted in $1.2 billion in direct economic returns for the city and $1.4 billion for the state. The forty-one million square feet of new development built adjacent to the park represented a quarter of all new development in Manhattan during that period.

Property taxes in that area were growing 9 percent faster than Manhattan tax revenue below 59th Street and 28 percent faster than the entire borough. Approximately three thousand direct jobs were created in the park. The number of jobs was expected to grow to 5,000 with the completion of Piers 26, 55, and 57. A third of the park's 17 million visitors were tourists, generating approximately $60 million in spending annually. While it was wonderful to get a broader understanding of the breadth and depth of the park's economic impact, the study was another opportunity lost. The reconstituted Friends failed to recommend any mechanism to capture a portion of that documented public value and create a long-term funding stream for maintenance and operations.

Pier 40 Again

In the spring of 2017, the trust had established The Future of Pier 40 Working Group to set parameters for redevelopment. In November, the group held public hearings and received more than 3,100 responses to a questionnaire it had distributed. Respondents stated the importance of the park: 78 percent said they used the park regularly, and 81 percent said that the park was important to the future of the community and the city. A new goal for Pier 40 revenue was set at $12.5 million/year. The pier had not generated anywhere near that amount in the past, and the trust's revenue projections for the pier were not that high. The inflated revenue projection required more commercial development, although the respondents objected to tall buildings on the waterfront.[32]

When asked about acceptable uses, over 90 percent of respondents supported cultural events and performance spaces/venues, 89 percent wanted restaurants and cafes, and 70 percent supported art galleries, artist space, and studios. None of those uses, however, would generate significant revenue. Surprisingly, over half of the respondents supported commercial or government offices, which was what Madelyn was now encouraging. Residential development was not even mentioned.

Tobi Bergman was still playing a central role in the Pier 40 process. He had resigned from P3 and Pier 40 Champions and was now serving as the chair of the Pier 40 Working Group, whose final report was released in November and approved by CB 2.[33] The trust was expected to release a new request for proposals for Pier 40 the following spring, but the legislation had to be amended to allow for offices.

Big Changes Happen

The new year started off dramatically when Governor Cuomo, in his 2018 State of the State message, committed to completing the park. Praising the vision of then-Governor Mario Cuomo and Mayor David Dinkins, he stressed that Hudson River Park was a phoenix that rose from the ashes of Westway and became a blueprint for using open space as a catalyst to transform adjacent neighborhoods from Brooklyn to Buffalo. He proposed fulfilling his father's nation-leading vision working with the city through matching investments needed to complete the park and ensuring that the estuary was protected.[34]

There were major changes in the trust board as Joe Rose left earlier in 2017, and by November, de Blasio appointed Carl Weisbrod, who had stepped down as City Planning chair, to the trust board. Trust leadership recommended that Weisbrod sit on two board committees—Finance and Investment, and Governance.[35] In January of 2018, Manhattan Borough President Gale Brewer appointed Douglas Durst, a lifelong resident of Hell's Kitchen, to the trust board representing Community Board 4.

The appointment was approved by the Cuomo, but the trust, which traditionally issued a statement welcoming new board members, failed to comment on Douglas's appointment.[36] In May, Douglas attended a meeting of Community Board 2 and presented testimony regarding Pier 40 that must have made Madelyn pause. It was rare for a trust board member to appear before a local community board with their own testimony.[37]

In February, RXR and Youngwoo & Associates announced that, with the withdrawal of Anthony Bourdain's proposed market from Pier 57, Google would expand its presence and occupy the majority of the pier.[38] The rooftop park that the developers were planning and the public promenade might be great assets, but now more office space was being built in the park.

The Pier 57 press release was issued several days after Google announced its $2.4 billion purchase of nearby Chelsea Market. By year's end, Google proclaimed that it would invest another $1 billion to create a Hudson Square campus, expanding its footprint from Chelsea south to Tribeca.[39] The tech industry had washed ashore.

The Trust's Obfuscation

After the Google announcement, I lamented the fact that an interesting mixed-use project had become a horizontal office building and bemoaned the lack of transparency and public participation in the Pier 57 planning process.[40] I was corrected by Lowell Kern, chairman of Community Board 4, who stated that the trust had presented its revised plans to the board, and they had approved.

As for the issue of transparent public meetings, Kern said that anyone who wanted to review and comment on the trust's plans simply had to attend the board's Waterfront, Park, and Environment Committee meeting and/or their full board meetings. I repeated my concern that the trust was not exercising its responsibilities to ensure meaningful public involvement in the development and operation of the park.[41] If you were not on a particular community board's mailing list or did not check the trust website regularly, you would have no idea that the uses at Pier 57 were being modified. If you did attend the community board meetings, you had two minutes to state your concerns or suggestions.

Limiting the distribution of information to selected audiences enabled the trust to reduce public involvement in decision-making and to pit community boards and interest groups against one another. If someone questioned a decision, it was justified by stating that the issue had already been presented to the community board affected, and why should anyone else object?

Trust staff routinely insisted that a person seeking information only had to check its website regularly, but that put the responsibility on the citizen. If they wanted people to comment on their actions, they should send electronic notifications of their plans. They informed the public about educational, recreational, and cultural programs and sent invitations to Friends fundraising events, but you had to search their site to get information about planning, budget, construction, and policy initiatives?

In addition, the trust does not provide the email or direct office phone number for its senior staff on their website. Anyone without that information must call their switchboard, which is only staffed on business hours, to contact staff members—another subtle way to control public access. The trust is one of the few public park corporations in the city that does not participate in the Wayback Machine, a digital internet archive started in 1996 containing hundreds of billions of web pages and a critical tool for research.[42]

Cuomo Delivers $50 Million, Negotiations Continue

In March of 2018, Cuomo's proposed budget for the following fiscal year, running from April 1 to March 31, included $50 million in new funding for the park and a commitment to ensure that the Estuarine Sanctuary Management Plan was completed.[43] In April, the legislature approved the governor's request, providing that the state's financial commitment was matched by the city.[44]

In May, the "Second Floor" agreed to integrating the Hudson River Foundation's recommendations into the trust's updated plan for the estuarine sanctuary and repackaged three projects already in the trust's budget for an initial media splash. They allocated $10.2 million for shoreline habitat at Gansevoort Peninsula, $10 million toward the construction of the estuarium, and $9 million for an ecological feature at Pier 26.

However, the only "new" initiative proposed was a $1.5 million oyster habitat restoration project working with the Billion Oyster Project between Piers 26 and 32 in Tribeca.[45] Oysters are a critical, or keystone, species in the Hudson estuary, and that investment was a pleasant surprise.

Police Department Budget Request for Pier 76

The 1998 Hudson River Park Act required that the city police department make "best efforts" to relocate the tow pound from Pier 76, yet two decades later they had not even identified an alternative site. While reviewing the city's preliminary 2019 budget request, Community Board 4 members were shocked to find a request for $26 million to repair the pier's roof and electrical system without seeking funding to ensure the stabilization and safety of the pier itself.

Community Board 4 is starved for public open space, and the 2013 amendments to the act required that the pier be transferred to the trust when the property was vacated. At more than five acres, Pier 76 was a coveted public resource, and Community Board 4 objected to the police department's budget request, stating that any public investments in the pier should only be for the safety and stabilization of the pier itself—not tow pound maintenance.[46]

The Hell's Kitchen Neighborhood Association had been advocating for the public use of Pier 76 for years. On hearing about the community board's objections, Douglas made it clear that if the association wanted to force the relocation of the tow pound from Pier 76, the Durst family would support the effort.

Rebuilding the Playground at Chelsea Waterside

The first playground at Chelsea Waterside Park was built in 2002 by the original Friends of Hudson River Park with a generous $1 million donation from the Durst family. The money represented the first private philanthropic donation to the park, and the playground was accessible to kids of all ages. As the first water play park in the area, it was well used, but without adequate maintenance or reinvestment by the trust, the playground deteriorated. By 2017, many of the original water features were broken.

At the annual meeting of the Chelsea Waterside Park Association that June, the now rebranded Hudson River Park Friends announced they were working with the trust to rebuild the playground. The $3.4 million budget for the new facility was supported by $500,000 from Assemblyman Dick Gottfried and $800,000 from City Council speaker Corey Johnson.[47]

In June of 2018, the playground opened to rave reviews. The defining feature was a brightly colored, sixty-four-foot-long zoomorphic representation of a pipefish, a creature native to the Hudson estuary.[48] The fountain featured a pair of two-ton cows' heads, with water spouting from their mouths, that had been salvaged from the building that housed the New York Butchers' Dressed Meat Company on Eleventh Avenue at 40th Street—which had been demolished in 1991. The playground's climbing structures included winged granite cartouches that marked the entrances to the Miller Highway. Another pair of cartouches had been incorporated into the design of Washington Market Park in Tribeca.

When the Hudson River Park Conservancy completed the plan for the park in 1995, preservationists had urged that remaining artifacts from the Miller Highway be integrated into the park's design. I had heard that the state transportation department had stored some artifacts in a maintenance facility in Syosset, Long Island, so one day, on a trip out to the Hamptons, I visited the facility.

I introduced myself, mentioned the artifacts, and to my surprise, discovered that an entire wall of the building was lined waist-high with fifty-pound circular city seals that had decorated the sides of the highway. Each cast iron seal represented one of the four periods in the city's history, starting with the Dutch colonization and ending with the 1898 consolidation of the five boroughs to form Greater New York. In an overgrown lot adjacent to the building were several street signs, large concrete eagles, and winged cartouches.

Although I had informed the trust about my find, when I checked Google Earth while writing this book, I noticed that although the lot is still vacant and overgrown, the artifacts were not visible. Apparently, like most historic artifacts left unattended, they disappeared.

Air Rights Sale and Transfers Increases Density

In December of 2017, new plans were released for a residential mixed-use development on a site on Eleventh Avenue between 29th and 30th Streets that was owned by the Georgetown Company. The developers, now Douglaston and Lalezarian Properties, proposed two buildings, sixty-two and thirty-seven stories high, respectively, with 1,200 apartments.[49] The site was within the Special Hudson River Park District established by City Planning in 2016, and developers proposed buying air rights from the Chelsea Piers Complex between 18th and 23rd Streets a half mile to the south.

In June, the City Council approved the sale of 158,000 square feet of the trust's air rights from the Chelsea piers complex for $52 million.[50] The 2013 amendments to the act had created a new financing mechanism, and City Planning had created a special zoning district to facilitate the transfer, which insured the park would continue to reshape Manhattan's West Side— although not as initially intended.

By October of 2018, St. John's Center was again commanding attention. Earlier that year, with the market for condominiums being weak, Atlas and Westbrook had sold their development rights for the southern portion of the property to Oxford Properties, of Toronto, for $700 million.[51] Oxford planned a $2 billion, 1.3-million-square-foot, twelve-story office building on the site. The plan retained the lower floors topped by a new structure with 100,000-square-foot floor plates that were increasingly desirable in commercial offices. The anticipated 1,586 residential units were significantly reduced, as were the number of affordable units.

An Engineered Ecological Restoration at Pier 26

In October of 2015, the trust had announced that Citigroup would donate $10 million toward the reconstruction of Pier 26. The donation completed the projected $30 million reconstruction budget.[52] Two months later, the trust unveiled the plans for the reconstruction of Pier 26, which is located in Tribeca, the original home of The River Project.[53] The original plan had been for the pier and the estuarium to become a center for research and education regarding the estuary.

Marcha Johnson, a landscape architect with the city Parks Department, had worked with The River Project as a volunteer for nearly thirty years to maximize the pier's educational and ecological value. Their plans included

St. John's Terminal building across Route 9A from Pier 40. (Tom Fox)

incorporating various in-water textured fabrics and structures that were considered habitat-friendly, allowing light to penetrate the pier deck into the under-pier environment, establishing a nearshore area with native vegetation, and constructing pier edges to support the Hudson estuary ecosystem.

In October of 2018, construction of Pier 26 began.[54] But instead of showcasing sustainable and energy-efficient construction, with a design focused on restoration of Hudson River wildlife, it was first rebuilt as a generic pier with a rectilinear, solid concrete deck and standard piles that rendered several unique features originally proposed for Pier 26 impractical. The trust's refusal to allow dredging meant that accommodations for visiting research vessels was also dropped; as a result, the opportunity to facilitate research was diminished.

Although several plans for the pier, stressing ecological restoration and education, had been developed over the years, Madelyn Wils decided to start with a blank slate and design the entire pier anew. She had deep roots in the neighborhood: her family had lived on Duane Street, where her husband's "butter and eggs" business was located, and she was a former chairwoman of Community Board 1.

Madelyn opened the community design process to anyone who had an idea for the pier. The neighborhood had changed significantly since the theme of ecological restoration and environmental education was initially adopted.

With few active recreation areas in Tribeca and a growing population of young people, there was a conflict between environmentalists and local parents advocating for space where their children could play. Unsurprisingly, the environment lost. Two small playing fields, which were lighted and surrounded by twenty-foot-high bright blue netting, were placed right in the middle of the pier.

The trust should have focused on research, protecting and enhancing natural habitat, and environmental education. Environmental advocates had hoped that Pier 26 would introduce visitors to the wonders of the estuary and attract wildlife of various sorts, including migratory and resident birds, so that the full scope of the natural ecology at the water's edge might be understood and appreciated.

There were three primary funding sources for the pier: $10 million each from the Lower Manhattan Development Corporation, New York City, and Citibank, whose world headquarters was directly across Route 9A. The original plans included intertidal habitat in the shallow water near the bulkhead and the restoration of plants and animals indigenous to the riverbank.

For inexplicable reasons, the trust spent a fortune designing a "faux" ecological restoration and environmental education project at the tip of the pier, in the deepest portion of the park's waterway, where a new structure had to be engineered to support tidal wetlands. That area is constantly buffeted by wind-blown swells and vessel wakes and is an extremely precarious place to try to create a shallow water environment.[55]

In 2014, the trust had announced that Clarkson University, working with the Beacon Institute, would raise $40 million to design and build the estuarium, which the two institutions would then operate. In 2016, the trust announced that Rafael Vinoly Architects was now designing the facility. But two years later, with plans for Pier 26 moving forward, the estuarium was still unfunded.

Cuomo had earmarked $10 million towards the $50 million cost of the planned structure, but Clarkson could not raise the remaining $40 million. After waiting a quarter of a century for this facility to be built, it was profoundly disappointing to watch restaurants and commercial attractions take precedence over research and educational facilities as the trust bounced from donor to donor, looking for someone to pay for the estuarium.

When we next met with the "Second Floor" to discuss the details of Cuomo's funding commitment and the estuarium, we got the impression that the governor's office was advocating some type of indoor estuary classroom on Pier 26 without Clarkson.[56] Cuomo had committed his administration to the completion of the park, but it would not be finished without the estuarium. Nonetheless, the Hudson River Foundation and The River Project were delighted to hear that Clarkson was out of the picture. As the year ended, the trust issued a request for public comment and notice of hearings for *Day's End* as the community planning process for Pier 97 began.

Another Stealth Project at Pier 25

In March of 2018, the trust withdrew their request for proposals issued the previous December seeking a manager for maritime activities, including a water taxi dock, on the south side of Pier 25. Citigroup expressed interest in being a subcontractor for the water taxi dock, but no one responded to take overall responsibility, so the request for proposals failed. Soon afterward, a permit request to modify a dock in Jersey City was filed with the New Jersey Department of Environmental Protection. The purpose was to support a corporate waterborne shuttle for employees, guests, and invitees to travel between Citigroup's Jersey City office and their headquarters at 388 Greenwich Street in Tribeca.

The trust commenced negotiations with Citigroup on a direct basis for the installation of a public water taxi dock at Pier 25 with nonexclusive use rights.[57] Madelyn told Douglas that the trust had not presented the project to the Advisory Council because the trust did not have a seat on the council and did not participate in setting the meeting agendas. The trust did not inform Community Board 1 until mid-September, just before the dock's planned installation in October, and the board was understandably miffed by the delayed notification.[58] It confirmed my fears about the trust's approach to public review.

Community Board 1 was concerned about the potential impact on the nearby playground on Pier 25. Residents of nearby Battery Park City were suffering from exhaust, noise, and foot traffic generated by the Port Authority's ferry terminal, and the community board was sensitive to the potential impact of the private corporate service on a public pier. The trust responded that the site had been approved in the environmental review for the park twenty years earlier and that the trust had "carefully considered environmental and operational factors associative with locating the landing near the playground."[59]

The community board passed a resolution referring to the trust's statement that initial approvals for the park authorized the landing and service at that specific location and that the trust did not need to get the board's review or approval since the permits had already been secured. They requested that air quality monitoring devices be installed to assess emissions and that the results be made publicly accessible. They also asked that Citigroup consider expanding use of the water taxi outside weekday service hours to transport little league and soccer leagues teams to Governors Island on the weekends.[60]

What the trust chose to ignore, or misrepresent, was that a water taxi servicing various locations in the park was included in the park's General Project Plan and initial environmental impact statement. The water taxi was planned to move people north and south along the waterfront, but not commuters shuttling back and forth to New Jersey. In 1997, it was New York Water Taxi, not the trust, that received the required approvals and installed a water taxi dock at this site, but Pier 25 only had interim uses and no permanent location for a playground at the time.[61]

My October 2018 op-ed article in *The Villager* mentioned that during the past two decades, the neighborhood had changed dramatically, as had uses on the pier, and noted that the proposed dock had been permitted for a different maritime purpose. I voiced concerns that another major park project had been initiated without informing the Advisory Council; in fact, this time it had not even been discussed with the trust board.[62] I knew that because Douglas was surprised when he heard of the project, and he was a trust board member.[63]

The trust must have given Citigroup enough confidence regarding the outcome of their negotiations for them to spend upwards of $1 million building the dock and contracting for its installation. Why didn't they use that time for community review and approval as required by the Hudson River Park Act? I suggested that if the trust "wants to be trusted, it should work in an open and transparent manner with the local community and all stakeholders, not just their corporate partners." Diana Taylor, the trust chair, has been a director of Citigroup since 2009.[64]

Park's Twentieth Anniversary Gala

October saw the reconstituted Friends annual gala, an event at which the trust celebrated the twentieth anniversary of the 1998 Hudson River Park Act and the park's creation. The event was held at Pier 60 in Chelsea Piers and drew more than a thousand park supporters, including such celebrities as Martha Stewart and Jay Leno. It also raised more than $3.2 million for the park.

I was fond of Leslie Kameny's original park logo, which had been used for twenty-six years and was quite elegant, but a new logo and other branding items created by Pentagram, the celebrated design firm, were rolled out at the gala.[65] The park was now officially Hudson River Park, or HRPK, and new banners, uniforms, and signs in a blue and green color scheme were to be used throughout the park. The logo was incorporated into fifteen-foot-tall lighted stanchions, in welcome and directional signs along the piers and pathways as well as in large, illuminated signs on top of buildings like City Vineyard on Pier 26.

I had always enjoyed the original Friends annual gala, but I had not attended one since the start of our lawsuit involving Pier 55. I was persona non grata with both the trust and the reconstituted Friends, which, given my taste for being a bit of a renegade, made strolling around the cocktail party and dinner particularly enjoyable. I was seen but pointedly ignored by Taylor and Wils, which was fine with me. However, I enjoyed seeing old friends from various agencies, community boards, and environmental and park organizations with whom I had worked over the years.

17

Will the Incoming
Tide Return?
(2019–2023)

● ● ● ● ● ● ● ● ● ● ● ● ● ●

Over the past four years, the Hudson River Park has witnessed profound and constant changes in terms of financing, public support, and leadership. The changes have been so frequent, and have occurred on so many fronts, it can be hard even for a person deeply enmeshed in the project to follow the multiple twists and turns and to keep track of the myriad players in and out of government.

This is not surprising for such an ambitious undertaking, especially in a large and complex city like New York, where major projects invariably come to fruition only after a long and often contentious journey.

On the plus side, the park is more popular than ever, attracting seventeen million visitors a year and offering a wide variety of attractions ranging from sports fields and kayak launches to dog parks and playgrounds. Park staff implements environmental research and education programs and hosts popular food festivals and public gatherings while volunteers tend gardens and teach fishing. At the same time, many critical issues involving matters such as long-term financing, commercialization, transparency, coordination with other related infrastructure projects, and public involvement in decision-making remain unresolved and can detract from public use and enjoyment of the waterfront.

In his January 2019 State of the State address, Governor Andrew Cuomo pledged to provide another $23 million to the park in the state's capital budget for fiscal year 2020 if the city agreed to match it.[1] This action may have marked the return of the incoming tide that carries all ships. With a total of $146 million in new state and city budget appropriations in response to our Pier 55 litigation withdrawal, the funding necessary to complete park construction is almost in hand.

In January 2019, Douglas Durst responded to Madelyn Wils's letter defending the trust's public actions in the installation of the Citigroup water taxi dock at Pier 25. He noted that the trust board had played no role in the approval of the water taxi dock, said that the board should be notified of the trust's actions and involved in decision-making—not just informed— and expressed his desire to improve the trust's operating procedures, particularly as they relate to ensuring openness and transparency.[2]

In February, our negotiating team—Douglas, Richard Emery, and I—met again with members of the governor's senior staff to discuss the transparency and governance of the trust. In a memo, we detailed why we thought that the current leadership of the trust was undercutting the credibility of both the trust and the governor by failing to operate in an open manner and failing to include the trust's board in decision-making. We included backup information on the trust's omissions and misrepresentations to the public.[3]

We encouraged Cuomo to consider leadership changes to get the trust back on course as an accountable public entity. To reduce the possibility of serious blowback by the trust, our meetings were held at the governor's Manhattan office or by phone, and all correspondence was on plain paper marked "confidential." By the fall, our attention turned to long-term park funding, and we encouraged Cuomo to support efforts to secure a new revenue stream from adjacent real estate development.[4]

Continuing Changes at Pier 57

The year 2019 saw a series of significant changes with respect to the businesses in the park. In February, RXR informed the trust that they intended to "move away" from the initial concept of a master lease for a marketplace at Pier 57 and instead operate the marketplace themselves and sublet space to vendors.[5] RXR also proposed that City Winery, a music venue that was being forced out of its home in Tribeca, establish a 350-seat concert hall with a 150-person loft, a hundred-person restaurant and tasting room, and a winery on the pier.

City Winery signed a twenty-five-year lease to relocate to Pier 57 that April.[6] Although a restaurant and music venue—not the marketplace envisioned in the original redevelopment proposal—it introduced some diversity into what had become a horizontal office building topped by a quasi-public park. Madelyn claimed that City Winery was "part of a larger marketplace," but not the large public marketplace initially envisioned. A first-floor plan showed market activities and City Winery—a public space environmental education labs and classrooms—and another space at the pier's tip that will accommodate another restaurant.[7]

The owners were already operating City Vineyard restaurant at Pier 26 and were the second business with multiple operations in the park. Crew, a hospitality group, was operating a town dock and Grand Banks, a restaurant aboard a Canadian fishing trawler at Pier 26, as well as Drift In, a food and beverage concession at Pier 45.[8]

New Legislation for Piers 40 and 76

Meanwhile, local elected officials had begun meeting regularly to jump-start redevelopment of Pier 40. In January of 2019, they sent Madelyn Wils a long list of financial questions. They asked for information about the pier's revenue-generating potential, an accounting of the $100 million earmarked for pile repairs, annual budget projections, information regarding trust efforts to secure funding to enhance resiliency from the city, state, and federal government, and Friends' anticipated fundraising goals.[9]

Wils responded by setting 2029 as a target date for the completion of the park, including Piers 40 and 76 and the estuarium.[10] She stated that the Hudson River Park Trust expected that Pier 40 would contribute at least $12.5 million annually, which, given inflation, would amount to $16 million annually a decade hence, or 26 percent of the park's annual operating and capital maintenance budget.

In May, a group of officials led by state Assemblymember Deborah Glick and state Senator Brad Hoylman unveiled a draft amendment to the Hudson River Park Act to facilitate the redevelopment of Pier 40. The proposal was to allow construction of 700,000 square feet of commercial office space and a ninety-nine-year lease on the pier.[11] The amendment called for both the creation of a Pier 40 Task Force that included members of the community and an increase in public open space if there were major redevelopment on the pier to balance commercial goals with community needs.

A public hearing was held to review the proposed amendment. At this point, Tobi Bergman, the former cochairman of Pier 40 Champions, who opposed office development on the pier, resigned from Community Board 2.[12] The trust and Friends leadership complained bitterly that the proposal still was not adequate to meet the park's long-term financial needs and asked the governor to modify the legislation to generate more revenue for the park. On New Year's Eve, Cuomo surprised many by vetoing the proposed amendment altogether.

The tow pound on Pier 76 seems to be where he turned his attention. Pressure to remove the tow pound increased in October of 2019 when the police department announced that they would undertake a study to analyze how much space they needed in an alternative location. With the support of the Durst family, the Hell's Kitchen Neighborhood Association again rose to the park's defense and sued the city to force the tow pound's relocation.[13]

In January of 2020, Cuomo proposed transferring control of Pier 76, which he dubbed "the most expensive parking lot in the world," to the trust.[14] Cuomo encouraged local elected officials to work with the trust to develop a more comprehensive financial strategy for the park including both Piers 40 and 76 and set a deadline of May 1, 2020, for any legislative language that might be required from Albany.[15] By the end of January, he approved new state legislation that forced the removal of the tow pound.[16]

At this point, my op-ed in *Crains* urged increased support for the park from neighboring real estate interests and increased transparency from the trust.[17] The Hudson River Park Trust, which had been established as a model for community participation and independent financing, was now planning and negotiating deals in private and failing to capture any of the value the park had created.

Joe Rose, an original trust board member, pushed back against my assertion. "Instead of sniping at the public servants who work tirelessly to complete the miracle on the Hudson River waterfront," he responded in *Crains*, "those who care about the Hudson River Park should put their shoulders to the wheel and participate in the constructive dialogue that has already gotten us so far."[18]

Scrambling to meet Cuomo's deadline, the trust formed a Hudson River Park Strategic Planning Task Force, chaired again by Carl Weisbrod, to focus on redevelopment options for Piers 40 and 76.[19] By late March, they released yet another estimate of park revenue, expenses, and capital replacement costs and listed the possible public and private revenue sources, including the redevelopment of Piers 40 and 76.[20] The plan included potential commercial developments on both piers, but the governor failed to embrace the trust's proposals.

Green Initiatives

While the trust's approach to planning, budget, and policy issues left much to be desired, their park programming and operations supported a wide variety of activities that increased public use and enjoyment of the park and encouraged and supported volunteer involvement. Activities ranged from environmental education, sports leagues, and yoga to tango dance lessons and tennis. The trust operated quality environmental education programs and began expanding their environmental initiatives in the park.

The trust instituted a community composting program in 2018 that now has ten different locations in the park. That fall, they hosted their first annual pumpkin-smashing festival.[21] The theme was "Don't trash it, smash it," and young park visitors tossed, pummeled, and smashed their Halloween pumpkins and learned about the importance of compost for the park's landscape as they worked off youthful energy.

The trust also introduced an initiative called "Parks Over Plastics," stopped buying single-use plastics for their operations and park events and asked their vendors and the public to participate. Thirteen of the park's twenty-one restaurants and concessions agreed to stop selling plastic water bottles, cups, straws, stirrers, and flatware and to substitute environmentally acceptable alternatives. All new tenants were required to agree to the restriction. Portable hydration stations were placed along the waterfront so visitors could refill their water bottles, volunteers collected plastics from the shoreline, and a public education campaign was implemented.

In the spring of 2019, Cathy Drew, who founded The River Project in 1986, announced her retirement and the start of a transition during which the group would merge its operations and staff with that of the trust. It was a great opportunity to continue the work of this successful organization and increase the trust's estuary research and environmental education programs. The transition has been smooth and the impact evident.

In September of 2019, Governor Cuomo announced, with great fanfare, the oyster restoration project he had promised. The project had grown to

$2.9 million and was placed in the waters between Piers 26 and 34 in Tribeca. Oysters are a keystone, or critical, species for the rebirth of the Hudson estuary. The Billion Oyster Project, which began as a project of the New York Harbor School on Governors Island, worked with the trust to identify specific locations for a placement of reef balls and the cages, or gabions, used to support oyster generation.

Fox in the Hen House

Every entity established to redevelop the West Side waterfront since 1986 has had an independent citizens advisory group. The 1998 Hudson River Park Act established an Advisory Council to provide the trust board with guidance on "all matters regarding the planning, design, construction and operation of the park."[22] The Advisory Council is composed of fifty representatives from community and civic organizations and elected officials from districts bordering the park.

I had been told that many Advisory Council members considered meetings a waste of time. There were no agendas distributed with meeting invitations, trust presentations dominated meetings, and the Advisory Council had not passed a resolution in several years. Major issues such as the 2013 legislative amendments were presented to the council as a fait accompli the day before they were introduced in Albany, and issues like the Citigroup water taxi stop were not discussed at all.

That was not how I remembered citizen advisory groups working, so I attended the meeting in November of 2018 as a guest. Only nineteen of the fifty Advisory Council members attended, and the attendance sheets indicated that the same number of members had attended recent meetings. I thought the council might be a good venue to continue my advocacy.

In June of 2019, the Advisory Council requested applications from organizations interested in filling several vacant membership seats. As a member of the City Club of New York's Policy Committee, I volunteered to represent the club on the council.[23] Ten candidates were interviewed by the Membership Committee, and four nominees, including the City Club, were elected which required approval from the trust board. Diana Taylor and Madelyn Wils voiced concern about my participation on the council but ultimately agreed to my election.[24] As for me, I was determined to help the council resume its traditional role supporting the park.

Pier 97

In November of 2019, the trust selected the designer to complete Pier 97, one of the last original public piers in the park.[25] The final design and construction of the pier's surface had been delayed several years. Pier 97 was a very important open space for Hell's Kitchen and Community Board 4.

The construction of Little Island had eliminated berthing for historic ships envisioned at Pier 54, and in November of 2020, the trust issued a request for proposals for berths at Piers 25 and 97—the other two locations designated for historic ships in the park. The trust claimed that the historic ships do not need dredging and stated that the 1998 act did not allow it, but the act allows dredging to maintain navigation.[26] Historic ships float into their berth, leave periodically for maintenance, inspections, and repairs, and provide public sailings and need dredging.

The trust claims that vessels should pay for their own dredging. But the cost would be astronomical compared to the trust instituting a long-term dredging contract to maintain the depth of areas in the park designated for historic ships or visiting vessels. This approach also favors maritime operators engaged in commercial activities and penalizes nonprofit organizations devoted to historic preservation, interpretation, and education.

The trust has neither a historian on staff nor a historic consultant, yet it often makes decisions regarding historic ships. If a ship is listed on the National Register of Historic Places, the decision is easy, but most ships are not on the register because of the cost involved. The *Sherman Zwicker*, for example, a Canadian schooner built in Nova Scotia in 1942 to fish for cod on Newfoundland's Grand Banks, was moored at Pier 25 in 2014.[27] Although an older vessel, she is not eligible for listing on the National Register and does not provide public tours, historic programming, or public sails, but hosts Grand Banks, a restaurant and bar. Floating restaurants like Grand Banks generate revenue for the trust and provide a visual amenity, but the initial intent of designating berths for historic vessels was public education and historic preservation.

Berths for historic ships should not be appropriated by commercial enterprise, especially since the trust has recently banned nonprofit historic ships from fundraising activities like renting out their vessels for special events to support their public programs and operations. The trust should embrace the majority of the park that lies in the river.[28] Nonprofit organizations providing public services that the trust cannot, or will not, provide are critical to fulfilling the vision of a world-class maritime park.

Advisory Council Becomes Active

The chair of the Advisory Council rotates annually among the three community boards. The outgoing chair Daniel Miller of Community Board 2 had initiated the election of new members to fill vacant seats and suggested extending the term of the chair from one to two years, and the new chair agreed. This gave the council leadership much more stability because the chair scheduled meetings, set the agenda working with a small executive committee, and gave our report to the trust board at its meetings.

The Advisory Council sprung back to life in March of 2020 when Jeffrey LeFrancois of Community Board 4 became the chair. He quickly established a committee to update our twenty-five-year-old bylaws. Jeffrey accelerated our meeting schedule to address unfinished business, distributed agendas prior to meetings, and ran meetings well. Responding to the pandemic, the council convened via Zoom, which helped to increase participation especially during the winter and in bad weather. Since then, more than thirty members and guests have regularly attended Advisory Council meetings and sometimes as many as sixty people.

In May of 2020, we joined local Community Boards 1, 2 and 4 in requesting that the state Department of Transportation dedicate one traffic lane on Route 9A to micromobility vehicles that were traveling at high speeds, undermining public safety, and causing chaos on the park's bicycle path.[29] By September, state transportation representatives attended our Advisory Council meeting to discuss the issue, although they did not agree to any changes in the roadway.[30]

Trust Leadership Changes

During our negotiations with the governor's staff, we focused on the trust's failure to abide by the laws regarding public review and the fact that they were cutting deals out of the public eye. In August of 2020, Douglas Durst resigned from the trust board. He had hoped to increase transparency and collaboration between the trust and other stakeholders, but he said in his resignation letter that unfortunately, "The Board, while a component of the organization, is engaged only when necessary, and then usually post facto. . . . I believe I can be a better advocate for the park outside of the organization."[31]

A few weeks later, Cuomo replaced Diana Taylor with state Environmental Conservation Commissioner Basil Seggos as trust chair.[32] Seggos then wrote to Mayor de Blasio to remind him that the state had amended the 1998 act and that if Pier 76 was not vacated by December 31, 2020, the city would owe the state $12 million and would be charged $3 million a month after that.[33]

The seismic shift in trust leadership continued in January of 2021, when Madelyn Wils resigned after ten years as president.[34] Her relationship with Cuomo seemed to have grown rocky and her plans for Piers 40 and 76 had been rejected. Although many people had a difficult relationship with Madelyn, others believed that she was instrumental to the park's progress. Pamela Frederick, a long-time trust board member and now publisher of *Tribeca Citizen,* published a letter from Friends' president Connie Fishman praising Madelyn's accomplishments.[35]

However, most of Madelyn's contributions involved economic development and private sector investment in the park, including office development and a nightclub at Pier 57, the Classic Car Club at Pier 76, three theaters on Little Island, new restaurants and food and beverage concessions at Piers 25, 26, and 45, an extravagant $100 million investment in Pier 40's piles, and a private water taxi dock for Citigroup.

Amendments that she initiated to the 1998 act resulted in the creation of a Hudson River Park Special District—not to secure a portion of the value the park created for adjacent real estate but to increase density with air rights transfers from the park. They allowed the heliport to expand into the river, levied a new fee on maritime tour operators, and extended commercial lease terms to ninety-nine years. Madelyn completed public projects like Pier 26 and initiated the design of Pier 97 and the Gansevoort Peninsula, but her vision seemed to resemble an amusement park rather than a public park.

In April of 2021, Deputy Mayor Vicki Been replaced state Department of Environmental Conservation commissioner Seggos as chairman of the trust.[36] It was the first time since the project began in 1986 that a city official was appointed chair. Many park advocates were pleased when Noreen Doyle, who had been involved in the park since 1994, was appointed president and chief operating officer of the trust in June.[37] The "change at the top" continued as Dan Kurtz retired in July. His retirement removed the last senior staff member who actively promoted economic development interests in the park.

Toward the end of the year, the engineer responsible for much of the substandard in-water designs left the organization, Mike Novogratz announced that he was stepping down as chairman of the reconstituted Friends in March of 2022, and state Assemblymember Dick Gottfried announced that he would not run for reelection that November. It looked like the decks were clearing, which could be a good thing.

Cuomo Resigns

In August of 2021, Andrew Cuomo resigned in the face of multiple sexual harassment claims by state employees and others.[38] He had become the park's champion, but many people disliked his abrasive style and micromanagement, and few rose to his defense in the face of damning accusations. Lieutenant Governor Kathy Hochul of Buffalo became the first female governor in the state's history.[39] She has visited the park and voiced her support, so many are hopeful she will continue the state's interest and investment in the project.

In September, the trust and Chelsea Piers Management presented preliminary plans for a new long-term lease to the Waterfront, Parks, and Environmental Committee of Community Board 4.[40] Noreen Doyle said that the trust was giving Community Board 4 a courtesy briefing and would try to finalize the agreement and return. When I asked Noreen why the Advisory Council had not been briefed, she replied that it was posted on the trust's website and the council had not requested a briefing. That confused me because it seemed to be evasive rather than straightforward, which I have always expected from Noreen.[41] It reinforced a concern I had a year earlier when she said that she did not think it was the trust's role to provide the Advisory Council with administrative support. We are all volunteers working to support the trust.

Little Island Opens

I attended the community opening of Little Island as a guest of a fellow Advisory Council member. Several children, and even a few adults, rolled down the grassy hills, wandered along the undulating paths, and enjoyed breathtaking views. The landscape is magnificent, and the structure itself is an interesting engineering feat.[42] However, Little Island is a symbol of contemporary noblesse oblige, with tech companies behaving the way the owners of railroads or steel mills once did—facilitating fabulous wealth to be spent at the owner's discretion. Just $260 million down, and $120 million over twenty years allowed a patron to control the design and use of a public space in the Hudson River just blocks from his corporate headquarters.

Little Island (Tom Fox)

Visiting Little Island that summer required timed reservations, and gawking crowds taking selfies made Little Island feel less like a "public" space. They also have a 128-person staff responsible for programming, operation, and management.[43] At fifty-three staff members per acre, that is far beyond anything imaginable, or appropriate, for the trust to shoulder after the Diller von Furstenberg Family Foundation's largess ends in twenty years. This saga might end well if we take the suggestion of Fred A. Bernstein of *Architectural Record* and return those few acres to nature after the patron's largesse sunsets in 2041.[44]

Advisory Council Growing Pains

In March of 2019, I submitted testimony to the city Economic Development Corporation regarding their plans to add a NYC Ferry route from Staten Island to the Midtown West Ferry Terminal at Pier 79 in the park.[45] The corporation had built the ferry terminal in 2005, and the area between the terminal and the bike path was being used for daytime bus layovers and overnight parking.

The expansion of NYC Ferry promised to increase ferry traffic on the Hudson adjacent to the park. The Advisory Council proposed restricting ferries and tour boats from operating within a hundred yards of the tips of the piers to minimize the impact of ferry wakes on park infrastructure, the estuary, and human-powered boating. I reached out to regulators, maritime industry leaders, and the owners of Circle Line and New York Water Taxi; the council chair sent a letter to the city Economic Development Corporation, and Noreen reached out to NY Waterway. [46] The teamwork was great, and the operators agreed to honor the voluntary restriction. Monitoring and enforcement, however, will be required.

NYC Ferry also planned to use the existing NY Waterway bus fleet servicing Pier 79 to transport their new ferry riders to and from Midtown. This plan is economical and minimized bus traffic to and from the terminal. However, the 1998 act limits surface transportation at Pier 79 to pickups and drop-offs along the bulkhead. The bus layover and overnight parking will have to be removed for the trust to complete the park between 29th and 44th Streets.

It was sometimes difficult to get issues relevant to Community Board 4 on Advisory Council meeting agendas. The chairman preferred that Community Board 4 take a position on issues in their community that required public review rather than the Advisory Council weighing in.

However, in March of 2021, when the bus parking issue finally came up for discussion at the council, everyone agreed that the issue needed to be addressed, and the chairman sent a letter to the city transportation commissioner requesting the removal of the parking.[47] The trust staff told us that the city Department of Transportation had ignored repeated requests to relocate the parking, so the council requested a meeting with the commissioner to discuss five alternative parking locations that we had identified. We never received a response, and the issue has yet to be addressed.

At the same time, we were told that the trust had been negotiating a new thirty-year lease with the Intrepid Sea, Air & Space Museum but failed to bring the issue to the council and was planning to execute the lease. The chairman wanted the Advisory Council to review this issue because Community Board 4 had already voted against it. Council members tried to review the proposal and make recommendations at our March meeting, but the issues were complicated, and the time available was too short. We all agreed that the trust had again failed to provide adequate time for the Advisory Council to participate in decision-making and wrote to the trust board express our displeasure.[48]

In April, the trust presented its draft update of the Estuary Management Plan to the council. The decennial document, which guides research, education, and restoration efforts, called for a $30 million state commitment for estuary research, restoration, and protection; the remaining $100 million that Cuomo had promised was not identified.[49]

Friends' Challenge

As an advocacy group, the original Friends raised or leveraged over $100 million, helped removed noncompliant municipal uses, and played a critical role in supporting the creation of the park. Reconstituted as the trust's official fundraising partner, Hudson River Park Friends has been less effective. When they forced the restructuring of Friends ten years earlier, the trust leadership hoped to attract big-money players with access to significant capital to join a new Friends board and had lofty expectations for their new fundraising partner. In 2018, the last full year before the pandemic, in addition to promoting the park and volunteer programs, Friends contributed almost $4 million to the trust.[50]

They have built a network of important supporters, hosted successful social gatherings and events, funded specific capital projects, organized volunteer programs, supported programming, and promoted the park. However, as an instrument of the trust, their ability to leverage public funding is limited. Hudson River Park's budget was reduced during the pandemic, and several of us were surprised that during that time, Friends sent letters to its supporters soliciting contributions for increased funding for the New York City parks system.[51] They might have considered advocating for increased public funding to support the park's contribution to both physical and mental health during the pandemic instead.

In October 2021, Friends honored Madelyn Wils and Google at their annual gala. Madelyn's award was presented by Diana Taylor, the former trust chair, and Madelyn began her acceptance speech stating, "We finally completed it," even though the park was still not finished. She stated that if she were a man, people would have said she was persuasive, not intransigent, and she thanked Diana and her dear friend Carl Weisbrod who helped achieve that goal.

In March of 2022, Friends announced that Diana Taylor was replacing Mike Novogratz as chair.[52] It was a fitting choice because, as the trust chair, Diana had insisted that Friends become a fundraising organization and soon abandoned the effort to create the Neighborhood Improvement District. The pandemic slowed fundraising nationwide, and in 2022, Friends' fundraising total was $4.4 million. The estimated annual contribution from that district could have been $13 million by then. Even if Friends' overhead was the customary 25 percent, they would have to raise $17.5 million this year to contribute the same amount as the Neighborhood Improvement District was projected to generate annually.

The reconstituted Friends honored Hudson Yards at its 2022 annual dinner, even though their major contribution to the park has been increasing the demand for public open space and advocating for the retention of the heliport. We will see if Friends eventually works to establish the Neighborhood Improvement District, which many people believe is the only way to generate consistent annual support without increased commercial development in the park.

Original Chelsea Advocates Pass

In 2021, two pillars of the decades-long effort to create the park passed away. In January, Ross Graham, the former chair of Community Board 4 and vice-chair of the original Friends, died at ninety-three from complications of COVID.[53] She often said she hoped the park was completed before we were too old to be rolled down the waterfront in our wheelchairs, and in her late eighties, Ross was still walking to Chelsea Piers to swim daily.

In December, Bob Trentlyon—a friend, a fellow citizen member of the West Side Task Force, and the driving force behind the Chelsea Waterside Park—died at the age of ninety-two. He had served on the Friends board, had been a member of innumerable park advisory groups, and had been publisher of the *Chelsea Clinton News* and other local newspapers.[54]

The new year began with the passing of yet a third original Chelsea activist, Ed Kirkland, another nonagenarian and historic preservationist who had been instrumental in the efforts to create both the Hudson River Park and the High Line.[55] All three citizen activists cared deeply about their community and were champions of the entire park.

Pier 57's Rooftop Park

In spring of 2022, the new rooftop park opened atop Pier 57 opened. It looked nothing like the heavily landscaped rooftop park originally proposed when the trust awarded the lease for Pier 57 twelve years earlier.[56]

The rooftop park was an austere space. There is a large restaurant pavilion topped with a rooftop observation deck that has spectacular views occupying the center of the roof. On the west side of the roof, a concrete-lined path runs through two smallish lawns enclosed by eight-foot-high planters that block the wind but also block the views to the north and south. The river side of the roof is open and has great views over the Hudson. The eastern, or city, side of the Pier 57 rooftop park has a lawn with flush circular sky-lights that illuminate the floor below and is also enclosed by those high planters. That side of the rooftop has a grandstand for screenings at the annual Tribeca Film Festival.

The trust claimed that the National Park Service would not allow significant vegetation to grace the rooftop as initially proposed because Pier 57 is a historic pier on the National Register of Historic Places. A knowledgeable historian might have convinced the National Park Service that landscaping be exempt from those restrictions because it did not try to mimic the historic building itself, but as I mentioned earlier, the trust has no historic staff or consultants to advise them. However, the restoration of Pier 57 is an amazing example of adaptive reuse of a historic structure.

At two acres, the site was mistakenly billed as the largest rooftop park in the city.[57] Riverbank State Park atop the North River Water Treatment Plant, several miles north in Upper Manhattan is twenty-eight acres and includes an Olympic-size swimming pool, a 2,500-seat athletic complex, an ice-skating rink, two playgrounds, an educational greenhouse, and a carousel.[58]

Another Missed Opportunity at Chelsea Piers

In November of 2021, the trust informed Community Board 4 that they were in negotiations with Chelsea Piers Management for a new forty-four-year lease for the complex. The trust had inherited its existing lease from the state Department of Transportation, and Chelsea Piers had requested a new lease for the complex.

The trust explained that the existing lease lacked certain protections that were now common in contemporary commercial leases and that a new lease would guarantee long-term park funding of well over $800 million over its term. Dan Kurtz, who had recently resigned as the trust's chief financial officer and executive vice president of real estate, was now representing the trust in the negotiations as a consultant.

There had been controversy regarding changes to the original lease made in 1996. The final environmental impact statements for both Chelsea Piers and Route 9A had called for two vehicle lanes and a thirty-six-foot-wide bicycle and pedestrian path and buffer adjacent to the roadway. However, the modifications made by the state Department of Transportation allowed Chelsea Piers to build a third vehicle lane on the east side of the complex, significantly reducing the space planned for pedestrians and bicycles, and thus creating public safety issues.[59]

This time, Chelsea Piers commissioned a transportation analysis, which, not surprisingly, confirmed that three vehicle lanes were essential.[60] Community Board 4 recommended that a new lease not be signed unless one traffic lane was returned to public use.[61] The Advisory Council agreed and voted unanimously that the lease be signed only if at least one lane of vehicle traffic was returned to public use as initially intended.[62]

In response, Chelsea Piers unleashed its ice skaters, gymnasts, golfers, maritime operators, and other pier users to lobby local officials to support the new lease. A professional review of their transportation study confirmed the fact that interior parking was reduced. Movie and television support planned for the interior of the complex was relocated to trailers parked in the third vehicle lane and other revenue-producing uses were built in the spaces planned for those activities. Yet Chelsea Piers' self-imposed hardship had now become a justification to retain the three-lane frontage road.[63]

People agreed that Chelsea Piers was an important asset for both the park and the adjacent communities. However, its management had increased its profits by usurping public open space for the past twenty-five years. And their claim that they needed three lanes of vehicle traffic between their complex and Route 9A to operate was not supported by the facts.

As the title of this chapter suggests, I had high hopes that the change in trust leadership would result in a return to the original open public planning process in pursuit of a grand public waterfront. But the jury is still out. In May of 2022, nine trust board members approved the new lease—an indication that private, rather than public, interests remain a trust priority. However, the former chair of Community Board 4 who served on the trust board did not support the new lease. As a minor concession, the trust included periodic reviews of the need for the third roadway to address public access concerns during the new lease term.

The previous fall, Eric Adams defeated three other Democratic primary challengers and Guardian Angels founder Curtis Sliwa in the general election to be elected mayor. Meera Joshi, who had spearheaded the Vision

Zero initiative for the De Blasio administration, became Adams's Deputy Mayor for Operations and was appointed as the new trust chair in the summer of 2022.

Con Edison and Pier 98

I served on the Advisory Council's historic preservation resources group to help the trust identify opportunities to integrate public education regarding the rich history of the West Side waterfront into new facilities under construction. After completing our recommendations for the Gansevoort Peninsula in May 2022, the trust asked to consider public education elements at Pier 97, which was scheduled to open the following year.

Adjacent Pier 98 has a profusion of pipes on its deck and a fuel barge docked alongside to supply Con Edison's 59th Street power plant directly across Route 9A. The initial plans for the park sought to preserve the industrial maritime infrastructure that had been the lifeblood of the waterfront for centuries, and marine refueling facility was deemed an allowable commercial use in the park. Very few park visitors have any idea what happens at Pier 98, and it was obviously "low hanging fruit" for interpretation.

However, an article in the *West Side Rag* stated, "According to Con Ed, cold water from the river is fed from the pier into a heat exchanger system, which cools the cables at a neighboring electrical substation and thereby allows the substation to handle substantially higher loads." That was both a surprise and a cause for concern.[64] Apparently, almost all the fuel used for the power plant is now provided by a natural gas pipeline, not by diesel fuel barges.

To better understand what was happening at Pier 98, Richard Emery, a fellow board member of the City Club, and I filed several Freedom of Information Law requests. We found that Con Edison was drawing up to four million gallons of water from the Hudson each day during warmer months to cool electrical cables and discharging the water back into the river at temperatures that were allowed to reach 104 degrees Fahrenheit. State Department of Environmental Conservation's regulations normally limit thermal discharges in the Hudson estuary to 90 degrees Fahrenheit.

Con Edison was also using one million gallons of city drinking water to create steam and flush their boilers and was discharging that water into the Hudson as well—water contaminated with conventional pollutants and various toxins.

The state Department of Environmental Conservation designated the in-water portion of the park as an estuarine sanctuary to protect its unique aquatic life and support preservation, research, education, and restoration efforts. The trust is the park's steward, but it was receiving more than $1.2 million in rent from Pier 98, which was emitting heated and polluted water into the sanctuary even though the trust's lease prohibits Con Edison from polluting the park. Fish are very sensitive to both temperature and toxic chemicals.

The trust failed to indicate the discharges in their decennial Estuarine Sanctuary Management Plan that the advisory council reviewed, and the trust approved in 2021. In addition, there is a kayak launch at Pier 96 in Clinton Cove Park just five hundred feet from Con Edison's outfalls.[65]

In August, the City Cub filed a sixty-day notice of our intent to sue Con Edison, the state Department of Environmental Conservation, and the trust to stop the pollution of the estuarine sanctuary.[66] Knowing the power of the press, we reached out to the *New York Times*, and after two weeks of detailed fact-checking, they broke the story.[67]

Local community boards, the Advisory Council, and the trust's Technical Advisory Committee all expressed surprise at not being informed of the discharges and requested a review of the situation. The trust said that the facility was what they called a "legacy industrial use" and that the pollution was approved by the state Department of Environmental Conservation.

Community Board 4 invited representatives of the trust, Con Edison, and the state Department of Environmental Conservation to meet with the board to discuss the issue.[68] At the September 2022 meeting, the representative from the state Department of Environmental Conservation seemed unprepared and evasive. The community board's major question was why the state Department of Environmental Conservation had not renewed Con Edison's 2016 permit after six years of internal technical review. The agency representative told Community Board 4 that the review was proceeding and that a public notice should be issued in the beginning of 2023.

But I was most surprised to see Venetia Lannon, the former deputy secretary of state for the environment, representing Con Edison.[69] Apparently, in 2011, Mayor Bloomberg had petitioned Governor Cuomo to replace the state Department of Environmental Conservation's regional director for New York City, whom he considered too environmentally friendly and opposed to business and development interests. Ms. Lannon was working for Madelyn Wils at the city Economic Development Corporation at the time and was the appointed replacement.[70] She served in that role for six years before overseeing the entire agency for another three years while serving as Cuomo's deputy secretary for the environment. She was now representing the utility she regulated for almost a decade.

State Department of Environmental Conservation representatives failed to attend the November 2022 Advisory Council meeting as requested, stating that they did not have the appropriate staff. The Advisory Council passed a resolution providing guidance and suggestions. "Most importantly, the Council urges that state DEC work more closely with Con Edison and in partnership with the Trust to facilitate the transition of Con Edison's operations at Pier 98 to state-of-the-art technologies that will conserve precious water resources and minimize impacts of wastewater discharges into the Hudson River Park estuarine sanctuary."[71]

The trust subsequently committed to monitoring water temperatures from the Pier 98 discharges. They also involved the Estuarine Sanctuary Management Plan's Technical Advisory Committee and committed to including the issue in future environmental education programs.

Assemblymember Deborah Glick, with a long history of efforts to preserve the Hudson's aquatic environment and protect the park from commercialization, became the chair of the state Assembly's Committee on Environmental Protection and urged the state Department of Conservation to work with the Advisory Council. Given the public response, the trust's actions, and the Advisory Council's commitment to actively participate in the permit renewal process, the City Club decided not to move forward with litigation.[72] Con Edison's public notice was finally issued March 29, 2023.[73]

Piers 92 and 94

The city Economic Development Corporation had controlled Piers 88, 90, 92, and 94 since the passenger ship terminals were removed from the park plan by the Giuliani administration in 1996. However, the corporation's stewardship of the piers has been questionable. In 2009, they leased Piers 92 and 94 to Vornado Realty Trust for redevelopment, but community improvements that the developer committed to never materialized. Pier 92 was abandoned due to structural deterioration, leaving the corporation with a derelict pier.[74] To add insult to injury, the city is allowing Vornado to create an entirely new partnership to redevelop Pier 94 as a publicly subsidized film and TV studio.[75] It might increase public access to the waterfront, but it will also increase traffic—and Vornado has reneged on its public space

Pier 57 community space (Tom Fox)

commitments to the community in the past. Hopefully, the community amenities are built quickly and maintained well.

The new Market Pier 57, spearheaded by the James Beard Foundation, is much smaller than initially envisioned, but the interior community space and environmental education classrooms provide a unique public amenity within the park and give Pier 57 more meaningful public use.[76] The new beach, boat launch, natural area, and ball fields at Gansevoort have recently opened, and the new Pier 97 is scheduled to open in the near future.[77] And new state legislation to remove the heliport from the park has been introduced by local elected officials.[78]

In the fall of 2023, the future of the Hudson River Park looks hopeful. The new trust leadership has found its footing, is assembling experienced planning and management professionals, and is working more closely with the Advisory Council.

18

Hope Springs Eternal
(2024 and Beyond)

● ● ● ● ● ● ● ● ● ● ● ● ● ● ●

When we completed the West Side Task Force recommendations in 1987, I had asked colleagues to sign my copy of the final report. Hank Dullea, Governor Mario Cuomo's director of state operations, signed with the phrase "Hope Springs Eternal." His words meant a lot to me. They helped me realize that achieving physical and social change was a marathon, not a sprint, and that it was important to continue the struggle. They also offered an important message for everyone working to protect and enhance the public realm.

After the defeat of Westway in 1985, the stage was set for the revitalization of Manhattan's West Side waterfront. Between 1986 and 1998, a unique public process had focused on the basics like designing an appropriate roadway, removing noncompliant municipal and commercial activities from the waterfront, implementing interim improvements, developing the park's first revenue-producing commercial area at Chelsea Piers, completing the public planning and environmental review processes, and passing the 1998 Hudson River Park Act—the legislation that officially created the park.

From 1999 to 2009, planning and construction budgets were limited but funded with public money and focused on creating active and passive recreation opportunities on the Greenwich Village and Tribeca waterfronts, as well as Chelsea Waterside Park, Pier 84, and Clinton Cove. Several boathouses expanded public access to the Hudson, and appropriate small-scale commercial activities such as miniature golf, beach volleyball, and food and beverage concessions were built on Piers 25 and 26 and at the restored historic Pier 66 float bridge in Chelsea.

The most recent phase of work, from 2010 to 2022, has focused on "development" both in and adjacent to the park as former staff members from the city's Economic Development Corporation were appointed to trust leadership and consulting positions. The push for economic development has brought Manhattan into the park with offices, nightclubs, and restaurants.

After lobbying for amendments to the act in 2013, the trust expanded economic development and private philanthropic initiatives at Piers 55 and 57, installed the Classic Car Club on Pier 76, permitted a private water taxi dock for Citigroup at Pier 25, and transferred air rights from the park to adjacent real estate developers in Greenwich Village and Chelsea, thereby increasing the density. However, Piers 26 and Pier 97 were reconstructed as open landscaped public piers, and improvements included new ball fields, estuary restoration, and river access at the Gansevoort Peninsula.

A lot has gone right in the decades-long effort to create the Hudson River Park. Now, the park is almost complete and is visited by seventeen million people annually. Park visitors run and stroll along the esplanade, garden paths, and open lawns, and they enjoy the playgrounds, dog runs, ball fields, tennis courts, and skate parks that grace the piers and upland park. Boathouses, historic ships, and environmental research and education programs have opened access to the Hudson, and the wide-open river rolling one way, or the other, frees the spirit and soothes the soul. As we have seen with the first year of operation at Little Island, the number of park visitors will only increase as Pier 57, the Gansevoort Peninsula, and Pier 97 open for a full season of public use next spring.

But a lot has gone wrong. The passenger ship terminals and most of their revenue were removed from the park, and the rezoning of adjacent neighborhoods failed to generate any revenue for the park while at the same time increasing the demand for public open space. There is still a heliport in the park, bicycle and pedestrian safety continues to be an issue, and after twenty-five years, the estuarium still is not fully funded. The redevelopment of Piers 40 and 76 holds the promise of expanded public recreation space but also poses potential threats if their commercial uses are not carefully selected.

Residents, corporations, and all adjacent property owners have a vested interest in completing and protecting the park—so do local businesses, elected officials, and the seventeen million people who use the park each year. The COVID pandemic reinforced our awareness of the importance of public open space for physical and mental health and the quality of urban life.[1] As the Hudson River Park nears completion, a course correction would help protect the park and increase its benefit to the public. Perhaps some of the following suggestions might prove to be helpful in the future.

Shift Gears

During the past twenty-five years, the trust has focused on design and development, but as the park construction ends, stewardship becomes the critical mission. After developing final plans for public space and commercial development at Piers 40 and 76 at Houston and 36th Streets, and completing park construction, the trust should transition into a traditional park entity.

The biggest challenge facing the park is ensuring that the land remains public in perpetuity. The 1998 Hudson River Park Act has already been amended five times and offers only weak legislative protection for the park. The state Department of Environmental Conservation's prohibition on landfill in the designated estuarine sanctuary provides some additional protection, but past efforts to designate the entire waterfront as public parkland have failed.

The city retains a 50 percent interest in the park property between Chambers and 36th Streets and owns all the park property from 36th to 59th Streets. Therefore, the city has the majority interest in the park (56 percent), and receives the lion's share of economic benefit from the park resulting from increased employment, real estate, and sales tax revenues and should therefore shoulder much of the responsibility of its long-term operation, maintenance, and capital replacement.

The Hudson River Park should be officially designated as city parkland, which will provide the most effective long-term protection. Using city parkland for any other purpose, a process called "alienation," requires the approval of the City Council and the mayor before being sent to the state legislature for approval and then the governor's signature. However, the city and state should also continue to share responsibility for estuary protection, legislative and regulatory issues, and major capital financing. The governance of the park should focus on planning, programming, public involvement, management, and maintenance—and minimize economic development or political interference in stewardship.

The Central Park Conservancy could be a good model for a restructured Hudson River Park Trust. This nonprofit organization is governed by an independent board and has a management agreement with the city Department of Parks and Recreation to oversee the park's programming, management, and maintenance. The organization receives annual funding from the city and secures other public and private money. Everyone working in Central Park is a conservancy employee or volunteer.[2]

The city has about a dozen such management agreements with other nonprofit organizations including the Prospect Park and Van Cortlandt Park Alliances. Any new entity should have all the powers and limitations enshrined in the 1998 act, including an Advisory Council and a requirement for meaningful community participation. Given the wealth of talented and resourceful individuals and corporations in adjacent communities and on the board of Friends, an independent nonprofit board should be easy to assemble.

A change in governance would open other possibilities as well. State Department of Transportation jurisdiction of the bicycle path has consistently been used as an excuse not to address pressing design and safety issues, and the bicycle path could be included in the park's jurisdiction with state transportation advising the trust on planning and securing federal and state funds for necessary maintenance and improvements to this element of a federal-aid highway.

Park enforcement police who currently oversee public safety do not provide the level of professional policing needed in the park given the increasing level of violent crimes.[3] In the short term, the trust should insist that these officers report directly to the trust's management staff and are precluded from being reassigned elsewhere by the city to support other events—something that frequently happens. The need to preserve the peace, maintain order, and enforce the law will continue to grow. If the park is designated as city parkland, the New York City Police Department could patrol the park and provide seasonal details, as is the case in other city parks.

Given its geography, it may be impractical for the park to be part of a designated precinct as Central Park is. The park property lies within several precincts, with the 10th Precinct having jurisdiction over a mile and a half of the waterfront, extending from 14th to 42nd Streets. A designated substation in the 10th Precinct could coordinate the activity of the involved precincts, as is done in Prospect Park. Mobile "command posts" could be set up in trailers for public events, as is done in Flushing Meadows Corona Park.[4]

Encourage Meaningful Community Participation

The Hudson River Park is the product of over three decades of meaningful community participation, and the 1998 act required that this successful strategy be continued. However, over the last decade, decision-making has become more insular and public access to information increasingly limited.

The balance of power between government and the public is constantly shifting. It is critical for the trust to revert to its initial practice of broadly distributing information regarding the schedule and content of public hearings, board meetings, Advisory Council meetings, new plans and proposed policies, regulations, and proposed legislative changes. An informed public is an involved public, and an involved public will advocate for public funding and protect the park. New Yorkers should not have to search trust and local community board websites to find important information or join multiple mailing lists to understand what is happening when it comes to park planning and policy.

The trust and Friends have an engaging and informative public outreach and education presence on social media. Current outreach primarily focuses on announcing scheduled programs, fundraising events, and volunteer opportunities, but it should also solicit public participation in planning, programming, and policy deliberations. For example, the trust reports presented at Advisory Council meetings could be distributed after council meetings without adding an administrative burden.

The trust's archives should be available in a searchable electronic database. While doing research for this book, I found it very difficult to retrieve information regarding past plans, projects, budgets, staff, or activities. The trust should participate in the Wayback Machine, a service that allows public access to archived versions of websites, just as the city's other public and nonprofit park organizations do. Providing access to historical information helps the public understand the context of current decision-making as well as the park's progress, challenges, and its evolving promise.

The trust has recently embarked on a closer working relationship with the Advisory Council. An independent sounding board is vital for public decision-making. By working with tenants and neighboring nonprofit organizations as partners, the trust can build on their recent success merging with The River Project, which is a great model for the future. A journalist who experienced The River Project as a City-As-School participant recently remembered that experience in a Twitter post twenty years later when she was an assignment editor at the *New York Times*.[5] Investments in environmental education often reap benefits in unpredictable ways.

Secure Self-Sufficiency

It is important to dispel the myth that the Hudson River Park is required to be self-sufficient. Although often repeated by elected officials and government agencies who do not want to share a portion of the financial benefits generated by the park, this contention is simply not true. The park was established to be self-sufficient to the extent practicable, with practicable defined as feasible or possible, given its public purpose.[6]

The 1998 Hudson River Park Act states that the city and state are responsible for capital funding and may allocate additional city and state money to meet the costs of operating and maintaining the park. The initial concept for financing the development, maintenance, and operation of the park had three components: public and philanthropic funds, retained revenue from limited park-related commercial development at three designated locations, and a creative financial mechanism to secure additional funding from inboard real estate appreciation.

The creative public financing options recommended by the West Side Waterfront Panel were designed to secure some of the appreciating real estate tax revenue to supplement public funding to build, maintain, and operate the park. Several creative public financing techniques have been implemented along the far West Side corridor just not to support the park that stimulated the area's transformation.

The trust's alternative "development" approach to longer-term financing comes at a heavy cost. Selling unused air rights from the piers and transferring them to adjacent rezoned real estate will provide a one-shot source of capital but will also increase population density, multiply demands on the park, lead to the casting of long morning shadows from taller buildings, and increase gentrification. The trust leadership initially estimated the amount of air rights available for transfer was 1.6 million square feet and later increased that amount to 3.5 million square feet. An independent review of the scale and value of the proposed air rights transfers would help clarify the situation.

The 1993 Zoning Resolution codifying the city's 1992 Waterfront Plan recommendations applied only to piers or platforms that are "structurally sound, and physically accessible from the shore with a surface that's capable of lawful occupancy."[7] Several of the piers in the park were either not structurally sound or not able to be lawfully occupied at that time and probably do not qualify for air rights transfers.

Many question the ability of the Hudson River Park Friends to raise the money necessary to meet the trust's annual budget gap year after year. Without a guaranteed source of reliable long-term funding for maintenance, operation, and capital replacement, the park is vulnerable to serious deterioration that would impact not only the park itself but the surrounding communities as well. We saw the effect of inadequate maintenance funding in Union Square, Bryant Park, Prospect Park, and even Central Park in the late 1970s and early 1980s, and it was not pretty. Deferring maintenance and allowing the park to deteriorate would also increase the cost of operations and eventual reconstruction.

A viable long-term public financial plan for the Hudson River Park that supports self-sufficiency without increasing commercialization and undermining public use is critical. The city, state, trust, and Friends have new leadership. Corporate and residential investments along Route 9A have matured and, after the redevelopment of Piers 40 and 76, commercial development in the park will be maxed out—that is, if we want the park to remain public.

The adjacent neighborhoods have been rezoned from warehousing, manufacturing, and transportation uses to residential and commercial office use. Thankfully, gentrification resulting from the creation of the park was minimal as few people were living along the waterfront when the park was conceived. However, West Side residential values that were similar to those in other areas of Manhattan in 1998 have doubled in the fifteen years after the completion of the Hudson River Park's initial phase.[8]

Corporate and philanthropic interest in the park appears to be growing. Citigroup donated $10 million to complete Pier 26 and paid for a water taxi stop at Pier 25 opposite their headquarters. The Diller von Furstenberg Family Foundation built and operates Little Island several blocks from Barry Diller's corporate headquarters, and the adjacent Meatpacking Business Improvement District celebrated a new crosswalk to access the park.[9]

Google has major investments in the former Chelsea Market, Pier 57, and St. John's Terminal where a new crosswalk on Route 9A will enhance access to the park.[10] The Hudson Square Business Improvement District is proposing a bridge to the park at Spring Street; Phase 2 of Hudson Yards, closest to the park, will eventually start construction; and Chelsea Piers has just signed a new long-term lease.[11]

A *New York Times* article on the 25th anniversary of the legislation establishing the park emphasized the contribution that Hudson River Park made to the revitalization of Manhattan's West Side.[12] The original Friends' 2008 study that documented the impact was mentioned, but there was no mention of the neighborhood improvement district recommended to secure the last critical piece of funding for the park.

A neighborhood, or park, improvement district requires a voluntary contribution from adjacent property owners to support the long-term maintenance, operation, and capital replacement needs of the park. Residential property is normally not included in this type of district. However, the new West Village Business Improvement District includes residential property, so there is a recent precedent.[13]

It is in the interest of those who have invested billions in redeveloping the West Side to protect the park and help identify and secure a stable, long-term source of park funding. Residents need to protect their quality of life and their property value. Corporations need to maintain their brand, employees' well-being, and property values. Develop any mechanism that works and call it what you will, but the last piece of the financial puzzle required to maximize the park's self-sufficiency and public benefit must be found to protect our collective accomplishments.[14]

Rather than championing a serious and sustained public funding solution, the reconstituted Friends continues to claim that park maintenance and operations depend on private funding and donations. As they celebrated the 25th anniversary of the 1998 Hudson River Park Act, a sign in their photo exhibit on a fence at opening of the Gansevoort Peninsula stated, "Celebrate Hudson River Parks 25th Anniversary . . . Hudson River Park is not a city run park and relies on private funds for its operations, maintenance and free public programing."[15]

There are many models for creative public financing that should be explored. The Trust for Public Land keeps a LandVote Database of public financing measures that voters have approved across the nation since 1988 and that have generated a staggering $86 billion for conservation.[16] People love parks, the quality of urban life depends on them, and citizens will vote to support public open space. Friends, now the trust's official fundraising organization, must work with all West Side stakeholders and insist that the city and state address this critical issue. The time for kicking the can down the road is over.

Leaders of the trust recently said they would be reviewing the park's commercial structure, precipitated primarily by the existence of competing tango clubs who were vying to control the trust's dance floor at Pier 45 and charging patrons to enjoy it.[17] As steward of the park, the trust is responsible for mediating conflicts regarding the use of public space. Precious public space should not be taken over for private revenue-producing uses, no matter how enjoyable the activity. Commercial operators have recently begun to offer bicycle tours on the Hudson River Greenway.[18] Public space should remain just that—public space, for public use, programs, events, and activities.

Private activities should take place in spaces designated for park-related commercial activities or hosted by nonprofit tenants—not in public spaces. The trust is fortunate to have nonprofit tenants in the park that provide services the trust cannot provide. They are not just tenants; they are partners that should be supported and celebrated.[19]

Regarding revenue generated in commercial areas within the park, the new concession agreement at Wollman Rink in Central Park might provide a useful model.[20] The joint venture partners involved are not seeking, or accepting, profit from operating Wollman Rink and have agreed that any net proceeds generated will be reinvested in the facility and the community.

Control Costs

The reclamation of the West Side waterfront has accomplished many important goals. It has provided major new public open space for active and passive recreation and maritime uses, and it has reconnected New Yorkers to the Hudson.[21] But costs must be kept under control.

Although the initial construction suffered from budget reductions, the design of newer park facilities has gotten quite expensive. In 2003, nine acres of the Greenwich Village waterfront—including Piers 45, 46, and 51—were designed and built for $46 million ($69 million in fiscal year 2022 dollars).[22] Recent projects have been costlier. For example, the initial reconstruction of Pier 97 cost $16 million, with $38 million being spent on the surface amenities or $54 million for the two-acre pier.[23] The cost to transform the 5.5-acre Gansevoort Peninsula's transformation to recreation facilities and natural areas is $73 million.[24]

More expensive capital improvements in the park will require increased long-term funding for both maintenance and capital replacement, especially since many of the new facilities are uniquely designed and do not share common elements with the rest of the park. For example, the trust recently spent $414,000 to restore "Private Passage," a sculpture at Clinton Cove.[25] Unfortunately, the restored sculpture was vandalized shortly after its return.

The selection, installation, and replacement of thin pavers continue to plague the park. The trust recently awarded a three-year contract for over a million dollars for paving block restoration.[26] The offshore wetlands at Pier 26 are also expensive to maintain. The trust approved a million-dollar contract just to monitor those engineered wetlands for five years.[27] Design and construction must take long-term maintenance and capital replacement needs into consideration.

Expanded programming also increases the trust's budget. In 2022, Friends contributed $800,000 to support the trust's plans to host 260 free public events during the peak park season. However, all the events require scheduling, coordination, management, setup, and cleanup.[28] Robust programming is great, but the funding must come from somewhere—consistently.

Some of the park's most important and least heralded assets are the nonprofit organizations engaged in activities help the trust meet its public mission. The trust should maintain the annual rent of $1 for nonprofit organizations that engaged in work that provides public services and finance and install the utilities and generic marine infrastructure necessary for their activities in support of the park. The trust should also assist with liability insurance and allow nonprofits to host fundraising and special events during hours that they are not normally open to the public to support their programming.

Embrace the River

Hudson River Park is a maritime park, and thanks to public advocacy and use, there are five boathouses in the park and a high concentration of kayakers and rowers. Although not cheap, providing adequate waterfront access, investing in infrastructure improvements, and enhancing public safety are necessary to encourage more visitors to enjoy and protect the over 70 percent of the park in the river.[29]

There is still a need for appropriate-scale fendering on all the piers, for the restoration of the marine hardware like bollards and cleats, and for the installation of removable railings to support emergency access. The West Side piers were designed for oceangoing ships, and those design elements can prevent smaller vessels from docking easily or safely. They have prevented the Hudson River Sloop Clearwater from providing its environmental programming and sailing trips that the trust has wanted in the park for years.

Navigable waterways also need maintenance, and that includes dredging. The trust has refused to consider dredging, but limited dredging in areas designated to host historic ships and visiting vessels is essential for the park to reach its potential. The increasing number of people falling, or jumping, into the river calls for a significant investment in water's edge safety investments to rescue individuals who for one reason or another find themselves "in the drink." The trust has recently begun going to address this concern at the Advisory Council's urging.

One major obstacle to greater use of the Hudson is the fear of litigation, and the cost of liability insurance impedes the mission of encouraging public access to the waterway. The 2013 amendments to the Hudson River Park Act tried, but failed, to address the issue. If the property is designated as city parkland, the city is self-insured, and this costly item could be eliminated from the park's annual operating budget.

Maritime uses have been retained and expanded in the park, which has a wide variety of activities ranging from recreational kayaking, rowing, and sailing to commercial tour and dinner boats, barges, ferries, and large passenger ships. However, the fences and security installations at the passenger ship terminals in Midtown prevent people from getting close to the water for a stretch of about a quarter of a mile. Public access there should be improved.

There are four park piers that have had their decks removed where the piles have been left in place to support biodiversity and serve as a placeholder for future pier construction. Rebuilding Piers 32, 42, 49, and 72 as public piers would add almost ten acres of public space in Tribeca, Greenwich Village, and Chelsea. A low-cost addition that is immediately available is opening the northern finger of Pier 34, which had been closed to the public since 1994. Installing simple amenities and opening the gates would provide a half-acre of new public space at Canal Street at minimal cost.

Con Edison has been encouraged to limit thermal discharges and transition to new technologies that will reduce water consumption and minimize the impact of wastewater discharges.[30] When Con Edison has successfully transitioned, if Pier 98 is no longer needed for industrial use, it should be added to Clinton Cove Park, making up for the loss of Pier 94, which was initially planned as a public pier. The need is great because new residential development has increased density in the adjacent neighborhood.

New Task Force Proposed

In the summer of 2022, there were concerns that flood protection proposals for Manhattan omitted the West Side waterfront north of Battery Park City.[31]

By September, the U.S. Army Corps of Engineers released a preliminary flood control plan for Manhattan's West Side waterfront in Hudson River Park between Battery Park City and West 34th Street. They proposed building a twelve-foot-high concrete wall along three miles of the waterfront—in the Hudson River Park.[32]

The wall would disrupt the busiest bike path in America, diminish public use and enjoyment of the park, impede public access to the river, increase air and noise pollution, and block views of the river. It would significantly change the function and appeal of the park, undermine the quality of life in adjacent neighborhoods, and erode both the value of adjacent real estate and the city's tax base.

My West Side adventure began in 1983 just before the U.S. Army Corps' Westway permit for an interstate highway buried under 234 acres of landfill in the Hudson River was withdrawn. The governor and mayor established a unique city/state task force to address the issue. That twenty-two-member body brought together senior government officials and commissioners, local elected officials, and community, environmental, business, and civic stakeholders to craft a new vision for the West Side waterfront.

The recommendations were bold: build a surface boulevard and turn the waterfront into a world class maritime park. The Hudson River Park transformed a dangerous and deteriorating waterfront, preserved the priceless Hudson estuary, made adjacent neighborhoods more livable, increased tourism, created jobs, and enhanced the city's tax base. That progress, and the continued vitality of adjacent West Side neighborhoods, will be undermined by the Army Corps' proposal.

The Hudson River Park Advisory Council voted unanimously, in February 2023, to request that the governor and mayor establish a new city/state task force to coordinate future public infrastructure investments to prevent coastal flooding, protect the Hudson River Park, and redesign Route 9A to meet changing transportation needs without increasing traffic congestion.[33] There are physical, environmental, and economic benefits to crafting a new vision that will enable the West Side waterfront to adapt and thrive for rest of this century.

In March 2023, Community Board 2 passed a resolution endorsing a task force approach, and U.S. Congressman Dan Goldman stressed the need to coordinate the activities of all the agencies to address issues of addressing the resiliency.[34] Community Board 1 requested a brief history of the Tribeca portion of the park and an overview of the task force concept and joined the Advisory Council and Community Board 2 in calling for the creation of the task force.[35] At the end of July, the nine city and state West Side elected officials whose districts border or include the park wrote to the governor and the mayor requesting the establishment of the task force recommended by the Advisory Council.[36]

The opportunity is unique because implementing three major public infrastructure projects together would be critical to the future of the park, the estuary, and adjacent West Side communities. Billions in public and private dollars have been invested in the park and in adjacent communities. Coordinating the planning and implementation of major public infrastructure improvements is critical to protecting and expanding the benefits that the Hudson River Park has created. Fortunately, new state and federal funding is available to help accomplish these goals.

In November 2022, New Yorkers passed a $4.2 billion environmental bond act that can help the state complete its commitment to research, preservation, and restoration of the park's estuarine sanctuary.[37] Over $30 million of the $134 million that the state committed toward estuarine research, restoration, and protection is being spent for new shoreline habitat at Gansevoort Peninsula, ecological improvements at Pier 26, oyster restoration, and the design of the estuarium in Tribeca.[38]

Increasing resiliency and flood protection on the West Side waterfront should include both in-water and shore-based measures, and mitigating the impact of tidal surges should start in the park's estuarine sanctuary. Existing aquatic systems must be preserved while implementing innovative environmental interventions, such as expanding the current oyster restoration initiative, and implementing near shore ecological enhancements.[39] In addition, pier piles and the bulkhead can be surfaced with materials that encourage and support the growth of marine and terrestrial flora and fauna.

Improve Water Quality

In-water environmental enhancements cannot succeed without improving water quality, which will require stopping the routine discharge from thirty-three combined sewer outfalls that dump untreated waste directly into the Hudson River. The city's combined sewer system mixes raw sewage with stormwater from local streets and normally routes the waste to municipal wastewater treatment plants for processing. However, too much water would overwhelm municipal water treatment facilities, so the untreated waste is discharged directly into the Hudson during periods of heavy rainfall, wreaking havoc on the marine and bird life and creating unsanitary conditions for fishers, boaters, and other park visitors.[40]

A stormwater holding system, like the one installed at Paerdegat Basin in East Flatbush Brooklyn, should be considered. There, a city Department of Environmental Protection installed a forty-eight-inch-diameter sewer line that captures and stores stormwater to prevent its discharge into Jamaica Bay. The sewage is then slowly routed to a wastewater treatment plant after the rainfall ends.[41] The agency issues bonds to raise the money to build its water treatment facilities and should design and finance this critical public infrastructure in the Hudson River Park as part of a comprehensive approach to resiliency and estuary restoration.

Redesign Route 9A

Almost forty years ago, the West Side Task Force recommended a surface-level boulevard to accommodate traffic along the West Side corridor and enhance waterfront access for adjacent communities. The future of the waterfront and the adjacent neighborhoods was unknown, and assumptions were made about what would take place on both sides of the roadway.

Some assumptions were accurate. But few envisioned the dramatic transformation of the Meatpacking District and Hudson Yards, redevelopment of Hudson Square, popular new attractions like the High Line and Little Island, or commercial offices at Pier 57. The state Department of Transportation's primary concern was moving traffic along the West Side corridor, and they chose an inexpensive roadway alternative. Development on both sides of the roadway has changed the nature of the area, both conventional biking and electric powered micromobility has increased exponentially, and congestion pricing is expected to reduce Manhattan vehicular traffic below 60th Street by about 20 percent.[42]

The roadway is approaching its expected fifty-year lifespan, and there have been calls for the city and state to address its shortcomings. For example, local community boards, the Hudson River Park Advisory Council, and the Manhattan Borough President have requested that one lane of Route 9A be dedicated for electric vehicles used to transport people or goods.[43] There are also opportunities for new pedestrian bridges at De Witt Clinton Park and for linking a redeveloped Pier 76 across Route 9A to the Javits Convention Center, and then over West 34th Street to the High Line, to connect these major attractions together.

Piers 76, 78, and 79 with the Javits Convention Center and High Line across Route 9A. (Tom Fox)

In New York City, there is always competition for public space. As we move away from automobile dominance, competition between pedestrians and bicycles has been exacerbated by the introduction of various electrically powered vehicles that have become commonplace.[44] Repurposing Route 9A's parking lane for these vehicles would support the current and future use of throttle-controlled electric bicycles and scooters, as well as food delivery and small "last mile" package delivery vehicles.[45] Bicycle and pedestrian safety in the park would also be enhanced. Thankfully, the new $1.2 trillion federal Infrastructure Investment and Jobs Act, passed in 2021, included $110 billion to improve the nation's transportation infrastructure and provides the opportunity to meet that need.

Over the short term, pedestrian, and bicycle safety in the park is a most pressing issue. It is not an accident waiting to happen; it is one that has already happened—and all too often. Public education, enhanced signage, and enforcement of existing park regulations are immediate needs.

Wherever possible, vehicle access to the park should be curtailed or eliminated. Traffic signals must be installed at all locations where commercial activities require that vehicles cross the bicycle and pedestrian paths. Traffic lights should be timed to facilitate vehicles turning from Route 9A, the roadway that runs along the park but should give priority to pedestrians and bicyclists. The new roadway design should also incorporate simple improvements like roadway safety grooves that are machine cut and oriented parallel to the flow of traffic. Such improvements will increase vehicle safety and reduce noise.

The original design speed limit on Route 9A was forty miles per hour, which was reduced to a posted speed of thirty-five miles per hour for safety. The city's Vision Zero initiative to reduce pedestrian fatalities brought the speed limit down to thirty miles per hour in October of 2020, partly in response to the ten fatalities that occurred on the roadway since 2013.[46] Lower speed limits, public education, and consistent enforcement contribute to roadway and pedestrian safety.

Expand the Park

As a public asset, Hudson River Park has created tremendous benefits for the environment, adjacent communities, the city, and the region's economy. Redesigning Route 9A could create an opportunity to expand the park as well. With changing urban transportation preferences and an anticipated reduction in vehicle traffic, the roadway could be narrowed and the park expanded to increase the room for more creative, and natural, shore-based flood control measures, both natural and engineered.

Route 9A was designed to accommodate 1980s traffic levels. The tree-lined, nineteen-foot-wide median was included to facilitate pedestrian safety and mitigate air and noise pollution from traffic. An anticipated 20 percent reduction in traffic from congestion pricing argues for a narrower roadway, and the increasing number of electrically powered vehicles means less noise and fewer exhaust emissions.

With less traffic, one vehicle lane and the median might be removed from the roadway. That could add thirty feet of width to the Hudson River Park. Except perhaps for the segment from 14th to 23rd Streets, where the park is extremely narrow, expanding the park would provide room for creative shore-based measures, such as bioswales and reinforced landscaped berms or hills.

It is premature to suggest specific designs for a comprehensive approach to implementing these public infrastructure improvements. A task force charged with this mission should be responsible for decision-making with the same meaningful and transparent community participation that led to the creation of Hudson River Park.

It is time for the city and state to work with key stakeholders from the local, environmental, transportation, civic, and business communities and complete a new vision for the West Side in the twenty-first century.[47] The U.S. Army Corps' simplistic approach to enhance resiliency on Manhattan's West Side should become a catalyst for developing a coordinated effort that respects natural systems, embraces new technologies, enhances the public enjoyment of the Hudson River Park, and protects the quality of life and municipal tax base in adjacent neighborhoods.[48]

Only the governor and mayor can assemble and empower senior-level government, civic, corporate, and community leaders to capture this opportunity to complete the park and the transformation of the West Side waterfront. No one else can ensure that the Hudson River Park Trust, the U.S. Army Corps, the city Department of Environmental Protection, the state Department of Environmental Conservation, the city and state transportation departments, and other involved agencies coordinate their efforts.

So this story ends as it began: with community and environmental advocates and local elected officials encouraging the mayor and the governor to take a new approach in response to a controversial U.S. Army Corps proposal for the West Side waterfront. If the mayor and governor can be encouraged to coordinate long-term public infrastructure investments in the West Side waterfront, we can build on the success of the park to protect natural systems and ensure a better quality of life for Manhattan's West Side into the next century.

Hopefully, we have learned how to work better together, and a resilient task force is something everyone can agree on. The challenges are real, but the benefits hold too much promise to ignore.

Hope Springs Eternal

Over the past two years since the changes in trust leadership and board membership, transparency and cooperation between the trust and the Advisory Council has grown. Many are hopeful that this change in course continues.

Progress on the Hudson River Park has often occurred when New Yorkers have taken ownership of the project and pushed it forward despite the inertia that is endemic to bureaucratic systems and changing political priorities. The ultimate success of the project will depend on the public continuing to assert its ownership of the park, as it did in the beginning.

Community participation has been a key element in the project and remains critical to continued success. The community includes park users, local residence, businesses, nonprofit organizations, and sports and civic groups. Embracing community participation and thinking outside the box turned Westway into the Hudson River Park. Continued cooperation and consultation will ensure the success of West Side redevelopment in the long term. Hopefully, the park will grow and continue to evolve to adequately, and equitably, provide an oasis for humanity and a celebration of nature.

Establishing a reliable long-term financing mechanism to support the park's maintenance, operation, and capital replacement, as well as the investments made to enhance resiliency and flood protection, are essential. Without it, the park will suffer either from lack of maintenance or from overcommercialization. If the Advisory Council, local elected officials, community boards, and civic organizations can galvanize public support for a new West Side Task Force focused on resiliency, and establish viable financing mechanisms to support the park, restore and manage the estuary, and maintain new flood protection infrastructure, it will insure its longevity. Private philanthropy has benefited the park greatly but is not up to that task.

The introductory quote for the book is a reminder of the importance of personal responsibility to protect those things that are most important to us. The future of the Hudson River Park—and indeed our planet in the face of accelerated climate change—depends on individual action.

Corporate and individual greed, government ineptitude and chicanery, and a misguided popular belief that someone else will take care of the things that are most important threaten all that we hold dear. The progress of the Hudson River Park has ebbed and flowed over the last four decades. The future calls for increased transparency, less kowtowing to developers, reduced emphasis on the bottom line, and on cooperation, creativity, and pursuing the common good. With open and constructive dialogue, enlightened government action, and increased individual responsibility, there is hope. Only time will tell.

Acknowledgments

My wife Gretchen and son Michael for their patience, love, encouragement and understanding.

Shane Smith and Charlotte Kahn, friends, urban gardeners, environmental advocates, and fellow Loeb Fellows who encouraged me to write this book as a first-person history.

Colleagues who provided advice and information during my five-year adventure writing this book. The original Friends of Hudson River Park—Douglas Durst, Ross Graham, Ben Korman, A. J. Pietratone, and Matthew Washington; former construction union leader Thomas P. (Tommy) Maguire; former city environmental commissioner and construction industry executive Francis (Frank) X. McArdle; Route 9A team members Richard (Dick) Maitino and Heather Sporn; river rats Graeme Birchall, Rob Buchanan, Cathy Drew, and Captains Huntley Gil, Mary Habstritt, Rip Haymen, and David Sharps; former Hudson River Park Conservancy staff members Arne Abramowitz, Noreen Doyle, Vincent McGowan, and Margaret Tobin; civic, park, and community leaders Kent Barwick, Anne Buttenweiser, Ernest Cook, Clay Hiles, Charles Komanoff, Daniel Miller, Rob Pirani, Peter R. Stein, Bob Trentlyon, and Pamela Wolff; former city park commissioner Adrian Benepe; attorneys Danny Alterman, Mark Baker, Mitchell (Mitch) Bernard, and Richard Emery; public servants Michael Marella and John McLaughlin; photographer Shelley Seccombe; marine engineer Malcolm (Mal) McLaren; architect Craig Whittaker; landscape architect Marcha

Johnson; journalists Lincoln Anderson, Josh Benson, and Tom Robbins; graphic designer Leslie Kameny; my computer guy Joe Mulholland; businessmen Tom DeMartino and Alvin Trenk; Laurie Kilcommons and Miriam Tuchman from the Neighborhood Open Space Coalition; and New Yorkers who wish to remain anonymous.

Special thanks to my talented editors Susanna Margolis, who helped shape the initial draft manuscript, and Constance Rosenblum, who helped craft the final text; Brooklyn College Archivist Colleen Bradley-Sanders; archival intern Vera Madey; professors Emily Tumpson Molina and Tony Wilson; Brian Ostrander of Westchester Publishing Services and copyeditor Heather Gladhill; and most importantly, the staff at Rutgers University Press, including my patient editor Peter Mickulas, cartographer Michael Siegel, production editor Vincent Neuhaus, and Brice Hammand.

I owe a great deal of gratitude to park opponents, especially Marcy Benstock, John Mylod, and Gene Russianoff. My positions would have seemed quite extreme if it were not for their positions being even more so.

Glossary

Maritime

Barge Flat-bottom boat for carrying freight either under its own power or towed by another vessel

Bits Square or cylindrical posts with smaller diameter crossbar resembling a lowercase letter *t* found on vessels and sometimes on docks

Boat Watercraft with a variety of shapes and sizes generally smaller than a ship

Bollards Short metal mushrooms, where a loop from a line is secured and the slack taken up at the other end, used to secure ships

Bulkhead Retaining wall that separates the land from the water

Chocks Flattened loops with a narrow opening on top to hold a line and prevent it from moving laterally, usually on vessels

Cleats Maritime hardware found on both docks and vessels and resembling a wide and short capital T.

Draft Depth of the keel when the vessel is loaded

Dredge Removing material from the bottom of the river

Freeboard Distance between the waterline and the main deck of a vessel; height of a pier or other over-water structure above the recorded high-water line

Headhouse Structure over a pier entrance that is not on the pier but generally over a relieving platform and provides access, sometimes including ticketing facilities, waiting areas, toilets, and baggage facilities for passenger vessels

Inboard Property and neighborhoods on the eastern side of Route 9A

In-water Anything outboard of the bulkhead

Keel Bottom of a vessel

Mariner A sailor; someone who sails or works on a boat or ship

Maritime Connected with the sea, especially seafaring, commercial, or military work

Navigable waterway Federally mandated navigable water that must be kept open to allow the unobstructed navigation of vessels

Outboard Park property on the river side of Route 9A

Pier Platform supported by piles leading out into the waterway to support the landing of vessels and the handling of their cargo and/or passengers

Pier deck Surface structure built over pier piles

Pierhead Tip or end of a pier

Pier shed Structure that covers a pier to provide protection from the elements

Pile field Piles left after the removal of a pier's decking

Piles Vertical wooden, steel, or concrete structures that hold up a pier

Relieving platform Loading deck on the land side of a retaining wall and supported partly by the wall (bulkhead) and partly by bearing piles

Ship Vessel larger than a boat used to carry cargo and/or passengers

Vessel A ship or large boat

Transportation

Crosswalk Area designated for pedestrian crossings

Federal-aid highway Roadway built using federal funds with state match

Grade separation Aligning two or more transportation axes at different heights so that they do not disrupt traffic flow when they cross each other

Jersey barrier Modular concrete barrier or barricades used to separate traffic and designed to minimize impact from vehicle incidents, reroute traffic, protect pedestrians, or thwart vehicles being used for suicide attacks

Marginal Way Property adjacent to Route 9A along the Hudson River

Median Central area that provides a physical barrier between opposing lanes on divided roadways

Miller Highway Original elevated roadway above West Street (Route 9A)

Right-of-way A legal easement granted over land for transportation purposes

Route 9A New York State Department of Transportation's designation of the West Side roadway

West Side Highway Common term for Miller Highway, West Street, and Route 9A

West Street Roadway below Miller Highway (Route 9A)

Adjacent Neighborhoods (from south to north)

Financial District Battery Place to Chambers Street inboard of Route 9A

Battery Park City Battery Place to Chambers Street outboard of Route 9A

TriBeCa (Triangle Below Canal) Chambers Street to Canal Street

Greenwich Village Canal Street to 14th Street

Chelsea 14th Street to 34th Street

Hell's Kitchen 34th Street to 59th Street (rebranded Clinton in the 1980s)

Community Boards

Community Board 1 The Battery to Houston Street

Community Board 2 Houston Street to West 14th Street

Community Board 4 West 14th Street to West 59th Street

Community Board 7 West 59th Street to West 110th Street

Notes

Reference materials without specific links that can be placed online can be found at https://tinyurl.com/Creating-the-Hudson-River-Park in the Brooklyn College Archives.

Chapter 1   Starting the Journey

1   "Piers 88, 90 and 92—New York NY," The Living New Deal, University of California Berkley, Geography Department, https://livingnewdeal.org/projects /piers-88-90-and-92-new-york-ny/.
2   Ryan Malane and Ginger Vaughn, "Black Ball: 200 Years Strong," Coho Ferry, https://www.cohoferry.com/img/pages/Black%20Ball%20Line%20History.pdf.
3   Bill Hine, "Fulton's Folly, and Now the Port Authority's," *New York Times*, August 15, 1987, https://www.nytimes.com/1987/08/15/opinion/fulton-s-folly-and -now-the-port-authority-s.html.
4   "The Erie Canal," Today in History—October 26, Library of Congress, https:// www.loc.gov/item/today-in-history/october-26/.
5   *Encyclopaedia Brittanica Online*, "John Ericsson: Swedish-American Engineer," https://www.britannica.com/biography/John-Ericsson#ref110997.
6   Madelyn Berg, "The History of Death Avenue," *The High Line* (blog), October 22, 2015, https://www.thehighline.org/blog/2015/10/22/the-history-of-death-avenue-2/.
7   "Hudson and Manhattan Railroad Years," Authority of New York and New Jersey, https://www.panynj.gov/path/en/about/history.html.
8   "This Week in History: Holland Tunnel Opens to Traffic," *People's World*, November 14, 2017, https://www.peoplesworld.org/article/this-week-in-history -holland-tunnel-opens-to-traffic/.
9   World Book, "Opening the Lincoln Tunnel," *World Book* (blog), December 22, 2017, https://www.worldbook.com/behind-the-headlines/Opening-the-Lincoln-Tunnel.
10 "The History of the George Washington Bridge," Port Authority of New York and New Jersey, https://www.panynj.gov/bridges-tunnels/en/george-washington-bridge /history.html.

11 "History of the Port Authority of New York and New Jersey," Port Authority of New York and New Jersey, https://www.panynj.gov/port/en/our-port/history.html.

12 "Sailing Back in History: A Look at South Florida's Ports, Ken Kaye, *South Florida Sun Sentinel*, August 23, 2015, https://www.sun-sentinel.com/local/broward/fl-south-florida-cruise-history-20150821-story.html.

13 Thomas J. Lueck, "New York Port Changes with Shifting Economy," *New York Times*, June 1, 1986, https://www.nytimes.com/1986/06/01/nyregion/new-york-port-changes-with-shifting-economy.html.

14 Paul Goldberger, "Robert Moses, Master Builder, Is Dead at 92," *New York Times*, June 30, 1981, https://www.nytimes.com/1981/07/30/obituaries/robert-moses-master-builder-is-dead-at-92.html.

15 Staff of the Regional Plan, *Regional Plan for New York and Its Environs*, vol. 1 (New York: Regional Plan Association, 1929), 219, figure 12, https://s3.us-east-1.amazonaws.com/rpa-org/pdfs/RPA-Plan1-v1-Regional-Plan-of-New-York-and-Its-Environs.pdf.

16 "Interstate 87, Major Deegan Expressway," NYC Roads, http://www.nycroads.com/roads/major-deegan/.

17 "History, Empire State Development Corporation," Empire State Development Corporation, https://esd.ny.gov/about-us.

18 Sam Roberts, "The Legacy of Westway: Lessons From its Demise," *New York Times*, October 7, 1985, https://www.nytimes.com/1985/10/07/nyregion/the-legacy-of-westway-lessons-from-its-demise.html.

19 Craig Whitaker (principal, Mills Whitaker Architects), discussion with Tom Fox, May 13, 2021.

20 West Side Highway Project, *Draft Environmental Impact Statement and Section 4(f) Statement for the West Side Highway, Interstate Route 478* (New York: U.S. Department of Transportation, Federal Highway Administration, 1974), 10–13, https://books.google.com/books?id=JdHvAMH6CqEC&pg=PA1&lpg=PA1&dq=West+Side+Highway+Project,+Environmental+Impact+Statement,"+Draft+Environmental+Impact+Statement+and+Section+4(f)+Statement+for+the+West+Side+Highway,+Interstate+Route+478,+April+25,+1974&source=bl&ots=EhrV5phhM4&sig=ACfU3U3DjnEgpwvJ6RWnLMTvTaydDEdDAw&hl=en&sa=X&ved=2ahUKEwit3MnvsKr1AhWuhOAKHdjLCiEQ6AF6BAgPEAM#v=onepage&q=West%20Side%20Highway%20Project%2C%20Environmental%20Impact%20Statement%2C"%20Draft%20Environmental%20Impact%20Statement%20and%20Section%204(f)%20Statement%20for%20the%20West%20Side%20Highway%2C%20Interstate%20Route%20478%2C%20April%2025%2C%201974&f=false.

21 "David and Nelson Rockefeller," American Experience, PBS, accessed October 11, 2023, https://www.pbs.org/wgbh/americanexperience/features/newyork-rockefeller/.

22 "David and Nelson Rockefeller."

23 Jeffrey Rosenberg, "The 1969 U.S. Downturn Can Tell a Lot about a Key Recession Indicator That's Flashing Yellow," *Business Insider*, June 5, 2018, https://www.businessinsider.com/recession-1969-downturn-can-tell-us-about-the-key-2018-6.

24 "Gateway National Recreation Area," National Parks Foundation, accessed October 11, 2023, https://www.npca.org/parks/gateway-national-recreation-area.

25 Laurie Johnson, "Brooklyn 4th Graders Get Close Look at Marine Life," *New York Times*, April 26, 1977, https://www.nytimes.com/1977/04/26/archives/brooklyn-4th-graders-get-close-look-at-marine-life.html.

26 John Lewis, "A Treat of a Trip 400 Cruise to Park," *Daily News*, July 22, 1976.

27 "Liz Christy Bowery Houston Community Farm and Garden," Liz Christy Community Garden, accessed October 11, 2023, http://www.lizchristygarden.us.

28 "How to Make a Seed Bomb," The Wildlife Trusts, accessed October 11, 2023, https://www.wildlifetrusts.org/actions/how-make-seed-bomb.

29 Institute for Local Self-Reliance (website), accessed October 11, 2023, https://ilsr.org.

30 Laura Vecsey, "Weinstein Unloads West Village Townhouse for $25.6M," *StreetEasy* (blog), March 28, 2018, https://streeteasy.com/blog/harvey-weinsteins-nyc-townhouse-sold-25-6-million/.

31 Meaghan, "Remembering the Original New Yorkers," *Village Preservation* (blog), November 26, 2014, https://www.villagepreservation.org/2014/11/26/remembering-the-original-new-yorkers/.

32 "Pre-Contact, Dutch, and the Eighteenth Century" and "The Federal Period," Greenwich Village History, The Greenwich Village Society for Historic Preservation, accessed October 11, 2023, https://www.villagepreservation.org/resources/neighborhood-history/#federal-period.

33 "Washington Square Park," Monuments, NYC Department of Parks and Recreation, accessed October 11, 2023, https://www.nycgovparks.org/parks/washington-square-park/monuments/1657.

34 "The Hangman's Elm, Manhattan New York," Atlas Obscura, accessed October 11, 2023, https://www.atlasobscura.com/places/the-hangmans-elm-new-york-new-york.

35 Holland Cotter, "He Captured a Clandestine Gay Culture Amid the Derelict Piers," *New York Times*, September 19, 2019, https://www.nytimes.com/2019/09/19/arts/design/alvin-baltrop-photographs.html.

36 "The Hudson Estuary, A River That Flows Two Ways," New York State Department of Environmental Conservation, accessed October 11, 2023, https://www.dec.ny.gov/lands/4923.html.

Chapter 2   Westway (1974–1985)

1 David W. Dunlap, "What David Rockefeller Wanted Built Got Built," *New York Times*, March 26, 2017, https://www.nytimes.com/2017/03/26/nyregion/david-rockefeller-development-nyc.html.

2 Jason M. Barr, "The Bedrock Myth and the Rise of Midtown Manhattan," Building the Skyline, July 29, 2019, https://buildingtheskyline.org/bedrock-and-midtown-i/.

3 "The World Trade Center," History, September 10, 2019, https://www.history.com/topics/landmarks/world-trade-center.

4 "New York, NY West Side Highway," Removing Freeways—Restoring Cities, Preservation Institute, October 10, 2023. http://www.preservenet.com/freeways/FreewaysWestSide.html#:~:text=The%20West%20Side%20Highway%2C%20officially,1936%2C%20connecting%20at%2072nd%20St.

5 "Truck and Car Fall as West Side Highway Collapses," *New York Times*, December 16, 1973, https://www.nytimes.com/1973/12/16/archives/truck-and-car-fall-as-west-side-highway-collapses.html.

6 "Who We Are, History," Association for Better New York, https://abny.org/History.

7   "Partnership for New York City, Our History," Partnership for New York City, https://pfnyc.org/our-history/.

8   Lynne B. Sagalyn, "The Cross Manhattan Expressway, Object Essay," Museum of the City of New York, November 14, 2016, https://www.mcny.org/story/cross -manhattan-expressway.

9   "Sierra Club v. United States Army Corps of Engineers, 541 F. Supp. 1367 (S.D.N.Y. 1982)," Justia US Law, https://law.justia.com/cases/federal/district-courts/FSupp /541/1367/2288539/.

10 "Durst Uses Times Page One Ads to Promote Housing and Oppose Westway," *Real Estate Weekly*, April 9, 1984.

11 "Backgrounder on the Three Mile Island Accident," U.S. Nuclear Regulatory Commission, accessed October 11, 2023, https://www.nrc.gov/reading-rm/doc -collections/fact-sheets/3mile-isle.html.

12 Paul W. Valentine, Karlyn Barker, and staff writers, "The Protestors," *Washington Post*, May 7, 1978, https://www.washingtonpost.com/archive/politics/1979/05/07 /the-protesters/b2ea631e-933c-4f07-b59e-e97bf1068b7e/.

13 "About Us," New York Public Interest Research Group, accessed October 11, 2023, https://www.nypirg.org/about/.

14 Robin Herman, "Nearly 200,000 Rally to Protest Nuclear Energy," *New York Times*, September 24, 1979, https://www.nytimes.com/1979/09/24/archives/nearly -200000-rally-to-protest-nuclear-energy-gathering-at-the.html.

15 Chris Kaltenbach, "Liberty Ship John W. Brown Has a Place to Moor in Baltimore. It Just Needs (At Least) $10 Million," *Baltimore Sun*, December 30, 2019, https:// www.baltimoresun.com/features/bs-fe-john-w-brown-ship-20191230-pycdmnqf andd3g7fabs75jgyme-story.html.

16 Paul L. Montgomery, "Throngs Fill Manhattan to Protest Nuclear Weapons," *New York Times*, June 13, 1982, https://www.nytimes.com/1982/06/13/world/throngs -fill-manhattan-to-protest-nuclear-weapons.html.

17 Constance "Coco" Eiseman (NYS Office of Parks, Recreation, and Historic Preservation), letter to Tom Fox, April 21, 1984.

18 Bunny Gabel, John Mylod, and Marcy Benstock, "Westway Park—Pie in the Sky; Would Drain Funds from Other State Parks If It Was Ever Built," press release, June 19, 1984.

19 New York State Office of Parks Recreation and Historic Preservation, "NYS Comprehensive Recreation Plan," March 1983, IV–4.

20 New York State Office of Parks Recreation and Historic Preservation, "Recreation Plan," IV–5.

21 *U.S. Army Corps of Engineers, New York District, Public Hearing*, June 26, 1984 (statement of Neighborhood Open Space Coalition).

22 Sam Roberts, "Battle of the Westway: Bitter 10-Year Saga of a Vision on Hold," *New York Times*, June 4, 1984, https://www.nytimes.com/1984/06/04/nyregion /battle-of-the-westway-bitter-10-year-saga-of-a-vision-on-hold.html.

23 "The Westway Project: Its History and Future," *New York Times*, August 1, 1981, https://www.nytimes.com/1981/08/01/nyregion/the-westway-project-its-history -and-future.html.

24 Edward A. Gargan, "Koch and Carey Sign Pact for Westway Construction Unless US Cuts Amenities," *New York Times,* August 1, 1981, https://www.nytimes.com /1981/08/01/nyregion/koch-and-carey-sign-a-pact-for-westway-construction-unless -us-cuts.html; "Text of the Agreement Between the State and City Regarding

Westway," *New York Times*, August 1, 1981, https://www.nytimes.com/1981/08/01
/nyregion/text-of-the-agreement-between-the-state-and-city-on-the-westway-project
.html.

25 "Text of the Agreement between the State and City Regarding Westway," *New York
Times*, August 1, 1981, https://www.nytimes.com/1981/08/01/nyregion/text-of-the
-agreement-between-the-state-and-city-on-the-westway-project.html.

26 Arnold Lubasch, "Judge Bars $90 Million U.S. Payment for Westway," *New York
Times*, April 21, 1982, https://www.nytimes.com/1982/04/21/nyregion/judge-bars
-90-million-us-payment-for-westway.html.

27 *Westway Project: A Study of Abuses in the Federal/State Relations: Hearings
before a Subcommittee of the Committee on Government, House of Representatives Ninety-eighth Congress First Session* (Washington: U.S. Government
Printing Office, 1984), 896–900, https://books.google.com/books?id
=dkUa1qmBE3MC&pg=PA898&lpg=PA898&dq=NYD+DOT+Westway+plan
%27s+statistics&source=bl&ots=rSL5XyzW1f&sig=ACfU3U13IVLVN9PQ6oj
AY6zr5fktwxGwew&hl=en&sa=X&ved=2ahUKEwiV56TUs4XwAhWLm
-AKHdVZC84Q6AEwBnoECBAQAw#v=onepage&q=NYD%20DOT%20
Westway%20plan's%20statistics&f=false.

28 Sydney H. Schanberg, "New York; Cuomo's Impasse arrives," *New York Times*,
May 1983, https://www.nytimes.com/1983/05/03/opinion/new-york-cuomo-s
-impasse-arrives.html.

29 Arnold H. Lubasch, "Corps Aide Sees No Alternative to Westway," *New York
Times*, May 23,1985, https://www.nytimes.com/1985/05/23/nyregion/corps-aide-sees
-no-alternative-to-the-westway.html.

30 "Excerpts from the Ruling by the Federal Appeals Court on the Westway Project,"
New York Times, September 12, 1985, https://www.nytimes.com/1985/09/12/nyregion
/excerpts-from-ruling-by-federal-appeals-court-on-the-westway-project.html.

31 "Sierra Club v. U.S. Army Corps of Engineers," Casetext, accessed October 11, 2023,
https://casetext.com/case/sierra-club-v-us-army-corps-of-engineers-13.

32 William W. Buzbee, "Fighting Westway, Environmental Law, Citizen Activism,
and the Regulatory War That Transform New York City," *Cornell University Press*,
2014, https://www.cornellpress.cornell.edu/book/9780801479441/fighting
-westway/#bookTabs=1.

33 William G. Blair, "Money Still Flows as Westway Battle Continues in Court,"
New York Times, August 25, 1985, https://www.nytimes.com/1985/08/25/nyregion
/money-still-flows-as-westway-battle-continues-in-court.html.

34 American Community Gardening Association (website), accessed October 11, 2023,
https://www.communitygarden.org.

35 Sam Roberts, Complications over Trade-in for Westway," *New York Times*,
September 19, 1985, https://www.nytimes.com/1985/09/19/nyregion/complications
-over-trade-in-for-westway.html?searchResultPosition=22.

36 Michael Oreskes, "Moynihan Sees No Way to Win a Westway Vote," *New York
Times*, September 19, 1985. https://www.nytimes.com/1985/09/19/nyregion
/moynihan-sees-no-way-to-win-a-westway-vote.html.

37 "Removing Freeways—Restoring Cities," New York, NY West Side Highway,
Preservation Institute, accessed October 14, 2023, http://www.preservenet.com
/freeways/FreewaysWestSide.html.

38 Owen Mortiz, "How the 'Soot Lady' and Striped Bass Defeated the Westway
Development Project," *New York Daily News*, August 14, 2017, https://www

.nydailynews.com/new-york/soot-lady-defeated-westway-development-project
-article-1.818854.

39 Buzbee, "Fighting Westway."

40 Martin Gottlieb, "A New Proposal for West Side Waterfront," *New York Times*,
December 1, 1985, https://www.nytimes.com/1985/12/01/nyregion/new-proposal-for
-west-side-waterfron.html.

41 "Comments on West Side Replacement Study," Presented at the Public Information
Meeting, Neighborhood Open Space Coalition, March 18, 1986.

42 New York State Department of Transportation, "West Side Highway Replacement Study, Public Information Meeting—March 18, 1986," meeting summary,
1986.

Chapter 3   The West Side Task Force (1986–1987)

1 West Side Task Force, "West Side Task Force—Scope of Study," July 27, 1986.

2 Michael Kruse, "The Lost City of Trump," Politico, August 18, 2018, https://www
.politico.com/magazine/story/2018/06/29/trump-robert-moses-new-york-television
-city-urban-development-1980s-218836/.

3 "Panel Will Study West Side Growth," *New York Times*, July 27, 1986, https://www
.nytimes.com/1986/07/27/nyregion/panel-will-study-west-side-growth.html.

4 West Side Task Force Meeting Minutes, July 30, 1986.

5 West Side Task Force Meeting Minutes, July 30, 1986, p. 5.

6 Thomas J. Lueck, "Koch Looks to Rivers for Development," *New York Times*,
February 12, 1989, https://www.nytimes.com/1989/02/12/realestate/koch-looks-to
-rivers-for-development.html.

7 Neighborhood Open Space Coalition, "New York State Department of Transportation, Public Information Meeting," comments, August 6, 1986.

8 Mary Connelly and Carlyle C. Douglas, "The Region: If Not Westway, Then What?,"
New York Times, August 10, 1986, https://www.nytimes.com/1986/08/10/weekinreview
/the-region-if-not-westway-then-what.html.

9 Tom Fox, "Issues That Should Be 'Put on the Table Early' in the Process," memo to
Curt Berger, August 27, 1986.

10 Tom Fox (Neighborhood Open Space Coalition), invitation to ad-hoc advisory
committee members, August 27, 1986.

11 West Side Task Force Meeting Minutes, September 3, 1986, p. 3.

12 West Side Task Force Meeting Minutes, July 30, 1986.

13 West Side Task Force, "Fact Sheet #3, Overview of October 8th Task Force Meeting,
October 9th Transportation Working Group Meeting, and the October 18 Community Workshop," October 2, 1986.

14 West Side Task Force Meeting Minutes, October 8, 1986, p. 1.

15 West Side Task Force Meeting Minutes, October 8, 1986, p. 2.

16 West Side Task Force, "Community Workshop October 18 Acceptance List,"
October 16, 1986.

17 West Side Task Force Meeting Minutes, November 5, 1986.

18 Alan Finder, "Developer Named for Hudson River Complex," *New York Times*,
February 11, 1987, https://www.nytimes.com/1987/02/11/nyregion/developers
-named-for-hudson-complex.html.

19 Neighborhood Open Space Coalition, "West Side Ad-Hoc Committee," meeting
notes, November 5, 1986.

20 New York State Department of Transportation, New York City Department of Transportation, and Department of City Planning, "West Side Replacement Study," public information meeting, August 6, 1986.

21 "Evolution of the Clean Air Act," United States Environmental Protection Agency, accessed October 11, 2023, https://www.epa.gov/clean-air-act-overview/evolution-clean-air-act.

22 West Side Task Force, "Fact Sheet #4 Overview of November 14–16 Task Force Retreat and Meetings Between October 18 and November 1," November 21, 1986.

23 Sam Roberts, "Westway Alternatives Raising New Questions," *New York Times*, September 20, 1985, https://www.nytimes.com/1985/09/20/nyregion/westway-alternatives-raising-new-questions.html.

24 Martin Gottlieb, "New Proposal for West Side Waterfront," *New York Times*, December 1, 1985, https://www.nytimes.com/1985/12/01/nyregion/new-proposal-for-west-side-waterfron.html.

25 New York City, Department of City Planning, "Transforming the East River Waterfront," accessed October 11, 2023, https://www1.nyc.gov/assets/planning/download/pdf/plans-studies/east-river-waterfront/east_river_waterfront_book.pdf, 15.

26 West Side Task Force, "Scope of Study."

27 West Side Task Force, "Principles for West Side Corridor Entity," draft memo, November 21, 1986.

28 "23 U.S. Code Section 319—Landscaping and Scenic Enhancement," Cornell Law School, Legal Information Group, accessed October 11, 2023, https://www.law.cornell.edu/uscode/text/23/319.

29 Tom Fox (Neighborhood Open Space Coalition), "Public Funds for Park and Open Space Development Associated with the West Side Highway," memo to task force members, November 21, 1986.

30 Tom Fox (Neighborhood Open Space Coalition), "Chart I—Expenditures for the Acquisition and Improvement of a Strip of Land Necessary for the Restoration, Preservation and Enhancement of Scenic Beauty Adjacent to the West Side Highway," memo to task force members, December 12, 1986.

31 Robert O. Boorstin, "Panel Agrees on Parts of West Side Road Plan," *New York Times*, November 27, 1986, https://www.nytimes.com/1986/11/27/nyregion/panel-agrees-on-parts-of-west-side-road-plan.html.

32 Curt Berger and Ann Buttenwieser (West Side Task Force), "Revised Draft Recommendations," memo, December 1, 1986.

33 West Side Task Force, "Speaker's Order, West Side Task Force," public hearing, December 17, 1986.

34 "Final Decision on West Side Road Shows Sharp Divisions over Plan," *New York Times*, December 18, 1986, https://www.nytimes.com/1986/12/18/nyregion/final-hearing-on-west-side-road-shows-sharp-divisions-over-plan.html.

35 Nancy Webster and David Shirley, *A History of the Brooklyn Bridge Park* (New York: Columbia University Press, 2016), 74–75, http://cup.columbia.edu/book/a-history-of-brooklyn-bridge-park/9780231171229.

36 Saul Morgenstern, Dewey Ballantine Bushby Palmer & Wood, "Preliminary Conclusions Regarding the Use of Federal Highway Funds for the Purchase of Property Adjacent to the Proposed West Side Highway," letter and memorandum, December 5, 1986.

37 West Side Task Force Meeting Minutes, December 8, 1986.

38 Tom Fox (Neighborhood Open Space Coalition), "Inclusion of the Landscaped Esplanade in the West Side Highway," memo to West Side Task Force Members, December 12, 1986.

39 Tom Fox (Neighborhood Open Space Coalition), letter to West Side Task Force members, "Concerns at the Conclusion of the Task Force," December 12, 1986.

40 West Side Task Force, "Estimated Public Esplanade Costs," December 1986.

41 Tom Robbins, "Westway's Second Round," *Village Voice*, December 23, 1986.

42 Richard Higgins, Battery Park City Authority, "West Side Corridor Entity," December 22, 1986.

43 Robert O. Boorstin, "West Side Panel Disagrees on Esplanade," *New York Times*, January 8, 1987, https://www.nytimes.com/1987/01/08/nyregion/west-side-road -panel-disagrees-on-esplanade.html?searchResultPosition=1.

44 Carol Polsky, "West Side Task Force to Release Final Highway Recommendations," *NY Newsday*, January 8, 1987.

45 Arthur Levitt Jr. (American Stock Exchange), letter to Tom Fox, December 16, 1986.

46 Roberta Brandes Gratz, "Concurring Opinion," January 1987.

47 West Side Task Force, "Final Report," January 7, 1987, p. 42.

48 Lillian Liberti, "Cover Inscription," January 8, 1987.

Chapter 4   The Letdown (1987–1988)

1 Carol Polsky, "West Side Road Plan Includes a Park," *New York Newsday*, January 9, 1987.

2 "Surprise Turn on the Highway," editorial, *New York Newsday*, January 9, 1987.

3 Chris Archer, "Task Force Gives Report Final OK," *The Villager*, January 15, 1987.

4 "Don't By-Pass the Community Boards," editorial, *The Villager*, January 15, 1987.

5 "At Last, a Westway Truce," editorial, *New York Times*, January 29, 1987, https:// www.nytimes.com/1986/11/29/opinion/at-last-a-westway-truce.html?search ResultPosition=1.

6 Arthur Levitt Jr., "Let's End the Westway War," *New York Times*, February 4, 1987, https://www.nytimes.com/1987/02/04/opinion/lets-end-the-westway-war.html ?searchResultPosition=1.

7 Robert O. Boorstin, "Panel Urges West Side Road; Cuomo Faults Esplanade Plan," *New York Times*, January 9, 1987, https://www.nytimes.com/1987/01/09/nyregion /panel-urges-west-side-road-cuomo-faults-esplanade-plan.html.

8 "Park Vanishes, Gov Suspected," editorial, *Village Voice*, January 20, 1987.

9 Tom Fox, letter to The Honorable Governor Mario Cuomo, January 29, 1987.

10 Tom Fox, letter to The Honorable Governor Mario Cuomo, September 17, 1987.

11 Tom Fox, Anne McClellan, and Maria Stanco, "Brooklyn/Queens Greenway, A Feasibility Study," Neighborhood Open Space Coalition, New York, NY, July 1987.

12 Sandra Bodovitz, "Park Plans: A Brooklyn-Queens Path," *New York Times*, July 26, 1987, https://www.nytimes.com/1987/07/26/nyregion/parks-plan-a-brooklyn -queens-path.html?searchResultPosition=1.

13 Tom Fox and Anne McClellan, "Brooklyn/Queens Greenway—A Design Study," Neighborhood Open Space Coalition, New York, NY, 1988.

14 Noel Grove, "Greenways: Paths to the Future," *National Geographic*, June 1990, 93.

15 Charles E. Little, "From Olmsted to Moses to Fox," in *Greenways for America* (Baltimore, John Hopkins University Press, 1990), 166–172.

16 "Silver Medalist, Rudy Bruner Award for Urban Excellence," Rudy Bruner Foundation, 1991, http://www.rudybruneraward.org/winners/?res=brooklyn -queens-greenway.

17 "3-inch/50 (7.62 cm) Marks 27, 33 and 34," Naval Weapons, Naval Technology and Naval Reunions, http://www.navweaps.com/Weapons/WNUS_3-50_mk27-33-34 .php.

18 Jim O'Grady, "100 Years Ago, Arrival of Titanic Survivors in NYC Set Off a Media Free-For-All," *WNYC*, April 15, 2012, https://www.wnyc.org/story/199399-100 -years-ago-arrival-titanic-survivors-nyc-set-media-free-all/.

19 Regional Plan Association, "The Region's Agenda," January 1987.

20 William Woodside (chairman of Regional Plan Association), letter to Governor Mario Cuomo and Mayor Edward Koch, February 3, 1987.

21 Marcy Benstock and NYC Clean Air Campaign, letter to U.S. Senator Daniel Patrick Moynihan, January 26, 1987.

22 "28th Annual Conference Agenda," Council of Planning Librarians, Sheraton Hotel, New York City, April 24–27, 1987.

23 Alan Finder, "Developers Named for Hudson Complex," *New York Times*, February 11, 1987, https://www.nytimes.com/1987/02/11/nyregion/developers -named-for-hudson-complex.html.

24 NYS Senate Minority Leader Manfred Ohrenstein to Port Authority Executive Director Stephen Berger, August 11, 1987.

25 "West Side Highway Story: A Possible Happy Ending," editorial, *New York Newsday*, August 1987.

26 "Joint Statement of New York State Senators Manfred Ohrenstein and Franz Leichter, New York State Assembly members William F. Passannante, Richard N. Gottfried, and Jerrold R. Nadler, New York City Council members Ruth Messinger, Miriam Friedlander, and Carol Greitzer Regarding Governor Cuomo and Mayor Koch's Announcement on West Side Highway Replacement and Esplanade," press release, August 23, 1987.

27 Governor Mario Cuomo, letter to Tom Fox, September 9, 1987.

28 Testimony to the New York State Senate Democratic Task Force on Waterfront Development, September 21, 1987 (statement of Neighborhood Open Space Coalition).

29 Thomas J. Lueck, "Battling Urban Development with Parks," *New York Times*, March 18, 1987, https://www.nytimes.com/1987/03/18/nyregion/battling-urban -development-with-parks.html?scp=55&sq=Tom%20Fox&st=cse.

30 Regional Plan Association to William S. Woodside, chairman to the Honorable Mario M. Cuomo and the Honorable Edward I. Koch, September 21, 1987.

31 The Parks Council, "Hudson River Esplanade Park—A Design Concept for the West Side Waterfront," December 1987.

32 Elizabeth Kolbert, "Cuomo Delays Esplanade Plan for the Hudson, Cites Goldin Efforts-Highway Talks Go On," *New York Times*, January 17, 1988, https://www .nytimes.com/1989/01/17/nyregion/cuomo-delays-esplanade-plan-for-the-hudson .html?searchResultPosition=1.

33 Municipal Art Society, "Wanted: A Waterfront for New York," exhibit invitation postcard, Urban Center through February 17, 1988.

34 Richard N. Gottfried, "New York State Assembly Memorandum in Support of Legislation, S. 6992, 6997 and A. 8980, 8981," February 10, 1988.

35   Marcy Benstock, "Bill Prohibiting Landfill or Platforms in Westway Area of Hudson River Introduced in the State Legislature February 10, 1988: Westway II Action Alert," March 2, 1988.

36   Mitchell Moss, "Snag for Westside Esplanade Proposal," *New York Newsday*, March 8, 1988.

37   Tom Fox, "Meet Westway's Grandson," *New York Newsday*, March 17, 1988.

38   Meyer S. Frucher and Robert Esnard, "All Systems Go," *New York Newsday*, March 30, 1988.

39   David N. Dinkins, "One for the Roadway," *New York Newsday*, April 8, 1998.

40   The New York Building Congress, "1988 Leadership Awards Luncheon, Grand Hyatt Hotel, The Empire Ballroom," agenda, March 29, 1988.

41   Peg Tyre and Jeannette Walls, "West Side Driver Back on Track," *Intelligencer, New York Magazine*, April 18, 1988.

42   Meyer S. Frucher, "Let the Possibilities for the West Side Waterfront Be Explored," *New York Times*, May 8, 1988, https://www.nytimes.com/1988/08/05/opinion/l-let-the-possibilities-for-the-west-side-waterfront-be-explored-366688.html?searchResultPosition=1.

43   Joyce Purnick, "No Westway Substitute on the Map for 10 Years," *New York Times*, May 30, 1988, https://www.nytimes.com/1988/05/30/nyregion/westway-substitute-not-on-map-for-10-years.html.

44   "Know-Nothings on the Waterfront," editorial, *New York Times*, June 25, 1988, https://www.nytimes.com/1988/06/25/opinion/know-nothings-on-the-waterfront.html?searchResultPosition=9.

45   "Fish Tales in Albany," editorial, *New York Post*, June 29, 1988.

46   "Dumb, Dumber and Dumbest," editorial, *New York Daily News*, June 30, 1988.

47   Chris Fallows, "Take Park Pleas to City Hall Steps," *The Villager*, June 30, 1988.

48   Mitchell Moss, "River Structure Gives Its Foes Their Platform," *New York Newsday*, June 26, 1998.

49   Marcy Benstock, Clean Air Campaign, "Sneak Attack by Battery Park City on Westway Area of Hudson River: Floating Prison in Hudson Also Hastily Certified by City Planning," press release, June 20–27, 1988.

50   Douglas Martin, "A Prison Barge on Hudson: 'Folly' or 'Ideal,'" *New York Times*, June 16, 1988, https://www.nytimes.com/1988/06/16/nyregion/a-prison-barge-on-hudson-folly-or-ideal.html.

51   Celestine Bohlen, "Board Backs Prison Barge near Pier 40," *New York Times*, October 28, 1988, https://www.nytimes.com/1988/10/28/nyregion/board-backs-prison-barge-near-pier-40.html.

52   Tom Robbins, "Wise Guys, Westway II: First Blood," *New York Observer*, June 20, 1988.

Chapter 5   The West Side Waterfront Panel (1988–1990)

1   Nancy Webster and David Shirley, *A History of the Brooklyn Bridge Park* (New York: Columbia University Press, 2016), 72–73, http://cup.columbia.edu/book/a-history-of-brooklyn-bridge-park/9780231171229.

2   Ted Weiss and Manfred Orenstein, "Legislators React with Mixed Feelings to Appointments to Newly Created City-State West Side Waterfront Panel," press release, July 8, 1988.

3   Carter Wiseman, "Sylvia Deutsch," *New York Magazine*, September 12, 1988.

4 Neighborhood Open Space Coalition, *Neighborhood Open Space Coalition*, membership brochure, 1989.

5 Jacob Gershman, "Main Cuomo Advisor Runs a Low Profile," *Wall Street Journal*, November 27, 2010, https://www.wsj.com/articles/SB1000142405274870469310457563909126418682.

6 Dennis Hevesi, "Orin Lehman, 88, Parks Steward, Dies," *New York Times*, February 23, 2008, https://www.nytimes.com/2008/02/23/nyregion/23lehman.html.

7 Heather Sporn, former associate landscape architect, New York State Department of Transportation, interview by Tom Fox, May 3, 2021.

8 "West Side Highway Replacement," Flexibility in Highway Design, U.S. Department of Transportation, Federal Highway Administration, accessed October 12, 2023, https://www.fhwa.dot.gov/environment/publications/flexibility/ch09.cfm.

9 Kelsey Campbell-Dollaghan, "The Forgotten 13th Avenue That New York City Built and Then Destroyed," Gizmo, January 29, 2015, https://gizmodo.com/the-forgotten-13th-avenue-that-new-york-city-built-and-1682556913.

10 "Chelsea Piers History 101," Chelsea Piers New York, accessed October 12, 2023, https://www.chelseapiers.com/company/history/.

11 George B. Adams, "Backgrounding a Waterfront Park," letter to the editor, *New York Times*, April 21, 1994, https://www.nytimes.com/1994/08/21/realestate/l-backgrounding-a-waterfront-park-994634.html.

12 Chelsea Waterside Park Group and Congressman Weiss Meeting Minutes, November 13, 1989.

13 Richard Maitino to Nancy Goell et al., December 5, 1989.

14 Richard Maitino, former executive director, New York State Deparment of Transportation, interview by Tom Fox, April 28, 2021.

15 Larry McShane, "Fateful 1976 Mob Commission Vote to Admit New Members Marked Mafia Turning Point in Retrospect," *New York Daily News,* May 21, 2020, https://www.nydailynews.com/new-york/nyc-crime/ny-mafia-commission-vote-20200531-4clj4l7f4fhcvh4llcxouczrky-story.html.

16 Alex Vadukul, "For Sale: Sexiest Hourly Rate Hotel in Manhattan," *New York Times*, August 10, 2022, https://www.nytimes.com/2022/08/10/style/hourly-rate-hotel-manhattan.html.

17 Tom Robbins, "The State Pays for Sex," *Village Voice*, August 7, 2007, https://www.villagevoice.com/2007/08/07/the-state-pays-for-sex/.

18 Elizabeth Kolbert, "Cuomo Delays Esplanade Plan for the Hudson," Elizabeth Kolbert, Special to *The New York Times*, January 17, 1989, https://www.nytimes.com/1989/01/17/nyregion/cuomo-delays-esplanade-plan-for-the-hudson.html.

19 "Growth and Fishes' Rights," editorial #89–4, *WPIX*, January 8, 1989.

20 "Poor Little Westway Jr.," editorial, *New York Times*, February 14, 1989, https://www.nytimes.com/1989/02/14/opinion/poor-little-westway-jr.html?searchResultPosition=10.

21 Elizabeth Kolbert, "Cuomo Favors Building Ban Along Hudson," *New York Times*, March 31, 1989, https://www.nytimes.com/1989/03/31/nyregion/cuomo-favors-building-ban-along-hudson.html.

22 Al Amateau, "Esplanade Signpost: Impasse!," *Battery News*, April 10, 1989.

23 "Westway Nihilists," editorial, *New York Times*, April 15, 1989, https://www.nytimes.com/1989/04/15/opinion/westway-s-nihilists.html.

24 Testimony to the New York City Planning Commission, 1989 (statement of Neighborhood Open Space Coalition).

25 The Parks Council, *Citizens for a Hudson River Park Esplanade*, membership brochure, 1989.

26 Hudson River Rally and Festival Committee, *June 10th Hudson River Rally and Festival*, brochure, June 10, 1989.

27 Chris Archer, "Plan a Bash for Hudsonside Park," *The Villager*, June 1, 1989.

28 Audrey Farolino, "Pier Pressure," *New York Post*, June 8, 1989.

29 Governor Mario Cuomo and Mayor Koch to Michael Del Giudice, letter, June 19, 1989.

30 "Park May Be Planned on Ex-Westway Land," *New York Times*, June 21, 1989.

31 David W. Dunlap, "West Side Panel Rules Out Landfill for Hudson Riverfront," *New York Times*, July 20, 1989, http://www.nytimes.com/1989/07/20/nyregion /west-side-planning-panel-rules-out-landfill-for-hudson-riverfront.html.

32 Tom Fox, Neighborhood Open Space Coalition, "The History of Scenic Easements and Their Application to West Side Waterfront Preservation—A Changing Situation," January 4, 1990.

33 West Side Waterfront Panel, "Policies for Improving the West Side Waterfront," August 19, 1989.

34 Frank Lynn, "The New York Primary: Dinkins Sweeps Past Koch for Nomination; Giuliani Easily Wins Republican Primary; Mayor Offers Help," *New York Times*, September 13, 1989, https://www.nytimes.com/1989/09/13/nyregion/new-york -primary-dinkins-sweeps-past-koch-for-nomination-giuliani-easily-wins.html.

35 Sam Roberts, "The 1898 Election: The New York Vote; Almost Lost at the Wire," *New York Times*, November 9, 1989, https://www.nytimes.com/1989/11/09 /nyregion/the-1989-elections-the-new-york-vote-almost-lost-at-the-wire.html.

36 David W. Dunlap, "Post-Westway Plan Offered by Panel for Hudson Shore," *New York Times*, November 1, 1989, https://www.nytimes.com/1989/11/01 /nyregion/post-westway-plan-offered-by-panel-for-hudson-shore.html.

37 Carr, Lynch, Hack and Sandell, *Active Uses from Chambers to 43rd Street*, map, 1989.

38 Carr, Lynch, Hack and Sandell, "Real Estate Development Analysis (25 Year Proforma)," December 12, 1989.

39 Brian Leichtweis, "Park Along Hudson Nixed," *City Sierran*, Winter 1990.

40 Al Amateau, "Center Profits Linked to Esplanade," *Chelsea Clinton News*, December 21, 1989–January 3, 1990.

41 NYC Clean Air Campaign, "West Side Waterfront Panel's 'Esplanade Park' Costs," December 1989.

42 Betsy Haggerty (West Side Waterfront Panel), "Members of the Civic Advisory Committee, Subcommittee Assignments," memo, December 8, 1989.

43 Kathryn Ludwig; Carr, Lynch, Hack and Sandell, "West Side Waterfront # 848, Conceptual Cost Estimates," December 12, 1989.

44 West Side Waterfront Panel, "Planning Strategy to Reach Final Options in March/ April 1990," February 15, 1990.

45 "Congressman Ted Weiss et al., letter to Michael Del Giudice," December 29, 1989.

Chapter 6   New Park Proposed (1990–1992)

1 Mitchell Moss, "Dinkins: Repay Westway Project Fund," *New York Newsday*, February 3, 1990.

2 Allen R. Gold, "Cuomo and Dinkins Back Hudson Park," *New York Times*, February 16, 1990, https://www.nytimes.com/1990/02/16/nyregion/cuomo-and -dinkins-back-hudson-park.html.

3 State of New York Executive Chamber, "Governor Mario M. Cuomo Proposes Legislation for a \$1.9 Billion Bond Act to Protect and Enhance New York's Environment into the Next Century," press release, February 15, 1990.

4 West Side Waterfront Panel, "Statement by the West Side Waterfront Panel," press release, February 15, 1990.

5 Mitchell Moss, "Park Plan for Westway Site," *New York Newsday*, February 28, 1990.

6 Peter Oblitz, Chair et al., Manhattan Community Board 4, letter to The Honorable David N. Dinkins, March 13, 1990.

7 Elizabeth Kolbert, "Park Funds May Fall Short in West Side Park Plan," *New York Times*, March 4, 1990, https://www.nytimes.com/1990/03/04/nyregion/funds-may-fall-short-in-west-side-park-plan.html.

8 *The Board of Commissioners of the Department of Public Parks, Third General Report* (New York: William C Bryant and Co, 1875), 15–17.

9 Tom Fox, *Urban Open Space: An Investment That Pays* (Neighborhood Open Space Coalition, New York, 1990), 11.

10 "Urban Open Space: An Investment That Pays," symposium invitation, New York University Law School, March 22, 1990.

11 J. Kevin Sullivan, "Fish and Wildlife Populations and Habitat Status and Trends in the New York Bight," Dynamic Corporation, Rockville, MD, September 1991, https://www.hudsonriver.org/wp-content/uploads/2018/10/FishWildlifePopul Habitat1991.pdf.

12 Tom Fox, "West Side Waterfront Park," memo to West Side Waterfront Panel, May 7, 1990.

13 Tom Fox (Neighborhood Open Space Coalition), "Continuing the City, State, and Civic Partnership to Rebuild Manhattan's Lower West Side Waterfront," memo to Michael Del Giudice, July 21, 1990.

14 John K. McLaughlin, managing director, Office of Ecosystem Services, Green Infrastructure and Research, New York City Department of Environmental Protection, interview by Tom Fox, April 25, 2021.

15 Tom Fox (Neighborhood Open Space Coalition), "Interim Esplanade in Greenwich Village," memo to West Side Waterfront Panel, 1990.

16 Tom Lyons (New York State Office of Parks Recreation and Historic Preservation), "SEQRA and Temporary Use Esplanade," memo, March 13, 1990.

17 Constance Hays, "Lower Manhattan Calls for More Parks," *New York Times*, April 14, 1990, https://www.nytimes.com/1990/04/14/nyregion/lower-manhattan-calls-for-more-parks.html?pagewanted=all&src=pm.

18 Tom Fox (Neighborhood Open Space Coalition), "Request for Pay-Back Waiver to Preserve Scenic Vistas as an Element of Route 9A Reconstruction," memo to West Side Waterfront Panel, March 19, 1990.

19 Kevin Sack, "New York Told to Repay Westway Funds," *New York Times*, August 11, 1990, https://www.nytimes.com/1990/08/11/nyregion/new-york-told-to-repay-westway-fund.html.

20 Sam Howe Verhovek, "Accord near on Preserving Westway Site," *New York Times*, May 15, 1990, https://www.nytimes.com/1990/05/15/nyregion/accord-near-on-preserving-westway-site.html?searchResultPosition=7.

21 Constance Hays, "Hudson River Park Plan Draws Critics," *New York Times*, September 29, 1990, https://www.nytimes.com/1990/09/29/nyregion/hudson-river-park-plan-draws-critics.html.

22   Constance Hays, "Panel Unveils Plan for Park Along Hudson Waterfront," *New York Times*, September 18, 1990, https://www.nytimes.com/1990/09/18/nyregion/panel-unveils-plan-for-park-along-hudson-waterfront.html.

23   West Side Waterfront Panel, "A Vision for the Hudson River Waterfront Park," November 1, 1990.

24   West Side Waterfront Panel, "A Vision," 11.

25   West Side Waterfront Panel, 32.

26   West Side Waterfront Panel, Appendix F.

27   West Side Waterfront Panel, 82.

28   West Side Waterfront Panel, 81.

29   West Side Waterfront Panel, 15–17.

30   West Side Waterfront Panel, 9.

31   West Side Waterfront Panel, 85.

32   Allan R. Gold, "The 1990 Elections in New York: New York- Bond Act New Math on Both Sides of the Hudson; Defeat of the Environmental Bond Act May Mean Higher Taxes in New York," *New York Times*, November 8, 1990, https://www.nytimes.com/1990/11/08/nyregion/1990-elections-new-york-bond-act-new-math-both-sides-hudson-defeat-environmental.html.

33   Constance L Hays, "Funds May Fall Short in West Side Park Plan," *New York Times*, March 4, 1990, https://www.nytimes.com/1990/03/04/nyregion/funds-may-fall-short-in-west-side-park-plan.html?scp=258&sq=Tom%20Fox&st=cse.

34   Deborah Borner-Ein, "Urban Open Space: Color It Valuable," *Urban Forests Magazine*, January/February 1991, 61–64.

35   West Side Waterfront Office, "Entity Transition Period," draft proposed work program, May 9, 1991.

36   New York State Governor's Office, "Memorandum of Understanding Implementation of the Recommendations of the West Side Waterfront Panel," draft, May 24, 1991.

37   Will Nixon, "The Greening of the Big Apple," *The Environmental Magazine*, September/October 1991, 31–39.

38   John Strausbaugh, "Water Sports," *New York Press*, July 3–9, 1991.

39   "History of the Downtown Boathouse," The Downtown Boathouse, Printed Fact Sheet, November 16, 2005.

40   Community Board 1, "Pier 25 Interim Use Summer 1990," resolution, May 8, 1990.

41   Josh Rogers, "Historic Ferry Owner Will Go from Ship to Shore," *The Villager*, November 25, 2003, https://www.amny.com/news/historic-ferry-owner-will-go-from-ship-to-shore/.

42   Betsy Terrell, "The Floating Family of Tribeca: They Made a River Life All Their Own," *Tribeca Trib*, August 9, 2016, http://tribecatrib.com/content/floating-family-tribeca-they-made-river-life-all-their-own.

43   Dan Janison, "State Rebukes DOT for Inadequate Property Oversight," *Albany Times-Union*, November 15, 1989.

44   Stephen Drucker, "Soothing Sips for a Sultry Night," *New York Times*, June 2, 1991, https://www.nytimes.com/1991/06/02/arts/bars-it-s-evening-it-s-sultry-it-s-time-for-a-tall-one.html.

45   James Barron, "Peter Obletz, 50, Lover of Old Trains, Dies," *New York Times*, May 4, 1996, https://www.nytimes.com/1996/05/04/nyregion/peter-e-obletz-50-a-lover-of-old-trains-dies.html.

46   "Safety Grooving," NASA, February 11, 2016, https://www.nasa.gov/offices/oct/40-years-of-nasa-spinoff/safety-grooving.

47 "The Texture of Concrete Pavement," U.S. Department of Transportation, Federal Highway Administration, accessed October 13, 2023. https://www.fhwa.dot.gov/pavement/concrete/trailer/resources/hif18038.pdf.

48 Heather Sporn, former associate landscape architect, New York State Department of Transportation interview by Tom Fox, May 3, 2021.

49 Betsy Haggerty, "Feedback on 10/17 Meeting," memo to Michael Del Giudice, October 21, 1991.

50 Robert W. Laird, "Dinkins Needs to Look Westward," *Daily News*, November 21, 1991.

51 Tom Fox, "Park Perspective," letter to the editor, *Downtown Express*, November 11, 1991.

52 Calvin Sims, "Idle, Angry Hard Hats Tell Off City Hall," *New York Times*, December 20, 1991, https://www.nytimes.com/1991/12/20/nyregion/idle-angry-hard-hats-tell-off-city-hall.html.

53 Lou Coletti, Peter Brennan, and William Canavan (The New York Building Congress), letter to Tom Fox, December 27, 1991.

54 The International Union of Operating Engineers, "GEB Open Session Details Issues, Goals, Innovations," February–March, 1992.

55 Frank Hanley (general president, International Union of Operating Engineers), letter to Tom Fox, February 7, 1992.

Chapter 7   Things Finally Start Happening (1992–1993)

1 Tom Fox, "City's Response to the State's Draft MOU," memo to Mary Ann Crotty and Michael Del Giudice, December 27, 1991.

2 Mark McCain, "Commercial Property: Public Development Corporation; An Agency with Large Successes in Small Projects," *New York Times*, October 4, 1987, https://www.nytimes.com/1987/10/04/realestate/commercial-property-public-development-corporation-agency-with-large-successes.html?searchResultPosition=3.

3 Tom Fox, "City's Response to the State's Draft MOU," memo to Gary Deane, January 3, 1992.

4 West Side Waterfront Office, "Tasks, Internal and External Process," April 1992.

5 David Nocenti, Assistant Counsel to the Governor, New York State Executive Chamber, "Fully Executed Memorandum of Understanding Regarding Implementation of the Recommendations of the West Side Waterfront Panel," letter to Tom Fox, May 19, 1992.

6 Nocenti, "Fully Executed Memorandum of Understanding."

7 Sam Roberts, "Cuomo and Dinkins Offer a New Plan for the West Side," *New York Times*, May 20, 1992, https://www.nytimes.com/1992/05/20/nyregion/cuomo-and-dinkins-offer-a-new-plan-for-the-west-side.html.

8 West Side Waterfront Office, "Tasks, Internal and External Process."

9 Sam Roberts, "Consensus Means Waterfront Project for West Side May Actually Get Built," *New York Times*, May 21, 1992, https://www.nytimes.com/1992/05/21/nyregion/consensus-means-waterfront-project-for-west-side-may-actually-get-built.html.

10 "Wisdom on the Waterfront," opinion, *New York Times*, May 21, 1992, https://www.nytimes.com/1992/05/21/opinion/wisdom-on-the-waterfront.html?searchResultPosition=1.

11 David W. Dunlap, "A Blueprint of the Future along the Hudson River," *New York Times*, May 24, 1992, https://www.nytimes.com/1992/05/24/nyregion/a-blueprint -of-the-future-along-the-hudson-river.html.

12 "It Might Work," editorial, *New York Newsday*, May 22, 1992.

13 "For the West Side, a Plan—and Hope," editorial, *New York Daily News*, May 26, 1992.

14 "This Time, Let's Have Less Talk and More Action," editorial, *The Villager*, May 27, 1992.

15 "A Glorious Park," editorial, *Chelsea Clinton News*, May 28–June 3, 1992.

16 Michael McAuliff, "Take Us to the River," *Downtown Express*, June 22, 1992.

17 Tom Fox, "The Greening of the Hudson Waterfront," Interview with Robert Hennelly, *New York Newsday*, July 1, 1992.

18 James Dao, "Bids Accepted to Develop 4 Chelsea Piers," *New York Times*, May 23, 1992, https://www.nytimes.com/1992/05/23/nyregion/bids-accepted-to-develop-4 -chelsea-piers.html.

19 "Silver Screen Studios," Chelsea Piers, accessed October 13, 2023, https://www .chelseapiers.com/studios/.

20 Wood et al., "Final Agreement of Lease, Blacklined," memo, July 27, 1992.

21 Tom Fox (Hudson River Park Conservancy), memo to Michael Del Giudice, September 23, 1992.

22 Herb Muschamp, "Summers Last Hurrah: The Final Fling before the Fall; Recircling the Globe," *New York Times*, September 2, 1994, https://www.nytimes .com/1994/09/02/arts/summer-s-last-hurrah-the-final-fling-before-the-fall -recircling-the-globe.html.

23 Claude Solnik, "'New Look' Waterfront Is Unveiled," *The Villager*, August 19, 1992.

24 David Firestone, "Public Lives; Environmental Entrepreneur Closes a Deal," *New York Times*, June 24, 1998, https://www.nytimes.com/1998/06/24/nyregion/public -lives-environmental-entrepreneur-closes-a-deal.html.

25 Andrew Locapo, "Don't Stall the Development of the Village Waterfront," letter to the editor, *New York Times*, July 27, 1992, https://www.nytimes.com/1992/08/08 /opinion/l-don-t-stall-development-of-village-waterfront-999192.html?searchResult Position=2.

26 Carol Gordon et al., "Why Not Relocate Flower Market on Pier 40?," opinion, *New York Times*, September 1, 1992, http://www.nytimes.com/1992/09/01/opinion/l -why-not-relocate-flower-market-on-pier-40-666792.html.

27 Scottotv, "Bungee Jumping at the First NASA Scotto Jumps into the Hudson," YouTube video, July 24, 1992, https://click.linksynergy.com/fs-bin/click?id =ysYzDGpG/sM&offerid=748597.20&subid=0&type=4&u1=bf_euekiz39ksg8nw p7iqj2fp5wzfwi5q76.

28 "The Right Step," editorial, *New York Newsday*, November 19, 1992.

29 "Pier 34 New York," Andreas Sterzing Photography, accessed October 13, 2023, https://www.sterzing.co.uk/asp/place_1./Pages/Pier_34_New_York.html.

30 West Side Waterfront Panel, "A Vision for a Hudson River Park," November 1, 1990, 22–26.

31 Linda Saslow, "Avianca Crash Leaves Questions on Response" *New York Times*, October 7, 1990, https://www.nytimes.com/1990/10/07/nyregion/avianca-crash -leaves-questions-on-response.html?pagewanted=all.

32 Alice Lipowicz, "World Trade Center Bombing, an Interview with Stanley Brezenoff, I Stood on a Desk and Said, 'I Am Your Landlord,'" *Crain's New York*

Business, March 25, 1995, https://www.crainsnewyork.com/article/19950327/SUB
/503270722/world-trade-center-bombing-an-interview-with-stanley-brezenoffi
-stood-on-a-desk-said-i-m-your-landlord.

33 Andrew Jacobs, "On a New Pier, Necessity Brings Amenity," *New York Times*,
August 20, 1996, https://www.nytimes.com/1996/10/20/nyregion/on-new-pier-a
-necessity-brings-amenity.html.

Chapter 8   Completing the Plan and Change at the Top (1994–1995)

1 Richard A. Maitino, executive director, Route 9A Project, New York State
Department of Transportation, "Invitation to an Open House and Environmental
Scoping Session," letter to community leaders and residents, November 7, 1988.

2 David W. Dunlap, "Jostling for Position on the Riverfront," *New York Times*,
July 11, 1993, https://www.nytimes.com/1993/07/11/realestate/jostling-for-position
-on-the-riverfront.html.

3 Reggie Nadelson, "The 200-Year-Old Bar Beloved by Book Editors and Longshoremen," *New York Times*, November 13, 2018, https://www.nytimes.com/2018/11/13/t
-magazine/ear-inn-new-york-history.html.

4 Barbara Benary, "Ballad of the Bollard," sung to the tune of "Gilligan's Island," July 1993.

5 David W. Dunlap, "What's a Bollard? Police Call It Harbor Larceny," *New York
Times*, July 17, 1993, https://www.nytimes.com/1993/07/17/nyregion/what-s-a
-bollard-police-call-it-harbor-larceny.html.

6 Dana Schulz, "A History of the Village Halloween Parade: Puppets, Performers and
NYC Pride," *6sqft*, October 22, 2019, https://www.6sqft.com/a-history-of-the
-village-halloween-parade-puppets-performers-and-nyc-pride/.

7 Todd S. Purdum, "The 1993 Elections: Mayor Giuliani Ousts Dinkins by a Thin
Margin; Whitman Is an Upset Winner over Florio," *New York Times*, November 3,
1993, https://www.nytimes.com/1993/11/03/nyregion/1993-elections-mayor-giuliani
-ousts-dinkins-thin-margin-whitman-upset-winner.html.

8 Chelsea Piers Management Inc., "The Chelsea Piers, a Sports and Entertainment
Complex," overview of the Chelsea Piers Complex, 1993.

9 Katherine E. Finkelstein, "Abe Hirschfeld Gets 1 to 3 Years in Plot to Kill Longtime
Partner," *New York Times*, August 2, 2000, https://www.nytimes.com/2000/08/02
/nyregion/abe-hirschfeld-gets-1-to-3-years-in-plot-to-kill-longtime-partner.html.

10 "Port Imperial Ferry Company," Reference for Business, accessed October 13, 2023,
https://www.referenceforbusiness.com/history/Pa-Ql/Port-Imperial-Ferry
-Corporation.html.

11 "Port Imperial Ferry Company."

12 Hudson River Park Conservancy, "What Do You Do If You Live by the West Side,
and You Love to Bike, Rollerblade, or Simply Stroll?," *VIEWS*, Fall 1994.

13 "Down by the Riverside," editorial opinion, *New York Times*, June 5, 1995, https://
www.nytimes.com/1994/06/05/opinion/down-by-the-riverside.html?searchResult
Position=8.

14 Stuart Waldman, "Why Can't We Have a True Waterfront Park on the Hudson?,"
New York Times, June 16, 1994, https://www.nytimes.com/1994/06/16/opinion/l
-why-can-t-we-have-a-true-waterfront-park-on-the-hudson-413046.html.

15 "About Environmental Education Advisory Council of New York," Environmental
Education Advisory Council of New York, accessed October 13, 2023, https://eeac
-nyc.org/home/about-eeac/.

16   David W. Dunlap, "Officials Approve Plans to Rebuild West Side Artery," *New York Times*, August 2, 1994, https://www.nytimes.com/1994/08/02/nyregion /officials-approve-plans-to-rebuild-west-side-artery.html?pagewanted=all&src=pm.

17   Dunlap, "Jostling for Position."

18   Richard Maitino, former executive director, New York State Department of Transportation, interview by Tom Fox, May 3, 2021.

19   Marvin Howe, "Neighborhood Report: Fear of West Side Plans, Park or K-Mart-on-the-Hudson?," *New York Times*, August 21, 1994, https://www.nytimes.com /1994/08/21/nyregion/neighborhood-report-fear-of-west-side-plans-park-or-k-mart -on-the-hudson.html.

20   "Neighborhood Report: Midtown; Intrepid Ideas of Floating Heliport," Bruce Lambert, *New York Times*, May 15, 1994, https://www.nytimes.com/1994/05/15 /nyregion/neighborhood-report-midtown-intrepid-idea-for-floating-heliport.html.

21   Bruce Lambert, "Neighborhood Report: Chelsea/Clinton; Wanted: Pier with a View," *New York Times*, December 4, 1994, https://www.nytimes.com/1994/12/04 /nyregion/neighborhood-report-chelsea-clinton-wanted-pier-with-a-view.html.

22   John Bowers, letter to NYS Senator Franz Leichter and NYS Assemblymember Dick Gottfried, January 11, 1995.

23   "International Longshoremen's Association," International Longshoremen's Association, accessed October 13, 2023, https://ilaunion.org/ila-history/.

24   Franz Leichter and Richard Gottfried, New York State Assembly to John Bowers, January 20, 1995.

25   David W. Dunlap, "The Hudson River Waterfront: What's Next," *New York Times*, June 26, 1994, https://www.nytimes.com/1994/06/26/realestate/the-hudson -waterfront-what-s-next.html?pagewanted=all&src=pm.

26   Kevin Shack, "The New Governor, The Overview; Happy Republicans, in from the Cold, Gather for Pataki's Inauguration," *New York Times*, January 1, 1995, https:// www.nytimes.com/1995/01/01/nyregion/new-governor-overview-happy-republicans -cold-gather-for-pataki-s-inauguration.html.

27   Thomas J. Lueck, "Ruling May Delay Decisions on Hudson Riverfront Park Plan," *New York Times*, January 14, 1995, https://www.nytimes.com/1995/01/14/nyregion /ruling-may-delay-decisions-on-hudson-riverfront-plans.html.

28   Lueck, "Ruling May Delay."

29   Peter Stanford, president, National Maritime Historical Society to George Pataki Governor, Governor's Mansion, Albany, NY 12200, telegram, January 13, 1995.

30   Thomas P. Maguire (president and business manager, International Union of Operating Engineers, Local Union 15, 15A, 15 B, 15-C, and 15-D), letter to Ambassador Charles Gargano, January 17, 1995.

31   Community Board 1, "Resolution Regarding Hudson River Park Conservancy," January 17, 1995.

32   Kent Barwick (president, Municipal Arts Society), letter to Ambassador Charles Gargano, January 19, 1995.

33   Edward J. Cleary (president, New York State AFL-CIO), letter to Ambassador Charles Gargano, January 20, 1995.

34   Samuel F. Pryor III, letter to Hon. Bernadette Castro, February 9, 1995.

35   Tom Fox to Ambassador Charles Gargano, "Individuals Who Offered to Write or Call on My Behalf," list, January 1995.

36   "Fox Fire Misguided," editorial, *Chelsea Clinton News*, January 26–February 1, 1995; "Repeat after Me: The Waterfront Needs Leadership," editorial, *The Villager*, January 25, 1995.

37 Tom Fox (president and chief operating officer, Hudson River Park Conservancy), letter to Ambassador Charles Gargano, January 24, 1995.

38 Bruce Lambert, "Manhattan Neighborhood Report: Manhattan Up Close; Park at Center of War over Waterfront," *New York Times*, February 19, 1995, https://www .nytimes.com/1995/02/19/nyregion/neighborhood-report-manhattan-up-close-park -panel-center-war-over-waterfront.html.

39 Hudson River Park Conservancy, "Proposed Schedule Hudson River Park Concept and Financial Plan Empire State Waterways," board and staff memo, February 1995.

40 Tom Fox (Hudson River Park Conservancy), "Regarding Groundbreakings, Ribbon Cuttings and Special Events in 1995," memo to Carolyn Bachan, February 14, 1995.

41 Tom Fox (Hudson River Park Conservancy), "Regarding Critical Issues for the Conservancy's Future," memo to Michael Del Giudice and Fran Reiter, April 11, 1995.

42 Tom Fox (president and chief operating officer, Hudson River Park Conservancy), resignation letter to Hudson River Park Conservancy Board of Directors, April 25, 1995.

43 Tom Fox (Hudson River Park Conservancy), letter to supporters, April 26, 1995.

44 Andrew C. Rifkin, "Chief of Hudson River Park Conservancy Ousted," *New York Times*, April 26, 1995, https://www.nytimes.com/1995/04/26/nyregion/chief-of -hudson-river-conservancy-ousted.html.

Chapter 9   A New Approach (1995–1997)

1   United War Veterans Council (website), https://uwvc.org/our-history/.

2   Douglas Martin, "Veterans Day Parade Tries for a Comeback," *New York Times*, November 10, 1995, https://www.nytimes.com/1995/11/10/nyregion/veterans-day -parade-tries-for-a-comeback.html.

3   "More Than 500,000 Watch Nations Parade," *UPI Archives*, November 11, 1995, https://www.upi.com/Archives/1995/11/11/More-than-500000-watch-Nations -Parade/4721816066000/.

4   Robert D. McFadden, "On Parade to the Beat of History," *New York Times*, November 12, 1995, https://www.nytimes.com/1995/11/12/nyregion/on-parade-to -the-beat-of-history.html.

5   David W. Dunlap, "Building a Business-Friendly New York," *New York Times*, June 4, 1995, https://www.nytimes.com/1995/06/04/realestate/building-a-business -friendly-new-york.html?pagewanted=all&src=pm.

6   "A Park's Guiding Light," editorial, *Chelsea Clinton News*, May 4–10, 1995.

7   Larry O'Connor, "Bargaining Chip in Chelsea," *Chelsea Clinton News*, May 4–10, 1995.

8   Vince McGowan, interview by Tom Fox, May 23, 2021.

9   Bruce Lambert, "Neighborhood Report: West Side; Deadline Nears on Fund Waiver for Westway," *New York Times*, September 24, 1995, https://www.nytimes .com/1995/09/24/nyregion/neighborhood-report-west-side-deadline-nears-on-fund -waiver-for-westway.html?searchResultPosition=2.

10 Andrew Jacobs, "Neighborhood Report: Tribeca; Pier Group: 3 Bring Sand and Ideas" *New York Times*, August 13, 1995, https://www.nytimes.com/1995/08/13 /nyregion/neighborhood-report-tribeca-pier-group-3-bring-sand-and-ideas.html.

11 Margaret Tobin, interview by Tom Fox, January 2021.

12 David Schyler and Paul Gallay, "The Battle for Storm King," *Scientific American*, August 30, 2018, https://blogs.scientificamerican.com/observations/the-battle-for -storm-king/.

13 Al Amateau, "Why Westway Sleeps with the Fishes," *The Villager*, June 16–22, 2004, https://web.archive.org/web/20160304122348/http:/thevillager.com/villager _59/whywestwaysleepswith.html

14 Tom Fox, "Request for Mitch," email messages to and from Mitch Bernard, November 9, 2022.

15 Margaret Tobin, interview by Tom Fox, January 2021.

16 Bruce Lambert, "Neighborhood Report: Waterfront; Pataki About to Remove Waterfront Park Plan from Limbo," *New York Times*, January 28, 1996, https:// www.nytimes.com/1996/01/28/nyregion/neighborhood-report-waterfront-pataki -about-remove-waterfront-park-plan-limbo.html.

17 West Side Waterfront Panel, "A Vision for a Hudson River Waterfront Park," November 1, 1990, p. 64.

18 Hudson River Park Conservancy, "Hudson River Park, Concept and Financial Plan," May 1995, p. 52.

19 Richard Perez-Pena, "The Future Home of Yankee Stadium? It's All in the Traffic Patterns," *New York Times*, April 14, 1996, https://www.nytimes.com/1996/04/14 /nyregion/the-future-home-of-yankee-stadium-it-s-all-in-the-traffic-patterns.html.

20 Douglas Freiden, "Westward Ho, the New Road," *Daily News*, March 29, 1996.

21 Garry Pierre-Pierre, "After Two Decades, Work Begins on Far Less Ambitious Westway," *New York Times*, April 2, 1996, https://www.nytimes.com/1996/04/02 /nyregion/after-two-decades-work-begins-on-far-less-ambitious-westway.html.

22 Thomas P. Maguire and Francis X. McArdle (General Contractors Association of New York /International Union of Operating Engineers), letter to Mr. Thomas Fox, September 6, 1996.

23 Joyce Purnick, "Metro Matters: Slowly Moving Down the Road to a Roadway," *New York Times*, April 4, 1996, https://www.nytimes.com/1996/04/04/nyregion/metro -matters-slowly-moving-down-a-road-to-a-roadway.html?searchResultPosition=17.

24 Tom Fox, "Let's Begin Work on the Hudson River Park," letter to the editor, *New York Times*, April 20, 1996, https://www.nytimes.com/1996/04/20/opinion/l-let-s -begin-work-on-the-hudson-river-park-087718.html.

25 Tom Fox, "Down by the Riverside," talking point, *The Villager*, April 24, 1996.

26 Tom Fox, "West Side Waterfront Plan a Must," op-ed, *New York Daily News*, June 17, 1996.

27 Frances Beinecke to Tom Fox, Note, Natural Resources Defense Council, July 2, 1991.

28 New York State Department of State, "Certificate of Incorporation of Citizens for a Hudson River Park," July 5, 1996.

29 Citizens for a Hudson River Park, "What We Want to Do," 1997 plan, October 31, 1996.

30 Douglas Martin, "State Panel to Announce Riverfront Plan," June 6, 1996, https://www.nytimes.com/1996/06/06/nyregion/state-panel-to-announce -riverfront-plan.html?searchResultPosition=10.

31 Hudson River Park Conservancy, "Hudson River Park, Concept and Financial Plan," May 1995.

32 Hudson River Park Conservancy, "Hudson River Park," 7.

33 Hudson River Park Conservancy, 56.

34 "Park on the Hudson River'" editorial, *New York Times*, June 21, 1996, https://www
.nytimes.com/1996/06/21/opinion/a-park-on-the-hudson-river.html
?searchResultPosition=1.

35 Ambassador Charles A. Gargano (chairman, Empire State Development), letter to
Mr. Tom Fox, June 20, 1996.

36 Douglas Martin, "TriBeCa Dairy Wholesaler a Link to Pushcart Past," *New York
Times*, September 27, 1996, https://www.nytimes.com/1996/09/27/nyregion/tribeca
-dairy-wholesaler-is-link-with-pushcart-past.html.

37 "Pioneer Profiles: Roland Betts," Texans for Public Justice, George W. Bush's
$100,000 Club, July 2000, http://info.tpj.org/pioneers/roland_betts.html.

38 David W. Dunlap, "Chelsea Piers: The Fight to Stay Afloat," *New York Times*,
August 11, 1996, https://www.nytimes.com/1996/08/11/realestate/chelsea-piers-the
-fight-to-stay-afloat.html?pagewanted=all&src=pm.

39 Al Amateau, "Trash on Public Route," *Chelsea Clinton News*, April 25–May 1, 1996.

40 Heather Sporn, former associate landscape architect, New York State Department
of Transportation, interview by Tom Fox, May 3, 2021.

41 Andrew Jacobs, "$100 Mistake Gives Piers a Walkway," *New York Times*, June 30,
1996, https://www.nytimes.com/1996/06/30/nyregion/100-mistake-gives-piers-a
-walkway.html.

42 Josh Rodgers, "Look What's Coming to the Waterfront." *Downtown Express*,
December 4–17, 1996.

43 Josh Benson, "Scholarly Beef Boss James Ortenzio Works on $400 Million Hudson
Park," *New York Observer*, April 26, 1999.

44 "Rock Garden Party, 12 Park Supporters Receive Emerald Award at 9th Annual
State of the Parks," *The Daily Plant*, January 22, 2002, https://www.nycgovparks
.org/parks/rock-garden-park/news.

45 Thomas P. Maguire (president and business manager, International Union of
Operating Engineers Local Union 15, 15A, 15B, 15C, and 15D), letter to Mr. James
Ortenzio, September 20, 1996.

46 James Dao, "In Pataki Bond Measure Cleaning Money for Everyone," *New York
Times*, September 15, 1996, https://www.nytimes.com/1996/09/15/nyregion/in
-pataki-bond-measure-cleaning-money-for-everyone.html?searchResultPosition=1.

47 James Dao, "Governor Claims Victory for Environmental Bond Act," *New York
Times*, November 6, 1996, https://www.nytimes.com/1996/11/06/nyregion
/governor-claims-victory-for-environment-bond-act.html.

48 Andrew Jacobs, "Down by the River: Park Solution?," *New York Times*, December
29, 1996, https://www.nytimes.com/1996/12/29/nyregion/down-by-the-river
-park-solution.html?searchResultPosition=1.

49 Michael Haberman, "Peter Keogh Resigns Hudson R. Park Post," *Downtown
Express*, February 4–February 17, 1997.

50 David Firestone, "Vallone Describes Vision of Floating Casino Fleet," *New York
Times*, February 8, 1997, https://www.nytimes.com/1997/02/08/nyregion/vallone
-describes-vision-of-floating-casino-fleet.html.

51 "Shipboard Gambling," New York City Business Integrity Commission, accessed
October 14, 2023, https://www1.nyc.gov/site/bic/industries/shipboard-gambling
.page.

52 Lyn Bixby, "New York Blocks Tribal Plan for High-Speed Ferry," *Hartford Courant*,
March 14, 1998, https://www.courant.com/news/connecticut/hc-xpm-1998-03-14
-9803140221-story.html.

53   Douglas Feiden, "New Wave of Taxis," *New York Daily News*, February 3, 1997.

54   "(Water) Taxi!," editorial, *New York Daily News*, February 6, 1997.

55   Thomas J. Lueck, "Cute but Slow, Water Taxis Take Early Retirement," *New York Times*, August 2, 1997, https://www.nytimes.com/1997/08/02/nyregion/cute-but-slow-water-taxis-take-early-retirement.html?searchResultPosition=1.

56   Tom Fox, "Sweep cleanup funds downstate," op-ed, *New York Daily News*, January 24, 1997.

57   Tom Fox, "This Is the Right Plan Let's Do It"; Marcy Benstock, "We Want a Clean River, Green Park," op-eds, *Daily News*, April 20,1997.

58   Andrew C. Revkin, "Civic Group Warns State Over Pier on Houston Street," *New York Times*, April 4, 1997, https://www.nytimes.com/1997/04/04/nyregion/civic-groups-warn-state-over-pier-on-houston-street.html.

59   Hudson River Park Alliance, "Hudson River Park Legislation," draft, April 21, 1997.

60   Carol Ash, Al Butzel, Paul Elston, Hudson River Park Alliance, "City Role in Hudson River Park," memorandum to David Klasfeld and Connie Fishman, April 22, 1997.

61   Hudson River Park Alliance, "HRPA Comments on the Draft EIS," discussion outline, November 5, 1997.

62   The Mayor and the River," editorial, *New York Times*, November 24, 1997, https://www.nytimes.com/search?query=The+Mayor+and+the+River.

63   Richard Gottfried, "'Non-Ownership' Options for the Hudson River Park Legislation," memo to interested parties, November 24, 1998.

64   Tom Fox (The Fox Group), "Hudson River Park Legislation," memo to Al Butzel, December 8, 1997.

65   Al Butzel (Hudson River Park Alliance), "Your Comments on Our Legislation," memo to Tom Fox, December 15, 1997.

66   Cara Lee, cc: Klara B. Sauer, Scenic Hudson Inc., "Hudson River Park Legislation—Habitat Protection and Jurisdiction of the Underwater Land within the Proposed Park Boundary," memo to Hudson River Park Alliance members, December 29, 1997.

67   Hudson River Park Alliance, "Accounting for 1997."

68   Hudson River Park Alliance. "Projected Budget 1/1/1998–12/30/1998."

Chapter 10   Hudson River Park Act (1998–2000)

1   Andy Darrell, Hudson River Park Alliance, "Summary of January 6 HRPA Steering Committee Meeting," January 13, 1998.

2   Andy Darrell, Hudson River Park Alliance, "Notice of Steering Committee Meeting Tuesday, February 10, 8:30 A.M. and Summary of January 20 Meeting," January 22, 1998.

3   HRPA Steering Committee Meeting, Hudson River Park Alliance, "Agenda—2/10/98," February 10, 1998.

4   Andy Darrell (Hudson River Park Alliance), "Notice of Meeting and Reminder about Draft Legislation," including January 5, 1998, memo and December 27, 1997, markup of draft legislation, January 6, 1998.

5   Carol Ash et al., Hudson River Park Alliance, "HRP Legislation," memo to Assemblyman Richard Gottfried and State Senator Franz Leichter, February 10, 1998.

6 Douglas Martin, "Hudson River Park Plan Moves Closer to Reality," *New York Times*, February 16, 1998, https://www.nytimes.com/1998/02/16/nyregion/hudson-river-park-plan-moves-closer-to-reality.html?searchResultPosition=1.

7 "Dream and Reality on the Hudson," editorial, *New York Times*, February 21, 1998, https://www.nytimes.com/1998/02/21/opinion/dream-and-reality-on-the-hudson.html?searchResultPosition=1.

8 Assemblyman Richard N. Gottfried and State Senator Franz Leichter, "Legislators Introduce Bill to Create Hudson River Park," March 8, 1998.

9 Linda Stone Davidoff, executive director, New York League of Conservation Voters, "Waterfront Park Press Conference and Rally—Sunday March 8," March 3, 1998.

10 Douglas Martin, "Hudson Park Plan Turns Friends into Foes," *New York Times*, March 9, 1998, https://www.nytimes.com/1998/03/09/nyregion/hudson-park-plan-turns-friends-into-foes.html.

11 "The Hudson Needs the Mayor," editorial, *New York Times*, March 10, 1998, https://www.nytimes.com/1998/03/10/opinion/the-hudson-needs-the-mayor.html?searchResultPosition=1.

12 Tom Hynes, "These Tiny Wood-Eating Creatures Want to Sink Brooklyn Bridge Park, *Gothamist*, September 20, 2016, https://gothamist.com/news/these-tiny-wood-eating-creatures-want-to-sink-brooklyn-bridge-park.

13 Friends of Pier 84, "Pier 84 Closed Due to Damaged Piles," *A View from the Pier*, June 1998.

14 HRPC Advisory Board, "Resolution," May 21, 1998.

15 American Institute of Architects, New York Chapter, "The Hudson Riverfront in Manhattan," *Oculus Magazine*, October 1998, 10.

16 "HRPC Advisory Board Design & Access Committee," Resolution, May 27, 1998.

17 Hudson River Park Advisory Board, letter to Mr. James Ortenzio, June 3, 1998.

18 Adam Brown, President, Working Waterfront Association, "Comments to Carolyn Bachan and Mike Dalia, Empire State Development Corporation," May 5, 1998.

19 Douglas Martin, "City and State Agree on Plan for Oversight of River Park," *New York Times*, June 14, 1998, https://www.nytimes.com/1998/06/14/nyregion/city-and-state-agree-on-plan-for-oversight-of-river-park.html?searchResultPosition=1.

20 Hudson River Park Act, Ch. 592, S. 7845, NY Legis 592 (1998), https://hudsonriverpark.org/app/uploads/2020/03/HRP-Act.pdf.

21 David Firestone, "Public Lives; Environmental Entrepreneur Closes a Deal," *New York Times*, June 24, 1998, https://www.nytimes.com/1998/06/24/nyregion/public-lives-environmental-entrepreneur-closes-a-deal.html.

22 Hudson River Park Alliance "Steering Committee Meeting Agenda—6/29/98."

23 "A Walk in the Park," editorial, *Daily News*, June 24, 1998.

24 U.S. Army Corps of Engineers, New York District, "Announcement of a Public Hearing and Request for Public Comment," Public Notice Number: 98-00290-Y2, June 16, 1998.

25 Andrew Darrell, executive director, Hudson River Park Alliance, "Statements in Support of Permits for Hudson River Park," July 16, 1998.

26 Hudson River Park Alliance, "Steering Committee Meeting," agenda, July 22, 1998.

27 Douglas Martin, "Park Plan Draws Closer to Reality; Proponents Celebrate Approval in Albany," *New York Times*, July 30, 1998, https://www.nytimes.com/1998/07/30/nyregion/hudson-park-draws-closer-to-reality-proponents-celebrate-approval-by-albany.html?searchResultPosition=1.

28 "A River Park Grows in Manhattan," editorial, *New York Times*, July 31, 1998, https://www.nytimes.com/1998/07/31/opinion/a-river-park-grows-in-manhattan.html?searchResultPosition=1.

29 Wolfgang Saxon, "Prof. Curtis Berger, Expert on Real Estate Law at Columbia," *New York Times*, July 12, 1998, https://www.nytimes.com/1998/07/12/nyregion/prof-curtis-berger-72-expert-on-real-estate-law-at-columbia.html.

30 HRPC Advisory Board Design Committee, memo to Howard Abel, Paul Buckhurst, Buckhurst Fish & Jacquemart Inc., July 21, 1998.

31 Hudson River Park Conservancy, letter to Friends of the Hudson River Park, August 26, 1998.

32 Andy Darrell, Hudson River Park Alliance, "Mark Your Calendar," meeting notice and park updates, August 14, 1998.

33 Paul Elston (New York League of Conservation Voters), memo to the environmental community, August 28, 1998.

34 Judith Enck, "Greens Should Crash the Hudson River Park Bill Signing Ceremony," August 27, 1998.

35 Al Butzel (Hudson River Park Alliance), "Urgent Request for Letters to Governor Pataki," September 1, 1998.

36 Andy Darrell (Hudson River Park Alliance), "Reminder of Upcoming Events," memo to HRPA members and liaisons, September 2, 1998.

37 Douglas Martin, "Plan for Hudson River Piers Hits Snag in City Council," *New York Times*, October 16, 1998, https://www.nytimes.com/1998/10/16/nyregion/plan-for-park-on-hudson-river-hits-snag-in-city-council.html.

38 Douglas Martin, "Pataki Signs Law Creating Hudson Park," *New York Times*, September 9, 1998, https://www.nytimes.com/1998/09/09/nyregion/pataki-signs-law-creating-hudson-park.html.

39 Andy Darrell (Hudson River Park Alliance), "Come Celebrate the Opening of Ball Fields on Pier 40!," memo, September 1, 1998.

40 Tom Fox, "A New Park Needs Green (Backs)," op-ed, *New York Daily News*, October 27, 1998.

41 Richard Perez-Pena, "The 1998 Elections: New York State—The Governor; Pataki Wins Election to a Second Term by a Hefty Margin," *New York Times*, November 4, 1998, https://www.nytimes.com/1998/11/04/nyregion/1998-elections-new-york-state-governor-pataki-wins-election-second-term-hefty.html.

42 Home and Garden, "A Pier Once Ignored Is Suddenly a Favorite," *New York Times*, December 10, 1998, https://www.nytimes.com/1998/12/10/garden/a-pier-once-ignored-is-suddenly-a-favorite.html?searchResultPosition=1.

43 Douglas Martin, "Work on Hudson Park Is Stalled as Officials Lag in Naming Board," *New York Times*, March 1, 1999, https://www.nytimes.com/1999/03/01/nyregion/work-on-hudson-park-is-stalled-as-officials-lag-in-naming-board.html.

44 "Show Us the Money," editorial, *New York Times*, March 27, 1999, https://www.nytimes.com/1999/03/27/opinion/show-us-the-money.html?searchResultPosition=4.

45 Michael A. Rivlin, "A Splendid Park—But at What Price?," *Gotham Gazette*, Spring 1999.

46 Rivlin, "A Splendid Park," 58.

47 Douglas Martin, "Work on Hudson Park Is Stalled as Officials Lag in Naming Board," *New York Times*, March 1, 1999, https://www.nytimes.com/1999/03/01/nyregion/work-on-hudson-park-is-stalled-as-officials-lag-in-naming-board.html.

48 Martin, "Work on Hudson Park," 51.

49 Douglas Martin, "Pataki and Giuliani Pick Hudson Park Board Members, *New York Times*, March 5, 1998, https://www.nytimes.com/1999/03/05/nyregion/pataki -and-giuliani-pick-hudson-river-park-board-members.html.

50 Josh Benson, "Scholarly Beef Boss James Ortenzio Works on $400 Million Hudson Park," *New York Observer*, April 26, 1999.

51 Richard Schwartz, Technology and Policy (website), accessed October 14, 2023, https://richardschwartz.net.

52 Vince McGowan, interview by Tom Fox, November 5, 2020.

53 Douglas Martin, "Be It Ever So Humble: Hudson Park Has New Office," *New York Times*, March 16, 1999, https://www.nytimes.com/1999/03/16/nyregion/be-it-ever -so-humble-hudson-park-has-new-office.html.

54 Office of NYS Governor George Pataki and New York City Mayor Rudy Giuliani, "Governor, Mayor Recommend Head of Hudson River Park Trust," press release, June 16, 1999, http://www.nyc.gov/html/om/html/99a/pr235-99.html.

55 Office of the Mayor of San Francisco, "Mayor Willie L. Brown Jr. Announces Park Renaissance Crusade." press release, April 28, 1999.

56 Department of Elections, City and County of San Francisco, "Consolidated Presidential Primary Election," March 7, 2000, http://sfpl.org/pdf/main/gic /elections/March7_2000short.pdf.

57 San Francisco Bay Area Planning and Research Association (SPUR), "Proposition C—Open Space Fund Charter Amendment," voter guide, March 1, 2000, https:// www.spur.org/publications/voter-guide/2000-03-01/proposition-c-open-space -fund-charter-amendment.

58 "William H. White," Placemaking Heroes, Project for Public Spaces, January 3, 2010, https://www.pps.org/article/wwhyte.

59 Barbara Stewart, "Hudson River Park on Restored Piers Approved by U.S.," *New York Times*, June 1, 2000, https://www.nytimes.com/search?query=Hudson+River +Park+on+Restored+Piers+Approved+by+U.S.%22+.

60 Jan Hoffman, "Public Lives: Persistence (And Striped Bass!) Wins a Park," *New York Times*, June 7, 2000, https://www.nytimes.com/2000/06/07/nyregion/public -lives-persistence-and-striped-bass-wins-a-park.html.

61 Deborah Netburn, "Richard Meier Builds Perry Street Palace for Calvin and Martha," *The Observer*, December 4, 2000, https://observer.com/2000/12/richard -meier-builds-perry-street-palace-for-calvin-and-martha/.

Chapter 11   The World Changes (2001–2003)

1 Scott Fallon, "Perfect Storm Boat Set to Be Sunk on Wednesday," northjersey.com, May 9, 2017, https://www.northjersey.com/story/news/2017/05/09/perfect-storm -ship-tamaroa-set-sunk-wednesday/313653001/.

2 Fallon, "Perfect Storm Boat."

3 "New York's Quarrelsome Duo," editorial, *New York Times*, January 15, 2001, https://www.nytimes.com/search?query=New+York%27s+Quarrelsome+duo+.

4 "DeWitt Clinton (1769–1928)," History, New Netherlands Institute, accessed October 15, 2023, https://www.newnetherlandinstitute.org/history-and-heritage /dutch_americans/dewitt-clinton/.

5 Friends of Hudson River Park, "Pier 94 Background for Discussion at FoHRP Board Meeting," February 19, 2001.

6 Al Butzel, "My Thoughts on Pier 94," memo, May 30, 2001.

7 Tom Fox, "Waste Side Highway Trashes Original Vision," op-ed, *Daily News*, April 5, 2001.

8 RoadtoResilience, "BOATLIFT, An Untold Tale of 9/11 Resilience," YouTube video, September 7, 2001, https://www.youtube.com/watch?v=MDOrzF7B2Kg.

9 "The 9/11 Rescue That We Need to Hear More About," op-ed, Jessica DuLong, *CNN,* May 12, 2021. https://www.cnn.com/2017/08/20/opinions/911-boatlift -rescue-opinion-dulong/index.html

10 Captain Huntley Gill of *John J. Harvey*, interview by Tom Fox, March and July 2021.

11 Vincent McGowan, former director of operations, Battery Park City Park Corporation, interview by Tom Fox, March 2021.

12 Robin Finn, "Public Lives; Role at Ground Zero for Master of the Piers," *New York Times*, April 4, 2003, https://www.nytimes.com/2003/04/04/nyregion/public-lives -a-role-at-ground-zero-for-the-master-of-the-piers.html?searchResultPosition=1.

13 Matt Flegenheimer and Maggie Haberman, "How a String of Flukes Helped Pave the Way for Mayor Michael Bloomberg," *New York Times*, December 22, 2019, https://www.nytimes.com/2019/12/22/us/politics/Michael-Bloomberg-nyc-mayor -election.html.

14 Al Butzel (Friends of Hudson River Park), "Comments on Pier 94/Dattner Study," memo to Friends Issue Committee, October 28, 2001.

15 Tom Fox, "To: Friends Board Members Regarding Transition," memo, July 18, 2002.

16 Al Butzel, email message to Tom Fox, January 28, 2002.

17 Hudson River Park Conservancy, "Concept and Financial Plan," May 1998, 42.

18 Denny Lee, "Neighborhood Report: "Meatpacking District; They Miss the Smoke, But Not the Stacks" *New York Times*, March 24, 2002, https://www.nytimes.com /search?query=They+Miss+the+Smoke%2C+But+Not+the+Stacks.

19 Al Butzel and Tom Fox, "Hudson River Park—Memo 1," July 8, 2002.

20 Simone Sindin, chair, John Doswell, and Pam Fredrick, Manhattan Community Board 4, letter to Hon. Ron Balachandran, January 13, 2002.

21 Valerie Brook, "Trust Sets Concerts; Plans Admission," *Crains New York Business*, January 18, 2003.

22 Jay Kriegel, NYC2012, letter to Tom Fox, July 10, 2001.

23 David Dunlap, "Launching a Flotilla of Ferry Terminals," *New York Times*, April 7, 2002, https://www.nytimes.com/2002/04/07/realestate/launching-a-flotilla-of -ferry-terminals.html.

24 Jim O'Grady, "Neighborhood Report: Brooklyn Up Close; for a Waterfront Angel, an Honor in the Harbor," *New York Times*, September 29, 2002, https://www .nytimes.com/2002/09/29/nyregion/neighborhood-report-brooklyn-up-close-for -waterfront-angel-honor-harbor.html.

25 New York City Department of City Planning, "Far West Midtown, A Framework for Development," Winter 2001, https://www1.nyc.gov/assets/planning/download /pdf/plans/hudson-yards/fwmt.pdf.

26 Steven Malanga, "Develop the Far West Side, Now," *City Journal,* Spring 2002, https://www.city-journal.org/html/develop-far-west-side-now-12253.html?wallit _nosession=1.

27 Charles V. Bagli, "Grand Vision for Remaking the West Side," *New York Times*, February 10, 2003, https://www.nytimes.com/2003/02/10/nyregion/grand-vision -for-remaking-the-west-side.html?searchResultPosition=1.

28 Mary Voboril, "On the Waterfront," *Newsday*, March 12, 2002.

29 Al Butzel, Hudson River Park Alliance and John Doswell, chairman, Friends of Hudson River Park, letter to Hon. Richard N. Gottfried and Hon. Deborah Glick, May 13, 2002.

30 Board of Directors, Hudson River Park Trust, "June 13, 2002, Meeting Notice," May 10, 2002.

31 Lincoln Anderson, "Trust Releases Seven Plans for Pier 40," *The Villager*, July 31, 2002.

32 Terry Pristin, "Big Box Retail but with Icing on the Cake," *New York Times*, November 24, 2002, https://www.nytimes.com/2002/11/24/nyregion/big-box-plan -but-with-icing-on-top.html.

33 Terry Pristin, "Big Box Store Backed for Pier 40 in Village," *New York Times*, February 14, 2003, https://www.nytimes.com/2003/02/14/nyregion/big-box-store -backed-for-pier-40-in-village.html.

34 New York City Department of Parks and Recreation, "Mayor Michael R Bloomberg and Governor George E. Pataki Open Greenwich Village Segment of Hudson River Park," press release, May 29, 2003, https://www.nycgovparks.org/news/press -releases?id=16911.

35 Michele Herman, "Feeling Low after Flying Frenzy in Hudson River Park," *The Villager*, November 11, 2003. https://www.amny.com/news/feeling-low-after-flying -frenzy-in-hudson-river-park/

36 "Perry Street Towers," Eclos, accessed October 15, 2023, https://enclos.com/project /perry-street-towers/.

37 Ashley Winchester, "Mounted Unit Hoofs It over to Hudson River Park," *The Villager*, November 18, 2003, https://www.amny.com/news/mounted-unit-hoofs-it -over-to-hudson-river-park/.

38 "Frying Pan and Pier 66 Maritime," History, Frying Pan, accessed October 16, 2023, https://www.fryingpan.com/frying-pan-and-pier-66-maritime/.

39 Barbara Stewart, "On the Waterfront, at Least for Now," *New York Times*, August 8, 2002, https://www.nytimes.com/2002/08/08/nyregion/waterfront-least -for-now-hudson-river-park-threatens-some-home-grown-free.html.

40 Josh Rogers, "Park Trust Lawyer Suspended after Incident," *The Villager*, October 2003.

41 John Freeman Gill, "The Charming Gadfly Who Saved the High Line," *New York Times*, May 3, 2007, http://www.nytimes.com/2007/05/13/nyregion/thecity/13oble .html?pagewanted=all.

42 "High Line 'Park in Sky' Gets a Hearing," Associated Press, *Daily News*, July 20, 2003 https://www.newspapers.com/clip/42081516/high-line-park-in-sky-gets-a -hearing/.

43 "Coulée verte René-Dumont," Paris Convention and Visitors Bureau, accessed October 15, 2023, https://parisjetaime.com/eng/culture/coulee-verte-rene-dumont -p977.

44 "Ideas Competition (2003)," High Line, accessed October 15, 2023, https://www .thehighline.org/design/.

45 Adam Sternberg, "The High Line: It Brings Good Things Together," *New York Magazine*, April 12, 2007, https://nymag.com/news/features/31273/.

46 "Silver urges L.M.D.C. to Fund Hudson River Park Construction," *Downtown Express*, August 18, 2003, https://www.amny.com/news/silver-urges-l-m-d-c-to-fund -hudson-river-park-construction/.

47 Lincoln Anderson "Trust Springs Rink Surprise," *Downtown Express*, October 6, 2003, https://www.amny.com/news/trust-springs-rink-surprise/.

48 Tom Fox, "An Unfinished Hudson River Park Needs You," *New York Daily News*, December 7, 2003.

49 Urban Outdoors, Neighborhood Open Space Coalition, "The Commercialization of Hudson River Park," December 2, 2003.

50 Lincoln Anderson, "Trust Head Hangs up Ice Skates," *The Villager*, November 26–December 2, 2003, https://www.amny.com/news/young-tattoo-artists-etch-out-a-niche-in-the-village-2/.

Chapter 12   Hope Renewed, Problems Continue (2004–2008)

1 Albert Amateau, "PIER PRESSURE: Activist Files Pier 40 Lawsuit," *The Villager*, January 7–13, 2004, https://www.amny.com/news/pier-pressureactivist-files-pier-40-lawsuit/.

2 Lincoln Anderson, "Hudson River Park: Pier 40 Field of Dreams Coming," *The Villager*, April 27, 2004, https://www.amny.com/news/hudson-river-park-pier-40-field-of-dreams-coming/.

3 Lincoln Anderson, "Development Boom Near the River," *Downtown Express*, February 13–19, 2004, https://www.amny.com/news/development-boom-near-the-river/.

4 Al Butzel (Friends of Hudson River Park), email message to Douglas Durst, September 20, 2004.

5 Al Butzel, Friends of Hudson River Park, "Hudson River Park Funding Strategy Meeting, News from Albany re Hudson River Park Funding," October 6, 2004.

6 Tom Fox, "To Al Butzel and Paul Elston Re: Park Financing," memo, October 10, 2004.

7 Anderson, "Development Boom."

8 "Hudson Yards Overview," City of New York, accessed October 16, 2023, https://www1.nyc.gov/assets/planning/download/pdf/plans/hudson-yards/hyards.pdf.

9 "Supporters of West Side Stadium Cheer for Jobs and Jets," Jennifer Medina, *New York Times*, September 30, 2004, http://query.nytimes.com/gst/fullpage.html?res=9C06EEDC1538F933A0575AC0A9629C8B63.

10 Duff Wilson, "City Unveils Its Last and Best Bid to Gain 2012 Sumer Olympics," *New York Times*, November 13, 2004, https://www.nytimes.com/2004/11/18/sports/othersports/city-unveils-its-last-and-best-bid-to-gain-2012-summer.html.

11 "Hudson River Park Receives Awards for Excellence," *The Villager*, January 11, 2005, https://www.thevillager.com/2005/01/hudson-river-park-receives-awards-for-excellence/.

12 Lincoln Anderson, "Pier 57 Plans Down to 2: Chelsea Piers vs. Cipriani" *The Villager*, September 28, 2004, https://www.amny.com/news/pier-57-plans-down-to-2-chelsea-piers-vs-cipriani/.

13 "Target Has Docked," full-page advertisement, *New York Times*, November 14, 2002.

14 Charles V. Bagli, "On the Waterfront, Dueling Developers," *New York Times*, February 5, 2005, https://www.nytimes.com/2005/02/05/nyregion/on-the-waterfront-dueling-developers.html.

15 Bagli, "On the Waterfront."

16 Charles V. Bagli, "Cipriani Wins Bid for Italian Makeover of a West Side Pier," *New York Times*, April 7, 2005, https://www.nytimes.com/2005/04/07/nyregion

/cipriani-wins-bid-for-italian-makeover-of-a-west-side-pier.html?searchResult
Position=1.

17   Parks–Leases–Pier 57, Ch. 288, A. 8927, Laws of New York (2005), https://
     hudsonriverpark.org/app/uploads/2020/03/HRPActAmendmentRePier57.pdf.

18   Lincoln Anderson, "Hudson River Park: Pier 40 Field of Dreams Coming," *The
     Villager*, April 27, 2004, https://www.thevillager.com/2004/04/hudson-river-park
     -pier-40-field-of-dreams-coming/.

19   Steve Kurutz, "Off the Waterfront," *New York Times*, July 31, 2005, https://www
     .nytimes.com/2005/07/31/nyregion/thecity/off-the-waterfront.html.

20   "Nadler Secure $5 Million for Hudson River Park," *The Villager*, July 26, 2005,
     https://www.thevillager.com/2005/07/nadler-secures-5-million-for-hudson-river
     -park/.

21   Connie Fishman (president, Hudson River Park Trust), letter to Friends of Hudson
     River Park, May 13, 2005.

22   "The Mayor's Mad Money," editorial, *New York Times*, May 22, 2005, https://www
     .nytimes.com/2005/05/22/opinion/nyregionopinions/the-mayors-mad-money.html
     ?searchResultPosition=1.

23   "A River in View," opinion, *New York Times*, May 22, 2005, https://www.nytimes
     .com/2005/05/22/opinion/nyregionopinions/a-river-in-view.html?searchResult
     Position=1.

24   Friends of Hudson River Park, *Hudson River Current*, June 2006.

25   Blair Golson, "Park Frozen as City Trucks Blockade Pier," *New York Observer*,
     April 12, 2004.

26   Albert Amateau, "Suit Filed to Get Garbage Trucks off of Gansevoort," *The
     Villager*, May 3, 2005, https://www.thevillager.com/2005/05/suit-filed-to-get
     -garbage-trucks-off-of-gansevoortby-albert-amateaufriends-of-hudson-river-park
     -on-tuesday-filed-a-lawsuit-against-the-city-to-force-the-department-of-sanitation
     -to-stop-construction/.

27   Francis X. Clines, "Imagination on the Waterfront," *New York Times*, August 11,
     2005, https://www.nytimes.com/2005/08/11/opinion/imagination-on-the-waterfront
     .html.

28   Josh Rogers, "Saying Bye to Pier 25," *Downtown Express*, October 10, 2005,
     https://www.amny.com/news/saying-bye-to-pier-25/.

29   Timothy Williams, "The Old Ferry Boat and a Sea: A Parable Updated as a
     Landlord-Tenant Dispute," *New York Times*, November 4, 2005, https://www
     .nytimes.com/2005/11/24/nyregion/the-old-ferryboat-and-the-sea-a-parable
     -updated-as-a.html?searchResultPosition=1.

30   Michael Kimmelman, "For New York's Best New Public Sculpture, Thank the
     Sanitation Department," *New York Times*, December 21, 2015, https://www.nytimes
     .com/2015/12/22/arts/design/in-sanitation-and-salt-complex-in-tribeca-a-salutary
     -lesson-in-urban-responsibility.html.

31   Hasani Gittens, "Pier into the Future," *New York Post*, November 2, 2005.

32   Lincoln Anderson, "Former Trust Chairperson Pleads Guilty to Fraud," *The
     Villager*, November 27, 2007, https://www.thevillager.com/2007/11/former-trust
     -chairperson-pleads-guilty-to-tax-fraud/.

33   Tara Bahrampour, "Garbage Plan Not Well Received Downwind," *New York Times*,
     August 18, 2002, https://www.nytimes.com/2002/08/18/nyregion/neighborhood
     -report-upper-east-side-garbage-plan-not-well-received-downwind.html?search
     ResultPosition=1.

34   Michael Bradley (Executive Director, Riverside South Planning Corporation), letter to Larry Szarpanski (Assistant Commissioner), July 9, 2004.

35   Tom Fox (Friends of Hudson River Park), "October 13th Meeting on Sanitation Facilities and Plans in the Hudson River Park," memo to Issues Committee Members, October 23, 2004.

36   Sewell Chen, "Transfer Station in Park Raises Doubts about City Waste Management Plan," *New York Times*, February 20, 2006, http://www.nytimes.com/2006/02/20/nyregion/20garbage.html.

37   City of New York Department of Sanitation Water-Dependent Marine Transfer Station, Ch. 596, A. 11773, Law News of New York, 231st Legislature, (2008), https://hudsonriverpark.org/app/uploads/2020/03/2008_Amendment_to_Hudson_River_Park_Act_Chapter_596_of_the_Laws_of_2008.pdf.

38   Lincoln Anderson, "Members Bite Back at Trust's 'Gag Order' Rule," *Downtown Express*, March 31–April 6, 2006.

39   Sam Roberts, "After 20 Years of Delay, a River Park Takes Shape," *New York Times*, May 16, 2005, https://www.nytimes.com/2006/05/16/nyregion/16westway.html.

40   "Water World at Pier 40," *The Villager*, June 3, 2006, https://www.amny.com/news/water-world-at-pier-40/.

41   Jill Priluck, "Pier 40: Overhaul or Just Upgrade," *Gothamist*, January 4, 2007, https://gothamist.com/arts-entertainment/pier-40-overhaul-or-just-upgrade-it.

42   Eliot Brown, "Battle of Pier 40 Heats up over Big Developments," *New York Sun*, April 27, 2007, https://www.nysun.com/new-york/battle-of-pier-40-heats-up-over-big-developments/53312/.

43   Ronda Kaysan, "Hudson River Park Center is Sinking," *Downtown Express*, August 17, 2006, https://www.thevillager.com/2006/08/hudson-parks-river-center-is-sinking/.

44   Matthew Fenton, "James Gill Floats Dramatic Idea for Expansion of Battery Park City," *Battery Park City Broadsheet*, October 13, 2006.

45   Hudson River Park Trust, "Ribbon Cutting Ceremony, Hudson River Park's North Chelsea Section," invitation, December 11, 2006.

46   Lincoln Anderson, "Drunk Driver on Hudson River Bike Path Mows Down Cyclist," *The Villager*, December 12, 2006, https://www.thevillager.com/2006/12/drunk-driver-on-hudson-park-bike-path-mows-down-cyclist/.

47   Brad Aaron, "Bus Driver Seriously Injures Bicyclist on the Hudson River Greenway," *Streetsblog NYC*, July 24, 2014, https://nyc.streetsblog.org/2014/07/24/bus-driver-seriously-injures-cyclist-on-hudson-river-greenway/.

48   Jen Chung, "Classic Steamroller: Spitzer a Bully During Troopergate Interview," *Gothamist*, May 20, 2009, https://gothamist.com/news/classic-steamroller-spitzer-a-bully-during-troopergate-interview.

49   "Frying Pan and Pier 66 Maritime," History, Frying Pan, accessed October 16, 2023, https://www.fryingpan.com/frying-pan-and-pier-66-maritime/.

50   Lincoln Anderson, "Gov Picks Woman with Ties to Mayor and Pataki for Park Post," *Downtown Express*, August 16, 2007, https://www.amny.com/news/gov-picks-woman-with-ties-to-mayor-pataki-for-park-post/.

51   Robin Pogrebin, "Rehabilitating Robert Moses," *New York Times*, January 27, 2007, https://www.nytimes.com/2007/01/23/arts/design/28pogr.html?pagewanted=all.

52   Anemona Hartocollis, "Former GOP Official Admits He Evaded Taxes," *New York Times*, November 16, 2007, https://www.nytimes.com/2007/11/16/nyregion/16indict.html.

53 "Air Pegasus of New York Inc. vs Liberty Helicopter Tours, Inc," unpublished opinion, *Westlaw*, August 1, 2007.

54 Adam Pincus, "Disgraced GOP Leader Sells Meatpacking Parcel," *The Real Deal*, June 24, 2008, https://therealdeal.com/2008/07/24/disgraced-gop-leader-sells -meatpacking-parcel/.

55 Reuters Staff, "UPDATE 1-NYC Deputy Mayor to Resign, Join Bloomberg's Firm," December 6, 2007, https://www.reuters.com/article/newyork-doctoroff /update-1-nyc-deputy-mayor-to-resign-join-bloombergs-firm -idUKN0622535520071206.

56 Adam Lisberg, "West Side Residents vs Bloomberg Rezoning Plan," *New York Daily News*, November 5, 2007, https://www.nydailynews.com/news/west-side-residents -bloomberg-rezoning-plan-article-1.257607.

57 Jen Chung, "What's Going On with Pier 40?," *Gothamist*, January 8, 2008, https://gothamist.com/news/whats-going-on-at-pier-40.

58 Lincoln Anderson, "Pier 57 Process Is Barely Afloat Three Years After," *The Villager*, December 25, 2007, https://www.amny.com/news/pier-57-process-is-barely-afloat -three-years-later-2/.

59 Anderson, "Members Bite Back."

60 Peter Kiefer, "Developer Quits Pier 57 Project, Big Setback," *New York Sun*, January 25, 2008, https://www.nysun.com/new-york/developer-quits-pier-57-project -a-big-setback/70147/.

61 "Hudson River Park: A Name That Works," *The Villager*, January 8, 2008, https:// www.thevillager.com/2008/01/hudson-river-park-a-name-that-works/.

62 Michael M. Grynbaum, "Spitzer Resigns Citing Personal Failings," *New York Times*, March 12, 2008, https://www.nytimes.com/2008/03/12/nyregion/12cnd -resign.html.

63 Dave Hogarty, "Pier 40 Plan 86'd by Hudson River Park Trust," *Gothamist*, March 28, 2008, https://gothamist.com/news/pier-40-plan-86d-by-hudson-river -park-trust.

64 Friends of Hudson River Park, "The Impact of Hudson River Park on Property Values," Fall 2008.

Chapter 13 Going from Bad to Worse (2009–2012)

1 Wendy Kaufman et al. and the Associated Press, "US Airways River Rescue: A 'Miracle on the Hudson,'" *NPR*, January 15, 2009, https://www.npr.org/templates /story/story.php?storyId=99432590.

2 "Miracle on the Hudson," Tribune News Services, *Chicago Tribune*, January 16, 2009, https://www.chicagotribune.com/news/ct-xpm-2009-01-16-0901160143-story .html.

3 Teri Thompson et al., "Ferry Changed Course to Help Save Passengers of US Airways Flight 1549, *New York Daily News*, January 16, 2009, https://www .nydailynews.com/new-york/ferry-changed-save-passengers-airways-flight-1549 -article-1.423186.

4 "46 US Code Section 2304—Duty to Provide Assistance at Sea," Legal Information Institute, Cornell University Law School, https://www.law.cornell.edu/uscode/text /46/2304.

5 Michael Duffy, New York Cruise Lines, Circle Line, interview by Tom Fox, April 2021.

6   Brendan Sexton, Friends of Hudson River Park, "Creating a BID to Support Hudson River Park," April 2009.

7   New York City Department of Small Business Services, "Starting a Business Improvement District, A Step-By-Step Guide," 2002, http://www.nyc.gov/html/sbs /downloads/pdf/BID_ANN_REPORT_FINAL_singlepage.pdf;

8   New York City Department of Small Business Services, "FY 2008 Report Summary of 64 Business Improvement Districts," 2008, http://www.nyc.gov/html/sbs /downloads/pdf/BID_ANN_REPORT_FINAL_singlepage.pdf.

9   Dana Rubenstein, "Special Tax Sought to Fund Hudson River Park," *Wall Street Journal*, March 14, 2011, https://www.wsj.com/articles/SB100014240527487035554 04576195520506542928.

10 Matthew Schuerman, "How New York, the Vertical City, Kept Rising Under Bloomberg," *WNYC News*, July 8, 2013, https://www.wnyc.org/story/300641-how -new-york-vertical-city-kept-rising-during-bloomberg/.

11 "Pier 57 Gets New Proposals for Development," Going Coastal, October 23, 2008, https://goingcoastal.wordpress.com/2008/10/23/pier-57-gets-new-proposals-for -development/.

12 The Durst Organization and C&K Properties, *Development Proposal for Pier 57*, vol. 1. October 17, 2008.

13 Jen Carlson, "A Look at the Future of Pier 57," *Gothamist*, August 11, 2009, http://gothamist.com/2009/08/11/pier_57.php.

14 Charles V. Bagli, "Rezoning Will Allow Railyard Project to Advance," *New York Times*, December 21, 2009, https://www.nytimes.com/2009/12/22/nyregion /22hudson.html.

15 Aria Bendix, "Hudson Yards Is the Biggest New York Development since Rockefeller Center. Here Are All the New Buildings in the $25 Billion Neighbor-hood," *Business Insider*, March 15, 2019, https://www.businessinsider.com/hudson -yards-rundown-major-buildings-finished-2018-10.

16 Sewell Chan, "New Section of Hudson River Park Opens," *New York Times*, May 5, 2009, https://cityroom.blogs.nytimes.com/2009/05/05/new-section-of-hudson -river-park-opens/.

17 Nicole Berskin, "Hudson River Park Unveils New Merry-Go-Round and Skate Park," *DNAinfo*, May 17, 2010, https://www.dnainfo.com/new-york/20100517/chelsea -meatpacking-district/hudson-river-park-unveils-new-merrygoround-skate-park/.

18 Hudson River Park Act, Ch. 592, S. 7845, Sec. 3 (g) and (v), NY Legis 592 (1998).

19 A. J. Pietrantone, "A 'Quiet Victory' Is Won for the Hudson River Park," *The Villager*, April 6, 2010, https://www.thevillager.com/2010/04/a-quiet-victory-is -won-for-the-hudson-river-park-2/.

20 "Lilac: Flower of the Delaware," Lilac Preservation Project, accessed October 16, 2023, http://www.lilacpreservationproject.org/history-1.

21 "Programming Begins on the Lilac, Newly Arrived at Pier 25," Waterwire, Metro-politan Waterfront Alliance, July 7, 2011, https://waterfrontalliance.org/2011/07/07 /programming-begins-on-the-lilac-newly-arrived-at-pier-25/.

22 Julie Schapiro, "New Pier 25 Brings Volleyball and Mini Golf to Tribeca" *DNAinfo*, November 2, 2010, https://www.dnainfo.com/20101102/downtown/new-pier-25 -brings-beach-volleyball-minigolf-tribeca/.

23 "NYC Bids Goodbye to a Waterfront Visionary" Waterwire, Metropolitan Waterfront Alliance, February 28, 2011, https://waterfrontalliance.org/2011/02/28 /nyc-bids-goodbye-to-a-waterfront-visionary/.

24 "Bernard Ente, 1951–2011" Waterwire, Metropolitan Waterfront Alliance, April 18, 2011, https://waterfrontalliance.org/2011/04/18/bernard-ente-1951-2011/.

25 Julie Shapiro, "Connie Fishman Leaves the Hudson River Park Trust to Work for the YMCA, *DNAinfo*, January 15, 2011, https://www.dnainfo.com/new-york/20110105 /downtown/connie-fishman-leaves-hudson-river-park-trust-work-for-ymca/.

26 "YMCA of the Greater New York Board of Directors Names Diana Taylor New Chair," June 11, 2011, https://www.businesswire.com/news/home/20110628006523 /en/YMCA-of-Greater-New-York-Board-of-Directors-Elects-Diana-Taylor-New -Chair.

27 Patrick McGeehan, "Hudson River Park Trust Picks a New Leader," *New York Times*, May 26, 2011, https://cityroom.blogs.nytimes.com/2011/05/26/hudson-river -park-trust-picks-a-new-leader/.

28 New York City Department of Small Business Services, "Starting a Business Improvement District."

29 Agreement between Friends of Hudson River Park and Hudson River Park Trust, September 12, 2011.

30 Matt Chaban "Libertarians Flood the Hudson River Park," *The Observer*, June 22, 2011, https://observer.com/2011/06/libertarians-flood-hudson-river-park/.

31 Charles V. Bagli and Lisa W. Foderaro, "Time and Tides Weigh on Hudson River Park," *New York Times*, January 27, 2012, https://www.nytimes.com/2012/01/28 /nyregion/hudson-river-park-after-early-success-faces-new-challenges.html ?pagewanted=all.

32 "Chelsea Piers vs Hudson River Park Trust," FindLaw for Legal Professionals, May 2, 2103, https://caselaw.findlaw.com/ny-supreme-court-appellate-division /1630099.html.

33 Joseph De Avila, "Struggling Trust Seeks Funds for the Hudson Shore," *Wall Street Journal*, April 18, 2012, https://www.wsj.com/articles/SB100014240527023035134 04577352150500426364.

34 Manhattan Community Board 4, letter to Taylor, Bloomberg, Cuomo, Silver and Skelos, June 8, 2012, https://www1.nyc.gov/html/mancb4/downloads/pdf2012 /june2012finalresos/MCB4%20Letter%20re%20Hudson%20River%20Park%20 Strategic%20Planning%20Task%20Force%20Recommendations.pdf.

35 C. J. Hughes, "On the Waterfront, Minus the Stevedores," *New York Times*, September 21, 2012, http://www.nytimes.com/2012/09/23/realestate/living-along -the-west-side-highway-on-the-waterfront-minus-the-stevedores.html.

36 Tom Fox, "Let's Return to the Vision of the Hudson River Park," *The Villager*, September 13, 2012, https://www.thevillager.com/2012/09/lets-return-to-the-vision -of-the-hudson-river-park/.

37 Pier 40 Champions, "Pier 40 Champions," videos, January 27, 2013.

38 Lisa Foderaro, "Repair Costs Could Bring Down a Popular Pier," *New York Times*, August 17, 2012, https://www.nytimes.com/2012/08/18/nyregion/repair-costs-could -bring-down-a-popular-pier.html.

39 McLaren Engineering, The Durst Organization, *Marine Engineering Report on Pier 40*, October 23, 2012.

40 Rafael Llopiz, The Durst Organization, "Pier 40—Summarized DLC Consulting Memo with comments," September 19, 2019.

41 Jessica Terrell, "Durst Presents His Own Rescue Plan for Crumbling Pier 40, *TribecaTrib*, http://tribecatrib.com/content/durst-presents-his-own-rescue-plans -crumbling-pier-40.

42 "Hurricane Sandy Taught One Devastated Queens Neighborhood More about Gain than Loss," Bahar Ostadan, *Daily News*, October 29, 2022, https://www.nydailynews.com/new-york/ny-hurricane-sandy-10th-anniversary-breezy-point-20221029-ljquftlvfba7bic6qhubuzspmu-story.html?utm_source=newsletter&utm_medium=email&utm_campaign=Don%27t%20Miss&utm_content=5631667058207.

43 Andrea Swalec, "Hudson River Storm Damage Estimated at $10 million," *DNAinfo*, November 30, 2012, https://www.dnainfo.com/new-york/20121130/west-village/hudson-river-park-storm-damage-estimated-at-10m/.

44 Matt Chaban, "Sinking Pier 40: Durst Leaves Hudson River Park Amid Mutiny over Its Future," *The Observer*, December 16, 2012, https://observer.com/2012/12/sinking-pier-40-durst-leaves-hudson-river-park-amid-mutiny-over-its-future/.

Chapter 14   The Trust Goes over to the Dark Side (2013–2014)

1 Matt Caban, "His Ship Comes In: Hedgie Michael Novogratz Named Chairman of Friends of Hudson River Park," *The Observer*, January 17, 2013, https://observer.com/2013/01/his-ships-come-in-hedgie-michael-novogratz-named-chairman-of-friends-of-hudson-river-park./

2 *The Real Deal* staff, "Former Highline Terminus Building Trades in $250 Million Deal," *The Real Deal*, January 3, 2013, https://therealdeal.com/2013/01/03/high-line-office-building-trades-in-250m-deal/.

3 James McKinley Jr., "More Concerts Coming to Hudson River Park," *Arts Beat* (blog), February 5, 2013, https://artsbeat.blogs.nytimes.com/2013/02/05/more-concerts-coming-to-hudson-river-park/.

4 Friends of Hudson River Park, "HRP NID Talking Points."

5 Friends of Hudson River Park, "HRP NID FAQ's," February 26, 2013.

6 Tom Fox, "Why Is Funding for the Hudson River Park So Contentious," op-ed, *The Villager*, March 14, 2013, https://www.thevillager.com/2013/03/why-is-funding-the-hudson-river-park-so-contentious/.

7 Charles V. Bagli and Lisa W. Forderaro, "Time and Tides Weigh on the Hudson River Park," *New York Times*, January 27, 2012, https://www.nytimes.com/2012/01/28/nyregion/hudson-river-park-after-early-success-faces-new-challenges.html.

8 "Hudson River Park Needs to Generate More Revenue," opinion, *The Villager*, April 4, 2013, https://www.amny.com/news/hudson-river-park-must-generate-more-revenue-2/.

9 "Hudson River Park NID: A Bad Idea," *Stop the Hudson River Park Neighborhood Improvement District* (blog), May 2013, http://nohrpnid.blogspot.com.

10 Pier 40 Champions, "Champions—WYX—Slideshow."

11 Ben Korman, email message to Douglas Durst, December 4, 2012.

12 Laura Kusisto, "Sports Groups Aim at Pier 40," *Wall Street Journal*, January 29, 2013, https://www.wsj.com/articles/SB10001424127887323375204578272163960769192.

13 Jaime Cone, "Pier 40 and the Clash of Views on How to Finally Save It," *Tribeca Trib*, March 5, 2013, http://tribecatrib.com/content/pier-40-and-clash-views-how-finally-save-it.

14 Lincoln Anderson, "The Two Towers: Pier 40 Plan Would Generate $115 Million for the Hudson River Park Upfront, Plus $10 Million Annually," *The Villager*, February 28, 2013, https://www.amny.com/news/the-two-towers-study-finds-pier

-40-plan-would-generate-115-million-for-hudson-river-park-upfront-plus-10-million
-annually/.

15 Tobi Bergman, email message to Douglas Durst, March 9, 2013.

16 David Dinkins and Richard Shaffer, *New York City Comprehensive Waterfront
Plan, Reclaiming the City's Edge* (New York: Department of City Planning, 1992),
148–149 and Map A.3, https://www1.nyc.gov/assets/planning/download/pdf/about
/publications/cwp.pdf.

17 "New York City Planning," Zoning Resolution, accessed October 18, 2023,
https://zr.planning.nyc.gov/article-vi/chapter-2/62-31.

18 State of New York, An Act to Amend Hudson River Park Act Amendments, A
8031, NYS Assembly (2013).

19 Arthur Schwartz (Hudson River Park Advisory Council), email message to Noreen
Doyle and the Advisory Council, June 18, 2013.

20 Richard D. Emery, Emery, Celli Brinkerhoff, Abady Ward & Maazel LLP, "For
Tomorrow's Discussion at Noon," memo to Jessica, January 18, 2021.

21 An Act to Amend the Hudson River Park Act, in Relation to the Rights, Powers,
Duties and Jurisdiction of the Hudson River Park Trust and the Boundaries and
Uses of the Hudson River Park, Ch. 517, Laws of New York (2013), https://
hudsonriverpark.org/app/uploads/2020/03/HRPA_Amendment_-_Chapter_517
_of_the_Laws_of_2013.pdf.

22 An Act to Amend the Hudson River Park Act.

23 Greenwich Village Society for Historic Preservation, Saint Chelsea, Council of
Chelsea Block Associations, and Greenwich Village Community Task Force, letter
to Governor Cuomo, October 31, 2013.

24 Theresa Agovino, "Hudson River Park is Still Sinking Financially," *Crain's New
York Business*, June 27, 2013, https://www.crainsnewyork.com/article/20130627
/REAL_ESTATE/130629893/hudson-river-park-is-still-sinking-financially.

25 Hudson River Park Act, Ch. 592, S. 7845, NY Legis 592 (1998), https://hudsonriver
park.org/app/uploads/2020/03/HRP-Act.pdf.

26 Hudson River Park Trust, "Pieces of the Puzzle: Why Pier 40 Matters" PowerPoint
for A. J. Pietratone.

27 Lisa Kisisto and Eliot Brown, "Hudson River Park Plan Is Questioned, Members of
Two Boards for Park Would Benefit from Air-Rights Sale" *Wall Street Journal*,
July 22, 2013, https://www.wsj.com/articles/SB10001424127887323848804578605843365387704.

28 Lisa Foderaro, "Preservationists Have Concerns about Plan to Sell Hudson River
Park Air Rights," *New York Times*, August 11, 2013, https://www.nytimes.com/2013
/08/12/nyregion/preservationists-criticize-plan-to-sell-hudson-river-park-air-rights
.html?searchResultPosition=2.

29 Paul Ullman, "Let's Embrace This key Moment for Hudson River Park," op-ed, *The
Villager*, November 2013, https://www.thevillager.com/2013/11/lets-embrace-this
-key-moment-for-hudson-river-park/.

30 Andrew Berman, "More Park Air Rights Mean More Safeguards are Needed,"
op-ed, *The Villager*, March 12, 2014, https://www.amny.com/news/more-park-air
-rights-mean-more-safeguards-are-needed/.

31 Joe Anuta, "Hudson River Park Trust Eyes Air Rights Rescue," *Crain's New
York Business*, February 1, 2014, https://www.crainsnewyork.com/article
/20140202/REAL_ESTATE/302029974/hudson-river-park-trust-eyes-air-rights
-rescue.

32 Miryea Navarro, "De Blasio's Pick for Planning Puts Focus on Housing," *New York Times*, February 7, 2014, https://www.nytimes.com/2014/02/08/nyregion/de-blasio-picks-revitalization-veteran-to-lead-planning-commission.html?_r=2&gwh=4EA44BB9811F9022B3E3F889DDBF934D&gwt=pay.

33 Lincoln Anderson, "Cuomo Pushes Deal for Pier 40 Air Rights Without ULURP," *The Villager*, May 22, 2014, https://www.amny.com/news/cuomo-pushes-deal-for-pier-40-air-rights-sale-without-ulurp/.

34 Lincoln Anderson, "Pier 40's Secret Agreement Is Now Dead, Opponent States," *The Villager*, June 9, 2014, https://www.amny.com/news/pier-40s-secret-deal-is-now-dead-opponent-says/.

35 Tom Fox, "Can the Hudson River Park Trust still be Trusted," op-ed, *The Villager*, June 19, 2013, https://www.amny.com/news/can-the-hudson-river-park-trust-still-be-trusted/.

36 Susanna Aaron, "Let's Work Together to Better Hudson River Park," op-ed, *The Villager*, June 26, 2014, https://www.amny.com/news/lets-work-together-to-better-hudson-river-park/.

37 Clarissa-Jan Lim, "Pier 26 Shows Rocked the Neighbors' World Too Much; Cancelled for 2014," *Downtown Express*, August 8, 2013, https://www.amny.com/news/pier-26-shows-rocked-neighbors-world-too-much-canceled-for-14/.

38 Jim Farber, "JBL Live Pier 97: Introducing New York City's Newest Music Venue," *Daily News*, July 3, 2014, https://www.nydailynews.com/entertainment/music-arts/jbl-live-pier-97-introducing-new-york-city-newest-music-venue-article-1.1854074.

39 Kelleigh Welch, "NJ Raises Ruckus over NYC Pier 97 Shows," *PROSOUND News*, July 29, 2014, https://www.prosoundnetwork.com/pro-sound-news-blog/2249.

40 Daniel Geiger, "Pier 57 Developer Adds Partner to Build Offices," *Crain's New York Business*, September 16, 2014, https://www.crainsnewyork.com/article/20140916/REAL_ESTATE/140919889/pier-57-developer-adds-partner-to-build-offices.

41 Benjamin Snyder, "Barry Diller Planning Fantasy Island on New York's Hudson River," *Fortune*, November 17, 2014, https://fortune.com/2014/11/17/barry-diller-planning-a-fantasy-island-on-new-yorks-hudson-river/.

42 Riverkeeper and NY/NJ Baykeeper, letter to the Hudson River Park Trust, January 15, 2015.

43 David Callahan, "The Billionaires Park," *New York Times*, November 30, 2014, https://www.nytimes.com/2014/12/01/opinion/the-billionaires-park.html.

44 Madelyn Wils, "River Park the Story of a Public Space," letter to the editor, *New York Times*, December 3, 2014, https://www.nytimes.com/2014/12/08/opinion/hudson-river-park-the-story-of-a-public-space.html.

45 New York State Comptroller Anthony DiNapoli, "Selected Financial Management Practices, Hudson River Park Trust," December 26, 2014, https://www.osc.state.ny.us/files/state-agencies/audits/pdf/SGA-2015-13s56.pdf.

46 Vincent McGowan, letter to Michael Terife, NYS Attorney General, Charitable Bureau, January 23, 2015.

Chapter 15   Public Resistance Builds (2015–2016)

1 "SS United States or QE2 Heading for Pier 57 in Manhattan?," *Cruise Industry News*, February 27, 2015, https://www.cruiseindustrynews.com/cruise-news/12274-ss-united-states-or-qe2-heading-for-pier-57-in-manhattan.html.

2 SS United States Conservancy (website), https://www.ssusc.org/the-ship.

3 Michael Tannenbaum, "Real Estate Developer Hints of Plans for Airbnb, Brewery in Docked SS United States," *PhillyVoice*, March 10, 2020, https://www.phillyvoice.com/ss-united-states-redevelopment-rxr-airbnb-beer-hall-philadelphia-ship/.

4 AKRF, Inc., for the Hudson River Park Trust, "Pier 54 Response to Comments Received during Public Review," February 10, 2015, https://silo.tips/download/pier-54-response-to-comments-received-during-public-review.

5 Riverkeeper NY/NJ Baykeeper, "Riverkeeper NY/NJ Baykeeper Comments on Proposed Lease between Hudson River Park Trust and Pier 55 Inc. and Proposed Amendment to the Parks Project Plan," January 23, 2015.

6 "Opposition to a Permit to Construct and Lease—Pier 54," Testimony to Hudson River Park Trust, January 12, 2015 (statement of Tom Fox).

7 James B. Stewart, "Cooper Union Inquiry Puts Nonprofits on Notice," *New York Times*, April 9, 2015, https://www.nytimes.com/2015/04/10/business/cooper-union-inquiry-puts-nonprofits-on-notice.html.

8 Corinne Ramey, "Groups Seeks to Block Hudson River Park," *Wall Street Journal*, June 12, 2015, https://www.wsj.com/articles/group-seeks-to-block-hudson-river-park-1434154177.

9 New York State, "Governor Cuomo Announces State Approval RXR Realty and Youngwoo & Associates Project to Redevelop Historic Pier 57 in Hudson River Park," press release, December 12, 2015, https://www.governor.ny.gov/news/governor-cuomo-announces-state-approval-rxr-realty-and-youngwoo-associates-project-redevelop.

10 Tom Fox, "Pier 57 Project Kept Changing, without New Bids," *The Villager*, February 25, 2016, http://thevillager.com/2016/02/25/pier-57-project-kept-changing-without-new-bids/.

11 Diana Taylor, "Fox Has His Facts All Wrong on Pier 57 Project," *The Villager*, March 3, 2016, https://www.amny.com/news/fox-has-his-facts-all-wrong-on-pier-57-project/.

12 Tom Fox, "This Is about Park and Public Process, Not Me," op-ed, *The Villager*, March 10, 2016, https://www.amny.com/news/this-is-about-park-and-public-process-not-me/.

13 "A Potential Win-Win for the West Side," Editorial, *New York Times*, December 14, 2015, https://www.nytimes.com/2015/12/14/opinion/a-potential-win-win-for-the-west-side.html.

14 Save Chelsea, "Commercial Enterprise Has No Place in Public Parks," op-ed, *The Villager*, August 12, 2015, https://www.amny.com/news/commercial-enterprise-has-no-place-in-public-parks/.

15 Daniel Geiger, "Westbrook Pays $200 Million for Majority Stake in St. John's Terminal, Eyes Big Redevelopment," *Crain's New York Business*, August 24, 2015, https://www.crainsnewyork.com/article/20150824/REAL_ESTATE/150829941/westbrook-pays-200-million-for-majority-stake-in-st-john-s-terminal-eyes-big-redevelopment.

16 "Josh French, Mike Novogratz: A 'Herd of Institutional Investors' Is Moving into Crypto," *The Street*, July 23, 2018, https://www.thestreet.com/investing/mike-novogratz-institutional-investors-heading-for-crypto-14656355.

17 Hannah Elliott, "This Old Horse Stable Will Be One of the Most Insane Clubs in New York," *Bloomberg*, April 5, 2016, https://www.bloomberg.com/news/articles/2016-04-05/classic-car-club-manhattan-new-location-at-nypd-stable-pier-57.

18 Lisa W. Foderaro, "How Diller and von Furstenberg Got Their Island in Hudson River Park," *New York Times*, April 3, 2016, https://www.nytimes.com/2015/04 /05/nyregion/how-diller-and-von-furstenberg-got-their-island-in-hudson-river -park.html?action=click&module=RelatedCoverage&pgtype=Article&region =Footer.

19 City Club of New York, "Affidavit of NYS Assembly member Deborah Glick," December 10, 2016.

20 Alexandra Lange, "Garden Bridge v. Pier 55: Why Do New York and London Think So Differently?," *The Guardian*, May 26, 2016, https://www.theguardian.com/cities /2016/may/26/garden-bridge-pier-55-new-york-london.

21 *The Real Deal*, "Pier 55, New York's First Floating Park, Gets the Go-Ahead," YouTube video, https://www.youtube.com/watch?v=lVtD-QIbm5g.

22 Judith Enk (Regional Administrator, United States Environmental Protection Agency, Region 2), letter to Colonel David A. Caldwell (U.S. Army Corps of Engineers New York District), November 4, 2015.

23 Richard Emery, letter to the Clerk of the Board U.S. Environmental Protection Agency Environmental Appeals Board, December 28, 2015, https://yosemite.epa .gov/oa/EAB_Web_Docket.nsf/Filings%20By%20Appeal%20Number/C3E12557A D66822685257F370068BB3D/$File/The%20City%20Club%20of%20New%20York . . . Petition . . . 1.pdf.

24 City Club of New York v. Hudson River Park Trust, ruling of Justice Joan B. Lobis (New York State Supreme Court, 2016).

25 City Club of New York v. Hudson River Park Trust, affirmation of Richard Emery, Index No. 101068/2015 (Court of Appeals New York State, 2016).

26 Carter Ledyard & Milburn LLP, "Brief of Amici Curia New Yorkers for Parks and the New York League of Conservation Voters in Support of Respondents-Respondents-Cross-Appellants Hudson River Park Trust Inc. and Pier55 Inc.," New York County Clerks Index No. 101–068\15, August 11, 2016.

27 Joseph J. Tanski, Henry J. Bokuniewicz, and Cornelia Schlenk, *Dredging Windows Workshop Summary*, Report NYSGI-W-11-001, (New York Sea Grant, April 2014).

28 "City Club of NY Inc. v. Hudson River Park Tr., Inc.," Opinion 101068/15 1710 1711 1709, Casetext, September 8, 2016, https://casetext.com/case/city-club-of-ny-inc-v -hudson-river-park-trust-inc-1.

29 Decision/Order/Judgment, Index No. 1776–16, RJI No. 01-16-ST7746 (State of New York Supreme Court, 2017).

30 Danielle Tcholakian, "City, Hudson River Park Trust Strike $100 Million Air Rights Deal for Pier 40," *DNAinfo*, October 21, 2015, https://www.dnainfo.com /new-york/20151021/hudson-square/city-hudson-river-park-trust-strike-100m-air -rights-deal-for-pier-40/.

31 "Testimony of Borough President Gale Brewer, Assembly member Deborah J. Glick, State Senator Brad M. Hoylman, Councilmember Corey Johnson, Congressman Jerrold Nadler, State Senator Daniel Squadron, regarding the 550 Washington St./Special Hudson River Park District Project, CEQR No.16DCP031M," November 20, 2015, https://www.amny.com/wp-content/uploads/2016/05/pier-40 -scoping-testimony.pdf.

32 Manhattan Community Board 2, "Community Board 2 to City Planning Commission Director Carl Weisbrod," November 24, 2015.

33 Daniel Geiger, "Developer Paying 33% above Market for Pier 40 Air Rights," *Crain's New York Business*, May 4, 2016, https://www.crainsnewyork.com/article/20160504

/REAL_ESTATE/160509940/developers-westbrook-partners-and-atlas-capital
-group-paying-33-above-market-for-pier-40-air-rights.

34 Greenwich Village Society for Historic Preservation, "FAQ: Pier 40/St. John's
Terminal/Hudson River Park Special District Plan," August 1, 2016, https://
vparchive.gvshp.org/_gvshp/preservation/hudson/hudson-07-28-16.htm

35 Danielle Tcholakian, "Here's How the St. John's Terminal-Pier 40 Deal Got Done,"
DNAinfo, August 31, 2016, https://www.dnainfo.com/new-york/20160831/hudson
-square/heres-how-st-johns-terminal-pier-40-deal-got-done.

36 Danielle Tcholakian, "St. John's Terminal Developers Outline Changes to
Proposal," *DNA info*, October 8, 2016, https://www.dnainfo.com/new-york
/20161008/hudson-square/st-johns-terminal-developers-outline-changes-proposal/.

37 Charles V. Bagli, "$100 Million Deal to Save Pier 40 in Manhattan Is Approved,"
New York Times, December 15, 2016, https://www.nytimes.com/2016/12/15
/nyregion/100-million-deal-to-save-pier-40-in-manhattan-is-approved.html.

38 Lincoln Anderson, "What the Hel(iport)? Operator to Pay $250K for Illegal Tourist
Flights," *amNY,* August 3, 2017, https://www.amny.com/news/what-the-heliport
-operator-to-pay-250k-for-illegal-tourist-flights/.

Chapter 16 A Court Battle Ends, and the Governor Delivers (2016–2018)

1 Matthew Fenton, "Trying to Wrest an Upside from Tragedy," *The Broadsheet*,
July 13, 2017, https://www.ebroadsheet.com/trying-wrest-upside-tragedy/.

2 Maya Rajamani, "Hudson River Greenway Crossings a 'Disaster Waiting to
Happen,' Group Says," *DNAinfo*, January 17, 2017, https://www.dnainfo.com/new
-york/20170117/hells-kitchen-clinton/hudson-river-greenway-intersections-traffic
-signals-chekpeds/.

3 Levar Alonzo, "Bike Begone! CB1 Endorses Plan to Steer Bicyclists Away from
Esplanade Towards the Hudson River Greenway," *Downtown Express*, September 28, 2017, https://www.thevillager.com/2017/09/bikes-begone-cb1-endorses-plan
-to-steer-bicyclists-away-from-esplanade-toward-hudson-river-greenway/.

4 "Hudson River Valley Greenway Train," New York State, accessed October 18, 2023,
https://hudsongreenway.ny.gov/trails.

5 Mark Lebetkin, "Top Urban Bypass across the USA," *USA Today*, July 23, 2013,
https://www.usatoday.com/story/travel/destinations/2013/07/23/best-urban-bike
-paths-across-the-usa/2576801/.

6 Benjamin Mueller, William K. Rashbaum, and Al Baker, "Terror Attack Kills 8 and
Injures 11 in Manhattan," *New York Times*, October 31, 2017, https://www.nytimes
.com/2017/10/31/nyregion/police-shooting-lower-manhattan.html.

7 Sharon Otterman, "Manhattan Terror Attack Exposes Bike Path's Vulnerable
Crossings," *New York Times*, November 1, 2017, https://www.nytimes.com/2017/11
/01/nyregion/manhattan-terror-attack-bike-path.html.

8 Reiter & Reiter Consulting Inc, *Rethinking Bollards—How Bollards Can Save
Lives, Prevent Injuries and Relieve Traffic Congestion in New York City* (2007),
https://www.reitercorp.com/uploads/1/3/1/6/131659429/rethinking_bollards_how
_bollards_can_save_lives_prevent_injuries_and_relieve_traffic_congestion_in
_new_york_city_transportation_alternatives.pdf.

9 Caroline Spivak, "Cyclists Rail against Narrow Hudson River Park Greenway Barriers,"
Patch, June 22, 2018, https://patch.com/new-york/west-village/cyclists-rail-against
-narrow-hudson-river-greenway-barriers.

10 Olivia Rizzo, "Prosecutors Will Seek Death Penalty for N.Y. Bike Path Terror Suspect," *NJ Advance Media*, September 29, 2018, https://www.nj.com/news/2018/09/prosecutors_will_seek_death_penalty_for_ny_bike_pa.html.

11 John Annese and Reuven Blau, "Victims of West Side Highway Bike Path Terrorist Sue City, Say Officials Should Have Known Popular Route Was Vulnerable to Truck Attack," *New York Daily News*, October 31, 2018, https://www.nydailynews.com/new-york/nyc-crime/ny-metro-bike-path-terror-victims-sue-city-20181031-story.html.

12 Manhattan Community Board 4, letter to City Planning, April 12, 2017, https://cbmanhattan.cityofnewyork.us/cb4/wp-content/uploads/sites/10/downloads/pdf/april_2017/23-WPE-Letter-to-DCP-re-Pier-92-94-Special-Permit-Recertification-RATIFICATION.pdf.

13 The City Club of New York et al. v the U.S. Army Corps of Engineers, Hudson River Park Trust, and Pier55 Inc., Opinion and Order (United States District Court Southern District of New York, March 2017).

14 Lincoln Anderson, "'Diller Isle' Dead in the Water? Judge Nixes Crucial Permit," *The Villager*, March 24, 2017, https://www.amny.com/news/fed-judge-torpedoes-pier55-plan-says-no-need-for-it-to-be-in-river/.

15 Tom Fox, "Mano a Mano to 'Novo': Public Participation Matters," *The Villager*, April 27, 2017, https://www.amny.com/news/a-message-mano-a-mano-to-novo-public-participation-matters/.

16 Charles V. Bagli, "Clash of Titans? Opponents of Pier 55 Have Secret Backer, Media Mogul Says," *New York Times*, September 4, 2016, https://www.nytimes.com/2016/09/05/nyregion/pier-55-park-chelsea-barry-diller-douglas-durst.html.

17 Lincoln Anderson, "Durst Admits Funding Pier 55 Lawsuit, Proving 'Novo' Suspicions True," *The Villager*, May 18, 2017, https://www.amny.com/news/durst-admits-funding-pier55-lawsuit-proving-novo-suspicion-true/.

18 Charles V. Bagli, "Question in Battle over 'Diller Island': Which Billionaire Blinks First?," *New York Times*, June 4, 2017, https://www.nytimes.com/2017/06/04/nyregion/pier-55-diller-island-performance-venues.html.

19 Tom Fox, "Pier Project on the Hudson," letter to the editor, *New York Times*, June 15, 2017, https://www.nytimes.com/2017/06/15/opinion/the-pier-project-on-the-hudson.html.

20 Richard Emery, Elizabeth Saylor, and Douglas E. Lieb, "Second City Club Federal Complaint, United States District Court, Southern District of New York," July 21, 2017.

21 Tom Fox, "Comments on 8-25-17 Privileged and Confidential Settlement Terms," August 28, 2017.

22 The Whitney Museum of American Art, "Gordon Meta Clark Days End | David Hammonds Days End," 2022, https://www.youtube.com/watch?v=uecdwXKuUco.

23 Jonathan Hillberg, "David Hammond's Ghostly Pier to Rise in the Hudson after All," *Architect's Newspaper*, June 8, 2018, https://archpaper.com/2018/06/david-hammons-ghostly-pier-rise-hudson-after-legislature-approval/.

24 Charles V. Bagli, "Diller's Plan for an Elaborate Pier in the Hudson Is Dead," *New York Times*, September 13, 2018, https://www.nytimes.com/2017/09/13/nyregion/diller-hudson-river-pier.html.

25 Julia Marsh, "Diller Upset He Wasted 'Way More than $40 Million' on Failed Park Plan," *New York Post*, September 14, 2017, https://nypost.com/2017/09/14/diller-upset-he-wasted-way-more-than-40m-on-failed-park-plan/.

26 Charles V. Bagli and Robin Pogrebin, "Billionaires, Bruised Egos and the Death of a Grand Project," *The New York Times*, September 23, 2017, https://www.nytimes.com/2017/09/24/nyregion/billionaires-bruised-egos-and-the-death-of-a-grand-project.html?mcubz=0.

27 Hudson River Park Trust, *Financing Plan FY 18* (February 1, 2017), https://hudsonriverpark.org/app/uploads/2020/03/Financing_Plan_FY2018.pdf.

28 Hudson River Foundation, "Advancing Science and Resource Protection in the Hudson River Park Estuarine Sanctuary," confidential draft, January 22, 2017.

29 "Statements from Governor Cuomo, Barry Diller, City Club Founding Member and Counsel Richard Emery, and Douglas Durst on Pier 55," press release, October 25, 2019.

30 Charles V. Bagli, "Diller Island Is Back from the Dead," *New York Times*, October 25, 2017, https://www.nytimes.com/2017/10/25/nyregion/diller-island-revived-cuomo.html.

31 Friends of Hudson River Park, *Realizing the Benefits of Hudson River Park* (2017), https://hudsonriverpark.org/app/uploads/2020/07/Realizing-the-Benefits-of-Hudson-River-Park.pdf.

32 Lincoln Anderson, "Pier 40 Report: Fields of Dreams . . . But Also Fears of Heights," *The Villager*, November 25, 2017, https://www.amny.com/news/pier-40-report-more-sports-fields-careful-on-raising-height/.

33 Tobi Bergman, "Resolution on the Future of Pier 40 Working Group," November 30, 2017, https://www1.nyc.gov/assets/manhattancb1/downloads/pdf/studies-and-reports/Pier%2040%20Working%20Group.pdf.

34 Andrew M. Cuomo, *Excelsior Ever Upward, 2018 State of the State Address* (January 3, 2018), 275, https://www.governor.ny.gov/sites/default/files/atoms/files/2018-stateofthestatebook.pdf.

35 Hudson River Park Trust Board of Directors Meeting Minutes, November 30, 2017, https://hudsonriverpark.org/app/uploads/2020/03/Minutes_of_November_30_2017_BOD_Meeting-1.pdf.

36 Joe Anuta, "Durst, Longtime Thorn in Side of Hudson River Park Trust, Is Named to Its Board," *Crain's New York Business*, January 14, 2018, http://www.crainsnewyork.com/article/20180115/REAL_ESTATE/180119938/developer-douglas-durst-longtime-thorn-in-side-of-hudson-river-park-trust-is-named-to-its-board.

37 Douglas Durst, "Manhattan Community Board 2, Full Board Meeting, Public Session Testimony Regarding Pier 40 Redevelopment," May 24, 2018.

38 Daniel Geiger, "On the Heels of a Megadeal, Google Does It Again," *Crain's New York Business*, February 8, 2018, https://www.crainsnewyork.com/article/20180209/REAL_ESTATE/180209882/on-heels-of-megadeal-google-reaches-agreement-for-major-expansion-on-west-side-pier#utm_medium=email&utm_source=cnyb-insider&utm_campaign=cnyb-insider-20180209.

39 Daniel Geiger, "Google to Invest More than $1 Billion in New York Expansion," *Crain's New York Business*, December 17, 2018, https://www.crainsnewyork.com/real-estate/google-invest-more-1-billion-new-york-expansion?utm_source=breaking-news&utm_medium=email&utm_campaign=20181217&utm_content=hero-headline.

40 Tom Fox, "From Park Pier to Horizontal 'Office Building,'" opinion, *The Villager*, March 22, 2018, 15 and 21, https://issuu.com/downtownexpress/docs/2018_03_23_tvg.

41 Tom Fox, "Park Trust Must Do Better on Transparency," op-ed, *The Villager*, May 31, 2018.

42 Carolyn Nicander Mohr, "The Wayback Machine Shows the History of the Internet," Voice of America Learning English, February 8, 2017, https://learningenglish.voanews.com/a/wayback-machine/3710648.html.

43 New York State Division of the Budget, "Cuomo Announces Highlights of the FY 2019 State Budget," March 30, 2018.

44 Zoe Rosenberg, "Cuomo Pledges $50 Million to Hudson River Park but Only If City Matches It," *Curbed New York*, April 6, 2018, https://ny.curbed.com/2018/4/6/17205806/hudson-river-park-funding-pier-55.

45 Venetia Lannon (Deputy Secretary for the Environment, State of New York Executive Chamber), letter to Paul Gallay (President, RiverKeeper), May 24, 2018, https://www.riverkeeper.org/wp-content/uploads/2018/05/201805241553.pdf.

46 Manhattan Community Board 4, letter to Mayor Bill de Blasio, April 6, 2018, https://www1.nyc.gov/html/mancb4/downloads/pdf/april2018/11-WPE-Letter-to-Mayor-de-Blasio-re-Pier-76.pdf.

47 Winnie McCroy, "Waterside Association Reels in Years of Park Plans," *The Villager*, May 31, 2017, https://www.thevillager.com/2017/05/waterside-association-reels-in-years-of-hudson-river-park-plans/.

48 Jane Margolies, "From the Slaughterhouse to the Playground," *New York Times*, June 20, 2018, https://www.nytimes.com/2018/06/20/nyregion/from-the-legacy-cow-heads-in-chelsea-waterside-park.html.

49 Nikolai Fedak, "New Details for 62-Story Multi-Tower Block 675 Development," *New York YIMBY*, December 5, 2017, https://newyorkyimby.com/2017/12/new-details-for-62-story-multi-tower-block-675-redevelopment-hudson-yards.html.

50 Joe Anuta, "City Council Approves $52 M Air Rights Deal for Hudson River Park," *Crains New York Business*, June 28, 2018, https://www.crainsnewyork.com/article/20180629/REAL_ESTATE/180629885/city-council-oks-52m-air-rights-deal-for-hudson-river-park.

51 Joe Anuta, "St. John's Project Shifts from Residential to Commercial," *Crains New York Business*, October 3, 2018, https://www.crainsnewyork.com/real-estate/st-johns-terminal-project-shifts-residential-commercial?utm_source=daily-alert-wednesday&utm_medium=email&utm_campaign=20181003&utm_content=article9-readmore.

52 Irene Plagianos, "Tribeca's Long-Stalled Pier 26 Gets $10M from Citigroup," *DNAinfo*, October 13, 2015, https://www.dnainfo.com/new-york/20151013/tribeca/tribecas-long-stalled-pier-26-gets-10m-from-citigroup/.

53 Patricia Lynch, "Plans Revealed to Transform Pier 26 into a New Park along the Hudson River in Manhattan," *ArchDaily Architecture News*, December 19, 2016, https://www.archdaily.com/801812/plans-revealed-to-transform-pier-26-into-new-park-along-the-hudson-river-in-new-york.

54 Caroline Spivack, "Construction Kicks Off for Pier 26's Ecology Themed Redesign," *Patch*, October 9, 2018, https://patch.com/new-york/downtown-nyc/construction-kicks-pier-26-s-ecology-themed-redesign.

55 "Pier 26 New York, NY," video, Design vs Build, https://www.designvsbuild.com/pier-26.

56 Carl Glassman, "Tribeca's Hoped-For River Study Center Is Many Millions of Dollars Away," *Tribeca Trib*, September 28, 2018, http://www.tribecatrib.com/content/tribecas-hoped-river-study-center-many-millions-dollars-away.

57   Madelyn Wils (Hudson River Park Trust), letter to Douglas Durst, December 20, 2018.
58   Anthony Notaro Jr. (chairman, Manhattan Community Board 1), letter to Madelyn Wils, October 3, 2018.
59   Madelyn Wils (Hudson River Park Trust), letter to Anthony Notaro Jr., October 12, 2018.
60   Manhattan Community Board 1, "Manhattan Community Board 1 Resolution," October 23, 2018.
61   New York Water Taxi, application information to US Army Corps of Engineers, 1997.
62   Tom Fox, "Park Trust Cut Public Out of Private Citi Dock Plan," op-ed, *The Villager*, October 23, 2018.
63   Douglas Durst (president and chief executive officer, the Durst Organization), letter to Madelyn Wils, December 6, 2018.
64   "Diana L. Taylor," Citigroup, accessed October 18, 2023, https://www.citigroup.com/citi/about/leaders/diana-taylor-bio.html.
65   "Hudson River Park—Branding, Signage and Environmental Graphics," *Pentagram*, October 28, 2018, https://www.pentagram.com/work/hudson-river-park/story.

Chapter 17   Will the Incoming Tide Return? (2019–2023)

1   Joe Anuta, "Olive Branch to Durst Tucked in State of the State," *Crains New York Business*, January 16, 2019, https://www.crainsnewyork.com/real-estate/olive-branch-durst-tucked-state-state.
2   Douglas Durst (The Durst Organization), letter to Madelyn Wils, January 22, 2019.
3   Douglas Durst et al., "Current Concerns with Transparency and Governance at HRPT," confidential memo to Alphonso David, Zach Knaub, and Jennifer Maglienti, February 19, 2019.
4   Tom Fox, "Memo by Beth Garvey on the Need for an Inboard Funding Source," October 11, 2019.
5   Scott Rechler (CEO and Chairman, RXR Realty), letter to Madelyn Wils, February 18, 2019.
6   Lincoln Anderson, "City Winery Moving to Pr. 57 in Hudson River Pk.," *amNY*, April 22, 2019, https://www.amny.com/news/city-winery-moving-to-pr-57-in-hudson-river-pk/.
7   RXR, "Pier 57 Ground Floor Plan," January 26, 2019.
8   Crew, "Ahoy, Grand Banks Is Open for the Season," electronic invitation, April 13, 2023.
9   Deborah Glick et al., letter to Madelyn Wils, January 17, 2019.
10   Madelyn Wils (Hudson River Park Trust), letter to Hon. Deborah J. Glick, Hon. Jerrold Nadler, Hon. Brad Hoylman, Hon. Corey Johnson, Hon. Gale A. Brewer, Hon. Brian Kavanaugh, February 8, 2019.
11   Lincoln Anderson, "Future Office Building O.K. for Pier 40," *The Villager*, July 1, 2019, https://www.thevillager.com/2019/07/future-office-building-o-k-d-for-pier-40/.
12   Lincoln Anderson, "Pr. 40: Mutiny on the Waterfront," *The Villager*, June 5, 2019, https://www.thevillager.com/2019/06/pr-40-mutiny-on-the-waterfront/
13   Lincoln Anderson, "Hell's Kitchen Sues to Rid Pier 76 of Police Tow Pound," *Village Sun*, December 6, 2019, https://thevillagesun.com/hells-kitchen-sues-to-rid-pier-76-of-police-tow-pound.

14 Lincoln Anderson, "Gov. Cuomo Vetoes Pier 40 Office Tower, Says Pier 76 Tow Pound Must Go," *Village Sun*, December 31, 2019, https://nypost.com/2020/01/02/cuomo-veto-of-pier-40-plan-sparks-new-development-fight/.

15 Caroline Spivak, "Pier 40 Redevelopment Bill Scuttles after Cuomo Kills Contested Bill," *Curbed New York*, January 6, 2020, https://ny.curbed.com/2020/1/2/21046633/hudson-river-park-pier-40-west-village-redevelopment.

16 Legislation to Vacate Pier 76, New York State Legislature, 12673-01-0 (2020), 424–425.

17 Tom Fox, "Hudson River Park Needs Community Input and Independent Funding," *Crain's New York Business*, January 16, 2020, https://www.crainsnewyork.com/op-ed/hudson-river-park-needs-community-input-and-independent-funding 2020/01/16.

18 Joseph B. Rose, "Stop Sniping at Public Servants Trying to Help and Work Together to Complete Hudson River Park," *Crain's New York Business*, January 27, 2020, https://www.crainsnewyork.com/letters-editor/stop-sniping-public-servants-trying-help-and-work-together-complete-hudson-river 2020/01/27.

19 Madelyn Wils, "Hudson River Park Strategic Planning Task Force," form letter, January 31, 2020.

20 Hudson River Park Trust, "Hudson River Park Planning Task Force Meeting #5," March 27, 2020.

21 Tequila Minsky, "The Mantra at the Hudson River Park's Pumpkin Composting Event: Don't Trash It Smash It," *amNY*, November 4, 2019, https://www.thevillager.com/2019/11/the-mantra-at-hudson-river-parks-pumpkin-composting-event-dont-trash-it-smash-it/.

22 Hudson River Park Act, Ch. 592, S. 7845, Sec. 15, NY Legis 592 (1998), https://hudsonriverpark.org/app/uploads/2020/03/HRP-Act.pdf.

23 Tom Fox, email message to Hudson River Park Advisory Council, September 24, 2019.

24 Tom Fox, conversation with Douglas Durst, November 2019.

25 Caroline Spivack, "Hudson River Park's Pier 97 Will Transform into 'Other Worldly' Green Space," *Curbed New York*, November 19, 2019, https://ny.curbed.com/2019/11/19/20971240/hudson-river-parks-pier-97-hells-kitchen-renovation.

26 Hudson River Park Act, Ch. 592, S. 7845, Sec 8.3 (c), NY Legis 592 (1998), https://hudsonriverpark.org/app/uploads/2020/03/HRP-Act.pdf.

27 Rick Spilman, "Grand Banks Oyster Bar on the Schooner Sherman Zwicker on the Hudson," website, *The Old Salt Blog*, July 9, 2014, http://www.oldsaltblog.com/2014/07/grand-banks-oyster-bar-on-the-schooner-sherman-zwicker-on-the-hudson-river/.

28 Tom Fox, "It's Time for the Hudson River Park Trust to Take the Plunge," *Village Sun*, July 9, 2020, https://thevillagesun.com/its-time-for-hudson-river-park-trust-to-take-the-plunge 2020/07/09.

29 Hudson River Park Advisory Council, letter to Governor Andrew Cuomo et al., May 6, 2020, https://hudsonriverpark.org/app/uploads/2022/01/HRPK-AC-Meeting-October-12-2021.docx-1.pdf.

30 Dave Colon, "State DOT Throws Cold Water on West Side Highway Bike Lane," *Streetsblog NYC*, September 10, 2020, https://nyc.streetsblog.org/2020/09/10/state-dot-throws-cold-water-on-west-side-highway-bike-lane/.

31 Douglas Durst, "Resignation from the Hudson River Park Trust Board," August 13, 2020.

32 Lincoln Anderson, "Diana Taylor Out, Basil Seggos in as Hudson River Park Trust Chairperson, Douglas Durst Resigns from Board," *Village Sun*, September 14, 2020, https://thevillagesun.com/diana-taylor-out-basil-seggos-in-as-park-trust -chairperson-douglas-durst-resigns.

33 Basil Seggos (Commissioner, New York State Office of Parks Recreation and Historic Preservation), letter to Mayor Bill De Blasio, September 17, 2020.

34 Lincoln Anderson, "Madelyn Wils to Resign from Hudson River Park Trust," *Village Sun*, January 21, 2021, https://thevillagesun.com/madelyn-wils-to-resign -from-hudson-river-park-trust.

35 Connie Fishman, "Open Letter: Madelyn Wils' Hard Work over Decades Made Life Better for New Yorkers," *Tribeca Citizen*, February 2, 2021, https:// tribecacitizen.com/2021/02/02/open-letter-madelyn-wils-hard-work-over-decades -made-life-better-for-new-yorkers/.

36 The official website of NYC, "Mayor de Blasio Appoints Vicki Been as Chair of the Hudson River Park Trust," press release, April 7, 2021, https://www1.nyc.gov/office -of-the-mayor/news/253-21/mayor-de-blasio-appoints-vicki-been-chair-hudson-river -park-trust.

37 Lincoln Anderson, "Noreen Doyle Named President and C.E.O. of the Hudson River Park Trust," *Village Sun*, June 7, 2021, https://thevillagesun.com/noreen -doyle-named-president-and-c-e-o-of-hudson-river-park-trust.

38 Luis Ferré-Saudirni and J. David Goodman, "Cuomo Resigns Amid Scandals, Ending Decade Long Run in Disgrace," *New York Times*, August 10, 2021, https:// www.nytimes.com/2021/08/10/nyregion/andrew-cuomo-resigns.html.

39 Debbie Walsh, "Glass Cliff or Rare Opportunity, Kathy Hochul's Challenge as New York's First Female Governor," *USA Today*, August 16, 2021, https://www .usatoday.com/story/opinion/2021/08/15/kathy-hochul-andrew-cuomo-resignation -female-women-governors-new-york/8130155002/.

40 Manhattan Community Board 4, "MCB4—September 2021 Waterfront Parks and Environment Committee Meeting," September 28, 2021, YouTube video, https:// www.youtube.com/watch?v=1AqQO_55Er8.

41 Noreen Doyle (Hudson River Park Trust), email message to Tom Fox, December 27, 2021.

42 Tom Fox, "My Visit to Little Island," *Village Sun*, July 6, 2021, https://thevillagesun .com/my-visit-to-little-island.

43 Little Island (website), https://littleisland.org/staff.

44 Fred A. Bernstein, "No Man Is an Island," commentary, *Architectural Record*, May 28, 2021, https://www.architecturalrecord.com/articles/15163-commentary-no -mans-is-an-island.

45 "CEQR No. 15DME009Y, NYC Ferry Service Expansion," Testimony, Final Scope of Work, Draft Supplemental Environmental Impact Statement, March 15, 2020 (statement of Tom Fox, Tom Fox & Associates).

46 Jeffery LeFrancois (Hudson River Advisory Council), letter to James Patchett (President and CEO NYC Economic Development Corporation), October 11, 2020.

47 Jeffrey LeFrancois (Hudson River Park Advisory Council), letter to Hank Gutman (New York City Transportation Commissioner), May 4, 2021, https:// hudsonriverpark.org/app/uploads/2022/01/DOT-Pier-79-Enforcement.pdf.

48 Jeffrey LeFrancois (Hudson River Park Advisory Council), letter to Commissioner Basil Seggos, Chair and Deputy Mayor Vicki Been, Vice Chair (Hudson River Park

Trust), March 22, 2021, https://hudsonriverpark.org/app/uploads/2022/01/Intrepid -Lease-Letter.pdf.

49 Hudson River Park Trust, "ESMP Action Agenda for AC," 2021–2030 action agenda, April 9, 2021, https://hudsonriverpark.org/app/uploads/2021/12/HRP-AC -April-9-2021-Minutes.pdf.

50 "Form 990, Return of Organization Exempt from Income Tax, Friends of Hudson River Park 2018," GuideStar, 2019, p. 1, https://pdf.guidestar.org/PDF_Images/2019 /134/112/2019-134112913-115e2589-9.pdf?_ga=2.76850453.1866328120.1605045287 -1621892298.1605045287.

51 Connie Fishman (Hudson River Park Friends), letter to Douglas Durst.

52 Lincoln Anderson, "Before Getting Crushed by the Crypto Collapse, Novogratz Stepped Down as Friends of Hudson River Park Chairperson Last Month," *Village Sun*, May 16, 2022, https://thevillagesun.com/novogratz-steps-down-from-hudson -river-park-friends-after-crypto-market-collapse.

53 Lincoln Anderson, "Ross Graham, 93, Former C.B. 4 Chairperson and Waterfront Activist, Dies of COVID," *Village Sun*, January 29, 2021, https://thevillagesun.com /ross-graham-93-former-c-b-4-chairperson-and-waterfront-activist-dies-of-covid.

54 Scott Stiffler, "In Publishing, Politics and Planning, Bob Trentlyon, 92, Put People First," *Chelsea Community News*, December 27, 2021, https:// chelseacommunitynews.com/2021/12/27/in-publishing-politics-and-planning-bob -trentlyon-92-put-people-first/.

55 Sam Roberts, "Edward Kirkland, Who Helped Preserve the Chelsea Historic District, Dies at 96," *New York Times*, January 14, 2022, https://www.nytimes.com /2022/01/14/nyregion/edward-kirkland-dead.html.

56 Karen Cilento, "Pier 57/Lot-EK and Young Woo Associates," *ArchDaily*, August 7, 2009, https://www.archdaily.com/31479/pier-57-lot-ek-young-woo-associates.

57 Matt Hickman, "New York City's Largest Rooftop Park Opens atop Historic Pier 57 in Chelsea," *The Architect's Newspaper*, April 19, 2022, https://www.archpaper.com /2022/04/new-york-city-largest-rooftop-park-opens-chelsea-pier-57/.

58 "Riverbank State Park (Denny Farrell Riverbank State Park)," New York State Office of Parks, Recreation and Historic Preservation, accessed October 22, 2023, https://parks.ny.gov/parks/93.

59 Al Amateau, "Trash on a Public Route," *Chelsea Clinton News*, April 25–May 1, 1996.

60 AECOM, "AECOM Ranked No. 1 by Fortune Magazine as the World's Most Admired Company in Its Industry," press release, February 1, 2021, https://aecom .com/press-releases/aecom-ranked-no-1-by-fortune-magazine-as-the-worlds-most -admired-company-in-its-industry/.

61 Jeffrey LeFrancois et al., "Significant Action Process for Chelsea Piers," March 11, 2022.

62 Daniel Miller, Tammy Meltzer, and Jeffrey LeFrancois, "Final Recommendation Regarding Chelsea Piers Lease," April 13, 2022, https://hudsonriverpark.org/app /uploads/2022/04/HRP-AC-Letter-to-HRPT-Board-CP-Lease.pdf.

63 BFJ Planning, "Review of Chelsea Piers Site Plan," prepared for Tom Fox & Associates, May 2022.

64 Daniel Katsive, "Not All Piers Are for Play: Keeping the Steam Up and the Lights On," *West Side Rag*, June 2, 2022, https://www.westsiderag.com/2022/06/02/not-all -piers-are-for-play-keeping-the-steam-up-and-the-lights-on.

65 James Barron, "Tiny Oysters Are a Hopeful Sign in the Hudson River," *New York Times*, August 11, 2022, https://www.nytimes.com/2022/08/11/nyregion/oysters -hudson-river.html?referringSource=articleShare.

66   Richard Emery, "60-Day Notice of Intent to File a Citizens Suit under the Clean Water Act," August 10, 2022.

67   Patrick McGeehan and Anne Barnard, "Con Ed Dumps Hot, Dirty Water from Hudson River Park Pier," *New York Times*, August 23, 2022, https://www.nytimes.com/2022/08/23/nyregion/coned-hudson-river-park-ny.html.

68   Sarah Beling, "ConEd in Hot Water after Polluting the Judson River for Years," *W42ndSt Magazine*, August 24, 2022, https://w42st.com/post/coned-in-hot-water-after-polluting-the-hudson-river-for-years/.

69   Manhattan Community Board 4, "MCB 4 Waterfront Parks and Environment Committee," Pier 98 Citizen's Suit, Con Edison presentation, minute 42:30 of Zoom meeting, YouTube video, September 8, 2022, https://www.youtube.com/watch?v=NtAAqLbK3sw.

70   "Is Scamardella Done with Power Plays?," SIlive.com, June 19, 2011, https://www.silive.com/opinion/strictly-political/2011/06/is_scamardella_done_with_power.html.

71   Hudson River Park Advisory Council, letter to Hudson River Park Trust, April 26, 2023, https://hudsonriverpark.org/app/uploads/2023/05/HRP-AC-reso-on-pier-98-w-date.pdf.

72   Hudson River Park Advisory Council Meeting, "City Club Statement on Con Edison's Pollution at Pier 98," memo, December 12, 2022.

73   "ENB Region 2 Completed Applications 03/29/2023, New York County" New York State Department of Environmental Conservation, March 29, 2023, https://www.dec.ny.gov/enb/20230329_reg2.html#262020003200004.

74   Jeffrey Lefrancois (chair, Manhattan Community Board Four), letter to Dan Garodnick (Chair & Director of the City Planning Commission and Department of City Planning Department) and Signe Neilson (President Public Design Commission of the City of New York), June 1, 2022, https://cbmanhattan.cityofnewyork.us/cb4/wp-content/uploads/sites/10/2022/06/20a-Exec-WPE-and-TRANS-Letters-to-DCP-and-PDC-re-Pier-92-94-With-Enclosure-20b.pdf.

75   Matthew Hag and Dana Rubinstein, "A Pier Deal Is Full of Developer's Perks, but Is It Good for the City?," *New York Times*, June 11, 2023, https://www.nytimes.com/2023/06/11/nyregion/soccer-stadium-film-studio-adams-nyc.html.

76   Pam Frederick, "Field Trip: Hudson River Park's Pier 57 in Chelsea (Part One)," *Tribeca Citizen*, March 1, 2023, https://tribecacitizen.com/2023/03/31/field-trip-hudson-river-parks-pier-57-in-chelsea-part-one/.

77   Clio Chang, "Maybe Manhattan Needed a Beach," October 3, 2023, https://www.curbed.com/2023/10/gansevoort-peninsula-manhattan-beach-review.html.

78   Assemblymember Tony Simone, "A 7277, An Act to Amend the Hudson River Park Act in Relation to Prohibiting a Heliport within the Boundaries of the Hudson River Park," New York State Assembly, October 5, 2023, https://assembly.state.ny.us/leg/?default_fld=&leg_video=&bn=A07277&term=2023&Summary=Y&Memo=Y&Text=Y.

Chapter 18   Hope Springs Eternal (2024 and Beyond)

1   Jake M. Robinson et al., "Nature's Role in Supporting Health during the COVID–19 Pandemic: A Geospatial and Socioecological Study," *Int. J. Environ. Res. Public Health* 18, no. 5 (2021): 2227, https://pubmed.ncbi.nlm.nih.gov/33668228/.

2   Adrian Benepe (former New York City Parks Commissioner), interview by Tom Fox, January 2022.

3   Phil O'Brien, "Murder Investigation: Man Dies after Stabbing on Pier 84," W42ST. NYC, July 13, 2023, https://w42st.com/post/murder-investigation-man-dies-after -stabbing-at-pier-84-in-hells-kitchen/; Female Jogger 52 Punched in the Face in Hudson River Park in Homophobic Attack," *Village Sun*, September 9, 2023.

4   Adrian Benepe (former New York City Parks Commissioner), interview by Tom Fox, May 2022.

5   Karen Zraick, "11 Million New Oysters in New York Harbor (but None for You to Eat)," *New York Times*, December 10, 2021, https://www.nytimes.com/2021/12/10 /nyregion/oysters-new-york-hudson-river.html.

6   Hudson River Park Act, Ch. 592, S. 7845, NY Legis 592 (1998), https://hudson riverpark.org/app/uploads/2020/03/HRP-Act.pdf.

7   "Bulk Computations on Waterfront Zoning Lots," New York City Planning Department Zoning Resolution 62–31 (b), https://zr.planning.nyc.gov/article-vi /chapter-2/62-31.

8   Jeffrey Steele, "Bank On It: Change Transforming Manhattan's East River Water-front," *Forbes*, December 28, 2021, https://www.forbes.com/sites/jeffsteele/2021/12 /28/bank-on-it-change-transforming-manhattans-east-river-waterfront/?sh =1a45bb4a6cf0.

9   WXY and Sam Schwartz, "Meatpacking District Western Gateway Public Realm Vision," Meatpacking District Management Association, 2023.

10   Lincoln Anderson, Safer West Side Highway Crossings Planned but Too Late for Senior Woman Killed by Truck," *Village Sun*, November 12, 2021, https:// thevillagesun.com/safer-west-side-highway-crossings-planned-but-too-late-for -senior-woman-killed-by-truck.

11   "Hudson Square BID Unveils $22M Streetscape Improvement Plan," *Real Estate Weekly*, September 28, 2021, https://rew-online.com/hudson-square-bid-unveils -22m-streetscape-improvement-plan/.

12   Jane Margolies, "How Hudson River Park Helped Revitalize Manhattan's West Side," *New York Times*, September 19, 2023, https://www.nytimes.com/2023/09 /19/business/hudson-river-park-development-manhattan.html?unlocked_article _code=U-_b0Z6ZJJFDsKLoS0FJ7Ip504tuglLZ4eCJR9fBXnnFzfslTtsY8edW GWrmZOmhxrkYZtyGqcPNX_BPa-Ky6SFEe8xeRRHkyEvjaqP5Dj2Dxx _ow44KbikTTecfhG-cQyqw1f-ojlhEzr-IOoGk4l8ec5EsoU5MngvsyPTwesdKT HCi00NzAmMiqxeOa81HBJw5SKV_I823pjrOgvUfKhAekuThH3JFhhgS8I900 8slcXw9keszzQh7KV7Ys6owPAiFxzlhMcHU_j4-FD490BthyQDGaZar7Uk3 -ipyUGxCQWkNAkbuz8_z6PPqgmhgdCaNFEGtnYjctFQS5R- _23rNJxo3ei88ZArYnB5dv6kx1g&smid=tw-share.

13   Lincoln Anderson, "West Village BID Won't Be Big, Will Focus on Sanitation 'Cultural History,'" *Village Sun*, January 23, 2022, https://thevillagesun.com/west -village-bid-wont-be-big-will-focus-on-sanitation-cultural-history.

14   Tom Fox, "Celebrate," email message to Noreen Doyle, October 6, 2021.

15   Tom Fox, *Celebrate Hudson River Parks 25th Anniversary*, October 2, 2023, photograph.

16   LandVote® Database, Trust for Public Land, https://tpl.quickbase.com/db /bbqna2qct?a=dbpage&pageID=8.

17   Hudson River Park Advisory Committee Meeting Minutes, October 12, 2021, https://hudsonriverpark.org/app/uploads/2022/01/HRPK-AC-Meeting-October -12-2021.docx-1.pdf.

18 "Hudson River Greenway Bike Tour, Viator, October 15, 2023, https://www.viator
.com/tours/New-York-City/Hudson-River-Greenway-Bike-Tour/d687-7274P29.

19 Graham Birchall, email message to Tom Fox, October 21, 2021.

20 "Central Park's Waldman Rank and Carousel Get New Operator after Trump
Organization Pushed Out," *West Side Rag,* July 7, 2021, https://www.westsiderag
.com/2021/07/07/wollman-rink-and-carousel-get-new-operators-after-trump
-organization-pushed-out.

21 Elissaveta M. Brandon, "New York City Is Reclaiming Its Piers," *Smithsonian
Magazine,* October 26, 2020, https://www.smithsonianmag.com/innovation/how
-new-york-city-is-reclaiming-its-piers-180976121/.

22 "Hudson River Park, Phase 1, Pier 45, 46, 51 + Upland Areas," Abel Bainnson Butz,
New York, NY, accessed October 23, 2023, https://www.abbnyc.com/hudson-river
-park-segment-4.

23 "'Frame Job' at Pier 76: Cuomo Announces Interim Recreation Space," *Village Sun,*
March 25, 2021, https://thevillagesun.com/cuomo-announces-pier-76-interim
-recreation-space.

24 Jane Margolies, "How Hudson River Park Helped Revitalize Manhattan's West
Side," *New York Times,* September 19, 2023, https://www.nytimes.com/2023/09
/19/business/hudson-river-park-development-manhattan.html?searchResult
Position=1.

25 Phil O'Brien, "Welcome Back—'The Bottle' Returns to Hell's Kitchen," W42ST.
NYC, April 27, 2022, https://w42st.com/post/welcome-back-the-bottle-returns-to
-clinton-cove-hells-kitchen/.

26 Hudson River Park Trust Board of Directors Meeting Minutes, May 22, 2022,
https://hudsonriverpark.org/app/uploads/2022/05/2022-May-19—Draft-Minutes
.pdf.

27 Hudson River Park Trust Board of Directors Meeting Minutes, May 19, 2022,
https://hudsonriverpark.org/app/uploads/2022/07/May-19—Final-Minutes.pdf.

28 Anna Rahmanan, "Hudson River Park Is Hosting 260 Free Events This Summer,"
Time Out New York, May 11, 2022, https://www.timeout.com/newyork/news
/hudson-river-park-is-hosting-over-260-free-events-this-summer-051122.

29 Adam Brown, "Comments to Carolyn Bachan and Mike Dalia, Empire State
Development Corporation," May 5, 1998.

30 Hudson River Park Advisory Council, letter to Hudson River Park Trust, April 26,
2023, https://hudsonriverpark.org/app/uploads/2023/05/HRP-AC-reso-on-pier-98
-w-date.pdf.

31 Dashiell Allen, "Coastal Resiliency Report: From Battery Park and Two Bridges to
Hudson River Park and Chelsea, Comprehensive Planning is Needed," *Village Sun,*
July 23, 2022, https://thevillagesun.com/coastal-resiliency-report-from-battery-park
-and-two-bridges-to-hudson-river-park-and-chelsea-comprehensive-planning-is
-needed.

32 "New York–New Jersey Harbor and Tributaries Coastal Storm Risk Management
Feasibility Study, Tentatively Selected Plan," Maps CS 107 (site plan 7 of 27) and
108 (site plan 8 of 27), https://www.nan.usace.army.mil/Portals/37/Appendix%20B3
_TSPPlanSet_HATS.pdf.

33 Hudson River Park Advisory Council, letter to Governor Kathy Hochul and Mayor
Eric Adams, February 14, 2023, https://hudsonriverpark.org/app/uploads/2023/02
/AC-letter-to-Governor-and-Mayor-regarding-West-side-resiliency.pdf.

34 Community Board 2, Manhattan, Quality of Life Committee, resolutions adopted at March 2023 meeting, March 6, 2023; Office of Congressman Dan Goldman, "Congressman Goldman Convenes Townhall to Improve Collaboration on Climate Resiliency Projects," press release, March 17, 2023, https://goldman.house .gov/media/press-releases/congressman-dan-goldman-convenes-townhall-improve -collaboration-climate.

35 Manhattan Community Board 1, "3/20 Environmental Protection Committee 2023," YouTube video, March 2023, https://www.youtube.com/watch?v =w1VUNpH5I_k; Matthew Fenton, "A Massive Change to Our Urban Land-scape," *The Broadsheet*, April 5, 2023, https://www.ebroadsheet.com/a-massive -change-to-our-landscape/.

36 Deborah J. Glick et al., letter to The Honorable Kathy C. Hochul and The Honor-able Eric L. Adams, July 31, 2023.

37 Clean Water, Clean Air and Green Jobs Environmental Bond Act," New York State Department of Environmental Conservation, November 8, 2022, https://www.ny .gov/programs/clean-water-clean-air-and-green-jobs-environmental-bond-act.

38 Venetia Lannon (Deputy Secretary for the Environment), letter to Paul Gallay (President, RiverKeeper), May 24, 2018, https://www.riverkeeper.org/wp-content /uploads/2018/05/201805241553.pdf.

39 Aliza Chasan, "How 'Living' Breakwaters Are Protecting NYC's Shores, 10 Years after Sandy," *PIX 11*, October 28, 2022, https://pix11.com/news/local-news/how -living-breakwaters-are-protecting-nycs-shores-10-years-after-sandy/.

40 "Heavy Rain & The City 'Spills Out' Trouble," The Freshkills Park Alliance, August 12, 2021, https://freshkillspark.org/blog/heavy-rain-the-city.

41 New York City Department of Environmental Protection, "DEP Completes Paerdegat Basin CSO Facility," press release, May 11, 2011, https://www1.nyc.gov /html/dep/html/press_releases/11-36pr.shtml#.Ye8nLC-BoQ8.

42 Tom Fox conversation with Charles Komanoff, Carbon Tax Center, February 3, 2023.

43 Jeffrey LeFrancois, letter to Governor Cuomo and Commissioners Dominguez and Kulleseid, May 19, 2020, https://hudsonriverpark.org/app/uploads/2021/04 /Greenway-request_Governor_FINAL.pdf; Gersh Kuntzman, "SEE IT! Manhat-tan BP to State: Take a Lane from Drivers on the West Side Highway," *StreetsBlog NYC*, August 1, 2022, https://nyc.streetsblog.org/2022/08/01/manhattan-bp-to -state-take-a-lane-from-drivers-on-the-west-side-highway/.

44 "The Basics of Micromobility and Related Devices for Personal Transport," Pedestrian and Bicycle Information Center, Chapel Hill, NC, accessed October 24, 2023, https://www.pedbikeinfo.org/cms/downloads/PBIC_Brief_Micromobility Typology.pdf.

45 Jack Ewing and Winnie Hu, "Ahoy! Your Air Fryer May Soon Arrive by Boat," *New York Times*, December 15, 2021, https://www.nytimes.com/2021/12/15/nyregion/nyc -packages-ferry.html.

46 "Vision Zero: West Side Highway Speed Limit Reduced in Manhattan," *WABC7NY*, October 12, 2019, https://abc7ny.com/west-side-highway-speed-limit-reduction -manhattan-driving/5613337/.

47 Tom Fox, "A Different Vision for Flood Protection on the West Side," opinion, *Village Sun*, March 5, 2023, https://thevillagesun.com/opinion-a-different-vision-for -flood-protection-on-the-west-side.

48 City Club of New York, "Comments on Proposals for Manhattan's West Side Waterfront Illustrated on US Army Corps Maps CS 107 (Site Plan 7 of 27) and 108 (Site Plan 8 of 27)," March 6, 2023.

Index

Page numbers in italics represent photographs.

About the Author

TOM FOX was an original member of the Green Guerillas and the first president of the Hudson River Park Conservancy. He designed the 40-mile Brooklyn/ Queens Greenway and was the founding cochair of the Brooklyn Bridge Park Coalition. Fox was the cofounder and CEO of New York Water Taxi; has served on nonprofit and corporate boards and public commissions; and has received recognition from the government and environmental, professional, and civic organizations.